A Companion to Medieval Popular Romance

Popular romance was one of the most wide-spread forms of literature in the middle ages, yet despite its cultural centrality, and its fundamental importance for later literary developments, the genre has defied precise definition, its subject matter ranging from tales of chivalric adventure, to saintly women, and monsters who become human. The essays in this collection seek to provide an inclusive and thorough examination of romance. They provide contexts, definitions, and explanations for the genre, particularly in, but not limited to, an English context. Topics covered include genre and literary classification; race and ethnicity; gender; orality and performance; the romance and young readers; metre and form; printing culture; and reception.

Studies in Medieval Romance
ISSN 1479–9308

Series Editors
Corinne Saunders

Editorial Board
Roger Dalrymple
Rhiannon Purdie
Robert Allen Rouse

This series aims to provide a forum for critical studies of the medieval romance, a genre which plays a crucial role in literary history, clearly reveals medieval secular concerns, and raises complex questions regarding social structures, human relationships, and the psyche. Its scope extends from the early middle ages into the Renaissance period, and although its main focus is on English literature, comparative studies are welcomed.

Proposals or queries should be sent in the first instance to one of the addresses given below; all submissions will receive prompt and informed consideration.

Professor Corinne Saunders, Department of English, University of Durham, Durham, DH1 3AY

Boydell & Brewer Limited, PO Box 9, Woodbridge, Suffolk, IP12 3DF

Previously published volumes in the series
are listed at the back of this book

A Companion to
Medieval Popular Romance

Edited by

RALUCA L. RADULESCU
CORY JAMES RUSHTON

D. S. BREWER

© Contributors 2009

All Rights Reserved. Except as permitted under current legislation
no part of this work may be photocopied, stored in a retrieval system,
published, performed in public, adapted, broadcast,
transmitted, recorded or reproduced in any form or by any means,
without the prior permission of the copyright owner

First published 2009
D. S. Brewer, Cambridge
Transferred to paperback and digital printing 2011

ISBN 978 1 84384 192 0 hardback
ISBN 978 1 84384 270 5 paperback

D. S. Brewer is an imprint of Boydell & Brewer Ltd
PO Box 9, Woodbridge, Suffolk IP12 3DF, UK
and of Boydell & Brewer Inc.
668 Mount Hope Ave, Rochester, NY 14604, USA
website: www.boydellandbrewer.com

The publisher has no responsibility for the continued existence or accuracy of
URLs for external or third-party internet websites referred to in this book,
and does not guarantee that any content on such websites is,
or will remain, accurate or appropriate.

A CIP catalogue record for this book is available
from the British Library

Papers used by Boydell & Brewer Ltd are natural, recyclable products
made from wood grown in sustainable forests

For Norah-Louise
and for Kevin

Contents

Acknowledgements		ix
Contributors		x
Abbreviations		xiii
Introduction *Raluca L. Radulescu and Cory James Rushton*		1
1	Popular Romance: The Material and the Problems *Rosalind Field*	9
2	Genre and Classification *Raluca L. Radulescu*	31
3	The Manuscripts of Popular Romance *Maldwyn Mills and Gillian Rogers*	49
4	Printed Romance in the Sixteenth Century *Jennifer Fellows*	67
5	Middle English Popular Romance and National Identity *Thomas H. Crofts and Robert Allen Rouse*	79
6	Gender and Identity in the Popular Romance *Joanne Charbonneau and Désirée Cromwell*	96
7	The Metres and Stanza Forms of Popular Romance *Ad Putter*	111
8	Orality and Performance *Karl Reichl*	132
9	Popular Romances and Young Readers *Phillipa Hardman*	150
10	Modern and Academic Reception of the Popular Romance *Cory James Rushton*	165
Bibliography		181
Index		205

Acknowledgements

The editors would like to thank Caroline Palmer, Editorial Director at Boydell & Brewer, for her initiative and enthusiastic support for this collective project, and Linda Jones, Research Administrator in the College of Arts and Humanities, Bangor University, for her invaluable assistance in bringing this volume to completion. Special thanks to Sheila Mackenzie from the National Library of Scotland for assistance with the reproduction image for the book cover, and to the Trustees of the NLS for permission to use the image. Raluca Radulescu would like to thank Pierre for providing cheerful advice and love, and Cory Rushton wishes to thank his wife Susan for her unending love, patience and support.

Contributors

Joanne Charbonneau, former professor at the University of Montana, is currently working on connections between romance and the Seven Deadly Sins tradition, especially those texts in Cambridge University Library MS Ff.2.38. Participating in the NEH summer seminar 'The Seven Deadly Sins as Cultural Constructions in the Middle Ages' provided the impetus for this line of inquiry. Her publications include notes to the *Franklin's Tale* for the *Riverside Chaucer*, a chapter on *Sir Gowther* in *The Matter of Identity in Medieval Romance* (2002), and 'Transgressive Fathers in Sir Eglamour of Artois and Torrent of Portyngale', in *Discourses on Love, Marriage, and Transgression in Medieval and Early Modern Literature* (2004).

Thomas H. Crofts is Assistant Professor of English at East Tennessee State University. His book *Malory's Contemporary Audience: The Social Reading of Romance in Late Medieval England* (2006), and several articles on Arthurian romance, investigate the contexts and contingencies of medieval literary production. He is currently at work on the Greek Arthurian poem 'The Ancient Knight'.

Désirée Cromwell, an independent scholar currently residing in Portland, Oregon, received her master's degree in English literature from the University of Montana, where she studied popular Middle English romance. Her work with twelfth-century romance won best presentation in UM's 2005 CAL graduate conference. She is working towards a doctoral degree.

Jennifer Fellows edits the Modern Humanities Research Association's *Annual Bibliography of English Language and Literature*. Her own published work is mostly on Middle English romance and on the theory and practice of editing medieval popular texts. She has also produced an edition of Richard Johnson's late Elizabethan prose romance *The Seven Champions of Christendom* (2003). Her most recent publication is *Sir Bevis of Hampton in Literary Tradition* (2008), a collection of essays co-edited with Ivana Djordjević.

Rosalind Field is Reader in Medieval Literature at Royal Holloway, University of London. Her publications include 'Romance in England, 1066–1400' in *The Cambridge History of Medieval English Literature*, ed. David Wallace (1999) and 'Romance' in *The Oxford History of Literary Translation in English*, Vol. I, ed. Roger Ellis (2008). She has recently co-edited *Guy of Warwick: Icon and Ancestor* (2007).

Phillipa Hardman is Reader in Medieval English Literature at the University of Reading. She has published articles on Chaucer, Lydgate, the *Gawain-*

poet, Middle English romances, manuscript history and illustration, medieval miscellanies, and Jane Austen, has edited *The Heege MS: Nat. Lib. Scot. MS Adv. 19.3.1* (2000), *The Matter of Identity in Medieval Romance* (2002), and *Medieval and Early Modern Miscellanies and Anthologies* (2003), and is co-author of *The Growth of the Tristan and Iseut Legend* (2003). Her current research interests are focused on the English Charlemagne romances.

Maldwyn Mills, Emeritus Professor at Aberystwyth University, has published articles and chapters on the Middle English romances, the *Linguistic Atlas of Late Medieval English*, and the crime novel; also editions of *Lybeaus Desconus*, *Horn Childe and Maiden Rimnild*, *Fragments of an Early Fourteenth-Century Guy of Warwick* (with Daniel Huws), *Troylus and Criseyde*, and the collections *Six Middle English Romances* and *Ywain and Gawain*, *Syr Percyvell of Gales*, *The Anturs of Arther*. He has taken part in recordings of *Horn Childe*, *Sir Gawain and the Green Knight*, and Chaucer's *Summoner's Tale*. At present his research and publication are most concerned with the post-medieval texts of earlier romances in Bodleian MS Douce 261 (of which he is preparing an edition), and the text of *Lybeaus* in the Percy Folio MS.

Ad Putter is Reader in English Literature at the University of Bristol. He is the author of *Sir Gawain and the Green Knight and French Arthurian Romance* (1995), *An Introduction to the Gawain Poet* (1996), and co-author (with Judith Jefferson and Myra Stokes) of *Studies in the Metre of Alliterative Verse* (2007). In the field of popular romance he has written various essays and is co-editor with Jane Gilbert of *The Spirit of Medieval English Popular Romance* (2000).

Raluca L. Radulescu is Senior Lecturer in Medieval Literature and Director of the Centre for Medieval Studies at Bangor University, UK. She is the author of *The Gentry Context for Malory's* Morte Darthur (2003), and co-editor of several collections of essays: (with Alison Truelove) *Gentry Culture in Late Medieval England* (2005), (with Kevin S. Whetter) Re-viewing Le Morte Darthur (2005), (with William Marx) *Readers and Writers of the* Brut Chronicles (2006), and (with Edward Donald Kennedy) *Broken Lines: Genealogical Literature in Medieval Britain and France* (2008). These publications as well as current work on spiritual journeys in medieval English romance reflect her interdisciplinary approach to medieval literature and culture.

Karl Reichl is Professor of Medieval Literature and Historical Linguistics at the Institute of English, American and Celtic Studies of the University of Bonn, Germany. Research interests include the medieval lyric, medieval romance and epic and oral poetry. Apart from work on medieval English literature, he has studied, edited and translated a number of oral epics from Central Asia. Among his major publications are *Religiöse Dichtung im englischen Hochmittelalter* (1973), *Turkic Oral Epic Poetry. Traditions, Forms, Poetic Structure* (1992), *Singing the Past: Turkic and Medieval Heroic Poetry* (2000) and *Edige: A Karakalpak Oral Epic as Performed by Jumabay*

Bazarov (2007). He has edited *A Concordance of Six Middle English Tail-Rhyme Romances* with W. Sauer (1993) and, with J. Harris, a collection of articles on *Prosimetrum: Crosscultural Perspectives on Narrative in Prose and Verse* (1997).

Gillian Rogers was formerly the English Faculty Librarian at the University of Cambridge. Her main research interests lie in the field of Middle English Arthurian romance, in particular the *Gawain*-poems, and in the transmission of these in the sixteenth and seventeenth centuries. She has published articles on the mid-seventeenth-century Percy Folio Manuscript, 'Golagros and Gawain', the Percy Folio version of 'The Grene Knight', and edited the chapter on 'Folk Romance' in *The Arthur of the English* (1999). She is currently working, with others, on an edition of the Arthurian items in the Percy Folio Manuscript.

Robert Rouse is Associate Professor of Medieval English Literature at the University of British Columbia in Vancouver, Canada. His research interests range across both Old and Middle English literature, addressing issues of historiography, nationalism and the medieval geographical imagination. He is the author of *The Idea of Anglo-Saxon England in Middle English Romance* (2005) and (with Cory J. Rushton) *The Medieval Quest for Arthur* (2005).

Cory James Rushton is Assistant Professor of English at St Francis Xavier University in Nova Scotia, Canada. In addition to numerous articles on the Arthurian legend and medieval romance, particularly Malory, he is co-editor (with Amanda Hopkins) of *The Erotic in the Literature of Medieval Britain* (2007), and editor of *Disability and Medieval Law: History, Literature, Society* (Cambridge Scholars Publishing). He co-wrote *The Medieval Quest for Arthur* with Robert Rouse (2005), and provided historical commentary for the recent DVD re-release of the film *First Knight* (2008).

Abbreviations

AN	Anglo-Norman
CUL	Cambridge University Library
Cultural Encounters	*Cultural Encounters in the Romance of Medieval England*, ed. Corinne Saunders, Studies in Medieval Romance (Cambridge: D. S. Brewer, 2005)
English Romance in Time	Helen Cooper, *The English Romance in Time: Transforming Motifs from Geoffrey of Monmouth to the Death of Shakespeare* (Oxford: Oxford University Press, 2004)
EETS	Early English Text Society
OS	Original Series
ES	Extra Series
SS	Supplementary Series
IMEV	*Index of Middle English Verse*, ed. Carleton Brown and Rossell Hope Robbins (New York: Columbia University Press for the Index Society, 1943)
Insular Romance	*Medieval Insular Romance*, ed. Judith Weiss, Jennifer Fellows and Morgan Dickson (Cambridge: D. S. Brewer, 2000)
Manual	*A Manual of the Writings in Middle English 1050-1500: I. Romances*, gen. ed. J. Burke Severs (New Haven: Connecticut Academy of Arts and Sciences, 1967)
Matter of Identity	*The Matter of Identity in Medieval Romance*, ed. Phillipa Hardman (Cambridge: D. S. Brewer, 2002)
ME	Middle English
MED	*Middle English Dictionary* (online version) <http://quod.lib.umich.edu/m/med/>
Middle English Romances	Dieter Mehl, *The Middle English Romances of the Thirteenth and Fourteenth Centuries* (London: Routledge and Kegan Paul, 1986)
OED	*Oxford English Dictionary*
ODNB	*Oxford Dictionary of National Biography*, online edition
OFr	Old French
Pulp Fictions	*Pulp Fictions of Medieval England: Essays in popular romance*, ed. Nicola McDonald (Manchester: Manchester University Press, 2004)
Riverside Chaucer	*The Riverside Chaucer*, gen. ed. Larry D. Benson (Boston: Houghton Mifflin, 1987)
Romance Reading	*Romance Reading on the Book: Essays on Medieval Narrative presented to Maldwyn Mills*, ed. Jennifer Fellows,

	Rosalind Field, Gillian Rogers and Judith Weiss (Cardiff: University of Wales Press, 1996)
Spirit	*The Spirit of Medieval Popular Romance*, ed. Ad Putter and Jane Gilbert (Harlow: Longman, 2000)
STC	*A Short-Title Catalogue of Books Printed in England, Scotland, & Ireland, and of English Books Printed Abroad, 1475–1640*, ed. W. A. Jackson, F. S. Ferguson and Katharine F. Pantzer, rev. edn, 3 vols (London: Bibliographical Society, 1976–91)

Introduction

RALUCA L. RADULESCU and CORY JAMES RUSHTON

The study of medieval popular romance, in Middle English or any other language, is a notoriously tricky business. Scholarly consensus over the apparent low aesthetic quality, unsophisticated form and limited conceptual framework exhibited by most medieval popular romances has affected many analyses of these texts until relatively recently. An impatience concerning the debate over the nature of their genre and classification, as well as their representative (or not) status in relation to English medieval literary culture, resulted in the selection of very few such texts for inclusion into the mainstream undergraduate curriculum – usually reserved for texts of high literary status, by authors like Langland and Chaucer. The oft-anthologized Breton lay *Sir Orfeo*, already distanced from other popular romances through a lack of purely chivalric focus, may be considered an exception, primarily due to its length and combination of elements – Celtic harping, magic and the fairy, links (however odd) with classical mythology, as well as the good stewardship motif – and despite the lack of any extensive descriptions of knightly combat (Orfeo's 'fighting' and winning of the lady is done by harp alone).[1] The absence of conveniently short, cheap and linguistically accessible editions until the arrival of Western Michigan University's TEAMS texts in 1964, with some notable exceptions, only partially accounts for the neglect popular romance has suffered.

While recent essay collections have gone some way towards mapping out this difficult territory, no comprehensive investigation of medieval popular romance is available to date. Ad Putter's and Jane Gilbert's collection, *The Spirit of Medieval English Popular Romance* (2000), addressed important issues in its introduction, including classification and the notion of 'popular', though overall it favoured studies of individual romances from a variety of perspectives rather than a systematic approach to the popular romance.[2] Nicola McDonald's edited collection *Pulp Fictions of Medieval England* (2004) similarly brought together a long overdue assessment of some popular romances, but, once again, without aiming for a hierarchy of themes or approaches (although her aptly named 'Polemical Introduction' provides

---

[1] For an assessment of the popularity of *Sir Orfeo* and the problematic nature of teaching romance, see Rosalind Field's chapter in this volume, pp. 9–30, and Cory Rushton's, pp. 165–79.
[2] See 'Introduction', in *Spirit*.

a number of interesting and provocative starting points).³ In addition, this collection emphasized the spectacular or controversial elements present in only some of the romances, at the expense of an overview of all popular romance, including the more down-to-earth, expected motif and trope combinations found throughout the genre. The *Cambridge Companion to Medieval Romance* (2000), edited by Roberta Krueger, is an interesting but diffuse collection of essays which, in its rather ambitious approach, covers all medieval romance in a variety of languages, but without enough specific guidance for the researcher of English popular romance.

The present Companion aims to address this perceived gap, while consciously questioning the concepts that shape 'popular' and 'romance' and the place of this genre in medieval culture and contemporary scholarship. Furthermore, it aims to provide a much needed guide to issues pertinent to the student and researcher of popular romance alike; although not exhaustive, the chapters are intended as comprehensive reviews of the state of play in the field, as well as pointers to areas that need further attention. Both editors and contributors start from the premise that the very definition of 'popular romance' is troubled by the conflicting definitions of its constituent parts: romance as a genre has defied final generic definition for decades, and the notion of popularity needs to be released from the modern associations of the term, and re-examined in its medieval context. The first two chapters in this Companion, by Rosalind Field (pp. 9–30) and Raluca Radulescu (pp. 31–48), provide a broad context for subsequent discussions by focusing respectively on the history of the genre and definitions of its admittedly-vague key terminology. Of equal importance is Ad Putter's exploration of metre and stanza forms, and the ways in which these issues can affect interpretation (pp. 111–31); the study of the popular romance is not the only critical area which might benefit from a renewed attention to poetry itself, and might even have something to teach scholars of later periods.

Contrary to older approaches, according to which it was preferable to keep a safe distance from the aesthetic nature of the popular romances' texts by taking refuge in textual or historical approaches, recent studies attest to an increased interest in what Middle English popular romance can reveal about contemporary culture, especially in relation to its evident lack of reverence for elite models of behaviour and its traditional 'appetite' for taboo issues. Traditional approaches tended to focus on respectable academic issues: editorial questions, comparisons with sources, relationships between manuscripts, their production, ownership and transmission, as well as language and dialect problems. In relation to these, more literary approaches (including the historical approaches favoured by the earliest editors) have preferred to find orderly and structured themes, such as happy endings, reunited families, and social and political order: in other words, 'tame' topics which seemed intrinsic to

---

3   See 'Polemical Introduction', in *Pulp Fictions*.

Introduction

popular romance as a genre. By contrast, recent work has turned to the very disturbing images – rape, incest, racial discrimination and religious intolerance – often encountered in these texts. As becomes evident to any newcomer to popular romance, both scholarly approaches are much needed, even if each requires an open attitude to, on the one hand, modern preconceptions about the nature of the archetypal text and its reconstruction, and on the other, the relationship between reality and the ideal or extreme in representations of gender, race and socio-political conditions in such texts. By becoming aware of our own tendency to fit popular romance into what can often be seen as the straightjacket of modern ideological and cultural fashions, we can try to retrieve some of the elements that made romance so popular in its own time. As Paul Freedman notes:

> Whether the medieval period is perceived as having a particular penchant for irrational persecution (the view of those emphasizing human progress) or as originating undesirable characteristics of modernity (the beginnings of colonialism, aggressive expansion, or intolerance), there is a temptation to look at the Middle Ages through the lens of contemporary concerns, through a certain hermeneutic of suspicion. While we cannot escape our own time and certain of its assumptions, there is more to be gained by looking at a period such as the Middle Ages as much as possible in terms of its own realities, not as a negative example or foundational model.[4]

In other words, it is not enough to acknowledge the repugnance felt by earlier generations of scholars towards romance,[5] and turn to rescuing popular romance from undeserved neglect by going in the opposite direction, which is equally dangerous – that of over-emphasizing the articulation of violence and taboo subjects in popular romances at the expense of their sometimes genuine entertainment value, and even a sometimes paradoxically refreshing lack of sophistication.[6] Our effort to redeem medieval popular romance forms an integral part of the modern project of recuperating 'medieval popular culture', a concept long acknowledged as problematic and vague. As Aron Gurevich rightly points out, 'In the first place, popular culture should not be regarded solely as a single identity distinct from official or "learned" culture: popular culture itself was composed of widely divergent components and tendencies.'[7] While Gurevich refers to mental structures in high versus

---

[4] Paul Freedman, 'The Medieval Other: The Middle Ages as Other', in *Marvels, Monsters and Miracles: Studies in the Medieval and Early Modern Imaginations*, ed. Timothy S. Jones and David A. Sprunger (Kalamazoo: Medieval Institute Publications, 2002), pp. 1–24 (p. 23).
[5] For a review of such older attitudes, see Nicola McDonald, 'Polemical Introduction', in *Pulp Fictions*, passim.
[6] See, for example, Paul Price's 'Confessions of a Godless Killer: Guy of Warwick and Comprehensive Entertainment', in *Insular Romance*, pp. 93–110.
[7] Foreword to Aron Gurevich, *Medieval Popular Culture: Problems of Belief and Perception*, trans. Janos M. Bak and Paul A. Hollingsworth (Cambridge: Cambridge University Press, 1988), p. xviii. Gurevich deliberately chose to 'dig deeper' into layers of subconsciousness: 'I have not focussed on the concrete cultural products usually studied by historians of literature, art and

popular culture in the Latin religious culture of the tenth and eleventh centuries, he in fact seeks to 'elucidate those mental constructs and customary orientations of consciousness, the "psychological equipment" and "spiritual rigging" of medieval people which were not clearly formulated, explicitly expressed or completely recognized'. In a similar fashion, scholars of medieval popular romance continue to unearth attitudes and behaviours that are not always completely articulated in these texts and indeed not always acknowledged even as a possibility. Joanne Charbonneau, for example, has pointed out how in two English popular romances (*Eglamour of Artois* and *Torrent of Portyngale*) suggestions of possible incest are always present, even if not actualized; she notes that 'despite this gesturing towards real cultural problems, these authors allow social concerns to slip away; the situation with problematic families with which the narratives open thus becomes a mere backdrop or background for the actions within the narratives'.[8] In fact, Charbonneau notes that there is even a tendency for 'the authors [to] turn to folklore motifs and archetypal forces of good and evil':

> It is as though these authors have created a space in which to explore painful realities, but are unwilling to write incest into their texts: it may be too painful a reminder of the precarious position of families and continuing family lines. Perhaps the authors felt that of the immediately available genres – *exempla*, allegory, hagiography, complaint, and historical and historiographical texts – romance seemed to fit best their need for inscribing cultural anxieties. (pp. 263–4)

Similar conclusions may be drawn from other popular romances, where a modern reader might perceive strikingly intolerant ways of dealing with women, children, the dispossessed, the 'Other'. The importance of critical engagement with these issues for the academic rehabilitation of the romance cannot be underestimated: in the present volume, Joanne Charbonneau and Désirée Cromwell provide a context for our current understanding of gender and the family in the popular romance, while Robert Rouse and Thomas H. Crofts discuss different and sometimes surprising formulations of race and nationality (the latter itself a much-debated word when it comes to the Middle Ages). Whether or not such 'cultural anxieties' were inscribed in these

---

philosophy; I have attempted instead to "dig down" to the intellectual, ideational, affective and socio-psychological soil in which culture arose and by which it was sustained. Perhaps it would be more precise to speak not about culture, but about that layer of consciousness in which its elements originated and were defined, namely the more amorphous, unstructured sphere of images, notions, beliefs and stereotypes hovering in social consciousness. To this end, I have sought that level of consciousness situated "lower" than the level of ideas and artistic works' (p. xix).

[8] Joanne Charbonneau, 'Transgressive Fathers in *Sir Eglamour of Artois* and *Torrent of Portyngale*', in *Discourses on Love, Marriage, and Transgression in Medieval and Early Modern Literature*, ed. Albrecht Classen (Tempe: Arizona Center for Medieval and Renaissance Studies, 2004), pp. 243–65 (pp. 262–3).

Introduction

texts in a visible way at the time of their inception, and recognized as such by their first audiences, forms part of the investigation we are conducting. What is evident, however, is that the popularity of these texts clearly attests to a widespread appetite for narratives likely to tackle some uncomfortable home truths, whether these are family issues or religious belief and practice. Indeed, as Jerome Jeffrey Cohen has aptly put it, romance can be seen as the genre 'that created a mode of being, transubstantiating social reality'.[9]

Thus we need to return to the term 'popular', and revisit its association with 'medieval romance', since in this context 'popular' has acquired some defined features, largely influenced by modern studies focusing on access to literature in the post-print era. As modern readers, critics and students alike, we understand the popularity of a text to refer to its accessibility to a wide audience, as witnessed by a particular text's circulation; the level of vocabulary and conceptual sophistication; and the appeal of the theme or topic it addresses. In other words, 'popular' has strong links with literacy levels but also with expectations and their fulfilment. Similarly, the term urges us to consider a middle-class audience, and, in a modern context, mass production and consumption. None of these terms is applicable as such to medieval romances. Only sometimes read by one individual, but more often recited, read aloud to a group, or performed, the medieval popular romance cannot be judged against the same principles we use for modern productions. Further, the charge of elitism often levelled at academic critics when they differentiate between 'high' and 'low' cultural productions takes on a peculiar tone when refracted through a historical lens: who, exactly, are the elites disparaging when they reject popular romance on aesthetic grounds? Neither the producers nor the audience for popular romance are defined universally in the same way, as Karl Reichl (on the orality of the romance, and the vexed question of the minstrel) and Rosalind Field (on the evolution of the romance from its Anglo-Norman origins to its Middle English manifestations) argue in this Companion.

Indeed, the typical structure (or 'grammar', as Derek Pearsall calls it) of romance would involve recognizable 'plot-patterns, [...] situations, [...] phrases':

> The reason for this close stereotyping [...] is to be found in the social context of Middle English romance, which is overwhelmingly popular and non-courtly. True courtly romance had no real vogue in English, since the audience who could appreciate it, at the time when it was fashionable, was French-speaking.[10]

---

9 Jerome Jeffrey Cohen, *Of Giants: Sex, Monsters, and the Middle Ages* (Minneapolis and London: University of Minnesota Press, 1999), p. 79.
10 Derek Pearsall, 'The Development of Middle English Romance', in *Studies in Medieval English Romances*, ed. D. Brewer (Cambridge: D. S. Brewer, 1988), pp. 11–35 (pp. 11–12).

Pearsall identifies the primary audience of popular romance as 'a lower or lower middle-class audience, a class of social aspirants who wish to be entertained with what they consider to be the same fare, but in English, as their social betters [...] a new class, an emergent bourgeoisie', and the heyday of romance in the fourteenth century, though the fifteenth also witnessed developments, either of a more sophisticated nature, or in the opposite direction, of more debased forms. Jennifer Fellows notes (this volume, pp. 67–78) that several romances retained their popularity throughout the sixteenth century, as witnessed by their appearance in print; at the same time, she argues, on the basis of several case studies, that the revision of some romances continued after they moved into print culture, testifying to the living nature of the genre. On the other hand, the popular romance also developed a reputation as literature for the young; Phillipa Hardman discusses the number of romances either centred on child-characters or focused on what we might now call developmental issues (pp. 150–64, and Charbonneau and Cromwell, pp. 96–110). As children's literature, the romance survived until readers like the young Walter Scott could be exposed to them, and from there they gradually moved back into the mainstream. The end of this movement, as discussed by Cory Rushton (pp. 165–79), is the new critical interest evidenced by the current Companion.

The popularity of a medieval text is commonly judged by scholars with reference both to the number of extant manuscripts and external references to the circulation or appreciation of the text in its own period and afterwards. According to this principle, religious works and later historical material like the *Brut* chronicle would rightly deserve the label 'popular', and have been called, alongside the Wycliffite Bible, best-sellers in late medieval England. The relatively low number of surviving popular insular romances pales in comparison with the hundreds of manuscripts of chronicles and religious material. Some critics, like Lee Ramsey, emphasize the high esteem in which devotional works were held by their audiences, by comparison with romances:

> Romances never pretended to give an accurate picture of life in their times, and they were not even the dominant form of medieval literature. To judge by the numbers of surviving manuscripts and the lists of library holdings during the Middle Ages, serious works in Latin and devotional works in the vernacular languages were more widely read, and both were certainly more esteemed, even among that part of the population which made up the principal audience for the romance.[11]

While religious and historical material commanded respect and in their turn gave respectability to those who owned them, the impact of romances on

---

[11] Lee Ramsey, *Chivalric Romances: Popular Literature in Medieval England* (Bloomington: Indiana University Press, 1983), p. 1.

their audiences was clearly visible, if we take into account the multiple copies that survive, sometimes in quite different variants and contexts, and their longevity over time, in the post-medieval period.

If a romance does survive in more copies in Anglo-Norman than in Middle English, as is the case, for example, with *Guy of Warwick* (see Field's chapter), one would be tempted to draw the conclusion that it was more popular with its Anglo-Norman audience. However, if we apply categories like 'open' and 'closed' to audience, they might help to bring our understanding of such a situation closer to what popular would actually mean in a medieval environment.[12] We can never be certain how many people heard a romance delivered in performance, for example, or how widely any given manuscript may have circulated. We propose, therefore, to judge 'popular' romances according to evidence of their widespread appeal in their own period (judged not just by number of copies, but through cross-references, evidence of readership and circulation), and the legacy they left in the post-medieval period, whether in the form of parody, ballad, or song. To take just one example, the Percy Folio witnesses to the popularity of several earlier texts, more than justifying its use as a case study in the survey chapter on manuscripts by Maldwyn Mills and Gillian Rogers. Indeed, the Percy Folio appears time and again in this Companion, along with other important manuscripts like the Auchinleck.

In brief, in this Companion we define 'popular romance' as those texts in Middle English, sometimes with origins in Anglo-Norman versions, which show a predominant concern with narrative at the expense of symbolic meaning. Such texts appear to have been widely read or heard, but have subsequently been ignored by scholarship as less worthy of study than the equivalent productions by Chaucer or the *Gawain*-poet, on the grounds of representing an inferior level of literary achievement, and lack of sophistication (see Rushton's chapter). In this collection we posit that popular romances were primarily aimed at a non-aristocratic audience, allowing that some themes and motifs travelled across social class boundaries. This definition, less stable than it is inclusive, aims to engender further debate. Most essays in this volume necessarily engage with theoretical approaches, hence offering multiple views of the 'popular' aspect of medieval romance. In this sense the collection serves to provide both an introduction to and a consolidation of the field, a reference point for establishing the parameters for the sub-genre and ground-breaking suggestions for further research. The topics covered in the Companion are very much the result of a dialogue between older and newer approaches; degrees of overlap or indeed some apparent disagreements in the chapters reflect, we believe, the ongoing debate about popular romance and its attributes. Rather than offer a monolithic view of popular romance at the

---

[12] Harriet E. Hudson, 'Toward a Theory of Popular Literature: The Case of the Middle English Romances', *Journal of Popular Culture* 23 (1989), 31–50.

beginning of the twenty-first century, this volume endeavours to present the healthy state of play in the field – in other words, a dialogue among established and younger scholars, urging modern audiences of medieval popular romance to delve deeper into this fascinating area of study.

1

Popular Romance: The Material and the Problems

ROSALIND FIELD

The Middle English verse romances of the thirteenth and fourteenth centuries have always posed a problem to academic study and modern readers. The majority are textually fragile, anonymous, and lack clear cultural and social contexts. Dealing with such textual and cultural problems is the business of scholarship, but these works remain resistant to an academic discourse that privileges difficulty in interpretation, an elite response, a professional readership. More seriously they are evidently the ancestors of a popular literary culture that academic discourse prefers to ignore, unless under the copious umbrella of cultural studies.

There are basic problems with the double meaning of 'popular' as both widely appreciated and culturally of 'the people', with an accompanying subtext of mediocrity: 'Rather than being only demographically descriptive, in critical practice, "popular" has tended to drag in its train the sense "unsophisticated".'[1] This perceived lack of sophistication has in turn generated some questionable assumptions about audience and reception, assumptions which have all too often served to mark the superior cultural level of critic and reader.

However, since 1971, when John Halverson was able to remark that '*Havelok the Dane* is one of a very small number of Middle English romances that still retain their charm', attitudes to the anonymous romances have moved considerably – Derek Brewer remarked on the 'explosion of interest' that took place in the 1980s,[2] and this has continued. The reasons have as much to do with new developments in critical approaches as with the romances themselves, especially the willingness to give serious consideration to works outside the canonical texts recognized as major Literature. At the same time a new appreciation of the power of narrative convention has altered attitudes, most notably in Helen Cooper's recent adaptation of the

---

[1] Ralph Hanna, *London Literature, 1300–1380* (Cambridge: Cambridge University Press, 2005), p. 107.
[2] John Halverson, '*Havelok the Dane* and Society', *Chaucer Review* 6 (1971–2), 142–51 (p. 142); Derek Brewer, 'Escape from the Mimetic Fallacy', in *Studies in Medieval English Romances*, ed. D. Brewer (Cambridge: D. S. Brewer, 1988), pp. 1–10 (p. 1).

'meme' to chart the movement of romance conventions from the Angevin period to the Renaissance.[3]

The initial problem has always been the unmanageable nature of the raw material and the sheer quantity of narratives of all shapes and none. Various taxonomic strategies have been used to organize Middle English romances. The clearest and most influential is by subject matter – as in the *Manual*, Hibbard (Loomis)'s *Mediæval Romance in England*, Barron's *English Medieval Romance* and numerous anthologies. Categorization by subject matter tends to adopt the Matters of medieval narrative: Rome, France, Britain, sometimes extended to England,[4] but this leaves a large and varied group of works under Miscellaneous or 'non-cyclic'. Hibbard (Loomis) adopted a more thematic approach to avoid this (Romances of Trial and Faith/ of Love and Adventure) and this approach is reflected in the titles of a number of recent collections – *Tales of Love and Chivalry* (Fellows), *Humorous and Sentimental Romances* (TEAMS), the homiletic or pious romances. The shifting, often subjective nature of this approach is avoided by other, more factual, categories, including classification by length (Mehl's Shorter Romances, Longer Romances, Novels in Verse), date – Early Middle English, fourteenth or fifteenth century (Pearsall) – and form – verse, tail-rhyme, alliterative (Mills).[5]

This presents further problems, as any attempt to organize or to select works that seem by one set of criteria or another to belong together shapes and controls the perception and reception of the romances. Another unacknowledged, but powerful, factor is the marketing of the romances. Anthologies and selections are put together with an eye to their accessibility to modern readers and especially their usefulness in courses; brevity is a strong survival factor here and many long romances are sadly neglected.[6] This is partly a pragmatic response to the realities of modern conditions of readership, and student courses and anthologies are the drivers which have established a 'canon' of standard texts. However, recent scholarship has moved beyond

---

[3] Cooper, *English Romance in Time*.
[4] Rosalind Field, 'The Curious History of the Matter of England', in *Boundaries in Medieval Romance*, ed. Neil Cartlidge (Cambridge: D. S. Brewer, 2008), pp. 29–42.
[5] *Manual*; Laura A. Hibbard (Loomis), *Mediæval Romance in England* (New York: Oxford University Press, 1924); W. R. J. Barron, *English Medieval Romance* (Harlow: Longman, 1987); Mehl, *Middle English Romances*; Derek Pearsall, 'The Development of Middle English Romance', *Medieval Studies* 27 (1965), 91–116; *Six Middle English Romances*, ed. Maldwyn Mills (London: Dent, 1973); *Of Love and Chivalry: An Anthology of Middle English Romance*, ed. Jennifer Fellows (London: Dent, 1993); *Sentimental and Humorous Romances*, ed. Erik Kooper, TEAMS series (Kalamazoo, MI: Medieval Institute Publications, 2006).
[6] The prime example of this is the tail-rhyme *Ipomadon*, generally recognized as one of the finest Middle English romances, extracts from which are to be found in only two student-level anthologies, *Middle English Metrical Romances*, ed. W. H. French and C. B. Hale (New York: Russell & Russell, 1930) and *Medieval English Romances*, ed. A. V. C. Schmidt and N. Jacobs (London: Hodder & Stoughton, 1980).

The Material and the Problems

this canon, to investigate largely neglected texts,[7] while the increasing availability of on-line texts in good editions is opening up a wider area to a larger readership.

Gaps in our knowledge about the occasions and conditions under which these texts were written and performed are inevitable, given the passage of time, but the anonymous nature of popular romance is in itself disorientating for modern readers, particularly perhaps in texts like these which deal with personal, family and social relationships. Arguably, medieval studies have long been familiar with the consequences of the Death of the Author, but modern theoretical developments have conferred respectability upon this situation. In the absence of an individual authorial voice, let alone the biographical dimension so vital to traditional literary study, the reader has to fill the gap with an attempt to historicize, to examine the audience, to deconstruct the texts' attitudes to power, gender, or society.

However, the conditions that are responsible for the anonymity of the majority of these texts also produce a narrative style that permits spaces and silences which modern narrative fiction would hasten to fill, but by which medieval popular romance engages its readers. We read into the conventional narrative, precisely because it is conventional narrative, the unspoken nuances that give the romance particularity and power. As will be indicated in this discussion, the result has been some critical readings of considerable subtlety and perception, as well as a constructive lack of agreement as to the meaning of some of the shortest and apparently simplest of romances.

We shall look at a selection of romances that have always been seen as 'popular' in the unsophisticated sense of the word and have proved popular with modern as well as medieval readers. We shall use them to examine the assumptions about popularity, the procedures of the long romance and the critical search for meaning and context in the romance of the family and the romance of the popular hero.

Popular romance in Anglo-Norman

If you give me some of your silver I shall now tell you more of the truth of this: if not, I shall leave it at that.[8]

The performer demanding money from his audience in the middle of his romance would seem a clear indicator of a popular level of literary produc-

---

7 *Pulp Fictions* contains studies on largely neglected romances such as *The King of Tars* (Jane Gilbert), *Richard Coeur de Lion* (Nicola McDonald) and *Le Bone Florence of Rome* (Felicity Riddy).
8 'Issi com vus me orrez a dreit conter / Si vus me volez de vostre argent doner, / Ou si noun, jeo lerrai issi ester', *Boeve*, 434–6; my translation. The complete romance is available in translation in *Boeve de Haumtone and Gui de Warewic*, trans. and intro. Judith Weiss (Tempe, AZ: Arizona Center for Medieval and Renaissance Studies, 2008).

tion and reception.⁹ And the romance in question, that dealing with the career of Bevis of Hampton, is a fast-moving narrative, with rather blunt and confused morality, little finesse of behaviour, and a direct appeal to a horse-loving, xenophobic, audience. The style is accessible with few pretensions of symbolic depth, there is no clearly individual authorial voice and the work has a confused textual history. All these are recognized features of 'popular' romance. As well as providing highly effective entertainment, the narrative deals with important issues of the day, and its later history shows it to be widely successful, that is, popular in the other meaning of the term.

But there is a problem here for modern systems of classification. This 'minstrel' demand is from the Anglo-Norman *Boeve de Hauntoun*, written in the vernacular associated with the higher ranks of post-Conquest society. Its subject matter links it firmly with a baronial family, and the name of the hero's horse with Arundel and its aristocratic owners.

The case of *Boeve* raises two issues around the definitions of popular literature. Firstly, the unexamined class-based assumptions according to which aristocrats, by virtue of their rank, have refined literary tastes. And secondly the question that arises from the peculiar situation in medieval England – in a bilingual culture can popular literature exist in the socially superior vernacular, a language largely inaccessible to the majority of the population? Rather than accepting the sophisticated tastes of the aristocracy as a given, it is more helpful to start with the distinction between 'open' and 'closed' narratives.¹⁰ Most Anglo-Norman romance originates as 'coterie' literature and has the named author and the identifiable patron to go with it.¹¹ The aesthetics of this 'closed' literature are exemplified in another AN romance, Hue de Rotelande's *Ipomadon*: well-informed literary references, in-jokes and a generally subversive humour, a named author, the flattery of a named patron: all indicative of a close and familiar audience with shared assumptions about fashionable courtly literature. It is a courtly aesthetic evident in several of the AN romances, but more likely to be familiar to readers through the later works of Chaucer or the *Gawain*-poet.

The clearest exceptions to this aesthetic amongst the AN romances of the late twelfth and early thirteenth centuries are *Boeve* and *Gui de Warewic*, translations of which are found in the Auchinleck MS and which go on to have a long history as popular English romances. The AN period thus indicates that romance in England held an appeal from the highest in the land to a wider audience for performed entertainment.

---

⁹ Nancy Mason Bradbury, 'The Traditional Origins of *Havelok the Dane*', *Studies in Philology* 90 (1999), 115–42 (p. 127), surveys work on the fictionality of such 'minstrel' remarks, but sees them as typical of Middle English romance.

¹⁰ Harriet E. Hudson, 'Towards a Theory of Popular Literature: The Case of the Middle English Romances', *Journal of Popular Culture* 23 (1989), 31–50.

¹¹ Rosalind Field, 'Romance in England, 1066–1400', in *The Cambridge History of Medieval English Literature*, ed. David Wallace (Cambridge: Cambridge University Press, 1999), pp. 152–76 (pp. 154–62).

The Material and the Problems

Nevertheless, the AN romances tend to be long, and length is often a marker of courtliness as it requires a given audience's attention over several occasions. But the AN *Gui* demonstrates that length can be turned into a feature of the popular narrative. The difficulties posed by a romance of some thirteen thousand lines to the medieval audience, or indeed the modern reader, can be met if we take into account the apparently careful structuring of a romance such as *Gui/Guy* into discrete episodes of a manageable length. To read a long romance, an episode at a time, over a length of time is to release its entertainment potential. These long works are not meant to be read at one sitting, any more than a television series is designed to be watched for ten hours.

We can examine this by looking at one of the typical episodes the accumulation of which make up the lengthy whole of *Gui/Guy*. Critical attention tends to focus on key episodes – Guy's declaration of love for Felice, his conversion, his fight with Colbrond, his death – but the sheer length of the romance is due to a number of quasi-independent adventures. We take as an example the episode in which Guy, disguised as a pilgrim, comes to the rescue of his old friend Terri of Worms (lines 9393–10775 in *Gui*, 1693–2788 in Stanzaic *Guy*). The episode is approximately a thousand lines in length, as could be delivered in a single performance. The 1095 lines of the ME is a reduction from the 1382 lines of the AN, some of which is the result of turning fast-moving couplets into tail-rhyme, but most of which relates to the more relaxed narration of the AN.[12] The synopsis of the episode is the same for both versions:[13]

> After another long pilgrimage, Guy reaches Germany where he encounters his sworn brother Tirri dressed as a pilgrim, begging for his bread, and full of sorrow. Unrecognized, Guy encourages him to explain the cause of his poverty and distress. Tirri describes how Emperor Reiner's steward Berard has falsely accused him of the death of his uncle, Duke Otes of Pavia (who in fact was slain by Guy previously). Tirri tells how, following his friends' appeal to Reiner, he has been released from prison on agreement that he find and bring Guy to defend him against Berard's accusation. Having searched far and wide, Tirri is convinced that Guy must be dead. As the time has now come to fulfill his agreement with Reiner, Tirri is desperate [stanzas 142–158].
>
> Guy offers comfort to his old friend. Tirri then has a dream which leads the two of them to a cave of treasure, from which Guy takes a magnificent sword. They head towards court together but Tirri becomes so fearful that Guy leaves him at an inn, with the sword in his possession. Guy therefore enters the court alone as an anonymous pilgrim. He enrages Berard with

---

[12] See *Ipomadon*, ed. Rhiannon Purdie, EETS OS 316 (Oxford: Oxford University Press, 2001), pp. lxvii–xx on the effect of translating Anglo-Norman couplets into Middle English tail-rhyme stanzas.
[13] Synopsis by Alison Wiggins in *Guy of Warwick: Icon and Ancestor*, ed. Alison Wiggins and Rosalind Field (Cambridge: D. S. Brewer, 2007), pp. 201–13.

reports of his bad reputation abroad and challenges his treatment of Tirri, whom he agrees to defend [stanzas 159–178].

Guy and Berard are prepared (Berard with a suit of 'double' armour and Guy with the sword from the treasure cave) and engage in a fierce battle. Tirri hides in a church and visits the battlefield only once, when he cannot believe that the fierce warrior he sees is the same pilgrim he met. Evening falls and it is agreed that combat will be resumed the next morning. During the night, through Berard's treachery, Guy is carried to the sea and set adrift in his bed. He awakes to see the stars above him but, by luck or providence, is rescued by a fisherman. At daybreak, finding the pilgrim gone, Reiner confronts Berard. The fisherman intervenes with the news of his rescue and the battle is resumed until Guy is victorious. Guy goes to tell Tirri the news of his defeat and, after correcting his fears of betrayal, has him instated as steward in place of Berard. Before departing, Guy reveals his identity to Tirri [stanzas 179–232].

In modern terms the episode is structured in relation to the whole as part of a series, not a serial. It develops several themes germane to the romance's purposes but it is not essential to the narrative structure: Guy's life-story would be complete enough without it. The cast of characters – Guy, Terri, Berard, the emperor – are familiar from the first half of the romance, so need, and receive, little introduction. Those in the audience who have missed the earlier episodes are brought up to speed by the back-story provided at the beginning, through the now well-worn device of Terri telling his story to the disguised hero whom he believes to be ignorant of it. The episode is marked out by its setting, beginning with a change of scene from Constantinople to Germany and ending as Guy sets out to return to England. The introductory information is fuller in the earlier version, possibly because the material is not yet as familiar as it will be by the fourteenth century, but the balance of the narrative components is similar in both versions. The relationships between the two versions are not direct enough to provide a line-by-line equivalence throughout, but the proportions are similar enough to indicate that the ME redactor(s) saw no need to alter the shape of the original.

The differences in tone and emphasis between the two versions are not such as to indicate significant differences in level of audience taste or literary competence. Both versions rely heavily on direct speech to convey information and emotion and the authorial voice is largely neutral. At some points the ME appears to clarify details in the AN, as in Guy's decision to keep the sword from the magic hoard [*Gui*, 9830; *Guy*, 2000], but it loses the neat narrative symmetry of the first and final conversations between Guy and Terri taking place at a roadside cross. Terri fears that Gui suffers from epilepsy when he swoons at their meeting: the ME omits this. The AN provides more names of people – the emperor is Reiner – and places (Speyer, Worms). The AN duel takes place on an island (perhaps a Tristan echo), which is normalized to a 'launde' in ME.

Gui's imitation of *chanson de geste* style means that the AN is more violent as much of the verbal aggression is lost in translation into English, and the AN tends to give a larger role to the choric onlookers of the emperor's court, another characteristic *chanson* technique. So the angry confrontation between the pilgrim Gui and the emperor and Berard at court is longer and more aggressive in the AN, although the ME Guy makes a telling jibe about boasting (2134–6), and Berard's defiance of the emperor the following morning, when accused of killing the pilgrim, is expanded in the ME into a sustained threat of feudal insurrection (2425–36). This may seem to suggest a stronger emphasis on aristocratic interests, although the ME then omits Gui's generously chivalric lament over the body of his foe. The bed on which Gui spends the night and goes to sea is described as richly furnished in AN, a description omitted in the English which adds its own extra flourish in describing the sea with 'winde and wateres wawe' (2352). In the AN the fisherman first thinks the floating bed is an object of enchantment, whereas the narrative voice in *Guy* ascribes the hero's rescue at sea to the intervention of Jesus (2365–7), and the ME versions rework Guy's prayer. While the ME may here be more pious in expression, the fact remains that it is the AN author who invents the main theme of the conversion of the hero.

These slight changes do not indicate a change in the social make-up of the audience and far more is unchanged: the emotional focus on Guy's relationship with Terri; the marvellous animal dream; the examination of the nature of good and bad rule, both in the criticism of the Emperor and in Guy's parting sermon to Terri; the comic cameo of the fisherman and the scolding of Terri by his wife at the end. The essential themes of the episode, the irony of Guy's disguised persona, the pious nature of his adventure, the repeated defence by the hero not only of his friend but of abstract justice, the bullying nature of his opponents are unchanged in detail or in emphasis. It is an episode that measures Guy's development – as Wiggins has noted, his awareness of the stars echoes the scene of his conversion.[14] But as an adventure it carries its moral message lightly, and the stage business by which the sleeping Guy ends up floating down to sea on a mattress is inescapably absurd – and entertaining.

This is the main point here. The episode is entertaining on several levels, quick-moving, emotional, sensational, violent or comic in places and comfortably moral or pious in others. This is (as I have argued more fully elsewhere[15]) the translation of popular romance from one vernacular into popular romance in another; both versions are 'open' narratives. The tally of extant manuscripts indicates that in the fourteenth century the AN *Gui* was more popular than the ME,[16] although of course it is in English that the story

---

[14] *Stanzaic Guy of Warwick*, ed. Alison Wiggins, TEAMS series (Kalamazoo, MI: Medieval Institute Publications, 2004), note to lines 2347–8.

[15] Rosalind Field, 'From *Gui* to *Guy*: The Fashioning of a Popular Romance', in *Guy of Warwick: Icon and Ancestor*, pp. 44–60.

[16] There are sixteen extant Anglo-Norman copies, five in Middle English; see further two chapters in *Guy of Warwick: Icon and Ancestor*: Marianne Ailes, '*Gui de Warewic* in its Manuscript

of Guy becomes a long-lasting and multi-media legend. The procedures of a romance like *Gui* establish the groundwork for popular romance as it is to develop in England, giving an episodic narrative, that is much copied, famous beyond the text, appealing to the immediate interests and tastes of a wide audience. It should not surprise us that the later history of Guy in English sees it taken up as an ancestral history by one of the most powerful baronial houses in the land; its very directness and lack of narrative ambiguity make the story of Guy into a powerful propaganda tool.

The Middle English Breton lay: the search for meaning

Guy is the model of the long episodic romance, but there are a large number of short verse romances that have been seen as more typical of the popular ME romance of the fourteenth century. Of these the so-called 'Breton Lais' have come to represent the most medieval and most romantic of the English medieval romances and as such have proved particularly popular with modern readers.

The self-identification as Breton Lai as expressed in the prologues to the Auchinleck *Sir Orfeo* and Chaucer's 'The Franklin's Tale' serves to draw attention to an antique origin and association with the marvellous or magical which signals to a medieval audience, not just a modern one, that these works operate symbolically and so require interpretation, and also that they may carry meanings at odds with the fourteenth-century world view. The problem has long been to find meanings which resonate with both the medieval poems and modern understandings of them.

The distance travelled in critical responses to *Sir Orfeo* has been vividly recalled by Derek Pearsall:

> ... over thirty years ago when I was teaching [*Sir Orfeo*] as a set text ... I had no idea why it should have been set or why I was teaching it, but I tried to make the best use of it I could in giving students a grounding in Middle English philology. I remember that the word *owy*, as a possible Kentish dialect form, was a very exciting feature of the poem ... my own individual contribution to the study of the poem consisted principally of scornful attacks upon its artlessness and naivety ... It has taken me a long while to realise that any analysis of those skills according to which *Sir Orfeo* falls short must be a bad analysis or must have chosen the wrong skills to analyse. For in truth *Sir Orfeo* is a small poetic miracle ...[17]

Context', pp. 12–26, and Alison Wiggins, 'The Manuscripts and Texts of the Middle English *Guy of Warwick*', pp. 61–80.

[17] Derek Pearsall, 'Madness in *Sir Orfeo*', in *Romance Reading*, pp. 51–63 (p. 51). Stephen Knight argued in 1966 that *Sir Orfeo* should be read and appreciated on its own terms: 'The Characteristic Mode of "Sir Orfeo"', *Balcony: The Sydney Review* 5 (1966), 17–24.

The Material and the Problems

The literary qualities, which Pearsall and others have recognized, are not those that lend themselves to easy identification or analysis. The problem with a poem like *Sir Orfeo* is simultaneously its particular strength: its apparent simplicity and transparency. It appears to lack the qualities of irony, verbal complexity, conscious artistry and ambiguity that are valued in writers such as Chaucer and of course those of the modern period. But some of this simplicity is not what it seems. The story of Orfeo's rescue of his abducted queen from the fairy otherworld is a deliberate reworking of the Orpheus myth into the romance mode. We may notice the turn in the narrative at precisely the mid-point of the poem,[18] the effective use of repetition with variation and the manipulation of a myth which is the possession of European culture, the appropriation of Celtic magic to make that myth accessible to an insular Christian audience, all evidence of the layered handling of the tale by successive generations of the multilingual culture of medieval England.

Moreover this version represents a move away from the potential for Christian allegory available in medieval readings of the Orpheus myth. The Auchinleck MS is sometimes chided not only for the line about King Juno (which is pretty irredeemable) but for re-situating 'Traciens' (Thrace) in Winchester. But as Rouse has shown in his detailed discussion of the use of Winchester in *Guy of Warwick*, this ancient capital of the Wessex dynasty held a significance for a fourteenth-century audience and this scribal alteration can be seen as part of the 'nationalistic agenda of the Auchinleck MS as a whole'.[19] Furthermore, the Winchester setting is particularly suitable for the story of Orfeo as handled in the ME version where it is no longer a myth of restoration operating on the level of emotional or spiritual fulfilment, but a romance that also examines the nature of kingship and good rule. When the classical Orpheus invades the kingdom of Dis he does not do so as an equal, but Orfeo and the Fairy King of the Otherworld are mirror images of each other. This is first established by one of those conscious repetitions that mark important narrative moments –

Castels & tours / Riuers, forestes, friþ wiþ flours (159–60; 245–6)

and then crucially by Orfeo's demand that the king act in accordance with royal codes of honour. The Rash Promise of folk-lore has transmuted into a test of royal credibility. But it is not only in the Otherworld that kingship is important; the nature of Orfeo's own rule as depicted in his departure and return is clearly exemplary. He does not leave his kingdom irresponsibly, and in appointing his steward as regent opens up the romance to the

---

[18] The turn in Auchinleck, 'And on a day he seiȝe him biside', is at line 303 out of a total of 604 lines. It is not so marked in London, British Library, MS Harley 3810 (line 289) or Oxford, Bodleian Library, MS Ashmole 61 (line 303). See *Sir Orfeo*, ed. A. J. Bliss (Oxford: Oxford University Press, 1954).

[19] Robert Rouse, *The Idea of Anglo-Saxon England in Middle English Romance* (Cambridge: D. S. Brewer, 2005), pp. 59–60.

topic of good rule in absolute terms, irrespective of birth. The testing of the steward on Orfeo's return is the emotional focus of the optimistic closure to the tale, much more so than the reunion with Herodis.[20] The childlessness of the central couple – usually the narrative sign of an unhappy marriage – is necessary to allow the steward to succeed to the throne through merit, not birth.

So the ancient themes of loss, love and restoration are given a positive outcome in *Sir Orfeo*, while the medieval pressure towards allegory and religious exempla is resisted in favour of extending the personal into the political. If, as seems likely enough, Chaucer knew this romance, he may well have mapped onto its structure the pattern that emerges in 'The Franklin's Tale' in order to expand the love triangle of a happy marriage threatened by a magically empowered rival with the addition of the non-noble but honourable figure of the clerk. Both lais demonstrate the power of the contagious nature of virtue, especially the virtue of loyalty exemplified by marriage, converting the predator to honourable behaviour and spreading out from the central couple to become a pattern for a post-feudal society.

A further complication in *Sir Orfeo* is that the supernatural is represented by the fairy otherworld and this contains its own interpretative problems.[21] For several influential readers the poem uses the fairy to construct a myth of madness.[22] Others have been concerned to explore the relationship of the fairy with the mythic kingdom of death, but noted that the 'taken' are presented as undead. I would suggest, however, that while the 'other' that establishes identity in medieval romance is often the traitor, the uncourtly, the Saracen, against which the identity of the loyal, the courtly, the Christian can be asserted, *Sir Orfeo* provides an 'other' which explores nothing less than the identity of being human. The interpretation of the elves of Celtic tradition familiar to modern readers from Tolkien's work is helpful here; and Tolkien, a translator of *Sir Orfeo*, drew heavily on that poem for his material. Here mortality is seen as the key to the human difference from the magical denizens of the otherworld – those taken by the fairy are not dead, because the fairy world knows nothing of the death that defines the human.[23] That Orfeo and Herodis do eventually die in the natural course of events at the

---

[20] Ralph Hanna sees this as Orfeo's 'climactic test', relevant to the world of provincial knighthood represented in the Auchinleck MS's romances, *London Literature*, p. 131; Lynne Staley reads it as speaking 'to many of the political anxieties that characterise late fourteenth-century literature', *Languages of Power in the Reign of Richard II* (University Park: Pennsylvania State University Press, 2005), p. 316; Oren Falk sees the childlessness as a negative, with references to the problems of the reign of Edward II: 'The Son of Orfeo: Kingship and Compromise in a Middle English Romance', *The Journal of Medieval and Early Modern Studies* 30 (2000), 247–74.

[21] See the detailed discussion of the critical difficulties of the supernatural world in *Sir Orfeo* and its place in the literary tradition of the fairy in Neil Cartlidge, 'Sir Orfeo in the Otherword: Courting Chaos', *Studies in the Age of Chaucer* 26 (2004), 195–226.

[22] Pearsall, 'Madness'; A. C. Spearing, '*Sir Orfeo:* Madness and Gender', in *Spirit*, pp. 258–72.

[23] For a recent analysis of the relationship between *Sir Orfeo* and Tolkien's concepts of elves in his own fiction, see Stuart D. Lee and Elizabeth Solopova, *The Keys of Middle Earth* (Basingstoke and New York: Palgrave, 2005), pp. 123–9.

end of the romance is a signifier of their humanity, of the processes of time, even of the possibility of resurrection,[24] at any rate of the re-establishment of the norms of human existence. This is a reading which, in its response to the intervening narrative of Tolkien and to contemporary anxieties about the boundaries of humanity, may well be seen as revealing more of the twenty-first century than the fourteenth.

Sir Orfeo thus requires interpretation which provides a balance between the mythical and the political. Whether it is seen primarily as one of Auchinleck's romances of social responsibility or a mythic exploration of the frontiers of human existence, it retains its ability to engage the reader in concerns that are far from trivial. Its narrative procedure of silences, repetition and patterning demands the readers' active engagement with finding meanings that are not necessarily confined to those available to the original audience.

Emaré is another work that identifies itself as a Breton lai and it is one that even more than *Sir Orfeo* teases by its silences and narrative gaps. It belongs to the narrative type of the 'flight from the incestuous father', in which the daughter flees or is exiled into a life of danger, and shares with many analogues the voyages of the exiled mother and child in a rudderless boat, the cruel mother-in-law and the final reunion of the fractured family.[25] The strong patterning of structural and verbal repetition would seem to suggest a purpose to the outrageous fate visited on a heroine whose only provocative action is to refuse an incestuous relationship with her father. But where most of the analogues, including Chaucer's 'The Man of Law's Tale', are exemplary tales demonstrating providential protection, the problem with *Emaré* would seem to be its failure to contain the power the narrative releases.

Emaré can be seen as one of those passive-aggressive heroines who expose the evils of their society, like the young Jane Eyre, and recent readings have focused on her power in the narrative, a power in excess of that shown by most calumniated heroines. For Robson, the events are a means by which female desire achieves its ends, for Tsai they are a strong expression of a parent-child tension which occupies many of the family romances. Putter views the repetition in the romance in Freudian terms as a trauma that has to be consciously reclaimed from the past, a process which Emaré herself sets up in the final sequences of reunions with her father and husband.[26] It seems that because this romance frees its tale of redemptive suffering from an explicit religious meaning (although Putter argues for a deep-structured

---

[24] For a different view of the resurrection theme in *Sir Orfeo,* see Cartlidge, 'Courting Chaos', p. 26.

[25] See Cooper, *English Romance in Time*, pp. 108–13 for a wide-ranging account of the motif of the sea voyage.

[26] Christine Li Ju Tsai, 'Parents and Children in Middle English Romance: Personal, National, and International Relations in the Thirteenth to Fifteenth Centuries' (unpublished Ph.D. thesis, University of Kent at Canterbury, 2006), pp. 33–42; Ad Putter, 'The Narrative Logic of *Emaré*', in *Spirit*, pp. 157–80; Margaret Robson, 'Cloaking Desire: Re-reading *Emaré*', in *Romance Reading*, pp. 64–76.

Christian meaning), it allows readers to move beyond regarding Emaré herself as a figure of simple goodness, to find instead a heroine capable of complex power-play and manipulation. The question then arises as to what extent this is a modern back-formation reflecting our tendency to look for empowered heroines, even if power detracts from moral probity. We may have lost the ability to recognize virtue itself as power, an ancient belief in many of the romances with female protagonists.

However, Emaré's power is further materialized in the mysterious gemmed robe which, with its embroidery of famous lovers and its intrinsic luxury, does not seem emblematic of simple virtue. This poses more problems as there is so little agreement as to the meaning of the robe as to demonstrate that it has no clear retrievable meaning. Putter notes that the robe confounds critical attempts to interpret it consistently, and chooses instead to take it at its narrative face value – 'the robe makes things happen ... because making things happen is what it does'. But the means by which the robe becomes a motive force in the narrative is not clear: because of what it symbolizes, or because it is supernatural? If, as has been noted by Amanda Hopkins,[27] the robe calls forth different responses in different characters in the romance, it has also given rise to a wide range of critical responses, often fuelled by a conviction that meaning exists to be found. It may be that we should be willing to be left in what is an entertaining and absorbing state of uncertainty and note the function of romance to provoke questions; to recognize that purpose may lie in the debate, not in the achievement of answers, is in itself a challenge to the critical ambition to fill in the gaps and find explanations.

In denying the straightforward interpretation of the suffering of the innocent as a vehicle for Christian meaning, *Emaré* is markedly different from the analogous 'The Man of Law's Tale'. The narrative spaces and lack of rationalizing or religious explanation leaves room for the reader's imaginative engagement, and this may explain why *Emaré* fascinates and attracts a range of reader responses, whereas Chaucer's tale is one of the less read of the *Canterbury Tales* and seems to attract respect rather than excitement.

These two romances are, in their different ways, romances about marriage, and it is noticeable that marriage and the family are as likely as courtship to provide the staple shape of many of these ME romances. Since the time of the Greek romances the narrative of the vulnerable and fractured family has been a strong element in romance.[28] The romance is characterized by an

---

[27] Ross G. Arthur, 'Emaré's Cloak and Audience Response', in *Sign, Sentence, Discourse: Language in Medieval Thought and Culture*, ed. Julian N. Wasserman and Lois Roney (Syracuse: Syracuse University Press, 1989), pp. 80–92; Mortimer J. Donovan, 'Middle English *Emaré* and the Cloth Worthily Wrought', in *The Learned and the Lewed: Studies in Chaucer and Medieval Literature*, ed. Larry D. Benson (Cambridge, MA: Harvard University Press, 1974), pp. 337–42; Putter, 'Narrative Logic of *Emaré*'; Amanda Hopkins, 'Veiling the Text: The True Role of the Cloth in *Emaré*', in *Insular Romance*, pp. 71–82.

[28] Margaret Anne Doody, *The True Story of the Novel* (Rutgers, NJ: Rutgers University Press, 1996).

occupation with personal relationships over public events, but it is a misconception to see this as necessarily 'romantic'; the relationships of families or of friendship can be as central as those of lovers.

Sons and lovers: the inter-generational romance

Among the shorter romances, the narrative themes of both exogamous courtship and the divided family provide a variety of structures and conventions.[29] The strength and repetition of the patterning of conventions indicate the perennial nature of the anxieties about intimate relationships, of problems with loss and destructive emotions and the need to test out ways of solving them. However, the domestic and intimate nature of the concerns in these romances are displaced onto a wide geographical and political canvas, a pan-European geography criss-crossing the Mediterranean sea and probing the boundaries of the familiar world, so that the division and restoration of the family unity have the potential to act metonymically for Europe seen as Christendom.

Octovian [or *Octavian*], taken from an OFr original (available in AN[30]), survives in two different versions, Northern and Southern, the latter attributed to Thomas Chestre, a writer distinguished by his available identity, rather than by his merits. Brevity and simplicity are not the aim here: it is three times the length of *Sir Orfeo* and a multilayered family romance using interlace to follow the separate fortunes of its protagonists. The tale opens with the narrative of the calumniated queen who gives birth to twin sons only to have them seized by wild animals, a stock feature of the divided family romance. The narrative then moves between the two as they grow into the mature heroes who will prove themselves in love and war, and finally reunite their parents. *Octavian* shares with *Emaré* many of the narrative ingredients of the family romance, and the problem here is that such a text can appear to be no more than a prefabricated construction of familiar elements.[31] Like *Emaré*, it occupies the romantic geography of mainland Europe, with its emperors, kings and allied kingdoms, thus finding opportunity for violence, warfare and heroism and the crusading response to the Saracens. But new variants are offered to provide a displaced examination of the difficulties of the parent-child relationship, in particular through the figure of the foster-parent.

The figure of the calumniated queen, exiled to give birth in the wilderness, is one of female suffering, and the mother as victim is a feature of

---

[29] Susan Wittig, *Stylistic and Narrative Structures in the Middle English Romances* (Austin: University of Texas Press, 1978).

[30] Ruth J. Dean, with Maureen B. M. Boulton, *Anglo-Norman Literature: A Guide to Texts and Manuscripts* (London: Anglo-Norman Text Society, 1999), p. 101.

[31] See Julie Burton, 'Folktale, Romance and Shakespeare', in *Studies in Medieval English Romances*, pp. 176–97.

popular romance as it is of popular religion. As Fellows has noted,[32] the queen in *Octavian* displays a courageous maternal love, which even the lioness respects, when she insists on going into the lion's den in search of her infant son. But the lioness herself bears closer scrutiny. A number of romance heroes have companion lions – Chrétien's Yvain in particular, closely imitated by Guy. Readers of these texts have been quick to find meaning in these animals, even if the meanings found may differ, and the lion can be read as an embodiment of the hero's nobility, ferocity or chivalry. A lioness is not such a usual companion, but this one fills that role once the queen has reclaimed her son. For the son is shared, the lioness accompanying them to Jerusalem and staying with them to join the son, Octavian, in his greatest battle and protecting him on the battlefield (an unfair advantage according to the steward in *Guy*). She operates in effect as an externalization of the queen's maternal love, not only nurturing the child in infancy, but fighting his corner with a robust energy as he grows to maturity. She fades out when he marries. So the lioness, as a symbolic expression of the fierce female protectiveness that holds the family together, provides some compensation for the passive, suffering mother of romance.

By contrast, and the contrast is a basic structure of the romance, the fostering of Florent, the child initially seized by an ape, lacks the regal touch, and the Northern version finds opportunity for humour and social commentary in the experiences of the lost prince reared in a bourgeois family. The figure of Clement, the Paris butcher and foster-father, veers from the brutal through the burlesque to the pathetic, as the parent figure moves from being a fearsome authority, to an embarrassment, to an object of pity in the narrative of maturity.[33] It is also a challenge to another easy assumption about the nature of popular romance, for here we find the bourgeois treated with sheer contempt as he is confused by the world of courtly etiquette. John Simons makes out a good case for envisaging a courtly and gentry audience for *Octavian*, in order to explain the treatment of Clement;[34] but in terms of narrative material and treatment it is nevertheless a romance that exemplifies the sensational, dramatic and humorous nature of the popular romance. So like the AN *Boeve* it challenges easy assumptions about popularity, language and social rank.

The two brothers provide contrasting portraits of the maturing hero. The winsome, precocious Florent, the Paris foster-child, demonstrates his innate superiority by preferring courtliness to profit. He goes on to prove his nobility

---

[32] Jennifer Fellows, 'Mothers in Middle English Romance', in *Women and Literature in Britain 1150–1500*, ed. Carol M. Meale (Cambridge: Cambridge University Press, 1993; 2nd edn 1996), pp. 41–60 (pp. 44–6).

[33] Derek Brewer, *Symbolic Stories: Traditional Narratives of the Family Drama in English Literature* (Cambridge: D. S. Brewer, 1980).

[34] John Simons, 'Northern *Octovian* and the question of class', in *Romance in Medieval England*, ed. Maldwyn Mills, Jennifer Fellows and Carol M. Meale (Cambridge: D. S. Brewer, 1991), pp. 105–12.

further by displaying the career of a successful lover, pursuing and winning that most enticing of brides, the 'belle sarrasine', daughter of the Sultan. However, Florent's military success fails and he, together with the kings and emperors of the Christian army, is captured; it falls to Octavian, the warrior reared in Jerusalem by his royal mother, to rescue them and Christendom. So the final reunion of parents and children is less emotional and personal than that in *Emaré*, but rather an assertion of the strength of the family and the empire.

Floris and Blancheflour provides a refreshing contrast after the battlefield triumphalism of the ending of *Octavian*. One of the earliest ME romances, it is another romance adapted from a French original available in England in an AN copy.[35] It is found in the Auchinleck MS with *Guy* and *Orfeo*, although not so clearly part of that collection's programme. The story of a Moorish prince in love with a Christian girl who is sold into the seraglio of the Sultan of Babylon, it is something of a rarity for several reasons: it is a simple courtship romance with no aim beyond the achievement of the union of the couple; it has children as its protagonists; and it is an Eastern story, and retains a positive and sympathetic, if wide-eyed, attitude to the lands and customs of the Saracens.

The problem for the modern reader here is not as a rule one of sympathy, for it is one of the most accessible and appealing of the ME romances, and its toleration of the Saracen other is refreshing, but rather how seriously to take it – the TEAMS edition is in a volume entitled 'Sentimental and Humorous Romances' which may, perhaps unintentionally, give grounds for dismissing it as more trivial than romances dealing with the fate of kingdoms.[36]

Like *Sir Orfeo* it oscillates between love and death, beginning with a false death, when Florent's parents pretend that Blancheflour has died, and ending with the threat of death defeated by a test of love, in this case as the children's mutual love moves the Sultan to pardon them. The cup that initiates Floris's quest is as exotic as Emaré's robe and carries the western world of Troy and Rome into the romance as the lover's quest takes him beyond the boundaries of the known world: Babylon here takes the place of fairy, and its strange eastern customs and marvellous plumbing the role of the supernatural. The harem is envisaged as a lively female community, represented by the warm and humorous relationship between Blancheflour and her confidante, Clarice. Despite this lightness of touch, the family is not presented positively. As with many courtship narratives, the parents are the obstacle and their moral confusion serves to highlight the single-mindedness of the hero-lover. There is no reunion with the parents: Floris's father must die in order for the couple to attain to the kingdom that symbolizes maturity. Courtship and the triumph of the younger generation dismantle the original, unsatisfac-

---

35 Dean and Boulton, *Anglo-Norman Literature*, p. 97.
36 Kathleen Coyne Kelly, 'The Bartering of Blauncheflur in the Middle English *Floris and Blancheflour*', *Studies in Philology* 91 (1994), 101–10, offers a darker reading.

tory, family. Like *Orfeo* and *Emaré*, *Floris and Blancheflour* is a romance in which love is important but violence is virtually absent; the lover is regained by the resourcefulness of the hero, not by displays of military valour, and in this it contrasts with the crusading strand in *Octavian* and the larger group of crusading romances.[37] These romances exemplify much that is typical and difficult about the shorter ME romances that lack the attractive symbolic implications of the Breton Lai. But the structuring around the generational clash between young and old, parents and children, is an important generic characteristic of romance, and these texts demonstrate the creative possibilities of the thematic variations that account for the sheer number of shorter romances.

While these romances are undeniably popular, in spread as well as aesthetic, they still lack any direct engagement with the social world of their audiences and thus contribute to the problems of defining the popular. All experience is viewed through the prism of aristocratic or royal identity and any attempt to break out of this, as in *Octavian*, is dealt with harshly. There are however a few romances that do deal with life from outside the charmed circle of romance courtliness, the most famous of which is *Havelok the Dane*.

Men of the people: the romance of the popular hero

Written at the turn of the thirteenth century,[38] *Havelok* derives from a chronicle tradition of a Danish prince, exiled to England in disguise, who regains his own kingdom and, in marrying the heiress to the English throne, establishes a joint Anglo-Danish kingdom in a manner somewhat reminiscent of Canute. It is one ME romance, agreed to be 'popular', which has received considerable scholarly attention from the earliest editions,[39] and continued to provoke a number of finely argued and important discussions.[40] There are two reasons

---

[37] For the importance of this theme, see Geraldine Barnes, *Counsel and Strategy in Middle English Romance* (Cambridge: D. S. Brewer, 1993).

[38] *Havelok*, ed. G. V. Smithers (Oxford: Clarendon Press, 1987), pp. lxiv–lxxii.

[39] David Matthews, *The Making of Middle English, 1765–1910* (Minneapolis: University of Minnesota Press, 1999), pp. 120–6.

[40] The following consider the historical context of *Havelok*: Robert Levine, 'Who Composed *Havelok* for Whom?', *Yearbook of English Studies* 22 (1992), 95–104; David Staines, '*Havelok the Dane*: A Thirteenth-Century Handbook for Princes', *Speculum* 51 (1976), 602–23; Halverson, '*Havelok the Dane* and Society'; John C. Hirsch, '*Havelok* 2933: A Problem in Medieval Literary History', *Neuphilologische Mitteilungen* 78 (1977), 339–49; Thorlac Turville-Petre, *England the Nation: Language, Literature and National Identity, 1290–1340* (Oxford: Clarendon Press, 1996), pp. 143–55, '*Havelok* and the History of the Nation', in *Readings in Medieval English Romance*, ed. Carol M. Meale (Cambridge: D. S. Brewer, 1994), pp. 121–34; Diane Speed, 'The Construction of the Nation in Medieval English Romance', in *Readings in Medieval English Romance*, pp. 135–57; Sheila Delany, 'The Romance of Kingship: *Havelok the Dane*', in her *Medieval Literary Politics* (Manchester: Manchester University Press, 1990), pp. 61–72.

The following consider the style and aesthetics of *Havelok*: Roy Michael Liuzza, 'Representation and Readership in the Middle English *Havelok*', *Journal of English and Germanic Philology* 93 (1994), 504–19; Judith Weiss, 'Structure and Characterisation in *Havelok the Dane*', *Speculum*

usually cited for this level of interest: its apparent or evident 'Englishness' which attracted the early editors and has formed the centre of discussions of the nature of insular literature ever since; and its 'realism' which seems to offer a respectable alternative to the escapist world of romance. It has thus provided material for both historicizing readings and for a discussion of popular aesthetic. Another reason is the story-telling ability of the poet (and most readers have a strong sense of authorship); *Havelok* is an entertaining, sensational, serious representative of the widespread tale-type of the male Cinderella.

Havelok shares many motifs with *Floris and Blancheflour* – the repetition-with-variation of scenes of eating as a measure of narrative development; the hero disguised as non-royal, a merchant or a mason; the voyeuristic viewing of the lovers in bed when the truth about them is discovered. But so different are the two romances that this serves mainly to illustrate the chameleon quality of narrative convention. *Havelok* is famously a narrative that engages with the realities of peasant and urban life and the world of the castle as seen from the perspective of the servants and is firmly based in a recognizable Lincolnshire. For much of the narrative, power and the court are associated with tyranny and the author draws two differentiated portraits of tyrannical usurpers to provide negative exempla against which the hero is to be measured. Havelok the lost heir seems to believe himself to be a peasant, reared by the eponymous Grim of Grimsby. He is of course of royal birth, and has the signs to prove it; this is no revolutionary text but a version of what in Arthurian romance is recognized as the tale-type of the 'fair unknown', a demonstration that royal birth will out (as in *Octavian*). But Havelok's education is in the school of hardship, his followers range across the social spectrum and he is that rarity in medieval story, a genuinely popular king.[41]

The events and the tone of narration imply the operation of a benign providence, protecting the weak, punishing the evil and restoring justice. The protagonists are orphans so there is no opportunity for the family romance pattern of loss and restoration; what is restored is the land to its rightful ruler. Havelok will triumph over his enemies and his kingdom of Denmark, but more importantly, Goldborough's kingdom of England will be saved from misrule. England is both clearly envisaged by this author – 'fro Douere to Rokesborw' (265) – and seen as under divine protection (as in *Guy*). There is a strong popular political creed at work here which links God, the realm and the king.

The materiality of the world of *Havelok* is matched by that of *Gamelyn*. As

---

44 (1969), 247–57; Anne Scott, 'Language as Convention, Language as Sociolect in *Havelok the Dane*', *Studies in Philology* 89 (1992), 137–60; Nancy Mason Bradbury, 'The Traditional Origins of *Havelok the Dane*'; A. C. Spearing, *Readings in Medieval Poetry* (Cambridge: Cambridge University Press, 1987), pp. 43–55.

41 This does not necessarily prove a 'popular' audience: see Hirsch, '*Havelok* 2933': 'Such romances as *Havelok* tell us not so much what the lower classes thought of the upper, as what the upper classes liked to think the lower classes thought of them' (p. 343).

recent studies of the poem have shown,[42] *Gamelyn* is an unusually realistic fiction that illustrates social conditions and changes in the later fourteenth century and has long been read as of historical interest, rather than appreciated for its literary qualities. However, it is a dramatic, humorous and idiosyncratic work that is a pleasure to read.[43] Its popularity in terms of manuscripts is considerable, due to its association with the *Canterbury Tales*, and its popularity in terms of direct expression of and appeal to non-aristocratic interests is evident. As with *Havelok* it expands the definition of romance away from the courtship or family romance with aristocratic protagonists towards a validation of the experience of those outside the courtly world.

Gamelyn is another male Cinderella story in which the youngest son of three is dispossessed of his inheritance on the death of his father by his grasping eldest brother, and put to work in the kitchens. Here, however, we have no *beau inconnu*, as the status of the protagonist and those around him is consistently that of the country gentry. Like Havelok, Gamelyn is too simple for his own good in a world of corruption and abuse of power. But where Havelok triumphs through his own innate virtues, Gamelyn is one of the founding figures of the outlaw tradition, and operates outside both the law of the realm and to a surprising extent, the moral law. *Gamelyn* is a darker work than *Havelok* although even more directly entertaining. There is no sense of providence at work in this tale, no supportive love or marriage, only the fellowship of a single servant and the slippery comradeship of forest outlaws.

The entertainments offered by these romances are in some ways problematic. Violence is uncourtly, unchivalric, often indiscriminating and totally celebrated in these poems.[44] The cloaking glamour of chivalry, of armour, horses and cavalry warfare is absent, and in its place is the physicality of hand-to-hand fighting with whatever weapon comes to hand: a doorpost in *Havelok*, a pestle in *Gamelyn*. Nor is the enemy spared – Havelok kills sixty would-be abductors in the defence of his wife, Gamelyn kills his brother's porter, and eventually the entire cast of a corrupt trial. The violence is fuelled by justified anger, against tyrants and thugs in *Havelok*, against corrupt clergy and self-serving local justices in *Gamelyn*.

Both heroes are displaced from the world of established power by corrupt usurpers who re-invent them as criminals – so Havelok is cast in the role of marauding Viking by Godric and Gamelyn is turned into an outlaw –

---

[42] Stephen Knight, '"Harkeneth aright": Reading *Gamelyn* for Text not Context', in *Tradition and Transformation in Medieval Romance*, ed. Rosalind Field (Cambridge: D. S. Brewer, 1999), pp. 15–27; Noël James Menuge, 'The Wardship Romance: A New Methodology', in *Tradition and Transformation*, pp. 29–43; T. A. Shippey, '*The Tale of Gamelyn*: Class Warfare and the Embarrassments of Genre', in *Spirit*, pp. 78–96.

[43] *Robin Hood and Other Outlaw Tales*, ed. Stephen Knight and Thomas Ohlgren, TEAMS series (Kalamazoo, MI: Medieval Institute Publications, 1997).

[44] Compare the moralistic treatment of violence in *Guy of Warwick*: see Paul Price, 'Confessions of a Godless Killer: Guy of Warwick and Comprehensive Entertainment', in *Insular Romance*, pp. 93–110.

'wolfshead' – by his brother the sheriff. The effect is to revolve the normal romance perspective to show the aristocratic world as corrupt – and furthermore to explode the vocabulary of feudal narrative; so descriptive terms such as 'king', 'lord', 'outlaw' (vividly expressed as 'dogges' or 'uten-laddes') are unreliable terms exploited by the corrupt and powerful. It is deeds that prove value and the action-laden careers of these heroes have meaning at this level and lead to the conclusions where Havelok becomes a worthy king and Gamelyn an honest justice.

Havelok, despite its positive and informed presentation of peasant life, comes across as a literary version of that life. The realistic detail is rhetorical display, none the less lively and entertaining for that but not necessary an authentic account of peasant life. Havelok's upbringing in the fisher settlement of Grimsby and his early career as a cook's assistant are part of the wider agenda of this deeply political romance, part of the training of an ideal king, a man who is marked out by destiny but whose experience gains him the trust of an entire people. The cohesive society that *Havelok* famously envisages –

> Erl and barun, dreng and þayn,
> Knict, bondeman, and swain,
> Wydues, maydnes, prestes and clerkes   (31–3)

– is embodied in a hero who moves upwards from country peasant, to court servant, to disguise as a merchant, to warrior and finally to king. The only social rank closed to him is that of cleric, but the authorial voice supplies that lack. Havelok is a good king, eventually, because he has experienced a time in the wilderness of poverty and servitude, but he is still destined to escape it and to remove his followers from it as he promotes his foster-brothers to the aristocracy.

Gamelyn has a less ambitious agenda and a narrower social range. The hero represents the dreams and resentments of a section of society rarely represented in fiction and if there is a wider moral it is that of the insecurity of a post-feudal society – 'many goode mannes child in care is brought' (619). Like Havelok, the hero is something of a simpleton, easily manipulated by the false words of his brother – 'the knyght thought on tresoun and Gamelyn on noon' (165) and responding to all situations with violence. His career does show some of the features of more chivalric heroes; he is motivated by the need to rescue the oppressed (the franklin's sons, his brother Ote) and he does grow up, for this is an unusually convincing romance of maturation.

These two romances undermine any definition of romance as the self-realization of aristocratic protagonists through adventure and love. Both present a popular hero and are read as appealing to a popular audience. That they are popular romances also accounts for their innate conservatism, another factor in the critical impatience with popular narrative. The corruption they expose is that of individuals not of systems and is corrected by replacing false kings or officials with the hero. In both poems, there is a strong ideal of kingship which is reasserted at the end in a display of justice and harmony. Such an unsubversive attitude is one of the characteristics of popular fiction. The dangers, scandals and exposures of the hero's career will settle into a familiar and reassuring stasis. Nevertheless what we seem to have here is evidence of the use of fiction to explore other possibilities, to move romance into areas of serious concern and wider social implications. If romance encourages the exercise of the imagination to conceptualize a world in which justice and virtue triumph over power and corruption, then a work such as *Gamelyn* shows such imaginings being transposed onto a different social scale and the working out of methods by which justice might be made to triumph.

These six representative romances of the thirteenth and fourteenth centuries demonstrate the flexibility and inherent interest of conventional narrative, but a different selection of romances would of course produce variations on these themes and types. If romances were totally predictable and conventional it would be sufficient to read one or two, and a knowledge of more would offer little; there are plenty of modern popular genres to which this applies. But the experience of reading these works is quite the reverse. We find something of a kaleidoscopic effect by which each work throws a new light and different perspective onto the others, accumulating a cultural and aesthetic depth. In this respect, the very size and categoric slipperiness of the corpus of popular romance become part of its particular quality.[45]

We can also recognize that however predictable a romance may be, it is grounded in the anxieties, aspirations and difficulties of its readers and audience. This applies as much to *Emaré* as to its distant cousin, *Jane Eyre*, as much to *Floris and Blancheflour* as to the parallel narrative in *Northanger Abbey*. Indeed, as the difficulties that *Gamelyn* has posed to later readers may indicate, it is the conventional tales set in distant lands and peopled with kings, queens and emperors that lend themselves to a clearly accessible symbolic coding of perennial human experience, whereas the realistic modulations into the recognizably contemporary medieval world remain rooted in that world and so require historical interpretation and contextualization.

While there is no need to look for, or regret the lack of, originality, there is evidence (as we have seen) of the creative use of convention and the awareness of audience expectation. Popular romances by definition are not written for audiences looking for verbal dexterity, artistic experimentation and literary innovation. The audience that supports the work of Chaucer and the *Gawain*-poet is always a minority in any culture. But there is plenty of evidence that medieval audiences were used to handling symbolic complexity and allusive

---

[45] See Nancy Mason Bradbury, *Writing Aloud* (Urbana: University of Illinois Press, 1998), p. 9: 'Each text is in a sense in its own category; each new text makes the old definition obsolete.'

depth,[46] and the concerns of the audiences of these romances are not trivial, nor are they narrowly localized. And of course, for the modern reader, verbal complexity can be an initial barrier as can coterie humour. The open appeal of the popular romance is that of a literature which is a window onto another culture, but also a mirror in which we see our own.

One of the problems with aligning the experience of reading ME popular romance with that of encountering its modern equivalents is the tendency to take the modern generic self-identification of 'romance' at its face value. But few, if any, ME romances resemble Mills & Boon (they are not so concentrated on female experience and desire to start with). The modern equivalent is to be found in deliberately non-mimetic novels, in fantasy and Science Fiction and in the developing genre of political romance. Adam Roberts's defence of the 'escapist' quality of modern fantasy can be applied to these earlier texts:

> Escapism isn't a very good word, actually, for the positive psychological qualities its defenders want to defend; it's less a question of breaking one's bars and running away (running *whither*, we might ask?); and more of keeping alive the facility for imaginative *play* ... What's wrong with Art that insists too severely on pressing people's faces against the miseries of actual existence is not that we shouldn't have to confront Darfur or Iraq, poverty or oppression; it's that such art rarely gives us the imaginative wriggle room to think of how things might be improved, or challenged ... Imaginative wriggle room, on the other hand, is something SF-Fantasy is very good at.[47]

While the world of the romances may be a heightened reality, it is one recognizably familiar to the original audience, but in the 'wriggle room' of constructive escapism, we can see a culture testing its boundaries and probing new possibilities. These romances offer entry into a world where justice triumphs over law, tyranny is vanquished, losses are restored. It is a world in which, by contrast with its contemporary experience, the young, the female, the loyal, triumph over the powerful and corrupt. This is not mere escapism, it is powerful imagination.

With popular romances we are not dealing with the more culture-specific issues that occupy courtly writers: chivalry, *courtoisie* and passionate love. These texts deal with the bases of human existence in society: getting born, surviving childhood, negotiating the family, finding a mate, facing threats, achieving justice and accepting mortality. And they demonstrate the enduring need to find meaning and even comedy in the narratives of human life.

The problem is not that there is so little to say about anonymous, conven-

---

[46] See for example Roy Liuzza's argument that the *Meditationes vitae Christi* provides a model for the realistic detail in *Havelok* in 'Representation and Readership', pp. 514–17.

[47] Adam Roberts, '*The Name of the Wind* by Patrick Rothfuss and *The Children of Húrin* by J. R. R. Tolkien', 16 July 2007. http://www.strangehorizons.com/. Accessed 23 May 2008.

tional works, but there is so much. The old complaint that such narratives do not seem important, intellectual or weighty enough to provide material for academic discourse has been invalidated by at least the last half century of editorial and critical work. But these works do present challenges to our skills as readers. 'This duality of historicity and timelessness'[48] requires us to work to fill the gaps in our cultural understanding in order to read works that are the expression of a distant culture not an individual voice, and at the same time to recognize the perennial significance of their concerns and more honestly the success of their appeal as entertainment. If we look around, the stories are still with us, sometimes in simpler and cruder form than those which appealed to medieval audiences.

---

[48] Corinne Saunders, ed., *A Companion to Romance: From Classical to Contemporary* (Malden, MA and Oxford: Blackwell, 2004), p. 539.

2

Genre and Classification

RALUCA L. RADULESCU

An attractive and, in some cases, defining feature of some medieval popular romances is (the intrusion of) the outrageous and the spectacular or unexpected, which unsettles the order of chivalric adventures encountered in these texts. The shocking twists and turns of popular romance have continued to appeal to medieval and modern audiences alike, and have prompted, at least in part, the revival of critical interest in these texts in recent decades. It is the anonymous romance authors and audiences that we should credit with the enduring appeal of texts that continue to 'unsettle our assumptions about, among other things, gender and sexuality, race, religion, political formations, social class, ethics, morality and aesthetic distinctions'.[1] Although not all popular romances include spectacular events or characters, or even purely chivalric exploits, the presence of such elements has produced strong responses of either dismissal or, more recently, positive appraisal from critics. As is now generally agreed, authors and audiences contributed to the creation of meaning in medieval texts and, unsurprisingly, the wide range of reactions to narrative elements in popular romances corresponds to the sheer variety of topics and taboos they challenge.[2] Read in this context, the adjective 'popular', when attached to particular romances, can be seen to indicate the spread of concerns tackled by these texts, and the wide application of their function: to entertain, to educate, to provoke repulsion and so on.[3] Traditionally, however, critics have used the term 'popular' in contrast to 'elite' to draw a negative comparison between the sophisticated content

---

[1] Nicola McDonald, 'A Polemical Introduction', in *Pulp Fictions*, pp. 1–21 (p. 17).
[2] It is generally agreed that popular romances were aimed at, and appealed to, a non-courtly audience, given their less sophisticated content and form. The question of what audience the authors of these popular romances had in mind remains open to debate. See, for example, Felicity Riddy's recent assessment of the middle-class, bourgeois, outlook in evidence in the Lincoln Thornton manuscript version of *Le Bone Florence of Rome*: 'Temporary Virginity and the Everyday Body: *Le Bone Florence of Rome* and Bourgeois Self-making', in *Pulp Fictions*, pp. 197–216. The Lincoln Thornton MS is Lincoln Cathedral MS 91, attributed to Robert Thornton, a fifteenth-century middling member of the gentry with a collector's tastes. See *The Thornton Manuscript (Lincoln Cathedral MS 91)*, intro. D. S. Brewer and A. E. B. Owen (London: Scolar Press, 1978), pp. vii–xvi.
[3] For a definition of the term 'popular' when applied to medieval romance, see the Editors' Introduction to this volume, pp. 5–7.

and form of *Sir Gawain and the Green Knight* and prose romances and the apparently low aesthetic value of the metrical romances that form the bulk of popular romances.[4] Distinctions have, therefore, been based on the low aesthetic of the popular romances, their presumed non-courtly audiences, their non-cyclic nature (as opposed to the great cycles of Arthurian or Charlemagne romances), highly formulaic structure, and 'popular' metre (couplet or tail-rhyme). This chapter contains a reassessment both of critical debates over generic features of medieval romance in general and of those particular elements that could be considered to define the core group of what critics have called 'popular romances' (identified as such by contrast to the cyclic romances, of Arthur and Charlemagne, for example, or those belonging to the alliterative tradition; see further below). The discussion will start with a brief review of the vexed definition of romance genre, to be followed by brief analyses of some representative examples that fall under the label of popular romance, and the equally contested and ever-reinterpreted functional sub-categories developed by various critics.

Critical work on Middle English literary works has established that medieval audiences of any social background were highly sensitive to the demands of certain genres, and were able to recognize texts for what they were. As Helen Cooper put it, '[r]omances could provide a secular forum analogous to academic debate. Their audiences expected to respond actively to them, and the writers encouraged such a response.'[5] By implication, the assumptions made in relation to the audiences for popular romance imply an awareness of certain demands on the genre, coupled with a demand from such audiences for particular types of topics and texts. Non-courtly audiences had at least some idea of what sophisticated literary forms were; the emulation of courtly values is a feature of gentry culture, the primary audience for popular romances, whose overall aim appears to be didactic or instructional as much as entertaining. Medieval audiences who could afford books or the exchange of books gave precedence to religious values and cultivated the exemplary element in material used for the instruction of their offspring. Just as the Bible offered examples of famous political and religious figures in the Old Testament – and the positive value of those examples to any social class in medieval society is uncontested – so the vulgarized versions of stories both religious and historical in outlook contained in Middle English popular romances (as opposed to more sophisticated models in Anglo-Norman or 'high' forms in Middle English) can be seen as appealing to a wide audience, irrespective of their predominantly upper-class characters.

When analysing the context for the composition and writing of the texts contained in one of the most well-known surviving collections containing romances, the Vernon MS (Oxford, Bodleian Library, English Poet 1.a.), A.

---

[4] For a more detailed investigation, see Cory Rushton's chapter in this volume, 'Modern and Academic Reception of the Popular Romance', pp. 165–79.

[5] Cooper, *English Romance in Time*, p. 13.

S. G. Edwards rightly points out that '[a]ny discussion of romances in the Vernon manuscript must, at the outset, acknowledge that the elasticity of the term "romance" in Middle English is so great as to rob it of much useful definitional capacity'.[6] The vexed question of romance as a medieval literary genre remains open – witness the continuing publication of genre-based discussions of romance including the existence of the present volume/chapter – though no evidence can be gleaned from extant texts and manuscripts as to a precise definition of the genre as understood by medieval authors and audiences, except that 'romance' designated the language in which some narratives were initially written. Critical examination of both lists of romances included in the body of medieval English texts as well as of generic titles given to romances in surviving manuscripts shows that medieval authors and audiences alike favoured a more flexible approach than modern critics would allow for. In his survey of terms associated with narratives that may be classed as romance, Paul Strohm has shown how difficult it is to classify Middle English Troy narratives according to the terms used by the narrators themselves:

> Middle English writers lacked any truly neutral terminology for describing narrative genres – *narratioun* emerged only at the end of the period, and the nearly synonymous *process* was never widely popular. As a result, Middle English writers classify their narratives with a number of different terms, reflecting such criteria as the relationship to actual events (*storie, fable*), mode of narration (*spelle, tale*), language (*romaunce*), literary tradition (*romaunce, legend, lyf*), proportion of represented action to argument (*geste, treatise*), and movement of the fortunes of the protagonist (*tragedie, comedie*).[7]

A similar perspective in analysing what romances say about their subject matter and their possible self-definition is given by Maldwyn Mills, who has examined generic titles in two romance miscellanies;[8] in fact, a close examination of titles has shown that only eight refer to the texts as 'romance' (see Mills's chapter below, pp. 49–57). However, as becomes evident from any analysis of such titles, a broad range of narratives modern critics consider to be under the umbrella of romance were seen by medieval authors and scribes as 'lives', 'histories', 'treatises' or 'jests', not to mention the more

---

[6] A. S. G. Edwards, 'The Contexts of the Vernon Romances', in *Studies in the Vernon Manuscript*, ed. Derek Pearsall (Cambridge: D. S. Brewer, 1990), pp. 159–70 (p. 159).

[7] Paul Strohm, '*Storie, Spelle, Geste, Romaunce, Tragedie*: Generic Distinctions in the Middle English Troy Narratives', *Speculum* 46:2 (1971), 348–59 (p. 348). See, also, his 'The Origins and Meaning of Middle English *Romaunce*', *Genre* 10 (1977), 1–28, and 'Middle English Narrative Genres', *Genre* 13 (1980), 379–88; John Finlayson, 'Definitions of Middle English Romance', *Chaucer Review* 15 (1980), 43–62, 168–81 and Robert B. Burlin, 'Middle English Romance: The Structure of Genre', *Chaucer Review* 30 (1995), 1–14.

[8] Maldwyn Mills, 'Generic Titles in Bodleian Library MS Douce 261 and British Library MS Egerton 3132A', in *Matter of Identity*, pp. 125–38.

controversial labels of 'legend' and 'chronicle'. Even more confusing is the fact that the same romance would, in one instance, be called a 'romance', and in another a 'life'; in the two extant copies of *Sir Gowther* we see the same hero as a saint and a secular hero, respectively.[9] The multiple facets of a popular romance become even more evident when studied in its manuscript context; as Murray Evans has shown, romances borrow features from and are affected by the characteristics of texts they are contiguous to in composite manuscripts.[10] This indicates not only the flexibility of the genre, but also the medieval audiences' expectations that generic boundaries could be adapted to suit the fabric of the miscellany in which they were included.

Six well-known lists of romances (or, to be more precise, romance heroes) have been scrutinized by critics over the decades in an effort to define the romance genre. Among them, the lists contained in *Richard Coeur de Lion* and *The Laud Troy Book* are most often cited, though Chaucer's parodic list of heroes in his 'Tale of Sir Thopas', and the negative connotations associated with romance in religious texts like *Cursor Mundi* and William of Nassington's translation of *Speculum Vitae*, are equally relevant and now as well known.[11] The difficulty in assessing the contents of these lists lies in discerning what portion constituted material grouped together on the basis of the popularity of its subject matter (heroes of the nation), whether romance was only associated with the language in which it was originally written (rather than a fixed or flexible set of generic features) and how critics might separate the popular from the courtly in these lists, since no evident hierarchy is imposed in any of them. A first example is the list in *Cursor Mundi*, a vast history of Creation in some 30,000 lines, which incorporates biblical stories and Christian legends, and famously deplores medieval audiences' desire to listen to stories focusing on great romance heroes rather than on morally edifying ones. Interestingly, the order of the list in this text appears to be in tune with modern critical opinion about the division of medieval romance into three matters: of Rome, of Britain, and of France, a classification based on the only available medieval classification of romances, that proposed by the medieval writer Jean Bodel, who referred to three 'matières', 'de France, de Bretagne, et de Rome la grant':[12]

---

[9] In London, British Library, MS Royal 17.B.43, fol. 131v: 'Explicit vita Sancti' and Edinburgh, National Library of Scotland, MS Advocates' 19.3.1, respectively. See the editions in *Six Middle English Romances*, ed. Maldwyn Mills (London: Dent, 1973), and *The Middle English Breton Lays*, ed. Anne Laskaya and Eve Salisbury (Kalamazoo, MI: Medieval Institute Publications, 1995).

[10] Murray Evans, *Rereading Middle English Romance: Manuscript Layout, Decoration, and the Rhetoric of Composite Structure* (Montreal and London: McGill-Queen's University Press, 1995); see also Mills's discussion in the chapter on manuscripts in this volume, pp. 49–57.

[11] Among the most recent, see Yin Liu, 'Middle English Romance as Prototype Genre', *Chaucer Review* 40 (2006), 335–53. See also John J. Thompson, 'The *Cursor Mundi*, the "Inglis tong", and "Romance"', in *Readings in Medieval English Romance*, ed. Carol M. Meale (Cambridge: D. S. Brewer, 1994), pp. 99–120.

[12] Jean Bodel, *La Chanson des Saisnes*, ed. A. Brasseur, 2 vols (Geneva: Droz, 1989), lines 6–7. For the first use of Bodel's 'matters', see W. H. Schofield, *English Literature from the Norman*

Man yhernes rimes for to here,	yearns
And romans red on maneres sere,	of various kinds
Of Alisaundur þe conqueror;	
Of Iuly Cesar þe emparour;	
O grece and troy the strang strijf,	
Þere many thousand lesis þer lijf;	lost their lives
O brut þat bern bald of hand,	
Þe first conquerour of Ingland;	
O kyng arthour þat was so rike,	
O ferlys þat hys knyghes fell,	wonders
Þat aunters sere I here of tell,	adventures
Als wawan, cai and oþer stabell,	
For to were þe ronde tabell;	
How charles kyng and rauland faght,	
Wit sarazins wald þai na saght;	
[Of] tristrem and hys leif ysote,	
O Ioneck and of ysambrase,	
O ydoine and of amadase	
Storis als o ferekin thinges	
O princes, prelates and o kynges;	
Sanges sere of selcuth rime,	
Inglis, frankys, and latine,	
To rede and here Ilkon is prest,	
Þe thynges þat þam likes best.[13]	

It is evident that at least in this case the classification of the traditional list of 'three matters' lacks a crucial member, now commonly known among modern critics as 'the matter of England' that we take for granted nowadays was unknown to medieval authors and audiences, and is purely a modern construct (albeit a much debated one).[14] The list also points to the language medium in which such texts were composed and circulated. In both respects *Cursor Mundi* reveals that our continued (modern) use of Bodel's labels only applies to works largely composed and circulating in his period and country, while the use of the same classification for texts composed much later is unsatisfactory. In addition, an examination of this and the other lists mentioned also reveals that, as Derek Brewer has shown, a lot of 'priority is given to stories of war and battle. The love stories come last, though the author adds that in general there are many other stories, "of princes, prelates and kings".'[15] Already this may be taken as an indication of the Middle

---

Conquest to Chaucer (London: Macmillan, 1906), p. 145, followed later by Albert C. Baugh, *A Literary History of England* (London: Routledge and Kegan Paul, 1948), p. 174.

[13] *Cursor Mundi*, in London, British Library, MS Cotton Vespasian A.iii; see the edition by Richard Morris, EETS OS 57 (London, 1874).

[14] Rosalind Field provides a much needed reassessment in 'The Curious History of the Matter of England', in *Boundaries in Medieval Romance*, ed. Neil Cartlidge (Cambridge: D. S. Brewer, 2008), pp. 29–42.

[15] Derek Brewer, 'The Popular English Metrical Romances', in *A Companion to Romance: From*

English romances' tendency to favour slightly different themes than their French counterparts. An identical focus, albeit devoid of the apparent order of the three 'matters', is evident in the other lists, and particularly in those contained in romances, like the two lists in *Richard Coeur de Lion*. In such texts it appears that the more popular heroes are given priority and the mix between the three 'matters' makes it difficult to ascertain if any hierarchy is intended. However, as Brewer has pointed out, one of the lists in *Richard* does establish the precedence of English over French heroes among the interests of the audience:

> In Frensshe bookys this rym is wrought
> Lewede men ne knowe it nou3t
> Lewede men cune Ffrensch non
> Among an hondryd vanethis on.
> Neuertheles, with glad chere
> Ffele of hem that wolde here
> Noble iestes, j. undyrstonde
> Off dou3ty kny3tes off Yngelonde...[16]

Lists are a feature of traditional literature, for the very reason that they help bring 'shape and a point' to the narrative,[17] though not enough survive to help modern critics to define the exact generic features that shaped popular romance for its initial audiences. In addition, one of the reasons why it remains hard to classify romances, whether into 'matters', according to the cycles they form or can be grouped into (cyclic and non-cyclic), or by meter, is that their French (and other language) models come from different genres, and influences on the resulting product may be given precedence according to the critic's preference for one or another. A good example is the Middle English *Amis and Amiloun*, whose antecedents in Anglo-Norman include, as its modern editor has pointed out, 'the most heterogeneous works, such as legends, tales in prose and metrical romances'.[18] A further gap is perceived between the high courtly style of the Anglo-Norman models and the low tone and poor artistic qualities displayed by their Middle English counterparts (a view questioned by Rosalind Field in her chapter above, pp. 9–30). The difficulty is compounded by the wide spectrum of features that can be referred to in any given example. In the popular *The Erl of Toulous* we are told 'the romaunse tellyth soo' (line 1197), but just a few lines later the same narrative is identified both as a 'geste' and a Breton lay: 'Yn Rome thys geste

---

Classical to Contemporary, ed. Corinne Saunders (Malden, MA and Oxford: Blackwell, 2004), pp. 45–64 (p. 50).

[16] Lines 21–7 in *Der mittelenglische Versroman über Richard Lowenherz*, ed. K. Brunner (Vienna and Leipzig, 1913), pp. 81–2 (cited in Brewer, 'Popular English Metrical Romances', p. 51).

[17] Brewer, 'Popular English Metrical Romances', p. 51.

[18] See Mehl, *Middle English Romances*, p. 32. See the discussion in the introduction to *Amis and Amiloun*, ed. MacEdward Leach, EETS OS 203 (London: Oxford University Press, 1937), Intro., p. xviii ff.

ys cronyculyd, ywys; / A lay of Bretayne callyd hyt ys' (line 1214–15).[19] Confusingly, the story is 'cronyculyd', a feature that indicates the desire to portray the story as 'history'. The discrepancy between these generic titles is evident in many romances – in the stanzaic *Guy of Warwick* in the Auchinleck MS (National Library of Scotland Advocates' MS 19.2.1), the narrative is said to be a romance right from the start: 'God graunt hem heuen-blis to mede / Þat herken to mi romaunce rede / Al of a gentil kniȝt' (lines 1–3). The author of *Havelok* does not refer to the genre of the text she is writing, but only informs the reader in the middle of his text of the importance of performing it, thus giving a context for our understanding of romance as general entertainment: 'Romanz-reding on þe bok. / Þer mouhte men here þe gestes singe' (lines 2328–9).[20] *Sir Gowther* identifies itself as a Breton lay but ends, in one version, by calling its protagonist St Guthlac ('Seynt Gotlake', line 726 in the Royal manuscript version; see above, note 9). The phrase 'in romaunce as we rede' functions, in many of these texts, as a pointer to authority as well as a formula signalling to the audience the parameters within which the action will take place. Romance is 'a highly formulaic and stylised genre', characterized by 'formalised and distinctive style' and a very self-conscious approach to its subject matter; according to Carol Fewster, the 'formulaic quality' of the line just mentioned has 'a double role – metrical, and as a comment on poetic creation'.[21] These examples and many more not mentioned here attest to a flexible approach to genre by medieval authors, and a similarly variable medieval response to their content by medieval audiences. Sometimes the term can also refer to the whole as much as a small part of the text, as in the romance of *Kyng Alisaunder* (line 663 reads: 'þis nis nouȝt ramaunce of skof', line 1916: 'Here begynneþ þe romaunce best', line 6159: 'Now ariseþ a gode romaunce').[22]

As the question of how romances/popular romances refer to themselves cannot be easily answered, critics have turned to comparisons between models and translations, as well as features such as metre, performance and theme. Unfavourable comparisons between models and translations shaped most critical debates in the first part of the twentieth century, to the extent

---

[19] Cited from *Of Love and Chivalry: An Anthology of Middle English Romance*, ed. Jennifer Fellows (London: Dent, 1993), by line number. In *Amis and Amiloun*, reference is made to the authority of the genre from the start: 'in romance as we reede' (line 27). Fellows notes that 'Middle English romances often contain such appeals to authority; the device goes back to late classical antiquity and, more directly, links the techniques of Middle English romance with those of early English hagiography' (n. to line 27, p. 289).

[20] *Havelok*, ed. G. V. Smithers (Oxford: Clarendon Press, 1987), p. 64.

[21] Carol Fewster, *Traditionality and Genre in Middle English Romance* (Cambridge: D. S. Brewer, 1987), pp. ix and 7. In *Athelston* the formula appears at lines 383, 569, 623, 779; see *Athelston: A Middle English Romance*, ed. A. McI. Trounce, EETS OS 224 (London: Oxford University Press, 1951, reprinted 1957, 1987, 2002). Formulae are discussed by Susan Wittig in *Stylistic and Narrative Structures in the Middle English Romances* (Austin and London: University of Texas Press, 1978).

[22] Mehl, *Middle English Romances*, p. 15. See *Kyng Alisaunder*, ed. G. V. Smithers, EETS OS 227 (London: Oxford University Press, 1952).

that the work of popular romance authors was merely classed as 'debased', or 'hack work', hence not worthy of academic study.[23] A further complication, when one considers the multiple narrative threads running in Middle English romances, is that the popular romances (or, as critics have called them, non-cyclic, or metrical) lend themselves to categorization by either theme, as proposed by Laura Hibbard (Loomis) – of Trial and Faith, Legendary English Heroes, and Love and Adventure – or by a combination of length, theme and format, as proposed by Dieter Mehl – long and short, homiletic and novels in verse (though he separates the 'homiletic romances' from the rest irrespective of their length), to take just two influential examples.[24] Hibbard's categories correspond to more recent labels used by critics: for Trial and Faith – penitential, pious, or hagiographical romance; for Legendary English Heroes – the romance of English local and national heroes like Havelok, Guy, Bevis and Richard; for Love and Adventure – the rest of the romances that feature love relationships as a primary interest. It soon becomes apparent that both Hibbard's and Mehl's categories are insufficient, as family as well as social concerns feature in each group, and themes like exile or incest, though prevalent in many romances, are not found in all texts. There are popular romances that straddle two (or more) genres, for example the 'secular legend' type,[25] just as romances whose protagonists are outlaws like Gamelyn do not really fit in with either the idea of knightly adventures or legendary heroes or, according to some critics, even with the notion of romance genre itself.[26] The Breton lay sometimes poses problems as it is usually classed and discussed together with popular romances, but its brief format and occasional lack of typical chivalric exploits does not always allow an easy fit into the genre; its magical/supernatural elements and the appearance of the unexpected do, however, justify its inclusion.[27] Recent editors of popular romances have brought in new labels and groupings, which, though functional, lead to further

---

[23] For an overview of attitudes, and their origins, see McDonald, 'Polemical Introduction', passim, and Rushton, below, pp. 165–79.

[24] Laura A. Hibbard (Loomis), *Mediæval Romance in England: A Study of the Sources and Analogues of the Non-Cyclic Metrical Romances* (New York and London: Oxford University Press, 1924); Mehl, *Middle English Romances*. Maldwyn Mills proposes to rename Hibbard's categories 'chivalrous' (for love), 'heroic' (for legendary heroes), and 'edifying' (for trial and faith) (*Six Middle English Romances*, ed. Mills, p. vii). However some romances still cross these boundaries, as will be shown in this chapter.

[25] See Andrea Hopkins, *The Sinful Knights: A Study of Middle English Penitential Romance* (Oxford: Oxford University Press, 1990); Susan Crane Dannenbaum, '*Guy of Warwick* and the Question of Exemplary Romance', *Genre* 17 (1984), 351–74 and a review of these attitudes in Rhiannon Purdie, 'Generic Identity and the Origins of *Sir Isumbras*', in *Matter of Identity*, pp. 113–24.

[26] For an analysis of the problems posed by these, see Field's chapter in this volume, pp. 9–30. See also T. A. Shippey, '*The Tale of Gamelyn*: Class Warfare and the Embarrassments of Genre', in *Spirit*, pp. 78–96.

[27] Elizabeth Archibald, 'The Breton Lay in Middle English: Genre, Transmission and the Franklin's Tale', in *Insular Romance*, pp. 55–70. The Middle English Breton lays are considered to be *Sir Orfeo, Lai le Freine, Sir Degaré, Emaré, Sir Launfal, Sir Gowther, The Erl of Toulous, Sir Cleges*, Chaucer's 'The Franklin's Tale' and sometimes even his 'Wife of Bath's Tale'. For a recent edition, see *Middle English Breton Lays*, ed. Laskaya and Salisbury.

Genre and Classification

general confusion about the nature and classification of the popular romance genre. In one such anthology *Floris and Blancheflour* appears side-by-side with *Sir Degrevant, The Squire of Low Degree, The Tournament of Tottenham* and *The Feast at Tottenham*; although the first three share an interest in love that conquers all barriers (mostly of social class in these cases), the last ones are actually widely considered as parodies of romance, hence sit uneasily alongside the others.[28]

A question that needs answering, therefore, is how the 'elasticity' of the romance genre more generally extends to popular romance, and what particular elements define the latter. An influential, though debatable, definition provides a functional understanding of the romance genre as 'a narrative about knightly prowess and adventure, in verse or in prose, intended primarily for the entertainment of a listening audience';[29] as a starting point of sorts, such a definition helps to sharpen our overall awareness of the characteristics that may shape popular forms. Four main elements are taken into account in this definition: movement, that is, 'adventure'; social class, 'knighthood'; form, 'verse or prose'; and delivery, 'listening audience', referring to performance. An expectation shared by medieval and modern audiences alike is that, broadly speaking, medieval romance deals with male aristocratic heroes who engage in some extraordinary exploits, usually in the service of ladies. A process of maturation is involved in most texts, allowing for the development of the (sometimes unknown or inexperienced) young knight into a recognized hero.

Popular romances, as mentioned at the beginning of this chapter, include unexpected elements, usually related to the manner in which the traditional trajectory of the story is handled, and the variety of perspectives the reader/listener is presented with. Popular romances share with their courtly, sophisticated counterparts preoccupations with, for example, penance and salvation, the breaking up of relationships or families, and much more. However, a distinct feature of popular romances appears to be the deliberate difference or deviation from the norm; for instance, at times plots have relatively little or nothing to do with male protagonists progressing through to maturation or through actual knightly exploits, but rather focus on disempowered heroines, who engineer their own careers or life paths. To take one example, the Middle English version of the Breton *Lai le Freine* (usually classified as popular romance) hardly qualifies as a romance, given that its protagonist is a rather passive female heroine, and the plot includes hardly any chivalric adventures or magic to justify the romance label. Moreover, contrary to the evidence

---

[28] The mini-anthology referred to here is titled *Sentimental and Humorous Romances*, ed. Erik Kooper (Kalamazoo, MI: Medieval Institute Publications, 2006). On the difficulty with studying parody in medieval romance, see Wim Tigges, 'Romance and Parody', in *Companion to Middle English Romance*, ed. H. Aertsen and Alasdair A. MacDonald (Amsterdam: VU University Press, 1990), pp. 129–51. Tigges discusses, among others, *Sir Cleges, The Squire of Low Degree* and Chaucer's 'Sir Thopas'.

[29] *Manual*, p. 11.

presented in the vast body of romances (and popular romances), the female heroine Freine lives in concubinage with Gouron, thus having 'no moral or legal claim over him', but she does not complain.[30]

If we continue to allow such flexible boundaries for popular romance, what generic elements may be said to define it and how can they be identified? Three main characteristics of the popular romance genre will be discussed in what follows: the mixed features which seem to (almost always) bring into focus social and family concerns into any romance; the widespread appeal of the presence of independently-minded female heroines in Middle English popular romance; and the self-consciousness of the narratives, whether expressed at the level of criticism against courtly or chivalric values or cultural taboos.

Pious heroes and social concerns: popular romance and authority

As a reflection of medieval audiences' concerns with spiritual matters and with the afterlife, chivalric romances also developed an awareness of, and sometimes even a narrow focus on, religion. Unlike the related genre of saints' lives or legends, popular romances use the features they borrow from their more pious counterparts in order to appeal to the audience to become more involved in the story. The strong homiletic (and hagiographic) strain has been a feature recognized as defining the Middle English romances by contrast with their French antecedents. Mehl points out that 'the narrative technique of the romances may help with defining the genre' and that Middle English metrical (popular) romances 'are characterized by an abundant wealth of plot and incident', 'a more concise mode of narration, a much sparser use of description and less reflection' by comparison with French models.[31]

In particular, the popular romances shaped as saints' lives, or those said to be a 'vita' or secular legend (*Havelok* and *Gowther* are in this category, even if *Havelok* is not a pious romance), the audience is moved to ponder on the hero's progress through various stages. In some of the pious texts, the audience is called to pray for the hero, as if 'praying for the hero implies that his fate is still open and can be influenced by intercession. In this way the dramatic tension is heightened and again the plot assumes a new importance.'[32] To this extent the romance involves the reader more than a saint's legend would (the latter functions by example, and requires meditation and imitation rather than active involvement), and thus ensures a more immediate response than the merely didactic, pious goal of saints' legends or lives. It is not without importance that texts like *Havelok* and *King Horn*, usually clas-

---

[30] Elizabeth Archibald, '*Lai le Freine*: The Female Foundling and the Problem of Romance Genre', in *Spirit*, pp. 39–55 (p. 52).
[31] Mehl, *Middle English Romances*, pp. 18–19, 22.
[32] Mehl, *Middle English Romances*, p. 27.

sified as popular romances concerned with a local hero, both feature main characters whose recognized primary concern is social and political order; to some extent it can be said that the coalescence of social and religious roles in the person of the leader or ruler of nations is of great importance to the author and audiences of such texts. Despite the fact that Gowther is usually associated with the penitential pattern familiar to readers in other pious romances (as he is indeed seen as a persecutor of the Church, who needs to do penance to expiate his sins), he is ultimately called to become a ruler in his own right, and to put right the wrongs he has done in society. Similarly, the eponymous hero of *Robert of Sicily* learns as much about his own need to reform inwardly as about becoming a good ruler through the various tests to which he is subjected.

These popular romances also address anxieties over heredity and the ruling of the country, which are, in typical romance fashion, satisfactorily resolved for all concerned. Political concerns with inheritance and succession are unavoidable in these popular romances, and it is not surprising to find that the Middle English Havelok is particularly shaped as a leader of the masses, while Gowther's restitution to humanity is accompanied not only by typical romance gains – a suitable heiress and an empire – but also by his restoration of political order in his home lands.[33] Alcuin Blamires has recently pointed out that *Sir Gowther* has largely suffered neglect in terms of its socio-political implications, and its reflection of medieval anxieties over male succession, to the extent that only its penitential vein, and the accompanying embodiment of medieval ideas of the 'wild man', have been debated and explored.[34] However, penance and social order together clearly signal the main focus of Middle English popular romance – dealing with authority, implying challenges to definitions of humanity (madness and 'wild'/devilish behaviour), heredity (whose features does the heir inherit?) and authority (paternal, religious, political). To some extent, a popular romance like *Sir Gowther* could be said, as Neil Cartlidge has proposed, to tackle even the issue of written authority in the form of the written law – whether referring to rape, slander[35] or, I would like to suggest, the applicability of all types of law (biological, religious, moral, political) to heirs of the highest rank, of royal blood.[36]

---

[33] For an examination of genealogical concerns in *Havelok* and other insular romances, see my 'Genealogy in Insular Romance', in *Broken Lines: Genealogical Literature in Medieval Britain and France*, ed. Raluca L. Radulescu and Edward Donald Kennedy (Turnhout: Brepols, 2008), pp. 7–25.

[34] See 'The Twin Demons of Aristocratic Society in *Sir Gowther*', in *Pulp Fictions*, pp. 45–62. For an examination of *Sir Gowther* as the wild man, see Joanne A. Charbonneau, 'From Devil to Saint: Transformations in *Sir Gowther*', in *Matter of Identity*, pp. 21–8.

[35] Neil Cartlidge, '"Thereof seyus clerkus": Slander, Rape and *Sir Gowther*', in *Cultural Encounters*, pp. 135–47.

[36] This forms the topic of my unpublished work in progress on the political appeal of popular romances like *Sir Gowther* and *Isumbras* to fifteenth-century audiences – henceforth referred to as 'Spiritual Journeys and Political Realities in the Pious Romances'.

Penitential romances thus appear as more complex than some critics might see them as loci of debate over all-encompassing issues of society and law, and in the private sphere (relationships between husband and wife, for example). A broadening of the definition of such texts is required in order to understand what features might constitute the backbone of popular romance, and whether narrow categories carry enough weight to be considered functional. An emerging feature in all penitential romances is the concern with social reintegration, healing and peaceful resolution, at the end of a long sequence of highly disturbing events. While such features might be said to inform most romances, the preponderance of unexpected, shocking developments can safely be assigned to the popular ones. *Sir Isumbras*, another popular romance usually classed as penitential, follows the Job-like journey of the main hero from his loss of high position in society, including his possessions and close relatives (wife and sons), only to regain everything at the end of a long and painful process of learning about (and climbing) the social ladder. Isumbras suffers a 'civil death', which leads him to become a pilgrim, then a smith; as Elizabeth Fowler put it, '[h]e forges armour as if he were reconstituting the social person of the knight he once was: he rebuilds his social body as he builds his armour.'[37] In view of this assessment, as well as the powerful combination of themes (Saracen fighting, friendship with and protection offered by symbolic animals, female agency in regaining power, to name but a few), *Sir Isumbras* cannot be considered just a penitential romance, but instead emerges as a popular romance which typically challenges the boundaries inherited from its model, the legend of St Eustace, and its other romance counterparts, by combining elements typical of family romance and crusading romance with the main character's penitential progress.[38]

The problematic nature of hagiographic romance is nowhere more evident, perhaps, than in *Amis and Amiloun*, usually considered as a romance variation of the stories about pairs of saints or apostles like Peter and Paul, Simon and Jude, Philip and Bartholomew, and many others.[39] The identical, though unrelated, heroes in this romance prefer their friendship to any other relationship, whether heterosexual (Amis weds Belisant, who had seduced him; Amiloun also weds a lady, who later abandons him on account of his leprosy) or homosexual (Amis rejects the erotically-charged proposal of friendship the steward offers him). In the midst of events which involve a great deal of

---

[37] Elizabeth Fowler, 'The Romance Hypothetical: Lordship and the Saracens in *Sir Isumbras*', in *Spirit*, pp. 97–121 (p. 102).

[38] For an investigation of the origins of *Sir Isumbras*, see Purdie, 'Generic Identity', references above, n. 25. A political interpretation of this romance is proposed in my 'Spiritual Journeys and Political Realities'; see reference above at n. 35.

[39] For an investigation of generic concerns in this romance, see Ojars Kratins, 'The Middle English *Amis and Amiloun*: Chivalric Romance or Secular Hagiography', *Publications of the Modern Languages Association* 81 (1966), 347–54. Kratins emphasizes the importance of the Christian dimension in the romance, by pointing out, among other things, the divine intervention in testing by leprosy with the test of 'trouthe', rather than seeing it as punishment (p. 350) and leprosy as a blessing rather than curse.

Genre and Classification

aggression (whether physical, verbal or emotional), including punishment for dishonesty with leprosy and killing one's children to save a friend (complete with the apparent divine miraculous revival of Amis's children), the main heroes' abandonment of earthly relationships and possessions, followed by their death and burial in the same grave, points the reader into the direction of saints' lives as well as a celebration of same-sex love, beyond all constraints – social, political or religious. In fact this popular romance seems to condone the choices its heroes make, to the point of subverting social order, which would favour concern over succession and the union of the family, not to mention models for children. In an original reinterpretation of this romance, Sheila Delany suggests that the story contains visible parallels between the relationship between Amis and Amiloun and the more famous and much reviled liaison between Edward II and his favourite, Piers Gaveston.[40] Interestingly, the Middle English version of this romance is contained in the Auchinleck MS, a collection regarded by critics alternatively as a 'handbook for the nation', or an instructional manual for the middling gentry.[41] Despite the presence of romance motifs (chivalric heroes, the notion of 'trouthe' in the form of pledged friendship, union between knights and ladies, challenges by duel, miraculous healing and revival), this popular romance actually subverts typical expectations by offering little in the way of chivalric adventures as such, or even educational material relating to spiritual, family or political matters, or indeed social order.

These representative examples of penitential romance show, on the one hand, that the Middle English versions fully achieve their popular potential/appeal by combining elements belonging to their original model (hagiographic, pious) with interests that are recognizably not sophisticated or courtly, and rather scandalous in one way or another, including inhuman social behaviour and taboo desires.

Feisty females

By contrast to French and Anglo-Norman romances, the Middle English versions are concerned with the effects of tension or aggression in the couple or in parent-child relationships, and rarely if ever with adultery, a dominant theme in the original stories.[42] Critics agree that Middle English popular romances in particular favour family values confirmed by authority – whether in the form of the customs of lay society, the Church or the law. The interven-

---

[40] Sheila Delany, 'A, A and B: Coding Same-Sex Union in *Amis and Amiloun*', in *Pulp Fictions*, pp. 63–81.
[41] See Thorlac Turville-Petre, *England the Nation: Language, Literature and National Identity, 1290–1340* (Oxford: Clarendon Press, 1996), p. 112 and Phillipa Hardman in this volume, p. 157.
[42] For a detailed analysis of gender roles, see the chapter on 'Gender and Identity' in this volume, pp. 96–110.

tion of divine providence is common in romances, so that the values of the couple can triumph; moreover, genuinely illegal births are a rarity in these texts. The nature of the union between the partners is very important, as it points to anxieties over social climbing, the debate about nobility by birth or virtue, and the desirability of having female heiresses choose their partner without outside intervention or constraint.[43] The heiresses of popular romance manifest independence and yield unexpected levels of power, despite frequent obstacles in their path. In particular, the heroines of the shorter romances or Breton lays (Emaré, the Empress Beulybon in *The Erl of Toulous*, Freine, as well as those in the longer romances like Belisant in *Amis and Amiloun*, Rimenhild in *King Horn*, Fere in *Ipomadon*, and the enterprising and strong-willed Melidor in *Sir Degrevant*) all exercise their independence in forging a path for themselves and their chosen partner, taking risks that sometimes involve near-death experiences. In some cases at least the strength of character of these heroines reminds the reader of the model of patient suffering typical of more pious heroines like Constance and Griselda (encountered in Chaucer's 'The Man of Law's Tale' and 'The Clerk's Tale', respectively), though it can be argued that the feisty heroines of popular romance exhibit more resourcefulness than their almost silent, compliant counterparts. Even the Princess in *The King of Tars* can be seen as an active agent, though a suffering one, who brings social unity and ultimately Christian redemption to both the Sultan's people and her own; as Jane Gilbert has shown, in the midst of the disaster brought about by the birth of a lump of flesh rather than a child and heir, the Princess exhibits moral strength to the point that 'she sees through her grief to seize the opportunity for ideological confrontation, and in her emotional muscularity she exemplifies the subordination of sentiment to doctrine which befits a Christian heroine'.[44]

The initiative taken by these women is typically related to their ancillary function in the romances, as they help the hero succeed in regaining his position, winning fame and the rule of a country, and reinstating social order. Female agency in achieving these goals should not be underestimated, however; in some romances, like the popular *Sir Isumbras*, the unnamed wife decides to wear armour and fight side-by-side with her husband in the battle against the Saracens. The presence of such acts is indicative, most critics agree, of an identifiable concern with contemporary social issues in late medieval England, when middling gentry women could be found in the position of administrators of lands and defenders of both family honour and property, and anxieties over the lack of male heirs justified the acceptance of lower-born males into gentle society.[45] In the same way *Le Bone Florence of*

---

[43] See Harriet E. Hudson, 'Construction of Class, Family, and Gender in Some Middle English Popular Romances', in *Class and Gender in Early English Literature*, ed. Britton J. Harwood and Gillian R. Overing (Bloomington and Indianapolis: Indiana University Press, 1994), pp. 76–94.

[44] Jane Gilbert, 'Putting the Pulp into Fiction: The Lump-Child and Its Parents in *The King of Tars*', in *Pulp Fictions*, pp. 102–23 (p. 113).

[45] Typical examples are found in the correspondence of the Paston family; see also Hudson,

Rome exhibits middle-class preoccupations with shaping female identity in the household (see references at n. 2 above).

Family relationships occupy centre stage in Middle English popular romances, and the pervasiveness of threats to unity, through evil mothers, step-mothers, and incestuous fathers, only adds more dramatic tension to the progress of the protagonist and refocuses attention on the interaction between the private and the public spheres, issues of perennial appeal to medieval audiences.

Self-conscious narrative in the popular romance

Popular romance can also be defined through its testing of the limits of the romance genre itself, by directly confronting prejudices against lower-class values as much as the upper-class, carefully crafted, notions of 'trouthe' and social duty. At times the challenge posed by popular romances relates to the extent to which the text under scrutiny can or should still be considered a romance; to take an example, *Sir Amadace*, typically seen by one modern editor as 'a commercial romance', talks rather unashamedly about financial problems and the implication of winning not only a social position but the material advantages that come with it.[46] Unlike *Sir Launfal* and *Sir Cleges*, where emphasis is placed on the knights' excessive liberality, but constant attention is paid to their lofty ideals, the chivalric values discussed in *Sir Amadace* are compromised through low ideals, and the traditional romance elements may appear as a cover for a persistent concern with a didactic lesson to be learned: no knight should underestimate the value of money. Despite the atypical emphasis on material values, a romance such as this one does in some ways relate to more complex issues explored in other romances, like recovering or discovering one's identity, social climbing and local violence, for example in *Sir Degaré*, *Libeaus Desconus* and *Sir Degrevant*, and even *Gamelyn*.[47]

Many other romances, such as *The King of Tars*, contain evidently self-conscious, ironic elements, which conduct a deliberate assessment of courtly values and their importance. The King of Tars is forced to send his daughter as a wife to the Sultan, following the defeat of the Christian forces and the Princess's willing act of self-sacrifice. At the Sultan's wedding feast the

---

'Construction of Class'; Joanne Charbonneau, 'Transgressive Fathers in *Sir Eglamour of Artois* and *Torrent of Portyngale*', in *Discourses on Love, Marriage, and Transgression in Medieval and Early Modern Literature*, ed. Albrecht Classen (Tempe: Arizona Center for Medieval and Renaissance Studies, 2004), pp. 243–65.

[46] See *Amis and Amiloun, Robert of Cisyle, and Sir Amadace*, ed. Edward E. Foster (Kalamazoo, MI: Medieval Institute Publications, 1997), Intro. to *Sir Amadace*.

[47] For a discussion of generic issues including links with the ballad in *Sir Degrevant*, see W. A. Davenport, '*Sir Degrevant* and Composite Romance', in *Insular Romance*, pp. 111–31.

lavish chivalric display cannot disguise the forced wedding.[48] The double meaning of the description is evident: on the one hand the Sultan's nobility and liberality can be admired, despite his heathen presentation; on the other questions are raised over what makes a noble knight and how heathens and Christians can be separated. In typical fashion, the habits and temperament of the Sultan and his followers (in the Auchinleck MS called 'knights', in the Vernon MS, 'Sarazins') justify their exclusion from the world known to medieval English audiences, Christian and white. It is evident that racial stereotypes in this romance are used, alongside other controversial elements, to confirm anxieties and prejudices about the Other, and justify the sermonizing aspect contained in the Princess's successful conversion of the Sultan. However, the same elements also suggest ambiguous interpretations of what chivalric and courtly values are, and who can display them, and in this way the author invites reflection on the very nature of romance and its purpose.

Last but not least the reflexivity of popular romance may be identified in its openness to other genres. The historical romances (known as either ancestral or as legendary), among which *Sir Bevis of Hampton*, *Guy of Warwick* and *Richard Coeur de Lion* are most prominent, were enthusiastically adopted by medieval audiences. In addition to these, the fascinating, though generically hard to place, *Romance of Thomas of Erceldoune* exhibits a complex mix of features (romance, prophecy and ballad). This text also marks a transitional moment between medieval and early modern prophecy later expressed in ballad form. As Helen Cooper has pointed out, instead of the usual tetrameter couplets or tail-rhyme encountered in popular romances, here we have quatrains typical of the ballad stanza (abab).[49] The text is not classed as a romance in *Manual* and the nineteenth-century editor of the text, James Murray, chose not to identify which part can be considered romance, which prophecy. More importantly, the medieval copyist of the only complete text of the romance plus prophecies, Robert Thornton, chose not to call his text a romance either but simply 'Thomas of Erceldoune' (Lincoln Thornton MS, fol. 149v), though he did identify other texts in his collection as romances (for example, 'The Romance of Sir Ysambrace' and 'The Romance of Sir Percyvelle of Gales' on fols 109r and 161r, respectively).

Murray identified a strong link between a historical character and the romance-teller; in 1286 a Thomas of Erceldoune is said to have predicted the terrible death of the King of Scotland, Alexander III, and the incident is noted in the *Scotichronicon* by John of Fordun, or more precisely by his continuator Walter Bower (b. 1385, wrote about 1430), who records that Thomas's skills were required by the Earl of March to prophesy about the

---

[48] Fewster, *Traditionality and Genre*, p. 12. For a summary of discussions of generic debates over this romance, see Karl Reichl, '*The King of Tars*: Language and Textual Transmission', in *Studies in the Vernon Manuscript*, ed. Pearsall, pp. 171–86 (pp. 171–2).

[49] See Helen Cooper, 'Thomas of Erceldoune: Romance as Prophecy', in *Cultural Encounters*, pp. 171–87 (p. 173). For an edition, see *The Romance and Prophecies of Thomas of Erceldoune*, ed. James A. H. Murray, EETS OS 61 (London, 1875), cited parenthetically below.

current political situation.⁵⁰ Similarly, Robert Mannyng of Brunne also seems to indicate widespread knowledge of Erceldoune in his preface to his *English Chronicle*, as did Thomas Grey in his *Scalacronica* of about 1355.⁵¹ Apart from his prophetic talents, Thomas was also credited with the authorship of the popular romance *Sir Tristrem*, itself contained in another mid-fourteenth century collection of romances, the Auchinleck MS.⁵²

The connection between romance-writing and prophecies influences our understanding of the flexible generic boundaries between the two types of texts, and in particular the medieval audiences' interest in the mixed genre. Murray notes that in the tripartite structure of the text attributed to Thomas, the beginning of the romance of Thomas resembles the prophecies which follow it in both style and meter, while in the third section, the ballad that usually follows the prophecies is markedly different, being much more 'interesting and lively' (p. xxvi). At the start of the *Romance of Thomas* we encounter strikingly typical features, such as the appeal to authority ('Gyff it als the storie sayes ...') and the meeting of the protagonist with the fairy queen under a tree, so often referred to in Breton lays, like *Sir Orfeo* and *Sir Launfal*. The prologue, only present in the Thornton MS, contains prayers for the 'ynglysche mene' twice (lines 14 and 24) and incorporates the typical minstrel address: 'Lystyns, Lordyngs, bothe grete and smale' (line 1), only to follow with a promise of 'Of doghety dedis þat hase bene done' (line 10) and 'Of felle feghtyngs and batells sere; / And how þat þir knyghtis hase wonne þair schone' (lines 11–12). The prayer for 'Englishmen' reminds us of the 'matter of England' romances, with their link between real historical events and characters of romance, and displays the attention paid to the nature of the story told and its impact on its audience. As Lesley Coote has shown

> The *Ersseldoune* romance connects king, people and nation with ideas of social class and regional loyalty, under the aegis of political prophecy. As a member of the northern gentry, the answers to Thomas's questions were precisely what interested Thornton himself, and they demonstrate how these potentially conflicting ideas and loyalties formed part of a single political consciousness.⁵³

Such a link is not surprising in the *Romance of Thomas*, even if this text remains on the borders between two genres; as scholars have shown, various romance heroes of the legendary type have counterparts in medieval histories.⁵⁴ Havelok is among the prominent examples, followed closely by Guy,

---

⁵⁰ Murray, Intro., pp. xiii–xiv.
⁵¹ Murray, Intro., pp. xx, xviii; Cooper, 'Thomas', p. 174.
⁵² Murray, Intro., p. xxi; Cooper, 'Thomas', p. 175.
⁵³ Lesley Coote, *Prophecy and Public Affairs in Later Medieval England* (York: York Medieval Press, 2000), p. 184.
⁵⁴ See the many articles by Rosalind Field on this subject, among them 'Romance as History, History as Romance', in *Romance in Medieval England*, ed. M. Mills et al. (Cambridge: D. S.

the ancestral hero adopted by the Warwick earls, and Bevis, the hero adopted by the Arundels. In Cooper's words:

> Yet romance and prophecy are not in practice so far adrift from each other. One of the most familiar forms of romance is the ancestral or genealogical variety: the association indeed goes back to before romance was invented as a formal genre at all, to the *Aeneid* as a founding legend of Rome. All the romances deriving from Geoffrey of Monmouth's *History of the Kings of Britain* have something of that foundational quality about them, not least the legends of Brutus and Arthur. [...] Not all of these romances contain explicit prophecies (although the *Aeneid* offers a model for such a process), but even when they do not, they tell stories set in an imaginary past to justify and explain the present of their writer and readers, just as prophecy sets itself in the past to demonstrate that the present is shaped and authorized by what has gone before. *Ancestral romance and prophecy both invent a past that contains the seeds of the present.* [...] both [romance and prophecy] are located backwards in time in order to look forwards, to the here and now.[55]

The flexibility of the popular romance genre may be said to have been once again tested and proven in the *Romance of Thomas* and the ancestral popular romances, while their appeal in the post-medieval period bears witness to the endurance of the topics they tackle.

Generic boundaries are hard to define when it comes to popular romance; however features such as those mentioned in this chapter do help to identify some of the texts, and shape our understanding of the vitality of the stories they tell us. The chameleonic nature of medieval popular romance, always on the verge of becoming something else, or taking on the resemblance of neighbouring narratives, is the key to the interpretation of a genre that continues to engage modern audiences.

Brewer, 1991), pp. 163–73 and 'The King Over the Water: Exile-and-Return Revisited', in *Cultural Encounters*, pp. 41–53.

[55] Cooper, 'Thomas', pp. 183–4 (my emphasis).

3

The Manuscripts of Popular Romance

MALDWYN MILLS and GILLIAN ROGERS

Popular romances survive in a number of manuscripts, both medieval and post-medieval, though the variety of contexts that result from their varied transmission has affected their modern interpretation. Chaucer's *Canterbury Tales*, for example, itself part of an often diffuse tradition, presents a basic identity which allows for interpretation of individual tales and the collection as a whole, and themes across common manuscript fragments. The individual romance, each a distinct tale which may share themes or even characters with other romances, can look very different in its manuscript context; scribes and collectors exerted a significant amount of power over how a text was presented to its initial audience, and therefore to posterity. This chapter will address some of the problems raised by the presence of popular romances in extant manuscripts, followed by an examination of the impact of one very influential post-medieval repository of romances, the Percy Folio manuscript.

Medieval manuscripts of popular romances

Maldwyn Mills
There are parallels between some of the romances discussed in this book and some of the MS collections in which they appear. Most particularly, perhaps, in the way in which the content of both will often seem more varied than unified. Individual romances may be written in more than one narrative mode, and about more than one kind of human experience: the two halves of *Le Bone Florence of Rome* are devoted in turn to large-scale fighting, and the sufferings of a pious heroine; those of *The Awntyrs off Arthure* to a stark warning against sin, and a combat between knights. This same variety is also to be found, not only in those manuscripts in which romances rub shoulders with works of other kinds, but in the (relatively rare) ones in which romances alone are to be found. London, British Library, MS Egerton 2862, the most substantial of these last, offers in sequence two stories of combative English heroes (*Kyng Richard* and *Beuous of Hampton*), one of love, chivalry, and the search for lost parents (*Sir Degarre*), another of mutual love, separa-

tion, and reunion (*Fflorence and Blanchefloure*), a chronicle of large-scale fighting (*The Batell of Troye*), a tale of male friendship and suffering (*Amis and Amiloun*), and a story telling of its hero's chivalry, its heroine's suffering, and their separation, reunion, and finding of a son lost (*Sir Egleamoure*). In this collection, as in some of the texts it contains, we can find both significant points of contact between the individual items, and a frequent diversity of content, and sometimes style.[1]

This diversity, in particular, could well have been 'popular' in sense 4 of those that the *OED* gives for the word: 'Intended for or suited to ordinary people'. Other senses are brought to mind by some more obvious features of these collections. Many are written on paper rather than parchment, lack any elaborate ornamentation or illustration, and look more amateur than professional in presentation – the lines unruled, the letter-forms not always consistent. It is true that sense 4b of 'popular' in the *OED* – 'Adapted to the means of ordinary people; low, moderate (in price)' – would not be apt here, since in marked contrast to the later prints and still later chapbooks of individual romance texts, such collections would have been beyond the means of all but a tiny minority. But they would not have been an aristocratic preserve.

Where the reception rather than the production or acquisition of these MSS is concerned, one part of *OED* sense 4a of 'popular' would seem most apt: 'intended for a general readership', and especially so to manuscripts that were commissioned (and in some cases written) by the head of a family for his and their entertainment and instruction. The most important example of such a collection is Lincoln Cathedral Library, MS 91; the most idiosyncratic, Oxford, Bodleian Library, MS Douce 261; the most varied, the 'commonplace book': the work of a (usually large) number of hands that might sometimes contain excerpts as well as whole texts. Exemplary here is Cambridge University Library, MS Ff.1.6 (the Findern MS), the work of no fewer than thirty contributors.[2] There are also a handful of manuscripts that might have been 'popular' in yet another way. These, again plain in appearance, and showing signs of hard usage, would also have been easily portable,[3] and

---

[1] This variety of content must be remembered when considering the romances in relation to the non-romance items with which they are juxtaposed; parts of them, at least, may have points of contact with these last. See below, pp. 52–55.

[2] See the Scolar Press facsimile, *The Findern Manuscript: MS Cambridge University Library Ff.1.6*, ed. Richard Beadle and A. E. B. Owen (London: Scolar Press, 1978), p. xi. Aberystwyth, National Library of Wales, MS Porkington 10, another example of such a collection, was the work of sixteen: see Daniel Huws, 'MS Porkington 10 and its Scribes', in *Romance Reading*, p. 189.

[3] The matter has been much debated, mostly with scepticism: compare the discussion of these 'holster books' (so called because of their long and narrow format) by Gisela Guddat-Figge in her *Catalogue of Manuscripts Containing Middle English Romances* (Munich: W. Fink, 1976), pp. 30–6 with that of Andrew Taylor in 'The Myth of the Minstrel Manuscript', *Speculum* 66 (1991), 43–73). The possibility that such collections might be meant for (less professional) reading aloud within a 'household' context is argued by Simon Horobin and Alison Wiggins in 'Reconsidering Lincoln's Inn MS 150', *Medium Ævum* 77 (2008), 30–53. See also Karl Reichl's chapter in this volume, 'Orality and Performance' (pp. 132–49).

easily read at sight.[4] As such they might have been intended for, and used by, professional reciters (*disours, gestours*) of the texts they contained, to audiences of people unable to read them for themselves; their contents would then be, 'favoured by people generally' (*OED* 'popular', sense 6b). Of all the manuscripts that have survived, the one that best meets these conditions is Oxford, Bodleian Library, MS Douce 228, which contains only a text of *King Richard*, and is the work of a single scribe.[5]

Of the single-scribe manuscripts of larger scope, only a handful contain romances and nothing else: the most significant is BL MS Egerton 2862, already mentioned; after this would come Princeton University Library, MS Robert H. Taylor Collection (1450–60) with *The Awntyrs off Arthure*, *Sir Amadace*, and *The Avowing of Arthur*;[6] and Bodleian Library, MS Douce 261, with *Syr Isenbras*, *Syr Degore*, *Syr Gawayne* and *Syr Eglamoure of Artoys*. This last manuscript, while post-medieval,[7] is in fact as densely 'popular' as any earlier collections in its actual choice of texts, since all but the third of them turn up quite often in other MS collections,[8] as well as in the form of

---

[4] In particular, by having their text set out in single columns. Other devices that would have helped a *disour* in performing these romances – paragraph-markers in the left-hand margins to divide the text into manageable units, bracketing rhyming lines in the right-hand margins, or setting tail-lines to the right of their couplets – would have been equally helpful to more private modes of reading. But larger divisions of the romance as a whole into 'fitts' might have been of particular help to a *disour*: these are found in both the BL Cotton Caligula and Cambridge University Library texts of *Sir Eglamoure* (at lines 343 and 634–6 in the first of these: see *Sir Eglamour of Artois*, ed. Frances E. Richardson, EETS OS 256 (London: Oxford University Press, 1965), pp. 27, 45). See particularly, Phillipa Hardman, 'Fitt Divisions in Middle English Romances: A Consideration of the Evidence', *Yearbook of English Studies* 22 (1992), 63–80.

[5] Even Taylor concedes that this MS may have been for 'minstrel' use. His only other candidate for such use is a lost book containing the originals of the texts of *Havelok* and *King Horn* in the second half of Bodleian Library, MS Laud Misc. 108 (op. cit., 60).

[6] A fairly coherent grouping of texts, with *Amadace* and the *Avowing* concerned with the testing of their heroes, and a strong supernatural element in the *Awntyrs* and *Amadace*.

[7] The date given on the verso of its final leaf is 1564; it is written in an italic hand, and derives all four of its texts from early sixteenth-century prints (which it resembles in format). Its one original feature is the sequence of large coloured line-illustrations that punctuate the narratives. The only other romance collection that it even superficially resembles is BL MS Cotton Nero A.x, also made up of four texts, broadly comparable in size (167 x 118 mm against 185 x 133mm in Douce) and also carrying a number of large, rather amateurish illustrations. But there are crucial differences, notably the fact that only one of the four texts in MS Cotton Nero is a romance, and that one (*Sir Gawain and the Green Knight*) both highly sophisticated and a unique copy.

[8] Nine medieval texts or fragments of *Isenbras* have survived, and four of both *Degore* and *Eglamoure*. All three items tell of the separation, hardships and reunion of a family, and of a tournament in which the hero distinguishes himself; the second and third also have a fight with a dragon, and the last-minute avoidance of a marriage between the hero and his mother. They appear together elsewhere: *Degore* and *Eglamoure* in BL MS Egerton 2862, and in the Percy Folio MS (BL MS Additional 27879); *Isenbras* and *Eglamoure* in Lincoln Cathedral Library MS 91, and in BL MS Cotton Caligula A.ii; *Degore* and *Eglamoure* in Cambridge University Library, MS Ff.2.38. Other romances of which four or more medieval copies have survived also tell of the sufferings of at least one of their principal characters (*Robert of Sicily* (10x), and *Amis and Amiloun* (4x)); others chronicle native English heroes (*Guy of Warwick* (5x), *Horn* (4x), *Bevis of Hamtoun* (7x), *Richard Coer de Lion* (7x)). Arthur and his knights appear in *The Awntyrs of Arthur* (4x), and *Lybeaus Disconus* (5x). More individual is the 'idyllic' romance of *Floris and Blancheflour* (4x). But in terms of surviving medieval copies (twenty-five in all), the most 'popular' of all Middle English

later prints, or transcripts of prints;[9] the first of them is also mentioned in earlier lists of popular romances.[10] And *Syr Gawayne* – which looks distinctly late (even post-) medieval – has itself survived in fragments of three earlier printed copies.[11]

More common, however, are single-scribe collections in which romances are set beside other kinds of text; of these three in particular stand out, all of the fifteenth century: Lincoln Cathedral Library, MS 91, already mentioned as a 'family' anthology; Cambridge University Library, MS Ff.2.38, and London, BL MS Cotton Caligula A.2.[12] But Edinburgh, National Library of Scotland, MS Advocates' 19.2.1 (the Auchinleck MS), the most important surviving repository of all, is at once of the early fourteenth century, and the work of six scribes,[13] probably working under the supervision of the one who did most of the copying.[14] This manuscript also shows how the actual scale and content of these collections might fluctuate over the years, generally from the loss of items (or parts of items), but sometimes from the introduction of new ones as well. At the beginning of the manuscript the loss of no fewer than five items is made plain by the late beginning of the sequence of item-numbers; the loss of parts of items is demonstrated by gaps in the narrative sense (and in the foliation), and often confirmed by the survival of narrow stubs from the leaves excised.[15] On the other hand, examples of the

---

romances would have to be *Gamelyn*, which C. W. Dunn discusses between *Guy of Warwick* and *Athelston*, in *Manual*, pp. 31–3, but which appears in none of the MSS listed in Guddat-Figge's *Catalogue*. It is in fact found only in manuscripts of the *Canterbury Tales* (in which it is generally ascribed to the Cook); these are listed in *Manual*, pp. 220–1.

[9] See Jennifer Fellows, 'Printed Romance in the Sixteenth Century', in this volume, pp. 67–78; also Gillian Rogers (for the Percy Folio transcripts of *Eglamoure* and *Degore*), later in this chapter, pp. 60–61.

[10] Some of the names given in these lists are those of characters from romances named after different ones. The best known list is of course the one given by Chaucer in *Sir Thopas*, which names *Horn Childe*, *Bevys of Hamtoun*, *Guy of Warwick* and *Lybeaus Disconus*, as well as the more surprising *Ypotis* and *Pleyndamour*. More extensive lists appear in *Cursor Mundi*, *The Laud Troy Book*, and at the beginning and end of *King Richard*. Between these four lists mention the first four titles in Chaucer's list at least once (*Guy* four times); *Isumbras* is noted twice. All of them are set out in *Sources and Analogues of the Canterbury Tales*, ed. Robert M. Correale with Mary Hamel, II (Cambridge: D. S. Brewer, 2005), pp. 704–6.

[11] None of which, unfortunately, supplies the lost opening of the Douce text.

[12] Facsimiles of the first two of these were published by Scolar Press, London in 1977 and 1979. See also John J. Thompson, 'The Compiler in Action: Robert Thornton and the "Thornton Romances" in Lincoln Cathedral MS 91', in *Manuscripts and Readers in Fifteenth-Century England*, ed. Derek Pearsall (Cambridge: D. S. Brewer, 1983), pp. 113–24; also his *Robert Thornton and the London Thornton Manuscript* (Cambridge: D. S. Brewer, 1987), *passim*, and 'Looking Behind the Book: MS Cotton Caligula A.ii. part 1, and the experience of its texts', in *Romance Reading*, pp. 171–87.

[13] See Alison Wiggins, 'Are Auchinleck Manuscript's Scribes 1 and 6 the same scribe? The advantages of whole-data analysis and electronic tests', *Medium Ævum* 73 (2004), 10–26. This article includes a useful bibliography of previous writing on this manuscript in the first of its notes.

[14] For an alternative, once popular, view of its making see Laura H. Loomis, 'The Auchinleck Manuscript and a Possible London Bookshop of 1330–1340', in *Adventures in the Middle Ages: A Memorial Collection of Essays and Studies* (New York: B. Franklin, 1962), pp. 150–87.

[15] A particular cause of the loss of text in the Auchinleck MS (MS Advocates' 19.2.1) was the removal of miniatures set at the head of many of its items, whether by cutting around them, or

late insertion of items before the gatherings were bound together are found on f. 146v, where the principal scribe passes from his incomplete couplet text of *Guy of Warwick* to its tail-rhyme continuation, and on f. 317v, where he passes from the couplet *Liber Regum Anglie* to the tail-rhyme *Horn Childe and Maiden Rimnild*. The gaps in time are attested by the fact that in each case the second item is in a version of his hand that is significantly larger than in the first.

Such diminution and augmentation of the range of individual manuscripts might also have taken place on a larger scale. On the one hand, a single manuscript may have been split into two or more: Oxford, Bodleian MSS Rawlinson D 82 (dominated by the *Seege of Thebes* and *Sege of Troye*), Douce 324 (containing only *The Awntyrs off Arthure*) and Rawlinson Poet. 168 (only Hoccleve, *The Boke of Governaunce*) had once formed a single manuscript. On the other, items originally separate, whether in the form of unbound gatherings, of 'booklets',[16] or of completed manuscripts, may later have been joined together. See, for example, Bodleian MS Laud Miscellany 108 (which links a manuscript of the *South English Legendary* with one dominated by the juxtaposed *Havelok* and *King Horn*), and Bodleian MS Rawlinson C 86 (where a collection dominated by the juxtaposed *Landavall* and *The Weddyng of Syr Gawen* is bound together with no fewer than four other collections).

Within the most important 'romance' manuscripts in their present form, individual romances may be grouped in a great variety of ways, as can be seen from the following summary accounts (in which contiguous items are separated by commas, those which are not, by one or more full stops):[17]

Auchinleck MS .. *King of Tars* ... *Amis and Amiloun* .. *Sir Degare*. *Floris and Blaunchefour* .. *Guy of Warwick, Reinbrun, Sir Beues of Hamtoun, Arthour and Merlin* .. *Lay le Freine, Roland and Vernagu, Otuel, [Kyng Alisaunder]* .. *Sir Tristrem, Sir Orfeo* .. *Horn Childe*. *King Richard*.

CUL MS Ff.2.38 ... *Erle of Tolous, Syr Egyllamore of Artas, Syr Tryamowre, Octavian, Bevis of Hamtoun. Guy of Warwick, Le Bone Florence of Rome, Robert of Sicily, Sir Degare*

---

by cutting or tearing off the leaves on which they stood. The illustrated leaves of Bodleian MS Douce 261 also seem to have been responsible for much of the damage done to the collection as a whole.

[16] For a detailed study of the way in which a manuscript of varied content might be built up of quires arranged as booklets, see Phillipa Hardman, 'A Mediaeval "Library In Parvo"', *Medium Ævum* 47 (1978), 262–73.

[17] As in all later references, slightly abbreviated titles for the MSS are given here; the two collections written by Robert Thornton (Lincoln Cathedral Library, MS 91 and BL MS Additional 31042) are henceforth given as Lincoln Thornton MS and London Thornton MS. The titles of individual items are usually presented (and spelt) as in the manuscripts concerned, though sometimes abbreviated; words in brackets are supplied to bring them in line with more familiar titles; whole titles in brackets, to replace Latin titles in the originals: *Octavian Imperator* and *Launfal Miles* in BL MS Cotton Caligula A.ii, *Bellum Troianum* in London, Lincoln's Inn, MS Hale 150, *Vita Ricardi Regis Primi* in Cambridge, Caius MS 175.

Lincoln Thornton MS *Lyf of Alexander. Morte Arthure, Octovyane, Sir Ysambrace, Erle of Tholous. Sir Degrevante, Sir Eglamour off Artasse .. The Awentyrs of Arthure, Sir Percyvelle ...*
BL MS Cotton Caligula A.ii . *Eglamour of Artas .. [Octavian], [Launfal], Lybeaus Disconus ...Emaré ...The Sege of Jerusalem, Chevelere Assigne, Isumbras ..*
Bodleian MS Ashmole 61 .. *Isombras ... Erle of Tolous, Lybeus Dysconus ...Sir Cleges ...Orfew ..*
Lincoln's Inn MS Hale 150 *[Libeaus Desconus], [Arthour and] Merlyn, [Kyng] Alisaunder, [The Seege or Batayle of Troye] ..* [18]
London Thornton MS *The Segge of Jerusalem, The Sege off Melayne . Rowlande and Ottuell ...Kyng Richerd*
Cambridge Caius MS 175 [*King Richard*], *Ysumbras .. Athelston, Beffs de Hamptoun ..*
BN (Naples) MS XIII.B.29 .. *Beuys of Hamptoun .. Libious Disconious . Sir Isumbras ..*
NLS MS Advocates' 19.3.1 ... *Sir Gowther ... Sir Ysumbras ... Sir Amadace ...*
Manchester Chetham MS 8009 ... *Torrente of Portyngale ... Bevys of Hampton, Ipomadon ...*

Some of the groupings of romances noted above are clearly meaningful, whether in respect of subject-matter, style, or both. Most impressive, perhaps, is that of *Erle of Tolous, Syr Egyllamore, Syr Tryamowre, Octavian* in CUL MS Ff.2.38, since all four contain the story of a wife falsely accused, and are written in tail-rhyme stanzas of twelve lines. The same is true of the group of *Octovyane, Ysambrace, Erle of Tholous* in the Lincoln Thornton MS, while in Lincoln's Inn, MS Hale 150, the conjunction of *Arthour and Merlyn* and *Kyng Alisaunder* brings together stories of two heroic kings of irregular birth, that are told (in couplets) in styles so alike that they have sometimes been ascribed to the same author.[19] Also striking is the juxtaposition of *Octavian, Launfal* and *Lybeaus Disconus* in BL MS Cotton Caligula A.ii, even though the verse-forms here are more diverse.[20] Other grouped texts may have only their subject-matter in common. In the Auchinleck MS, *Guy of Warwick, Reinbroun,* and *Beues of Hamtoun* all tell of native English heroes (as do *Kyng Richard* and *Beuous of Hampton* in BL MS Egerton

---

[18] This MS has sometimes been considered a 'minstrel' anthology. Its dimensions are not unlike those of MS Douce 228 (305 x 130mm against 288 x 100mm); it is unpretentious, written in single columns, shows signs of hard usage (especially at the beginning, where about half its text of *Libeaus Desconus* is missing), and its texts of *Arthour and Merlyn* and *Kyng Alisaunder* are notably shorter than their counterparts in the Auchinleck MS, and Bodleian MS Laud Misc. 622. At the same time, there are few clear signs of oral (rather than scribal) provenance for their (many) unique readings. The most important of these last are set out in *Kyng Alisaunder*, II, ed. G. V. Smithers, EETS OS 237 (Oxford: Oxford University Press, 1957), pp. 11–13.

[19] See *Of Arthour and of Merlin*, II, ed. O. D. Macrae-Gibson, EETS OS 279 (Oxford: Oxford University Press, 1979), pp. 65–75.

[20] For the possibility of common authorship here, see M. Mills, 'The Composition and Style of the 'Southern' *Octavian, Sir Launfal* and *Libeaus Desconus*', *Medium Ævum* 31 (1962), 88–109.

The Manuscripts of Popular Romance

2862). In the Auchinleck MS the conjoined *Rouland and Vernagu* and *Otuel* are both Charlemagne romances, while in the London Thornton MS the *Sege off Melayne* not only has obvious links with the preceding *Segge of Jerusalem*, but with *Rowlande and Ottuell* (which follows almost immediately) makes up another pair of Charlemagne romances. Some of these groups of romances may have previously existed as self-contained, unbound 'booklets', in which a degree of unity would be natural; especially relevant here are the two quite distinct groups of three consecutive texts found in BL MS Cotton Caligula A.ii and in the Lincoln Thornton MS.[21] But the inner variety that was noted earlier as typical of many of the romances also means that some of them may have quite different points in common with the texts with which they are associated. This comes out very clearly in the varied company that *Isumbras* keeps in the manuscripts in which it appears.[22] As a romance of trial and suffering, it can meaningfully be set between *Octovyane* and *Erle of Tholous* in the Lincoln Thornton MS, directly follow *Chevelere Assigne* in MS Cotton Caligula A.ii, and directly precede Chaucer's *Clerk's Tale* in Naples, Biblioteca Nazionale, MS XIII.B.29. And in Bodleian MS Ashmole 61, where it appears close to no other romance, it can still be set only a few leaves after *Seynt Ewstas*, which while a pious 'life' and not a romance, tells a story often very like its own. On the other hand, since it also celebrates militant Christianity for much of its length, it can also appear next to the bellicose *King Richard* in Cambridge, Gonville and Caius College, MS 175; since it tells of the separation of a whole family, come immediately before *Degore* in Bodleian MS Douce 261.

The physical and thematic proximity of *Seynt Ewstas* and *Isumbras* in Bodleian MS Ashmole 61 reminds us that the impact of individual romances may also be heightened by the presence of items which, while not romances themselves, have features in common with romances.[23] Chronicles and exemplary tales are both relevant from this point of view, and significant examples of both – in the form of collections of short narratives – are set next to romances in the Auchinleck MS. The historical item is the *Liber Regum Anglie* ('Book of the Kings of England'), which comes immediately before *Horn Childe* in the later part of the manuscript. This is a version of the *Short English Metrical Chronicle*,[24] but a uniquely expansive one, both in its

---

[21] It is possible that the second of these groups of three texts had already circulated as a separate booklet: see the introduction by Frances McSparran and P. R. Robinson to *Cambridge University Library MS Ff.2.38* (London: Scolar Press, 1979), p. xvi.

[22] An account of the romance in its various narrative contexts is given in Murray J. Evans, *Rereading Middle English Romance* (Montreal: McGill-Queen's University Press, 1995), pp. 51–82.

[23] For a consideration of the relation of romance to non-romance narratives within a single manuscript, see Lynne S. Blanchfield, 'Rate revisited, the compilation of the narrative works in MS Ashmole 61', in *Romance Reading*, pp. 208–20.

[24] Edited by M. C. Carroll and R. Tuve in 'Two Manuscripts of the Middle English *Anonymous Riming Chronicle*', *Proceedings of the Modern Language Association* 46 (1931), 115–54 (pp. 117–45); for the other texts, see *An Anonymous Short English Metrical Chronicle*, ed. Ewald Zettl, EETS OS 196 (London: H. Milford for Oxford University Press, 1935).

chronological range, and in the increased number (and sometimes length) of its component biographies: its account of Richard I is much longer than any other, and makes an interesting comparison with the romance *King Richard*, three items further on in this manuscript. The collection of exemplary tales is *The Seven Wise Masters*[25] which is set between *Sir Degare* and *Floris* here, between *Bevis* and *Guy* in CUL MS Ff.2.38, and immediately follows *Ywain and Gawain* in BL MS Cotton Galba E.ix. This close association with romances may be why it was included by Henry Weber in the third volume of his *Metrical Romances of the 13th, 14th and 15th Centuries* (Edinburgh, 1810). In fact, its constituent tales are generally more like fabliaux, some, like 'Puteus' and 'Avis', familiar as separate stories told by Boccaccio and Chaucer respectively.

These overlappings of genre bring us to the generic terms that are attached to the romances in the manuscripts themselves. In fact, very few of them are here labelled as romances; altogether, the title appears only eight times, seven of them within the two Thornton collections.[26] In the Lincoln Thornton MS it is used of *Octovyane*, *Ysambrace*, the *Erle of Tholous* and *Sir Percyvelle*; in the London Thornton MS, of *Rowlande and Ottuell* and *King Richerd*, as well as turning up (confusingly) in *The Romance of the childhode of Jesus Criste þat clerkes callys Ipokrephun*, which immediately follows *King Richerd*.[27] However, the three romances contained in Manchester, Chetham's Library, MS 8009 (*Torrente of Portyngale*, *Bevys of Hampton* and *Ipomadon*) are at least made to stand out by having their titles prefixed by '*A Good Tale of*', a phrase attached to no other title in this manuscript.

Precise indications of the dates of these collections are very rare, although Naples BN MS XIII.B.29 carries one (1457) on its final page, and MS Douce 261 another (1564) at the same point. Sometimes, however a date may be suggested less directly: since the range of the original of the *Liber Regum Anglie* in the Auchinleck MS has been extended to the death of Edward II this last text cannot have been written before 1327. Elsewhere the use of precisely dateable material within the manuscript may be helpful, as with Bodleian MS Ashmole 33, where parts of the binding allow this last to be placed c. 1380. Otherwise we may have to rely on the broader kind of dating suggested by the evidence of handwriting and watermarks.

While both kinds of evidence may also help to establish the *geographical* provenance of our manuscript collections, the most important resource here

---

[25] See *The Seven Sages of Rome*, ed. K. Brunner, EETS OS 191 (London: H. Milford for Oxford University Press, 1933). O. D. Macrae-Gibson has suggested that it may be by the author of *Kyng Alisaunder* (op. cit., p. 75). In CUL MS Ff.2.38 it has at least one point of contact with the *Bevis* that immediately precedes it: see my review of the Scolar Press facsimile in *Medium Ævum* 51 (1982), 247.

[26] The only other example is *The Sowdoun of Babylone*, in Princeton University Library, Garrett Collection, MS 140.

[27] Compare the equally unexpected presence in Chaucer's *Sir Thopas* list of *Ypotis* (the story of a wise child (in reality, Christ himself) who instructs the emperor Hadrian in the Christian faith).

will be linguistic in nature; most specifically, the phonetic values, and the spellings and grammatical forms of the words of the manuscript copies. The second and third of these (in particular) have been recorded on an impressive scale in the *Linguistic Atlas of Late Mediaeval English*,[28] and jointly used there to fix the places of origin of a very large number of manuscript collections (including a number of the most important of those containing romances). The chief concern is with variant forms of words of very high frequency; these are recorded in various ways throughout the four volumes of the *Atlas*, but for our purposes the volumes of most interest are the third (which sets out the detailed manuscript evidence as 'linguistic profiles' ('LPs')), and the fourth (at the end of which the presumed place of origin of these MSS is pinpointed on 'key maps' that cover the whole range of English counties, as well as some Welsh and Scottish ones). There are, however, some difficulties in the way of always interpreting the findings of the *Atlas* literally, most particularly the fact that the part of England that is suggested by the scribe's 'language' need not always be identical with that in which the MS to which he contributed was produced. Here, once again, the Auchinleck MS is of particular importance. This manuscript is acknowledged to be a London product, and – as mentioned earlier – is now accepted as the work of six scribes, four of whom are between them responsible for all the romances that it now contains. But while three of these four have been located in roughly the same part of the country – scribe C in NW London itself (LP 6500), scribe A in SE Middlesex (LP 6510), scribe E in S Essex (LP 6350) – the fourth (scribe F) is placed as far afield as the extreme south of Worcestershire (LP 7820).[29] Native habits of speaking and writing might clearly survive the geographical displacement of any scribe.[30]

The Percy Folio Manuscript (BL MS Additional 27879)

Gillian Rogers

The manuscript (known as the Percy Folio), transcribed c. 1640–50, is a tall narrow book of some 520 pages, containing 195 items of varying lengths, written on paper, by an unknown scribe, in a mixed secretary and italic hand, the same hand throughout.[31] Its present state, with each leaf separately

---

[28] Angus McIntosh, M. L. Samuels and Michael Benskin, *A Linguistic Atlas of Late Medieval English*, 4 vols (Aberdeen: Aberdeen University Press, 1986). For a detailed account of how the manuscripts were localized, see Michael Benskin, 'The "Fit"-Technique Explained', in *Regionalism in Late Medieval Manuscripts and Texts*, ed. Felicity Riddy (Cambridge: D. S. Brewer, 1991), pp. 9–26.

[29] See *Linguistic Atlas*, III, pp. 301, 305, 129, 563 (for the LPs of the contributions of these scribes), and II, pp. 387–8 (for their placing on Key Maps 5 and 6).

[30] See Loomis, *Adventures*, p. 184.

[31] With the exception of fols 124 (in Percy's hand, replacing the end of *Durham Feilde* (PF 79), which he had torn out), 188v and 265, both in later hands. The manuscript will be referred to as PF (Percy Folio) throughout this section.

mounted in a frame and covered with gauze, makes it difficult to ascertain its precise make-up, and the fact that its finder, Thomas Percy, sent it to 'an ignorant bookbinder' who pared its margins, means that the lines at both top and bottom of many of the pages are cropped to incomprehensibility. To make matters worse, the housemaids of its former owner, Sir Humphrey Pitt of Shiffnal, used half of each of what are now the first twenty-eight leaves to light the fire;[32] as a result, the contents of those leaves are in a very mutilated state.[33]

F. J. Furnivall, who, together with J. W. Hales, was the first editor of the manuscript, felt that it was almost certain that much, if not all, of it was written from dictation, and hurriedly, 'from the continual miswriting of ... *rought* for *wrought*, *Knight* for *night* ... *justine* for *justing* ...', which might suggest that the compiler had an amanuensis and dictated his material from manuscript, print or memory. Mistakes like 'pan & wale' for 'wan & pale' (*Eger and Grine* (= Grime) (PF 40, line 1082) certainly suggest hasty dictation.[34] A case might be made out for considering Waller's *Cloris* (PF 50) to have been orally transmitted.[35] But the majority of items would appear to have been copied, somewhat carelessly, presumably by the compiler himself, either from a printed version or from a manuscript. The splendid word 'imuptelasze' ('immortalise') (*Hero & Leander* (PF 141), line 118), for instance, must surely have been copied from a manuscript in which that word was illegible; some of the medieval romances (see below, pp. 60–61), and most of the broadside ballads, can be shown to have been copied from prints: the latter differ but little from surviving examples, such as those in the Pepys, Roxburghe, Wood and Bagford collections.[36]

This section will examine 'reader reception' with reference to one reader only, the Percy Folio compiler himself, a mid-seventeenth-century man, with

---

[32] S. G. St Clair-Kendall thinks it likely that folios 1–10 are the eighth to final leaves surviving from a gathering of sixteen of which the first seven are missing. See her 'Narrative Form and Mediaeval Continuity in the Percy Folio Manuscript: A Study of Selected Poems' (unpublished Ph. D. dissertation, University of Sydney, 1988), p. 9.

[33] For a more detailed, though by no means exhaustive, description of the MS, and of its contents, see Gillian Rogers, 'The Percy Folio Manuscript Revisited', in *Romance in Medieval England*, ed. Maldwyn Mills, Jennifer Fellows and Carol M. Meale (Cambridge: D. S. Brewer, 1991), pp. 39–44. Some of the following is based on material discussed there. For the 'pre-history' of the MS before Percy obtained it, see Leslie Shepard, 'The Finding of the Percy Folio Manuscript: A Claim of Prior Discovery', *Notes and Queries* 212 (1967), 415–16. For Percy's account of the finding of the MS, see *Bishop Percy's Folio Manuscript: Ballads and Romances*, ed. J. W. Hales and F. J. Furnivall, 4 vols (London, 1867–8), I, p. xii; for his theory as to the compiler, see the same, pp. xiii–xiv. The only mark of ownership occurs on p. 284 of the MS, where 'my sweet brother, sweet cous Edward' (Revell) is named as the owner by his sister/cousin Elizabeth Revell.

[34] *Bishop Percy's Folio Manuscript*, ed. Hales and Furnivall, I, Forewords, p. xiii. The initials PF followed by a number, in parentheses, refer to the item number in the MS.

[35] Substitution of words like 'needs' for 'now' (line 1), 'were I but sure', for 'Could I be sure' (line 12), and confusions such as 'that I to thee vnconstant proue' for 'That thou didst thus inconstant prove' (line 18), suggest an imperfectly remembered poem.

[36] See Robert A. Schwegler, 'Sources of the Ballads in Bishop Percy's Folio Manuscript' (unpublished Ph.D. dissertation, University of Chicago, 1978), for a detailed examination of this topic.

very wide-ranging, not to say eclectic, tastes. Overall, the contents of the manuscript exist in two dimensions, the medieval past and the (seventeenth-century) present. The contemporary, or near-contemporary, items present a broad spectrum of the interests of the age, both popular and literary, shared by this man. The past, represented by the many 'historical' ballads and the medieval romances, reflects his strongly antiquarian turn of mind, and his main interest. Almost all the items are popular (in the senses defined by Maldwyn Mills, above, pp. 50–51) and secular in character; all are in verse. Much of his material comes from sixteenth- and seventeenth-century sources, but many of the sixteenth-century items have roots in the fourteenth and fifteenth centuries, particularly the latter.

The manuscript appears to be the private collection of an antiquary, not intended for publication, but possibly to be shown to a select circle of like-minded friends, which might perhaps explain the attempt to give it, despite the execrable handwriting, some kind of orderly presentation, in the form of large, flamboyant italic titles, within horizontal rulings, equally large italic first words, extending into the left margin, and catchwords. Also, careless as the scribe was, he went back over many of the items, correcting eye-slip, inserting missing words, and, on occasion, reversing the order of lines or stanzas, with instructions in the left margin. There is, however, little attempt to organize the contents thematically, although the compiler seems to have started with that intention.

Nevertheless, a few groups *are* discernible in the manuscript, there, presumably, because the compiler found them together in other collections or printed miscellanies. The seven Robin Hood ballads which now begin it are followed by a loose grouping of Arthurian items, but then things start to fall apart. The only other Robin Hood ballad, *Guye of Gisborne* (PF 84), unique to the manuscript, comes considerably later in the sequence, the two other 'outlaw' ballads, *Adam Bell, Clime of the Cloughe & William off Cloudeslee* (PF 115), and its sequel, *Younge Cloudeslee* (PF 116), later still, and Arthur does not put in an appearance again until *Kinge Arthurs Death* (PF 43), there, possibly, as a result of the compiler wanting to fill in the gap left by the *Merline* (PF 41), which finishes before Arthur's birth.[37] Some of the 'historical' ballads, those taken from Thomas Deloney's *The Garland of Good Will*,[38] and dealing mainly with earlier English history, appear towards the end of the manuscript, although again, not in a continuous sequence, as one might have expected, but interspersed with other items. There are several clusters of Percy's category, 'Loose and Humorous' songs, indicating that,

---

[37] Suggested by Joseph Donatelli, 'The Percy Folio Manuscript: A Seventeenth-Century Context for Medieval Poetry', *English Manuscript Studies, 1100–1700* 4 (1993), 114–33 (p. 128).
[38] Entered in the Stationers' Register in 1593; the first extant edition, 1631. See *The Works of Thomas Deloney*, ed. F. O. Mann (Oxford: Clarendon Press, 1912), pp. 295–380.

a true man of his time, the compiler was well-acquainted with the popular verses that came to be known as 'drolleries'.[39]

The romance material, together with many of the 'historical' ballads, carries the burden of representing the past in the compiler's two-way collection. In some ways he seems to have perceived these two genres as two sides of the same coin, as narratives of times past.[40] That he preferred his history in the form of verse narrative, is clear, and perhaps to him romance was simply another aspect of that history. He seems, furthermore, to have seen no generic difference between the medieval romances in his collection and those ballads with a strong romance flavour. Not without reason, since, in some cases, the two genres were beginning to merge, the prime example here being *The Squier* (PF 135), reduced from 1131 lines (as in the Copland print of 1555–60) to 170. With its deliberate selection of couplets from the immensely long speeches of the king and his daughter, a short sharp exchange is created between them; the king's blandishments are interspersed with the daughter's laconic response, effectively creating a refrain: 'ffather ... godamercy, / but all this will not comfort mee'. The original is well on its way to becoming a ballad.[41]

The two most significant groupings in this extraordinarily multifaceted manuscript, neither of which one would expect to find in a mid-seventeenth-century miscellany of this nature, are the six full-length romances deriving directly from medieval sources, together with one, *Eger & Grine*, which must have had medieval forebears, probably Scottish, but is now the earliest known version; and the group of eleven Arthurian poems. The six romances, with known antecedents but no known exact source, are: *Sir Lambewell* (PF 21), couplets; *Merline* (PF 41), couplets; *Sir Triamore* (PF 72), 6-line tail-rhyme; *Eglamore* (PF 101), 12-line tail-rhyme; *Libius Disconius* (PF 105), 12-line tail-rhyme; and *Sir Degree* (PF 111), couplets. The first four of these, together with *Sir Degree*, all have both manuscript and printed antecedents; *Sir Lambewell*, *Sir Triamore* and *Eglamore* seem all to have been derived from prints; the closest affinities of *Merline*, a version of *Of Arthour and Merlin*, are with London, Lincoln's Inn, MS Hale 150, up to the death of Vortigern, and the de Worde print of 1510; and the various versions of *Sir Degree*, both manuscripts and prints, are recognizably affiliated to each other.

---

[39] See Donatelli, 'The Percy Folio', pp. 125–6, for a more extended discussion of the compiler's groupings.

[40] See Helen Cooper's chapter, 'Romance after 1400', in *The Cambridge History of Medieval English Literature*, ed. David Wallace (Cambridge: Cambridge University Press, 1999), pp. 690–719, for a lucid discussion of the way history and romance tended to merge in the early modern period, citing the examples of *Ladye Bessiye*, *Scotish Feilde* and *Bosworth Feilde*.

[41] See David C. Fowler, *A Literary History of the Popular Ballad* (Durham, NC: Duke University Press, 1968), chapter 4: 'The New Minstrelsy', pp. 94–131, for a detailed analysis of the gradual transformation of romance into ballad, and chapter 5: 'The Percy Folio Manuscript', pp. 132–82, for an application of that analysis, in particular, Fowler's comments on *The Squier*, pp. 134–7. St Clair-Kendall has an interesting discussion of the *Squyer*-into-*Squier* transformation in 'Narrative Form', pp. 314–33.

There are no extant printed versions of *Libius Disconius*.[42] The fact that some of the romances are very close to antecedent prints, however, does not preclude the possibility that they may have been copied from a manuscript of a print, as the example of Oxford, Bodleian Library, MS 261, discussed by Maldwyn Mills above (p. 51, n.7), shows.

Eglamore, *Sir Triamore* and *Sir Degree* perhaps share the greatest number of common themes of all the romances in the manuscript, which is probably why they are found together elsewhere in one combination or another. All three appear in Cambridge University Library, MS Ff.2.38 as well as in PF (although in neither are they grouped together);[43] *Eglamore* and *Sir Degree* are two of the four romances in Oxford, Bodleian Library, MS Douce 261, (see p. 51 above), and *Eglamore* and *Sir Triamore* both formed part of the collection of Captain Cox, the Coventry mason, which is described in wonderfully eccentric spelling by Robert Laneham, or Langham, on the occasion of Elizabeth I's visit to Kenilworth in 1575.[44] *Eglamore* and *Sir Degree* both feature a tournament, held by the Earl in the former, by Degree's grandfather in the latter. It is of no particular consequence in *Eglamore*, serving merely to stress the hero's knightly qualities, but in *Sir Degree* it leads to his marriage with his mother. This forms another link with *Eglamore*, in that the hero's son Degrabell marries *his* mother as a result of winning a tournament. Fortunately, in both cases, there is a recognition scene before the marriage can be consummated. Eglamore, Triamore and Degree all slay giants. For Eglamore, it is just the first of his three tasks set by Christabell's father, the Earl, but Degree wins his bride by doing so. Triamore's giant is called Marradas, Eglamore's Marras. In both *Sir Triamore* and *Eglamore* women are cruelly banished for supposed sexual misdemeanours: Triamore's mother, heavily pregnant, is packed off on horseback into exile; Christabell's father sets her and her newborn son adrift in a boat. Both Triamore and Degree unknowingly defeat their own fathers in combat. Eglamore defeats his son Degrabell in a tournament, thereby winning back his wife Christabell. Both Triamore's and Degree's parents are reunited at the end.

The Arthurian items are: *King Arthur and King Cornwall* (PF 8), c. 1500, ballad, unique copy, no known immediate antecedents, but ingeniously adapted from the plot of *Le Pèlerinage de Charlemagne*; *Sir Lancelott of Dulake* (PF 11), printed in Deloney's collection, *The Garland of Good Will*, but not necessarily copied from it, a ballad version of Sir Lancelot's fight

---

42 See Rogers, 'The Percy Folio', pp. 45–53, for a fuller discussion of the transmission history of the romances in this list. A perhaps surprising omission from it is *Bevis of Hamptoun*, possibly the most popular romance to come through into the early modern period.
43 In PF *Sir Triamore* is no. 72, preceded by *The Grene Knight*, *Eglamore* is no. 101, and *Sir Degree* no. 111. In CUL MS Ff.2.38 *syr Egyllamoure of Artas* and *syr Tryamowre* are nos 35 and 36, but *Sir Degare* does not appear until the end of the MS, at no. 43.
44 See *Robert Laneham's Letter: Describing a Part of the Entertainment unto Queen Elizabeth at the Castle of Kenilworth in 1575*, ed. F. J. Furnivall (London: Chatto and Windus, 1907), pp. xii–xiii. Captain Cox's list contains six other items that appear also in PF.

against Sir Turquin, drawn from Malory's *Le Morte Darthur*, fragments only; *The Turke & Gowin* (PF 12), c. 1500, a short 6-line tail-rhyme romance, unique copy, no known antecedents (although it has much in common, structurally with the late-fourteenth-century alliterative *Sir Gawain and the Green Knight*), fragments only; *The Marriage of Sir Gawaine* (PF 13), a ballad version of the mid-fifteenth-century tail-rhyme romance, *The Weddynge of Sir Gawen and Dame Ragnell*, fragments only; *Merline* (see above, p. 60); *Kinge Arthurs Death* (PF 43), a combination of 'The Legend of King Arthur' recounted in the first person by Arthur himself, from Richard Lloyd's *The Nine Worthies*, 1584, and a third person account of the last battle, drawing upon Malory's account; *The Grene Knight* (PF 71), tail-rhyme, a deliberate adaptation of *Sir Gawain and the Green Knight*;[45] *Boy & Mantle* (PF 94), a unique copy of a sixteenth-century (?) ballad based on medieval sources, but not taken directly from any, and including an episode, the boar's head, not otherwise known; *Libius Disconius* and *Sir Lambewell* (see above); and *Carle off Carlile* (PF 139), couplets, based on the same source as the tail-rhyme *Syre Gawene and the Carle of Carelyle*, c. 1400, another deliberate adaptation, for a different audience, with much structural, ballad-like, repetition not present in the earlier version.[46]

Romance, as understood in the Middle Ages, was out of fashion if not dead by the mid-seventeenth century, and Arthurian romance was particularly moribund. Arthur was more often referred to than written about in the literature of the period. When not still being used for political purposes, an increasingly forlorn enterprise, he was a figure of fun, a figure from the 'olden times', a figure of folklore. In Richard Johnson's *Tom a Lincolne* (1599–1607), for instance, he is an adulterer, begetting Tom on his mistress and leaving the infant at the door of a shepherd to be brought up. But in 1634, Thomas Stansby published his edition of Malory (the last until 1816), his principal purpose in so doing being to renew public interest in Arthur. He seems not to have had much success, although it may have been this event which inspired in the compiler a desire to find out more about him. His inclusion of *Kinge Arthurs Death* and *Sir Lancelott of Dulake* certainly suggests this. We must be grateful to him for preserving for posterity three otherwise unknown Arthurian pieces (*The Turke & Gowin*, *King Arthur and King Cornwall* and *Boy & Mantle*), and variant versions of others, the most significant of which is *The Grene Knight*. This romance demonstrates the way in which even 'high art' medieval romance could be adapted, somewhat disastrously in this case, to suit the tastes of a different audience.[47] Here is Raluca Radu-

---

[45] See Gillian Rogers, 'The Grene Knight', in *A Companion to the Gawain-Poet*, ed. Derek Brewer and Jonathan Gibson (Cambridge: D. S. Brewer, 1997), pp. 365–72.

[46] See *The Arthur of the English*, ed. W. J. R. Barron (Cardiff: University of Wales Press, 1999), chapter 6, 'Folk Romance', pp. 197–224, for discussions of *King Arthur and King Cornwall*, *The Marriage of Sir Gawaine*, *The Turke & Gowin*, *The Grene Knight*, *Carle off Carlile* and *Boy and Mantle*; and chapter 4, 'Dynastic Romance', pp. 71–111 (pp. 72–4), for *King Arthurs Death*.

[47] For a different view of the importance of *The Grene Knight*, see Rushton, below).

lescu's 'vertical channel of communication between what are traditionally seen as "high" and "low" classes and their values' in operation.[48]

Aside from these two groupings, a small number of items, adapted or recast anew, are drawn from earlier romances: *Lord of Learne* (PF 24), a broadside ballad based on the late-fifteenth-century Scottish romance *Roswall and Lilian*, in short couplets; *The Emperour & the Childe* (PF 103), couplets, adapted from the prose romance, *Valentine and Orson*, which exists in a print of 1502, possibly by Wynkyn de Worde; *Guy & Colebrande* (PF 108), tail-rhyme; *The Squier*, couplets, a version of *The Squyer of Lowe Degree*, c. 1500, of which I have spoken briefly above, p. 60; and *Patient Grissell* (PF 170), another ballad contained in Deloney's *The Garland of Good Will*. With the possible exception of the last, all demonstrate a process of creative transformation of their medieval sources. The most interesting of these, apart from *The Squier*, is *Guy & Colebrande*, a skilful adaptation of an episode from some earlier version of *Guy of Warwick*, which adds details from Guy's combat with the giant Amaraunt, and a short resumé of Guy's life before and after his conquest of Colebrande which owes little or nothing to any extant version. It certainly shows considerably more creative power than does Samuel Rowlands's *Guye & Amarant* (PF 73) or Guy's first-person account of his life in the incomplete *Guy & Phillis* (PF 80), both usually considered fairly deplorable specimens.

The final group of romance items in PF consists of: *Sir Lionell* (PF 9), ballad; *Sir Aldingar* (PF 22); *King Estmere* (no longer in the manuscript, having been torn out by Percy to send to the printer and subsequently lost); and *Sir Cawline* (PF 110). *Sir Cawline* was believed to be the earliest known version until 1972, when Marion Stewart published her discovery of a sixteenth-century Scottish version, more complete than the one in PF.[49] It shares both its slightly eerie atmosphere and the detail of the severed finger with *Eger and Grine*; *Sir Lionell* also contains a severed finger, but is otherwise singularly devoid of atmosphere of any kind. *Sir Aldingar*, one of the most powerful pieces in the manuscript, has many Scandinavian analogues, and shares with *Triamore* the themes of the 'Treacherous Steward' and the 'Calumniated Wife', and with *Boy & Mantle*, a mysterious 'boy' who acts as *deus ex machina*. A treacherous steward also appears in *Lord of Learne*, although it is the young lord himself who is the victim, not his mother. Treachery, in the form of the 'little foot-page', is also rife in a small group of ballads: *Lord Barnard & the Little Musgrave* (PF 14),[50] *Old Robin of Portin-*

---

[48] Raluca L. Radulescu, 'Ballad and Popular Romance in the Percy Folio', *Arthurian Literature* 23 (2006), 68–80 (p. 75).

[49] Marion Stewart, 'A Recently-Discovered Manuscript: "ane taill of Sir colling ye kny^t"', *Scottish Studies* 16 (1972), 23–39.

[50] A Scottish version of this, *Litel Musgray*, from Robert Edwards's Music Commonplace Book, c. 1630, was edited by Marion Stewart and Helena M. Shire, in *King Orphius, Sir Colling, The brother's lament, Litel Musgray: Poems from Scottish Manuscripts of c. 1586 and c. 1630 lately discovered* (Cambridge: The Ninth of May, 1973), pp. 24–6.

gale (PF 26), much of which is adapted from *Little Musgrave*)[51] and *Childe Maurice* (PF 106); a slightly older version of the 'litle foot-page', the 'lither ladd', betrays Glasgerion (PF 29).

There are other thematic connections between all these romance items. Thus, 'The young hero sets out to prove himself and win a bride and a kingdom' is the theme of *Sir Triamore*, *Eglamore*, *Libius Disconius*, *Sir Degree*, *The Squier* and *Sir Cawline*. Two poems that subvert this theme are: *Eger & Grine*, where the would-be hero at first fails in his quest, and only succeeds eventually through the efforts of his 'blood-brother', Grime, and a certain amount of trickery; and *The Turke & Gowin*, where Gawain, although not aspiring to a bride in this instance, is offered the Kingship of Man – correct romance procedure – but refuses it on the grounds that he has done nothing to deserve it. Sometimes the hero is of lower social status than his prospective bride, as in *Eglamore*, *The Squier* and *Sir Cawline*, and this related theme of upward social mobility is reflected in ballads that do not fit into the romance category, *Thomas of Potte* (PF 121) being a notable example. Upward social mobility of a slightly different order appears in *Kinge & Miller* (PF 75), and, at its most entertaining, in *John de Reeue* (PF 109), which, although not a romance as such, is structurally (but not thematically) so similar to one, *Carle off Carlile*, as to merit a mention in a romance context. As a result of encountering the king, the fortunes of each of these characters are radically improved, a theme that also surfaces in some of the Robin Hood ballads, and in *Adam Bell*. The satirical intent behind this *rapprochement* between king and subject is clear. It is evident that these themes, the very stuff of romance, held a great fascination for the compiler, and the many links between both romance and non-romance texts serve to strengthen the impression that he was deliberately seeking out such material.

The presence of a small group of 'Cavalier' poems (by Waller, Cleveland, Lovelace, Wither and Herrick) about a third of the way through the manuscript suggests that he had, for a time at least, some contact with those literary 'coteries' who circulated their poems in manuscript; Lovelace's *To Althea from Prison* (PF 49: *When Love with Unconfined Wings*), for example, is caught in an intermediate stage of development between composition and print.[52] A satirical poem, *To Oxfforde* (PF 153), by a Cambridge man, William Lake, on James I's visit to Oxford in 1605, may indicate a man with university connections. The alliterative poem, *Death & Liffe* (PF 114), also suggests a man of some education with access to the sort of library that would have contained such a work. Considering that the manuscript was transcribed during the 1640s, a time of great social, political and religious upheaval, strangely little of this turmoil is reflected in it, although items such

---

[51] See Fowler, *Literary History*, pp. 175–7, who also sees the influence of *Little Musgrave* on *Childe Maurice*, pp. 177–80.

[52] See Harold Love, *Scribal Publication in Seventeenth-Century England* (Oxford: Clarendon Press, 1993), for a full discussion of this practice.

as *Hollowe me Fancye* (PF 55), *Conscience* (PF 78), *The Fall of Princes* (PF 125), *Darkesome Cell* (PF 119), a 'Tom of Bedlam' poem, and *In Olde Times Paste* (PF 118) suggest a certain unease with the way the world was going, a hankering after the old ways, and perhaps a touch of melancholy. Some lines from *Hollowe me Fancye*, addressing the poet's wandering fancy, may reflect the compiler's state of mind during this time:

> Sithe itt will noe better bee,
> come, come away! Leave of thy Lofty soringe!
> come stay att home, & on this booke be poring!
> for he that gads abroad, he hath the lesse in storinge.   (44–7)

The inclusion of the well known political ballad, *The Kinge Enjoyes his Rights Againe* (PF 51), by the ballad-writer Martin Parker, which first appeared in 1643, and a satirical sideswipe at the Parliamentarians, *The Worlde is Changed* (PF 58), together with two Civil War poems, *Newarke* (PF 56) and *The Tribe off Banburye* (PF 59), indicates Royalist sympathies, and Richard Corbett's satire, *The Distracted Puritan* (called *O Noble Festus* in PF (no. 137)), describing the excesses of Puritanism, might suggest that the compiler's sympathies did not lie in that direction, possibly rather the opposite.[53]

Hales and Furnivall were the first to suggest a connection with the Stanley family, who owned a good deal of both Lancashire and Cheshire, principally on the grounds that the manuscript contains several 'historical' ballads relating to them (*Scotish Feilde* (PF 25), *Flodden Feilde* (PF 39), *Bosworth Feilde* (PF 132), *Ladye Bessiye* (PF 154) and the allegorical *The Rose of Englande* (PF 127)), together with Lancashire dialect forms, such as 'thoust' for 'thou shalt', and 'youst' for 'you will', 'unbethought' for 'umbethought', etc. David Lawton, indeed, calls the manuscript 'the main repository of the verse of Stanley eulogy'. One non-'historical' ballad item that also suggests the connection is *The Grene Knight* (PF 71). After the Green Knight and Gawain have reached an accord, they repair to 'the castle of hutton' (line 494). Edward Wilson puts forward the idea that Hutton may refer to Hooton, at Storeton in Cheshire, the former residence of the Stanleys ('Hutton' being a variant spelling of Hooton). The Stanleys were also hereditary Chief Rangers of the Forest of Delamere, in which most of the action of *The Grene Knight* takes place. Taking up this idea, Stella St Clair-Kendall suggests that the *Grene Knight* was composed to celebrate the raising of a Stanley to the Order

---

[53] The compiler seems to have made little attempt to excise references to Catholic religious practices. *Sir Degree* (PF 111) contains explicit references to the Mass at lines 37 (where the scribe has written *masques* instead of *masses*), 124 and 125, and significantly, at lines 409–15, he retains intact from his copytext the scene in which Degree goes to hear 'a Masse to the trinitye', and offers a florin each to the 'ffather', the 'sonne' and the 'holy ghost' in turn, despite the Parliamentary Bill of 24 April 1643, which 'required' people to 'take away, and demolish ... all images and pictures of any one or more persons of the Trinity ...' (W. H. Hutton, *The English Church from the Accession of Charles I to the Death of Anne (1625–1714)* (London: Macmillan, 1903), p. 126).

of the Bath, the creation of which Order is described in the poem.[54] So the poem may have been chosen for inclusion in his collection by the compiler because of its local associations. One might suggest also that if *The Grene Knight* was written for a Stanley patron, it might well have ended up in a Stanley library, conveniently to hand for the compiler who must, surely, have had access to the family's collection.[55]

This brief survey has merely touched upon some of the many issues involved in assessing the role of 'popular' romance in this enormous collection. There is much more to be found out and said about this fascinating record of one man's individual tastes, and about contemporary attitudes towards the matter of 'the olden time' against which his choice was made. The interplay between the 'historical' ballads and the romance material in it is a fruitful avenue to explore, given a stimulating boost by Helen Cooper's discussion of this issue. There is more to be said about the relationship of the non-romance ballads to the compiler's interests, more, too, perhaps, to be found out about his methods of transcription. To what extent did he tinker with the texts he copied?[56] I finish with the plea with which I ended my previous discussion of this manuscript, that it needs to be assessed as a whole and not just piecemeal as it so often has been in the past. Only by so doing can we hope to get closer to understanding the mentality of the compiler, and the background against which he worked.

---

[54] *Bishop Percy's Folio Manuscript*, ed. Hales and Furnivall, I, p. xiii; David A. Lawton, '*Scottish Field*: Alliterative Verse and Stanley Encomium in the Percy Folio', *Leeds Studies in English*, n.s. 10 (1978), 42–57 (p. 51); Edward Wilson, '*Sir Gawain and the Green Knight* and the Stanley Family of Stanley, Storeton, and Hooton', *Review of English Studies*, n.s. 30 (1979), 308–16 (pp. 314–15); St Clair-Kendall, 'Narrative Form', p. 303, n.732.

[55] Other items with a Stanley connection are: *The Turke & Gowin* (PF 12), where the Kingship of Man is at issue (the Earls of Derby were hereditary Kings, later Lords, of Man); *Panders come away* (PF 164), which lists Sir Kenelm Digby's wife, Venetia Stanley, of a younger branch of the family, among the contemporary prostitutes of London, possibly not a very tactful inclusion; and *Sir John Butler* (PF 129), a Chester ballad with Stanley associations. Child Waters, in the ballad of that name (PF 90), offers Ellen Cheshire and Lancashire rather than marry her, an offer she rejects. This incident does not occur in any of the other versions printed by Child (II, 63). The fragmentary *Thomas Lord Cromwell* (PF 16) refers to the 'Earle of darby' (line 9).

[56] See *Of Arthour and of Merlin*, ed. O. D. Macrae-Gibson, EETS OS 279 (Oxford: Oxford University Press for EETS, 1979), II, pp. 50–1, and *Libeaus Descounus*, ed. Maldwyn Mills, EETS OS 261 (Oxford: Oxford University Press for EETS, 1969), p. 27, note to line 1295, for indications of the ways in which the Percy Folio compiler may have adapted these texts.

4

Printed Romance in the Sixteenth Century

JENNIFER FELLOWS

Although there have been a number of studies of Middle English romance in the sixteenth century from the point of view of printing history or of descriptive bibliography,[1] very little attention has been paid to the actual texts in relationship to earlier manuscript traditions or to one another.[2] In this chapter I offer a textual characterization of the post-medieval versions of the five romances in Cambridge University Library, MS Ff.2.38 (*Sir Eglamour of Artois*, *Syr Tryamowre*, *Sir Bevis of Hampton*, *Guy of Warwick* and *Sir Degaré*) that were printed in the early Tudor period. My own work on *Bevis* has shown that textual relationships between manuscripts and prints of the romance are far from straightforward, with apparently 'original' features occurring uniquely in late printings, and that the text was substantially modified at or near the point of transition from manuscript to print.[3] I shall attempt here to establish whether any common patterns of transmission and adaptation can be identified among the five romances under consideration and thereby to throw some light on the practices of sixteenth-century printers in the selection and treatment of Middle English romance texts.

CUL MS Ff.2.38, generally thought to have been produced in the late fifteenth or the early sixteenth century,[4] is not the direct source of any of the printed texts discussed here, but it is significant in indicating the continued manuscript circulation of the romances that it contains in the early years of the printing era. This in turn suggests a degree of popularity that might otherwise be obscured by the vagaries of manuscript survival. (*Tryamowre*,

---

[1] E.g. Ronald S. Crane, *The Vogue of Medieval Chivalric Romance during the English Renaissance* (Menasha, WI: University of Wisconsin Press, 1919); Carol M. Meale, 'Caxton, de Worde, and the publication of romance in Late Medieval England', *Library* 14 (1992), 283–98; A. S. G. Edwards, 'William Copland and the Identity of Printed Middle English Romance', in *Matter of Identity*, pp. 139–47.

[2] A notable exception is Nicolas Jacobs, *The Later Versions of 'Sir Degarre': A Study in Textual Degeneration*, Medium Ævum Monographs, n.s. 18 (Oxford: Society for the Study of Medieval Languages and Literature, 1995).

[3] Jennifer Fellows, '*Bevis redivivus*: The Printed Editions of *Sir Bevis of Hampton*', in *Romance Reading*, pp. 251–68 (pp. 251–4), and 'The Medieval and Renaissance *Bevis*: A Textual Survey', in *Sir Bevis of Hampton in Literary Tradition*, ed. Jennifer Fellows and Ivana Djordjević (Cambridge: D. S. Brewer, 2008), pp. 80–113 (pp. 83, 94–9).

[4] See *Cambridge University Library MS Ff.2.38*, intro. Frances McSparran and P. R. Robinson (London: Scolar Press, 1979), p. xii.

for instance, survives in only one other (fragmentary) manuscript antedating the advent of print.)[5] It is a reasonable assumption, therefore, that printed romance was considered 'commercially viable because the texts had already been disseminated widely in manuscript, and thus the printer could be assured that there was a demand to which he could safely respond'.[6]

The giants among the sixteenth-century printers of romance were Wynkyn de Worde, who took over Caxton's business in 1492 and died in 1534/5,[7] and William Copland, who between 1553 and the mid-1560s produced twenty-two surviving editions of medieval romances.[8] Each of them produced at least one edition of *Eglamour*, *Degaré*, *Guy* and *Bevis*; de Worde also printed *Tryamowre* and *Torrent*. A direct line of descent, via William's father (or elder brother) Robert Copland, can be traced between the publishing activities of these two men.[9] As might therefore be expected, the relationships between their respective texts of any given romance are generally close.

There is evidence that de Worde, the first to print 'popular' romances such as those considered here,[10] took some care in preparing his texts for the press. Nicolas Jacobs speculates, in the case of *Degaré*, that he had 'sufficient regard for professional standards to ensure that the copy was edited to a decent standard of technical competence';[11] and, although only a fragment survives of his edition of *Eglamour*, this is sufficiently closely related to later printed texts to warrant the assumption that, as the first to print this romance, de Worde may well have been responsible for the considerable revision that it has undergone.[12] The nature and extent of the impact of such revision on the romances under consideration vary from text to text, as does the amount of textual variation within the printed tradition.

Sir Eglamour of Artois

Texts of *Eglamour* are found in London, British Library, MS Egerton 2862, in Lincoln Cathedral Library, MS 91 (the Lincoln Thornton MS), in London,

---

[5] Oxford, Bodleian Library, MS Eng. Poet. D.208, on which see below.
[6] Meale, 'Caxton, de Worde, and the Publication of Romance', p. 288; cf. Crane, *The Vogue of Medieval Chivalric Romance*, p. 2.
[7] *ODNB*, s.n. 'Worde, Wynkyn de (*d.* 1534/5)'.
[8] Edwards, 'William Copland and the Identity of Printed Middle English Romance', p. 139.
[9] *ODNB*, s.n. 'Copland, William (*d.* 1569)'.
[10] Caxton, who appears to have been catering for a more aristocratic clientèle, confined his printing of romance to works of Continental provenance: see Crane, *The Vogue of Medieval Chivalric Romance*, p. 3.
[11] Jacobs, *The Later Versions of 'Sir Degarre'*, p. 87; cf. John Finlayson, 'Legendary Ancestors and the Expansion of Romance in *Richard Coer de Lyon*', *English Studies* 79:4 (1998), 299–308 (p. 307).
[12] It would appear also that de Worde had a particular agenda in his treatment of the text of *Richard Coer de Lion*: his edition is based on a manuscript version akin to that in Cambridge, Gonville and Caius College, MS 175, but it excises many of the fictive and romance elements relating to the Multon and D'Oyly families that are found in that version: see Finlayson, 'Legendary Ancestors', pp. 306–7.

British Library, MS Cotton Caligula A.ii and in CUL MS Ff.2.38. Four complete editions survive from the sixteenth century; these were produced by the Edinburgh printers Chepman & Myllar (1508?), by John Walley (1550?) and by William Copland (1555? and 1565?).[13] Only two leaves of a de Worde edition (1500) are extant.[14] *Eglamour* was licensed to John Charlwood in 1581/2,[15] and therefore was clearly still considered saleable in the late sixteenth century; but if this edition ever appeared, it has not survived. None of the extant prints of *Eglamour* is illustrated, except on the title-page.

In her account of the text of *Eglamour*, Frances E. Richardson distinguishes two principal versions of the printed tradition, one represented by the Chepman & Myllar edition, the other by the de Worde, Walley and Copland prints.[16] The differences between the English *Eglamour* prints are very slight; this group is generally further from the earlier versions than is the Scottish text and is more inclined to agree with MSS Cotton Caligula A.ii and CUL Ff.2.38 than with the other manuscripts.[17] As in the case of *Bevis* (on which see below), the second of Copland's two editions was not set up from his first; it is, in fact, closer to Walley's print and is described in *STC* as a 'paginary reprint of STC 7542.7 with various lines omitted through negligence'. The Chepman & Myllar text, on the other hand, has particular affinities with MSS Egerton 2862 and Lincoln Cathedral Library 91.[18]

The bipartite nature of the printed *Eglamour* tradition is probably due to the fact that, from the early years of the sixteenth century, there were separate English and Scottish printing/publishing industries.[19] The guild system among English printers (whereby not only the right to copy and sell a text, but also the associated capital stock, fonts, presses and woodblocks, were heritable and tradeable) would tend to encourage textual stability. Until 1710, however, Scottish editions were produced under a different jurisdiction;[20] they would have been regarded in England as 'piracies'.[21]

There are no substantial narrative differences between the manuscript and the printed versions of *Eglamour*. Although the English and Scottish editions are occasionally in agreement in additions to the text as it appears in the manuscript tradition,[22] this is on the whole more characteristic of the Scottish print.[23] Variation between the English editions and the manuscripts tends

---

13 *STC* 7542, 7542.7, 7543 and 7544.5.
14 *STC* 7541.
15 Edward Arber, *A Transcript of the Registers of the Company of Stationers of London 1554–1640 AD*, 5 vols (London: privately printed, 1875–94) (hereafter Arber), II, 405.
16 *Sir Eglamour of Artois*, ed. Frances E. Richardson, EETS 256 (London: Oxford University Press for the EETS, 1965), p. xviii.
17 *Sir Eglamour of Artois*, ed. Richardson, p. xviii.
18 *Sir Eglamour of Artois*, ed. Richardson, p. xviii.
19 William St Clair, *The Reading Nation in the Romantic Period* (Cambridge: Cambridge University Press, 2004), p. 105.
20 St Clair, *The Reading Nation*, p. 105.
21 I am grateful to Mr St Clair for his help on this point.
22 Cf., e.g., *Sir Eglamour of Artois*, ed. Richardson, line 243.
23 Cf., e.g., *Sir Eglamour of Artois*, ed. Richardson, lines 735, 780, 1131.

to be in phraseology – even where the language of the manuscripts is not notably difficult. For example, where MS Lincoln 91 has

> This nobyll knyghte he sayde noght naye,
> Bot one the morne when it was daye
>   His wayes then wendes hee. (358–60)

the English prints read:

> Sir Eglamore would not gainsay
> His leaue he tooke, and went his way
>   To his iourney went he.[24]

Sometimes variation of this kind appears to be in the interests of metrical smoothness, as at lines 448–9, where LCL MS 91's 'Þou art doghety vndir þi schelde / Hase slayne thi fa and wonn þe felde' becomes in the English prints 'thou hast manfully vnder sheeld / Slayne the bore heer in the feeld'.[25] The manuscript tradition as a whole is irregular in its handling of tail-rhyme: the basic unit is a twelve-line stanza, but nine- or six-line stanzas also occur.[26] Where the two principal manuscript versions (as represented by LCL MSS 91 and BL Cotton Caligula A.ii respectively) agree in having a short stanza,[27] no attempt at regularization is made in the printed texts.

Syr Tryamowre

Syr Tryamowre is to be found in CUL MS Ff.2.38, in London, British Library, MS Add. 27879 (the Percy Folio) and (in fragmentary form) in Oxford, Bodleian Library, MS Eng. Poet. D.208. The only full sixteenth-century printed text of the romance is that produced by William Copland (c. 1565),[28] but the correspondences of this edition to the text in the Percy Folio, itself copied from a print, as well as to surviving fragments of editions by Pynson (1503?) and by de Worde (c. 1530),[29] are sufficiently close to indicate that it is representative of the printed tradition as a whole.

The text of *Tryamowre* in MSS CUL Ff.2.38 and Bodl Eng. Poet. D.208 seems to be fairly corrupt: there are many textual obscurities, and in both manuscripts the initial twelve-line tail-rhyme stanza breaks down at line 120; thereafter the stanza varies in length from three to eighteen lines.[30] The

---

[24] Quoted from *STC* 7543, sig. A[iv]ᵛ. Cf. *Sir Eglamour of Artois*, ed. Richardson, lines 442–6.
[25] Quoted from *STC* 7543, sig. B[iv]ʳ.
[26] E.g. *Sir Eglamour of Artois*, ed. Richardson, lines 406–11, 811–19 (Lincoln); 1153–61, 709–17 (Cotton).
[27] Cf., e.g., *Sir Eglamour of Artois*, ed. Richardson, lines 241–6, 376–81.
[28] *STC* 24303.
[29] *STC* 24301.5 and 24302.
[30] See *Of Love and Chivalry: An Anthology of Middle English Romance*, ed. Jennifer Fellows, Everyman's Library (London: Dent; Rutland, VT: Tuttle, 1993), pp. xvii, 303–9. The text of *Syr Tryamowre*, edited from CUL MS Ff.2.38, appears at pp. 147–98.

surviving portions of the text in MS Eng. Poet. D.208 correspond pretty much line for line to the version of the romance in MS CUL Ff.2.38, though there is considerable lexical variation within the line. The two manuscripts are closer to each other than either is to the prints.

The romance has been substantially rewritten for the press; the purpose of this revision seems mostly to be the replacement of obsolete language and obscure syntax and modes of expression, as in the following passage:

Yf ye be so hardy	She sayd treaytoure yf euer thou be so hardy
To wayte me wyth velanye,	To shewe me of suche a velany
Fowle hyt schall the rewe!	On a galowes thou shalt hange
Y trowe y schall never ete bredd	
Tyll thou be broght to the dedd.	
Soche balys then schall y the brewe,	
Y may evyr aftur thys	Yf I may knowe after this
That thou woldyst tyse me to do amys.	That thou tyce me to do a mysse
No game schulde the glewe.	Thou shalt haue the lawe of the londe.
(CUL MS Ff.2.38)[31]	(*STC* 24303, sig. Aii[v])

As in the case of *Eglamour*, the modifications in the printed text have no major impact on the narrative. There is, however, a rather touching addition as Queen Margaret takes leave of the fallen body of the aged Sir Roger, who has died in battle defending her against the wicked steward, Marrok:

> Ryght on the grounde there as he laye dede
> She kyssed hym or she from hym yede.[32]

There are substantial differences too in the details of Tryamowre's encounters in his first tournament.[33]

No attempt is made in the *Tryamowre* prints to regularize the tail-rhyme stanzas: Pynson's, de Worde's and Copland's editions all have a mixture of six- and nine-line stanzas – though this is not reflected in the layout of the text, which is printed in unbroken columns.[34] In the Percy Folio, the scribe (or Percy himself?)[35] has marked the divisions so that the text is broken up (in appearance at least) into regular six-line stanzas. The layout of Hales and Furnivall's edition reflects these divisions, even though they are frequently at odds with the rhyme scheme, as in the following example:

---

[31] Quoted from *Of Love and Chivalry*, ed. Fellows, p. 150 (lines 100–8).
[32] *STC* 24303, sig. Biii[r].
[33] See *Bishop Percy's Folio Manuscript: Ballads and Romances*, ed. John W. Hales and Frederick J. Furnivall, 3 vols (London: Trübner, 1868), II, 109–10.
[34] Cf. the account of Copland's handling of the six-line tail-rhyme stanza in his edition of *Syr Isenbras* (*STC* 14282) given in Maldwyn Mills, '*Sir Isumbras* and styles of tail-rhyme romance', in *Readings in Medieval English Romance*, ed. Carol M. Meale (Cambridge: D. S. Brewer, 1994), pp. 1–24 (pp. 21–3).
[35] I am grateful to Dr Gillian Rogers for this suggestion.

att fflome Iorden & att Bethlem,
& att Caluarye beside Ierusalem,
   in all the places was hee;—

then he longed to come home
to see his Ladye that liued at one;
   he thought euer on her greatlye.
soe long thé sealed on the fome
till att the last they came home;
   he arriued ouer the Last strond.

the shippes did strike their sayles eche one,
the men were glad the King came home
   vnto his owne Land.
there was both mirth & game,
the Queene of his cominge was glad & faine,
   Eche of them told other tydand.[36]

The printed texts of *Tryamowre* as we have them are not illustrated.

Sir Bevis of Hampton

The text of *Sir Bevis of Hampton* is found, in whole or in part, in Edinburgh, National Library of Scotland, MS Advocates 19.2.1. (the Auchinleck MS), in Naples, Biblioteca Nazionale, MS XIII.B.29, in MS Caius 175, in MS Egerton 2862, in Cambridge, Trinity College, MS O.2.13, in Bodl MS Eng. Poet. D.208, in Manchester, Chetham's Library, MS 8009 and in CUL MS Ff.2.38. It was printed in the sixteenth century by Wynkyn de Worde (three times: twice c. 1500 and once c. 1533), by Richard Pynson (c. 1503), by Julian Notary (twice: c. 1510 and c. 1515), by William Copland (twice: c. 1560 and c. 1565) and by Thomas East (1582?). A printed edition, now lost, seems to have been in existence by 1498;[37] the text was licensed to Thomas Marshe in 1558/9, to John Tysdale in 1561 and to John Alde in 1568/9, though none of these three editions survives if it was ever produced;[38] and the inventory of the Edinburgh printer Robert Gourlaw (d.1585) also includes an edition of *Bevis*.[39]

The relationships between the *Bevis* manuscripts are extraordinarily complex, and those between them and the printed texts, and between the

---

[36] *Bishop Percy's Folio Manuscript*, ed. Hales and Furnivall, II, 85.
[37] See H. R. Plomer, 'Two Lawsuits of Richard Pynson', *Library* n.s. 10 (1909), 115–33 (pp. 122, 126–8).
[38] Arber, I, 95, 156 and 389.
[39] Cf. Priscilla Bawcutt, 'English Books and Scottish Readers in the Fifteenth and Sixteenth Centuries', *Review of Scottish Culture* 14 (2001/2002), 1–12 (pp. 2, 8); Rhiannon Purdie, 'Medieval Romance in Scotland', in *A Companion to Medieval Scottish Poetry*, ed. Priscilla Bawcutt and Janet Hadley Williams (Cambridge: D. S. Brewer, 2006), pp. 165–7 (pp. 169–70). I am grateful to Dr Purdie for these references.

printed texts and one another, hardly less so.⁴⁰ Briefly, Notary's fragmentary texts seem to have corresponded quite closely to Pynson's edition, while Copland's two printings are more inclined to agree with those of Pynson's rival de Worde.⁴¹ As in the case of *Eglamour*, the second of Copland's editions does not seem to have been set up from his first. On the contrary, it retains many readings that have manuscript authority but do not survive in earlier printed texts; these may well have derived from lost portions of de Worde editions.⁴²

The version represented by the prints seems to have been adapted from a late medieval text akin to that in MS CUL Ff.2.38 round about the point of the advent of print in England; relationships between the texts of *Bevis* in CUL MS Ff.2.38 and Chetham's MS 8009 suggest that the romance was not rewritten specifically for the press.⁴³ There is little variation between the printed texts of *Bevis* except at a lexical level, so they can be regarded as representing a single version of the romance. The salient characteristics of this version are the rewriting of the stanzaic opening found in most manuscripts, a tendency to name and provide motivation for minor characters, some modification of the way in which Bevis's character and his relationship with the Saracen princess Josian are portrayed, and an emphasis on the gruesome details of injury in battle,⁴⁴ as in the following immortal lines:

> And they that stode him agayne
> they were all maymed and slayne
> Some theyr shankes by the knee
> And some quartered in thre
> Some their nose and some their lyppe
> the king of scotland had a shyppe ...⁴⁵

That is to say that the printed *Bevis* represents a version of the romance in which the narrative has been more substantially changed than is the case for *Eglamour*, for *Tryamowre* or, as we shall see, for *Degaré*.

Several of the woodcuts in Pynson's edition seem to have been made specifically for *Bevis* – that of Ascopard carrying Bevis, Josian and Arundel to the ship, for example, or that of Josian holding two horses while Bevis fights Ascopard⁴⁶ – while others are 'generic' (i.e. they deal with stock subjects,

---

[40] See Fellows, 'The Medieval and Renaissance *Bevis*', esp. pp. 94–9.
[41] Fellows, 'The Medieval and Renaissance *Bevis*', pp. 97–8.
[42] Fellows, 'The Medieval and Renaissance *Bevis*', p. 98.
[43] See Fellows, 'The Medieval and Renaissance *Bevis*', pp. 94–6; and cf. Fellows, '*Bevis redivivus*', pp. 251–68 (p. 254).
[44] Cf. Fellows, 'The Medieval and Renaissance *Bevis*', p. 96.
[45] Quoted from *STC* 1989, sig. Oiᵛ. These lines are singled out for ridicule by Thomas Nashe in *The Anatomie of Absvrditie*: see *The Works of Thomas Nashe*, ed. R. B. McKerrow, 2nd edn, rev. F. P. Wilson, 5 vols (Oxford: Blackwell, 1958), I, 26; and cf. Philip Massinger's *The Picture* (*The Plays and Poems of Philip Massinger*, ed. Philip Edwards and Colin Gibson, vol. V (Oxford: Clarendon Press, 1976), pp. 193–292), II.i.20–3.
[46] *STC* 1988, sigs Giiiʳ, Giᵛ.

such as a wedding or a battle, and recur in a wide variety of texts). Some of Pynson's woodcuts are recycled in later *Bevis* editions.⁴⁷

Bevis is, apart from *Guy of Warwick*, the longest of the Middle English metrical romances to have been printed in the sixteenth century. (At 4234 lines, the printed version is only some four hundred lines shorter than the text in the Auchinleck MS.) Uniquely, it continued to be reprinted in essentially its late medieval form throughout the sixteenth and seventeenth centuries and into the eighteenth.⁴⁸

Guy of Warwick

The Middle English *Guy of Warwick* is found in the Auchinleck MS, in Cambridge, Gonville and Caius College, MS 107/176, and in CUL MS Ff.2.38; in fragmentary form, it occurs also in London, British Library, MS Sloane 1044, in Aberystwyth, National Library of Wales, MS 572 and in London, British Library, MS Add.14408. It was printed by Richard Pynson (c. 1500), by Wynkyn de Worde (c. 1500) and by William Copland (1565).⁴⁹

Although *Guy* is much the longest metrical romance to have been printed in the Tudor period, the version represented by Copland's edition (the only complete sixteenth-century print to have survived) is, at a mere 7976 lines,⁵⁰ considerably shorter than the texts in the Auchinleck MS and in MS CUL Ff.2.38, both of which weigh in at well over 10,000 lines. In his 1873 study of *Guy*,⁵¹ Julius Zupitza identified four English versions of the romance, one of them consisting of Copland's text and the fragment in MS Add.14408; to this group must now be added the Aberystwyth binding fragments identified as part of *Guy* by Daniel Huws and edited with the MS Add.14408 fragment by him and Maldwyn Mills.⁵²

Mills and Huws adduce further evidence to support Zupitza's conclusions as to the close relationship between the fragments (referred to collectively as F) and Copland's print. They enumerate common errors, in passages where the Auchinleck and Caius texts are closer to the Anglo-Norman *Gui de Warewic*,

---

⁴⁷ On the *Bevis* woodcuts, see further Fellows, 'The Medieval and Renaissance *Bevis*', pp. 99–101; Siân Echard, 'Of Dragons and Saracens: Guy and Bevis in Early Print Illustration', in *Guy of Warwick: Icon and Ancestor*, ed. Alison Wiggins and Rosalind Field (Cambridge: D. S. Brewer, 2007), pp. 154–68.

⁴⁸ The last extant printing of the metrical *Bevis* was produced in Aberdeen in 1711. For a list of editions of the metrical *Bevis* from the advent of print until 1711, see Fellows, 'The Medieval and Renaissance *Bevis*', pp. 109–13.

⁴⁹ *STC* 12540, 12541 and 12542.

⁵⁰ Cf. *Guy of Warwick: Nach Coplands Druck*, ed. Gustav Schleich, Palaestra 139 (Leipzig: Mayer & Müller, 1923).

⁵¹ Julius Zupitza, *Zur Literaturgeschichte des Guy von Warwick* (Vienna: Karl Gerolds Sohn, 1873).

⁵² *Fragments of an Early Fourteenth-Century Guy of Warwick*, ed. Maldwyn Mills and Daniel Huws, Medium Ævum Monographs, n.s. 4 (Oxford: Blackwell for the Society for the Study of Mediæval Languages and Literature, 1973).

and draw attention to a particularly extensive example of agreement between F and Copland against those manuscripts.[53] While confirming Zupitza's point that F is not the direct source of Copland's text,[54] they conclude: 'It is quite certain that F, like [Copland], was an unusually terse version of this romance story.'[55] It would seem, then, that the text of *Guy* (like that of *Bevis*) was not revised specifically for the press.

Very little is added in the F/Copland version, whose author 'shows no real preference for one kind of story-material over another'.[56] In characterizing this version, Mills and Huws conclude:

> Altogether, then, it seems that the abbreviated version ... was rather arbitrary from the thematic point of view, as well as being one that was more and more prone to omission as it went on. Which suggests that the true *raison d'être* of the author's approach was an acute consciousness of the scale of his undertaking and, in consequence, a growing impatience with minor, expendable detail that was likely to slow down his progress through it. The relative integrity of the sentimental effusions probably owes more to their position near the beginning of the story than to any positive sympathy that the redactor may have had with them ... Predictably, this approach to the original results in a rather stark piece of work, that sticks firmly to the narrative business in hand, prefers to deal in facts than in hypotheses, and has little time for literary graces.[57]

There are seven woodcuts in the Copland *Guy* – not a large number in a book of 282 pages; none of them seems to be specific to this text. Indeed, the one used at sig. Ii.i^v to illustrate Guy's climactic battle with Colbrond occurs also in editions of *Bevis*, where it corresponds closely to the account of Bevis's fight with a giant outside the latter's castle, after the giant's wife has refused the hero hospitality.[58]

Despite the abbreviation that *Guy* had undergone before it achieved the dignity of print, it may well be that either its still considerable length or its lack of 'literary graces' explains why there is no evidence of its having been, like *Bevis*, frequently reprinted in sixteenth-century England.

Sir Degaré

Complete texts of *Sir Degaré* are contained in the Auchinleck MS, in Oxford, Bodleian Library, MS Rawlinson Poet. 34, and in the Percy Folio; there are

---

[53] Mills and Huws, *Fragments*, pp. 7, 8–9.
[54] Mills and Huws, *Fragments*, p. 9.
[55] Mills and Huws, *Fragments*, p. 10.
[56] Mills and Huws, *Fragments*, p. 13.
[57] Mills and Huws, *Fragments*, p. 14.
[58] This woodcut is reproduced as plate 10 in *Guy of Warwick: Icon and Ancestor*, ed. Wiggins and Field. For a fuller discussion of the *Guy* woodcuts, see Echard, 'Of Dragons and Saracens', esp. pp. 156–9.

fragments in MS Egerton 2862 (two leaves), in CUL MS Ff.2.38 (just over half the romance), and in Oxford, Bodleian Library, MS Douce 261 (probably transcribed, like the text in the Percy Folio, from a print). It was printed (as *Syr Degore*) by Wynkyn de Worde (1512/13), by John King (1560) and by William Copland (1565).[59] There is also an unattributed two-leaf fragment, which has been dated to c. 1535, in the library of Stonyhurst College, Lancashire.[60] These have all been collated by Jacobs.[61]

The variants noted by Jacobs between the manuscript and printed texts of *Degaré* are mostly lexical, prosodic, rhetorical or in the interests of greater explicitness;[62] there are no major changes to the narrative substance of the romance. There are, however, substantial expansions (classified by Jacobs as 'sophistications') in the dragon episode, 'the most consistently unstable portion of the poem'.[63] The presence here of lines influenced by the description of Bevis's dragon indicate that the printed *Degaré* texts are more closely related to the versions of the romance in MSS Egerton 2862 (late fourteenth- or early fifteenth-century) and Rawlinson Poet. 34 (late fifteenth-century) than to those in the Auchinleck MS and in CUL MS Ff.2.38.[64] Within the printed tradition, the text of *Degaré* is remarkably stable, even the page-breaks occurring at exactly the same points in the King and Copland editions.

The de Worde edition is the only one to have illustrations elsewhere than on the title-page, but there are no precise correspondences between image and text to suggest that the woodcuts were made specifically for this romance. Indeed, the one on sig. Ciii[r] of a knight fighting in a forest had earlier been used in de Worde's edition (c. 1502) of *Robert the Deuyll*;[65] and the one on sig. Bi[r] is identical to that on sig. Kii[r] of Richard Pynson's edition (c. 1503) of *Bevis*.[66] There are two distinct styles of woodcut in the de Worde text, the cuts on sigs Ciii[r] and Bii[v] being heavier in line, cruder and more old-fashioned in appearance than those elsewhere; that on sig. Di[r] is alone in having an ornamental border.

An unusual feature of the woodcuts in de Worde's *Degaré* is that they always occur in close proximity to in-text headings and correspond in their

---

[59] *STC* 6470, 6472 and 6472.5.
[60] *STC* 6470.5.
[61] Jacobs, *The Later Versions of 'Sir Degarre'*, pp. 65–87.
[62] Jacobs, *The Later Versions of 'Sir Degarre'*, pp. 68–84.
[63] Jacobs, *The Later Versions of 'Sir Degarre'*, p. 76.
[64] Cf. G. P. Faust, *Sir Degare: A Study of the Texts and Narrative Structure*, Princeton Studies in English 11 (Princeton, NJ: Princeton University Press, 1935), p. 22; Nicolas Jacobs, '*Sir Degarre, Lay le Freine, Beves of Hamtoun* and the "Auchinleck Bookshop"', *Notes and Queries*, n.s. 29 (1982), 294–301 (pp. 297–301).
[65] Cf. Edward Hodnett, *English Woodcuts 1480–1535* (Oxford: Oxford University Press, 1973), p. 305 (no. 1240). This woodcut could appropriately have been used for the death of Sir Guy in *Bevis*; unfortunately, this part of the text has not survived in any of the extant fragments of de Worde editions of *Bevis*.
[66] *STC* 1988.

subject-matter to the content of those headings. Thus a woodcut of two armed knights engaged in single combat immediately follows the heading

> ¶ How syr Degore fought with his fader & how his fader knewe hym by the broken swerde.[67]

The headings, therefore, seem almost to serve a dual function – as picture captions and as markers of textual divisions.[68] This feature of the positioning of woodcuts is considerably less common in the other illustrated texts under consideration here.

There are, then, both similarities and diversity in the ways in which these Middle English romance texts were handled by their early printers. *Eglamour*, *Tryamowre* and *Degaré* seem to have been revised at the point of their transition from manuscript to print, most of the textual changes being lexical and stylistic and apparently motivated largely by a desire to render these texts readily comprehensible to a contemporary readership. Within the printed tradition of *Tryamowre* and *Degaré* (particularly the latter) there is little textual variation; in the case of *Eglamour* there are two printed versions, English and Scottish, but the differences between the English prints are very slight. No attempt is made in *Eglamour* or in *Tryamowre* to regularize the way in which the tail-rhyme stanza is used. By contrast, the printers of the much longer romances of *Guy* and of *Bevis* seem to have used existing versions in which the narrative had already been substantially modified, and where (in the case of *Bevis*) prosodic irregularities had already been ironed out. The rival editions by de Worde and by Pynson generated more textual diversity within the printed tradition of *Bevis* than has been found for any of the other romances considered here. *Bevis* is the only one of these five texts to include any 'tailor-made' woodcuts; *Eglamour* and *Tryamowre* are illustrated only on their title-pages.

There are considerable differences in the subsequent fates of the romances from CUL MS Ff.2.38 that found their way into print. Only *Bevis*, the most frequently printed of these in the early part of the sixteenth century, continued to appear in its late medieval form until long after the period of William Copland's romance-publishing activities in the 1550s and 1560s, though *Eglamour* was clearly still considered commercially viable in the 1580s. Chapbooks of *Bevis*, as well as longer prose adaptations, were produced from the late seventeenth century until near the end of the eighteenth.[69] *Degaré* and *Tryamowre* seem to have disappeared from view after being consigned to 'that great dustbin of romance, the Percy Folio';[70] while *Eglamour* and

---

[67] *STC* 6470, sig. [Ciiii]ᵛ.
[68] Professor Maldwyn Mills has pointed out to me that the headings remain unchanged in the unillustrated *Degaré* prints.
[69] See Fellows, '*Bevis redivivus*', pp. 261–4.
[70] Jacobs, *The Later Versions of 'Sir Degarre'*, p. 87.

Guy survived in a variety of forms and genres – *Eglamour* in ballad and dramatic form,[71] and *Guy* in devotional literature,[72] as a play and in Samuel Rowlands's twelve-canto *Famous Historie of Guy of Warwick*,[73] as well as in a number of prose retellings (including chapbooks), which continued to appear until well into the nineteenth century.[74]

Why these particular romances were still sufficiently popular by the end of the fifteenth century to be selected for publication by the printers of Tudor England, and why their ultimate fates were so different, are questions that it would be hard to answer.[75]

---

[71] Cf. *Sir Eglamour of Artois*, ed. Richardson, pp. xli–xlii. Writing in the mid-1960s, Richardson (p. xlii) claims that ballads of Eglamour 'are still sung in schools and Boy Scout camps today'.

[72] See A. S. G. Edwards, 'The *Speculum Guy de Warwick* and Lydgate's *Guy of Warwick*: The Non-Romance Middle English Tradition', in *Guy of Warwick: Icon and Ancestor*, ed. Wiggins and Field, pp. 81–93.

[73] On the play and on Rowlands's poem, see Helen Cooper, 'Guy as Early Modern English Hero', in *Guy of Warwick: Icon and Ancestor*, ed. Wiggins and Field, pp. 185–99.

[74] E.g. *The Noble and Renowned History of Guy Earl of Warwick* ... (Warwick: H. T. Cooke; Warwick and Leamington: John Merridew; Coventry: Henry Merridew, 1829).

[75] I am grateful to Professor Maldwyn Mills and to Dr Gillian Rogers for commenting on earlier drafts of this chapter.

5

Middle English Popular Romance and National Identity

THOMAS H. CROFTS and ROBERT ALLEN ROUSE

Popular romance and medieval national identity

'Who are the English; where do they come from; what constitutes the English nation?' Such were the questions regarding Englishness that Thorlac Turville-Petre posed in 1994 when he observed that 'the establishment and exploration of a sense of a national identity is a major preoccupation of English writers of the late thirteenth and early fourteenth centuries'.[1] Turville-Petre's work, which found its most expansive form in his seminal study *England the Nation*,[2] established medieval English nationalism as a vibrant field of interest, and has led to the proliferation of studies of the development of medieval Englishness over the past decade or so. Important work by scholars such as Siobhain Bly Calkin, Geraldine Heng, and Kathy Lavezzo – amongst others – illustrates the degree to which the study of nationalism has become embedded within the practice of medieval scholarship.[3]

However, the validity of attempting to discern the origins of the English 'nation' within the literature of the medieval period has not been without its critics. Can one read the beginnings of English 'nationalism' – in the classic Andersonian sense[4] – in such pre-modern texts? Views on the issue have been polarizing: while many scholars have been quick to take up the search for a nascent medieval English national identity, others have remained more cautious. Derek Pearsall, in a response to the profusion of identifications

---

[1] Thorlac Turville-Petre, '*Havelok* and the History of the Nation', in *Readings in Medieval English Romance*, ed. Carol M. Meale (Cambridge: D. S. Brewer, 1994), pp. 121–34 (p. 121).

[2] Thorlac Turville-Petre, *England the Nation: Language, Literature, and National Identity, 1290–1340* (Oxford: Clarendon Press, 1996).

[3] Much of this work has focused on the role of romance as the vehicle for such discourse: see Siobhain B. Calkin, *Saracens and the Making of English Identity* (London and New York: Routledge, 2005); Geraldine Heng, *Empire of Magic: Medieval Romance and the Politics of Cultural Fantasy* (New York: Columbia University Press, 2003); Kathy Lavezzo (ed.), *Imagining a Medieval English Nation* (Minneapolis: University of Minnesota Press, 2004); Thorlac Turville-Petre, 'Afterword: The Brutus prologue to *Sir Gawain and the Green Knight*', in *Readings in Medieval English Romance*, pp. 340–6; Robert A. Rouse, *The Idea of Anglo-Saxon England in Middle English Romance* (Cambridge: D. S. Brewer, 2005).

[4] Benedict Anderson, *Imagined Communities: Reflections on the Origin and Spread of Nationalism*, rev. edn (London: Verso, 1991).

of medieval national sentiment appearing in the late 1990s, comments that 'while particular circumstances produced a momentary surge in assertions of Englishness around 1290–1340 and again in 1410–20, there was no steadily growing sense of national feeling'.[5] The debate seems – in essence – to be over what medievalists mean when they use terms such as 'nationalism' and 'national identity': are they implying 'momentary surges' or a 'steadily growing' sense of national identity? The question of whether nationalism can indeed be identified as a developing discourse in medieval English texts is further complicated by the postulated post-medieval origins of nationalism itself. Benedict Anderson, in his influential *Imagined Communities*, sums up the view that it was the Enlightenment that engendered nationalism: 'in Western Europe the eighteenth century marks ... the dawn of the age of nationalism'.[6] In response to such periodized objections, medievalists have been quick to dismantle Anderson's temporally-constrained formulation, and have argued for studies on 'the discourse of the nation' to be extended back beyond the traditional eighteenth- and nineteenth-century origins of the modern nation state. Diane Speed, arguing the case for the presence of medieval nationalisms in romance, considers 'that it could be reasonably taken back to the literature of the late thirteenth and early fourteenth centuries, especially to the early romances'.[7]

The widening of the use of 'nation' as a critical tool has encouraged medievalists such as Geraldine Heng to further challenge the rigorously modern definition of nationalism, arguing that nationalist ideology is discernible in earlier literature. Heng has argued that a form of English medieval nationalism can be seen in romances such as *Richard Coer de Lyon*.[8] She writes that 'medievalists agree that from the thirteenth century onward, discourses of the nation are visible and can be read with ease in medieval England...'[9] However, Heng also points out that the medieval nationalism that she advocates is not the same as that envisaged by theorists such as Anderson:

> That nation is not, of course, a modern state: among the distinguishing properties of the medieval nation – always a community of the realm, *communitas regni* – is the symbolizing potential of the king, whose figural status allows leveling discourses and an expressive vocabulary of unity, cohesion, and stability to be imagined, in a language functioning as the linguistic equivalent of the nation's incipient modernity.[10]

---

[5] Derek Pearsall, 'The idea of Englishness in the fifteenth century', in *Nation, Court and Culture: New Essays on Fifteenth-Century English Poetry*, ed. Helen Cooney (Dublin: Four Courts Press, 2001), pp. 15–27 (p. 15).
[6] Anderson, *Imagined Communities*, p. 11.
[7] Diane Speed, 'The Construction of the Nation in Medieval Romance', in *Readings in Medieval English Romance*, pp. 135–57 (pp. 135–6).
[8] Geraldine Heng, 'The Romance of England: *Richard Coer de Lyon*, Saracen, Jews, and the Politics of Race and Nation', in *The Post-Colonial Middle Ages*, ed. Jeffrey J. Cohen (New York: St Martin's Press, 2000), pp. 135–72.
[9] Heng, 'Romance of England', p. 150.
[10] Heng, 'Romance of England', p. 139.

Heng argues that an English narrative, written in English, concerning an important English figure, both reflects and contributes to a wider English national identity. Something analogous to modern nationalist ideology is at work in these texts, and while it may not be the process of national identity formation as delineated by Anderson, it can certainly be understood as an example of the development of an imagined group identity.[11]

The place of medieval romance within the discourse of medieval Englishness has been highlighted from the beginnings of the debate. From Turville-Petre's reading of *Havelok the Dane* to the often-critiqued nationalist fantasy of *Richard Coer de Lyon*, romance has proved to be a particularly fecund ground for the analysis of the nature of medieval Englishness. Heng comments that the 'characteristic freedom of romance to merge fantasy and reality without distinction or apology, and the ability of the medium to transform crisis into celebration and triumphalism, mean that romance has special serviceability for nationalist discourse'.[12] The nationalist content of Middle English popular romance should show itself, if it shows itself anywhere, deployed against the Frenchness of the Charlemagne romances of the fourteenth and fifteenth centuries. It might reasonably be expected that the Hundred Years' War (1337–1453) may have conjured in popular romance – if not in Chaucer, Gower or the *Gawain*-poet – some war-time expression of Englishness, oriented against the French. If the popular romance of this period did shape an English national identity, the existence of Middle English romances which treat the Matter of France (stories of Charlemagne, the great French king, and his knights) in neither chauvinistic terms nor with any especial praise of Frenchness must be explained. Heng's 'special serviceability' does not place itself in the service of any nationalism in the Andersonian sense.

Complex Englishness(es)

Amongst the romances of the fourteenth century, much recent work has focused upon those that are to be found in the Auchinleck MS (Edinburgh, National Library of Scotland, MS Advocates' 19.2.1). Describing this celebrated manuscript, which includes some sixteen different romances, as 'a handbook of the nation', Turville-Petre argues that the manuscript's narrative of England, written in English, 'does not simply recognise a social need but is an expression of the very character of the manuscript, of its passion for England and its pride in being English'.[13] Produced during the 1330s,

---

[11] Heng suggests that it is Anderson's concept of the nation as essentially an 'imagined community' that permits the notion of a medieval 'nation' ('Romance of England', p. 150).
[12] Heng, *Empire of Magic*, p. 67.
[13] Turville-Petre, *England the Nation*, pp. 112, 138. Phillipa Hardman discusses the national character of the Auchinleck MS and examines Englishness within a number of other miscellany manuscripts in 'Compiling the Nation: Fifteenth-Century Miscellany Manuscripts', in *Nation, Court and Culture*, ed. Cooney, pp. 50–69.

the Auchinleck MS represents a confluence of the height of the popularity of romance within England with the burgeoning sense of English national identity that developed in response to the historical crises of the previous decades.[14] Romances such as *Richard Coer de Lyon*, *Guy of Warwick*, *Bevis of Hampton* and others have been examined as sites of the articulation and negotiation of English identity, both within and without their manuscript context.[15] The Auchinleck romances are deployed within the manuscript to provide a set of powerfully articulated answers to Turville-Petre's questions as to the nature and origins of the English people.

Popular romance plays an important role in the development of English identity during the Middle Ages. What, however, is the nature of this Englishness? Do we envisage a homogeneous construction of national identity – Anderson's 'imagined community' of shared values and experience – or should we expect to find a more fragmented, disparate, and complex manifestation of group identity? As more work has been performed upon the romances of English heroes, a clearer – or perhaps murkier – picture of the nature of medieval Englishness has begun to emerge: one that is complicated by ties between England and the continent, regionalisms within England itself, and even worrying similarities with the Saracen Other. While much work has been done to map the limits of English identity, many questions remain to be answered as to its disparate shapes and forms.

The troublesome task of trying to map identity in medieval romance is well illustrated in the romance of *Guy of Warwick* through the series of epithets with which the text identifies its hero, who is progressively – and simultaneously – *Gij of Warwike* (157), *Gij þe Englisse* (3889), and Guy the *Cristen* (110:5), thus representing a complex hierarchy of group affinities, from region, to country, to Christendom. These overlapping identities – Guy's ever-expanding 'territories of the self'[16] – are in no way contradictory when applied to the individual knight, reflecting a historical reality of the multiple allegiances demanded of such chivalric figures. However, when applied to the idea of a developing Englishness, we can immediately see the potential conflicts in such a formulation of group identity: what occurs – one asks – if the interests of region and nation conflict? Is one first and foremost

---

[14] The historian Maurice Powicke identifies the expression of Englishness witnessed during Edward I's crises of the 1290s as an early form of nationalism, declaring that 'it was in Edward's reign that nationalism was born' (*The Thirteenth Century, 1216–1307*, 2nd edn (Oxford: Clarendon, 1962), p. 528).

[15] Of the Auchinleck romances, *Guy of Warwick* and *Bevis of Hampton* have attracted much recent attention, as can be seen in two comprehensive treatments of the romances and their wider narrative traditions: *Guy of Warwick: Icon and Ancestor*, ed. Alison Wiggins and Rosalind Field (Cambridge: D. S. Brewer, 2007); *Sir Bevis of Hampton in Literary Tradition*, ed. Jennifer Fellows and Ivana Djordjević (Cambridge: D. S. Brewer, 2008).

[16] A term taken from Erving Goffman: 'Territories of the Self', in his *Relations in Public: Microstudies of the Public Order* (New York: Basic Books, 1971), pp. 28–41.

English, or a man of Warwick? And what happens to the fantasy of Christendom when an English knight is called upon to fight the French, as was so often the case during this period? Just such anxieties as to the coherence and stability of identity categories come to the fore in the romances, and in *Guy of Warwick*, at least, we find the solution embodied in the form of the Saracen.[17] Jeffrey Jerome Cohen reads images of the Saracen in romance as acting to simplify the inherent complexities of individual and national identity.[18] By adhering to the binary paradigm of Christian as good and Saracen as evil, the oppositional model of identity formation produces a construction of identity that, while reductive, allows a clearer and less problematic definition of self and nation. In relation to the English romances, Cohen has suggested that 'protracted, messy nearby wars in Ireland, Spain, and especially France spurred the English romancers to dream of a time when self-identity was easy to assert, because the enemy was wholly Other (dark skin, incomprehensible language, pagan culture) and therefore an unproblematic body to define oneself against'.[19] *Guy of Warwick* acts to elide the inherent complexities of fourteenth-century English national identity, producing a cultural fantasy in which English subsumes Christian, and presents the reader with an avatar of Englishness that retains its corporeal integrity even after death in the sanctified body of Guy.

However, not all romances are as clearly fantastic in their identity politics as *Guy of Warwick* is, and its manuscript bedfellow *Bevis of Hampton* provides a wonderful counter-piece to the simplicity of *Guy*'s conception of Englishness. Some of the problems in positing a homogeneous Englishness are brought into relief within the curiously hybridized body of Bevis. Bevis is, in many ways, a strange and unsettling example of an English knight. Born the son of an English earl, he is exiled as a boy and brought up in a Saracen kingdom; he marries a Saracen princess, and – after a brief and turbulent return to the land of his birth – ultimately abandons England for the lands of the East. *Bevis* stands as a complex narrative of Englishness, drawing our attention to some of the many difficulties and anxieties within the fantasy of English national identity during the medieval period.[20]

There are two chief complicating factors that impact upon the coherence of the medieval fantasy of Englishness in this romance. First, there is the question of Bevis's connections with the Saracen East – his upbringing, his

---

[17] For an analysis of the use of the Saracen in *Guy of Warwick*, see Robert A. Rouse, 'Expectation vs Experience: Encountering the Saracen Other in Middle English Romance', *SELIM: Journal of the Spanish Society for Medieval English Language and Literature* 10 (2002), 125–40, and 'An Exemplary Life: Guy of Warwick as Medieval Culture Hero', in *Guy of Warwick: Icon and Ancestor*, ed. Wiggins and Field, pp. 94–109.

[18] Jeffrey J. Cohen, *Of Giants: Sex, Monsters, and the Middle Ages* (Minneapolis: Minnesota University Press, 1999), pp. 132–3.

[19] Cohen, *Of Giants*, p. 133.

[20] For a full account of the complex identities found within *Bevis of Hampton* see Robert A. Rouse, 'For King and Country? The Tension between National and Regional Identities in *Sir Bevis of Hampton*', in *Sir Bevis of Hampton in Literary Tradition*, ed. Fellows and Djordjević, pp. 79–88.

marriage, his horse, and his kingdom – connections which, we argue, raise serious concerns about the cultural identity of Western knights who spend a prolonged period of time in the Orient. To encounter the Other physically is to enter into what has been termed a 'contact zone',[21] and such proximity brings with it risks of external contamination of one's own culture. In a recent reading of *Bevis* through the lens of postcolonial theory, Kofi Campbell argues that 'this text functions as an early example of narrating the nation. It seeks to educate its audience as to what comprises Englishness and, equally importantly, what does not ... The Saracens are there to make clearer the bounds of England and Christianity.'[22] For Campbell, *Bevis* is primarily a text that concerns itself with the delineation and the territorial expansion of Englishness. Campbell points out the theoretical commonplace that romances such as *Guy of Warwick*, *The Sultan of Babylon*, and *Richard Coer de Lyon* utilize the figure of the Saracen in an early form of Orientalism, situating in the racial and religious Other all those things against which medieval Christendom was defined. However, in working hard to reconcile the difficulties of the narrative with a postcolonial reading of the text, Campbell too readily sutures the inherent fractures within the rhetoric of identity with which *Bevis* presents its readers. Colonial expansion, the fantasy of which Campbell rightly identifies as an important ideological concern in *Bevis*, brings its own fears and anxieties to the populace of the imperial homeland. While it is indeed true that encounters with the Saracen Other are an important part of the medieval poetics of otherness, there are also concomitant fears of cultural infection and miscegenation. While Campbell argues that Bevis after his fashion makes the East English, we must remind ourselves that acculturation is rarely unidirectional, and even the dominant culture in the process is itself changed through colonial and other forms of cultural interaction.[23] Calkin notes that Bevis and Josian – 'the convert–Christian couple' – seem ill-suited to life in Christian England, but must instead depart to 'a kingdom close to Saracen lands and interests'.[24] Bevis stands within his romance as a complex manifestation of hybrid English–Eastern identity, seemingly never comfortable upon his return to the land of his birth, and continually forced back to the East in order to carve out a new Christian kingdom that can accommodate him and his converted bride.

While the Englishness embodied by Bevis can be seen to be subject to anxieties relating to external contamination, this is not the only problem-

---

[21] A 'contact zone' is a space of cultural encounter, in which peoples geographically and historically distanced come into contact and establish ongoing relations: cf. Marie Louise Pratt, *Imperial Eyes: Travel Writing and Transculturation* (London and New York: Routledge, 1992), p. 7.

[22] Kofi Campbell, 'Nation-building Colonialist-style in *Bevis of Hampton*', *Exemplaria* 18:1 (2006), 205–32 (p. 232).

[23] The two-way street of acculturation is also evident in other medieval romances. For a discussion of this phenomenon in *Havelok the Dane*, see Robert A. Rouse, '*In his time were gode lawes*: Romance, Law, and the Anglo-Saxon Past', in *Cultural Encounters in Medieval English Romance*, ed. Corinne Saunders (Cambridge: D. S. Brewer, 2005), pp. 69–83.

[24] Calkin, *Saracens*, p. 85.

atic aspect of national identity raised in the romance. The homogeneity of Englishness is also at issue within the bounds of England itself. *Bevis*, a narrative with an avowedly regional focus (Hampshire), manifests an anxiety concerning centralized power in the body of the king and the locus of London. Through this regional narrative of identity, the text is forced to negotiate claims of group identities other than that of simply 'English'. Rosalind Field's statement that medieval romance operates 'to create a history for a country, a family, a city' at once identifies the broad scope of the romance mode of narrative history and alerts us to the competing historiographical voices that such romances may contain.[25] The importance of an appreciation of the tension between national and regional voices within medieval historiography is clear. Michelle Warren has highlighted the importance of recognizing the regional origins of writers such as Geoffrey of Monmouth, Robert of Gloucester, and Layamon, to name but three.[26] A powerful regional discourse can be seen to run through *Bevis* – one that manifests itself in Bevis's repeated conflicts with centralized royal authority in the form of King Edgar. In her analysis of *Richard Coer de Lyon*, Heng identifies the figure of the king as occupying a central and symbolic place within the articulation of the medieval English nation.[27] In *Bevis*, however, the figure of King Edgar is anything but a unifying symbol of English identity: he does not act when Bevis's father is murdered; he does nothing to return Bevis's usurped lands and title until Bevis confronts him over his inaction; he intemperately and illegally attempts to prosecute Bevis for Arundel's killing of his larcenous son; and he stands by impotently while the people of London attempt to murder Bevis at the instigation of one of his vassals. An examination of the interactions between Bevis and King Edgar illustrates the inherent tensions between region and centre that exist in *Bevis*. In its presentation of its hero's similarities with the Saracen and his differences from his fellow Englishmen, *Bevis* can be read as representing the internal tensions and external anxieties that were important concerns for the nascent fantasy of English identity during the Middle Ages. If we can derive one important conclusion from these complexities, it is perhaps that we should be careful not to ascribe to the medieval English national identity portrayed in medieval romances such as *Bevis* the monolithic homogeneity that we have come to expect from the forms of nationalism prevalent in the modern age.

---

[25] Rosalind Field, 'Romance in England, 1066–1400', in *The Cambridge History of Medieval English Literature*, ed. David Wallace (Cambridge: Cambridge University Press, 1999), pp. 152–76 (p. 162).

[26] Michelle Warren, *History on the Edge: Excalibur and the Borders of Britain, 1100–1300* (Minneapolis: University of Minnesota Press, 2000).

[27] Heng, 'Romance of England', p. 139.

Thomas H. Crofts and Robert Allen Rouse

The Problem of the French: The Middle English Charlemagne

Any expectation that these romances will show anti-French sentiment is soon disappointed: Auchinleck itself includes two Middle English Charlemagne romances, *Roland and Vernagu* and *Otuel a Knight*.[28] Points of contact between the Matter of France and the reading material of the English suggest that either a) it was a non-issue for romance, which was very busy doing other things, or that b) appropriation, rather than polarization, was the chief register of national difference. There is not scope here for an exhaustive demonstration, but we should preface the following analysis of *The Sege off Melayne* with the few points enumerated below, which can be taken to be representative of this commonality among the Charlemagne romances: that when a specifically English or British national spirit is found, it is neither a hostile nor even a separatist one.

> Auchinleck's inclusion of Charlemagne romances *Otuel* and *Roland and Vernagu* along with English romances such as *Guy of Warwick*, *Arthour and Merlin*, and *Sir Tristrem*, as well as the metrical chronicles *Liber Regum Anglie* and *Richard Coer de Lyon*.
>
> Writers across and between genres were happy to find, or to invent, genealogical threads uniting the French and English heroes: in the Middle English *Turpine's Story* Roland's father Milo de Angleris is claimed as an Englishman, 'Milo of Engelond, a worthy warriure' (fol. 328rb);[29] in *Sir Tristrem* the eponymous hero is Roland's own son.[30]
>
> In William Caxton's chivalric and 'Worthies' books, Charlemagne sits next to King Arthur as an exemplar of good kingship.
>
> In *The Sege of Melayne* the English poet, who habitually refers to French heroes as 'oure ferse men', 'oure worthy men', 'oure folke', does not otherwise invest his lyric identity with nationality. The single surviving copy of *Sege* is in a manuscript noted for its religious materials, the London Thornton manuscript (British Library, MS Additional 31042); these include

---

[28] Marianne Ailes and Phillipa Hardman, 'How English Are the English Charlemagne Romances?', in *Boundaries in Medieval Romance*, ed. Neil Cartlidge (Cambridge: D. S. Brewer, 2008), pp. 43–55 (p. 45, n. 10).

[29] Stephen H. A. Shepherd, 'The Middle English Pseudo-Turpin Chronicle', *Medium Aevum* 65:1 (1996), 19–34. The translator makes him back into a Frenchman at fol. 330vb, but not before repeating the 'mistranslation' (at fol. 329ra) with an unmistakable relish: 'þere where on kynge Charlis parte martird for þe Feythe and for þe loue of God .xl. thousonnde Cristen men, and amonge þem Duke Milo, a worthi warriure, a worthi Englyssh lorde, fadur of þat worshipfull knyht Rowlonde (f. 329ra)'. Shepherd is right to detect 'a nationalistic fervour intent on laying claim to that greatest of heroes, Roland', and he observes that 'One senses that the later passage which identifies Milo as a Frenchman was left untouched by mistake' (p. 26).

[30] For a recent exploration of Tristram's connection with Roland in both *Sir Tristrem* and *Castleford's Chronicle*, see Caroline D. Eckhardt and Bryan A. Meer, 'Constructing a Medieval Genealogy: Roland the Father of Tristan in "Castelford's Chronicle"', *Modern Language Notes* 115:5 (2000), 1085–1111.

The Siege of Jerusalem, *Cursor Mundi*, and *The Northern Passion*, as well as a second Charlemagne romance, *Rowlande and Ottuell*.[31]

Nevertheless, criticism has supposed enough nationalist feeling in and around English romance that some special explanation for the existence of the Charlemagne poems must exist. The traditional explanation is that their popularity came from a Christian militancy shared by England and France. It was, Dieter Mehl writes, 'chiefly the militant and completely intolerant Christianity of the Charlemagne stories that interested the English adapters, and it seems very likely that most of the English versions are to be attributed to clerical authors'.[32] This characterization sounds right. As Alan Lupack observes, 'almost all the Charlemagne romances are couched in terms of religious struggle'.[33] Whatever of the nature of the *Chanson de Roland* is lacking in Middle English Charlemagne romances, religious warfare remains the defining virtue of the Matter, explaining their presence in London Thornton, at least.

The crusade-style conflict between Christendom and Islam is indeed the characteristic feature of the Matter of France; it is, in Helen Cooper's usage, the matter's oldest and most recognizable *meme*. But this does not mean that the holy-war convention guarantees any one particular kind of poem. Rather, it informs the reader of the conventional background the poet will be working with or against:

> The very familiarity of the pattern of the motif, the meme, alerts the reader to certain kinds of shaping and significance, and sets up expectations that the author can fulfill or frustrate. The same motif will not always mean the same thing, or in the same ways: familiarity with the model is used precisely to highlight difference. The infinite adaptation of narrative material becomes a kind of shorthand for meaning, since it draws on what the audience already knows but reconfigures it in different ways.[34]

This is a familiar effect: medieval romancers have shown that you can reinvent King Arthur with no loss of recognition – or participation – as long as one or more of the regular features is present: Gawain, Guinevere, a feast. If it is a Charlemagne romance, there *will* be a holy war of some kind (and also, usually, a moment when Charlemagne is separated from his peers),[35]

---

[31] On the London Thornton MS, see John J. Thompson, *Robert Thornton and the London Thornton Manuscript* (Cambridge: D. S. Brewer, 1987). This manuscript is not to be confused with the Lincoln Thornton, as discussed in Mills and Rogers in this volume.

[32] *Middle English Romances*, p. 152.

[33] *Three Middle English Charlemagne Romances*, ed. Alan Lupack (Kalamazoo: Medieval Institute Publications, 1990), p. 4.

[34] *English Romance in Time*, p. 15.

[35] *Rauf Coilyear*, for instance, lacks the immediate context of war against the Saracens – though there is a fight with one – but takes its cue from the motif of Charles being cut off from his men by a storm; see also the 'straung wedur' episode in the Middle English *Song of Roland* (lines

but this element is subject to as many variations as there are romances. It is perhaps the very constancy of the holy-war *meme* that gives the Middle English Charlemagne-poet license to change things, to move things around, to cover up or expose this or that area of familiar wallpaper.

Robert Warm identifies a paradox in the production of the Middle English Charlemagne romances:

> Why was it that during a period of prolonged Anglo-French hostility, in a conflict which many commentators have defined as being instrumental in establishing a sense of English identity, romances which dealt with French heroes, French military successes, were being composed, copied, circulated and read throughout England?[36]

Such observations constitute a paradox only if the following things are assumed: that 'national identity' is necessarily equated with a simplistic and intolerant chauvinism – as we see, for example, in *Richard Coer de Lyon*; that such chauvinism is in turn promoted, and in a knee-jerk manner, by cultural productions such as chivalric romances; and that late medieval Anglo-French hostility had a universally polarizing effect on French and English subjectivity.

Nevertheless, simplifying Mehl's conclusion, Warm argues that Middle English Charlemagne-romancers overcome their nationalist, anti-French feelings by means of a transcendent piety: 'They are deliberately ignoring the deadly rivalry between the two countries, and constructing an idealized vision of the past, within which true Christian knights fought the infidel rather than one another.'[37] It requires the higher seriousness of religion and piety to heal, if only provisionally, the mutual hatred of the English and French. This – artificially, perhaps – puts the reader of Middle English Matter of France romances in the position of looking for both a nationalist content within the poems and a transnational piety which effaces it.

But a wide view of the material strongly suggests that the romances in question are too various in their plots, innovations, and areas of emphasis to be defined according to either agenda, and that, if anything, the agenda which these romances do serve (more or less) is neither national nor religious, but *chivalric*. An instructive comparison between *The Sege off Melayne* and the cognate Middle English 'crusade-romance' *Capystranus* is made by Stephen H. A. Shepherd. The subject of *Capystranus* is the Turkish siege of Belgrade, which was raised in 1456 (the *terminus a quo* of the poem), and while it is

---

846–62). See *The English Charlemagne Romances, Part II: 'The Sege off Melayne' and 'The Romance of Duke Rowland and Sir Otuell of Spaine' together with a fragment of 'The Song Roland'*, ed. Sidney J. Herrtage, EETS ES 35 (London, 1880).

[36] Robert Warm, 'Identity, Narrative and Participation: defining a context for the Middle English Charlemagne romances', in *Tradition and Transformation in Medieval Romance*, ed. Rosalind Field (Cambridge: D. S. Brewer, 1999), pp. 87–100 (p. 87).

[37] Warm, 'Identity, Narrative', p. 87.

thus not a Charlemagne romance, it shares many otherwise uncommon plot elements with *Sege*.[38] A comparison between the first stanza of *The Sege off Melayne* and that *Capystranus*, while not conclusive, will gesture towards the present argument.

> O Myghty Fader in heven on hye,
> One God and Persones thre
>   That made bothe daye and nyght—
> And after, as it was thy wyll,
> Thyn owne Sone thou sent us tyll
>   In a mayden to lyght;
> Syth, the Jewes that were wylde
> Hanged Hym that was so mylde,
>   And to dethe Hym dyght;
> Whan He was deed, the sothe to saye,
> To lyfe He rose on the thyrde daye
>   Thoroughe His owne might   (*Capystranus*, 1–12)

> All werthy men that luffes to here
> Off chivalry that before us were
>   That doughty weren of dede—
> Off Charlles of Fraunce, the heghe Kynge of alle
> That ofte sythes made hethyn men for-to falle
>   That styffely satte one stede—
> This geste es sothe; wittnes the buke,
> The ryghte lele trouthe, whoso will luke,
>   In cronekill for-to rede.
> Alle Lumbardy, thay made thaire mone,
> And saide thair gammunes weren alle gone,
>   Owttrayede with hethen thede   (*The Sege off Melayne*, 1–12)

The secular leaders of the *Capystranus* are entirely subordinated to the invocation of Christ quoted above, which continues until line 35, when Charlemagne is invoked as a past leader against Islam. *The Sege* never takes its eyes from Charlemagne or his men for any similar length of time. While the relationship between these poems is far more complex than can be told in a bare juxtaposition, it is worth noting that, in their respective opening lines, two distinctly different games are afoot.

The Sege off Melayne

Of the three groups into which the English Charlemagne material falls,[39] *The Sege off Melayne* belongs to the so-called 'Otinel' (or 'Otuel') family of

---

[38] In *Middle English Romances*, ed. Stephen H. A. Shepherd (London: W. W. Norton, 1995), pp. 391–408.
[39] The other two are the 'Sultan of Babylon' (or 'Ferumbras') group and the 'detached' romances based on Laban and his son Firumbras.

French Charlemagne romances, in which a Saracen knight of that name does battle with a Christian hero (here Roland), and is defeated and converted. In fact, this combat does not occur in *The Sege off Melayne*, which is placed in the Otinel group based on its having Garcy as the ruler of Lombardy (which is the case in all the Otinel stories). *The Sege off Melayne* records a story not found in any of the French originals, and which, according to Mehl, probably originated in England.[40]

As mentioned above, the Middle English *Sege*-poet's tendency throughout the narrative is to refer to French heroes as 'our': in direct discourse (not in speeches) the first person plural pronoun occurs twenty-two times as 'oure', twice as 'us'. Shepherd, noting that 'the density of such reference [in *The Sege*] is unmatched in other Middle English romances', suggests it is meant 'to evoke from us a strong sense of partisanship with the Christian forces'.[41] In addition, the first-person plural can also have an 'English' possibility. The genitive form is used with special emphasis in the phrase 'Oure Bretons' – signalling the arrival of reinforcements from Brittany – which occurs five times in fifty-three lines (1495–1545). Without wishing to impugn either the honesty or geographical knowledge of the poet or his audience, it is worth pointing out that *Breton*, which properly means 'from Brittany', is recorded in Middle English romance as a spelling of *Briton*, 'someone British',[42] and that this was an imprecision, or an ambiguity, of which the *Sege*-poet (or his scribes) might have made some use:

> Oure Bretons bolde that fresche come in
> Thoghte that thay wolde wirchipp wyn
>   And gatt the cante of the hill.   (lines 1525–27)

Even if it is a momentary or accidental effect, the repetition of 'Oure Bretons', in a war-like romance such as this, has an ambiguous capability which – especially if the poem was read aloud – would be hard to miss.

The main protagonist of *The Sege off Melayne* is Archbishop Turpin. As Lupack observes, the romance 'achieves some originality through its emphasis on Turpin as the military, political, spiritual, and moral center of the poem' (107).[43] Turpin was never a minor character: in *Chanson de Roland* he is, with Roland and Oliver, one of the three Franks still alive, if barely, when the Saracen attack is turned. His deeds in combat and his rousing speeches, which include colourful battlefield taunts, are among the *Chanson*'s most memorable features. The poetry of the crusade tradition allows (and the

---

[40] *Middle English Romances*, p. 153.
[41] *Middle English Romances*, ed. Shepherd, p. 275, n. 1. See also Ailes and Hardman, 'How English Are the English Charlemagne Romances?', p. 53.
[42] *Alliterative Morte Arthure*, line 1449: 'Thane the Bretons brothely brochez theire stedez'; *Arthur*, ed. Frederick J. Furnivall, EETS OS (London, 1869), line 15: 'Bretones haf hym þat name'. Malory used *Bretayne* to signify either place.
[43] Lupack, *Three Middle English Charlemagne Romances*, p. 107.

Chanson-tradition requires) Turpin to be priest and a warrior at the same time. His clerical status only adds to his heroism: Turpin has always been a puissant and unconflicted killer on the battlefield. The Middle English *Song of Roland* fragment vigorously affirms this:

> turpyn turnyd hym, and met him again,
> sat sadly in his sadill, soothe for to sayn:
> man and horse doune he laid,
> from the croun to the brest: 'Ly þer!' he said.
> hym he cursed, and rode further still,
> And bad the fleyng fend fetche hym to helle.   (lines 970–5)

Thus Turpin assumes his place among the lay heroes of the poem. In *The Sege off Melayne*, however, it is Turpin himself who embodies, to an almost Homeric degree, the time-honoured mixture of heroism and mental unbalance.

Considering that the protagonist of *The Sege off Melayne* is a cleric (as Mehl has observed the author probably was also), Warm's notion that the ruling principle of Charlemagne romances is their piety is presumably, in this case at least, a safe suggestion. *The Sege* is frequently noted for its fervently Christian aspect, in which 'hagiographic, devotional, and Eucharistic themes are used to depict a Christian community characterized by strength in the face of adversity'.[44] Turpin takes centre stage as the main conduit of Christian grace, administering a miraculously-supplied battlefield Eucharist. He also undergoes saint-like physical suffering and retains a formidable capacity for endurance, which includes refusing medical attention after receiving a grievous wound in fighting, addressing an exasperated Charles thus:

> 'What! wenys thou, Charls,' he saide, 'that I faynte bee
> For a spere was in my thee [thigh]
>   A glace thorowte my syde.
> Criste for me suffered mare.
> He askede no salve to His sare
>   Ne no more sall I this tyde.'   (lines 1342–7)

He also refuses to eat or drink until Milan is retaken. Turpin's mental and physical turbulence drive the poem, supplying the martial prowess and access to the divine proper to an ideally imagined crusade.

At the same time, that propriety is exceeded by a blasphemous invective right about the middle of the poem. When Turpin learns of the slaughter of French troops at Milan, the Archbishop throws down his mitre and crozier and begins to curse the Virgin Mary, expressing a wish that she had never been born:

---

[44] Suzanne Conklin Akbari, 'Incorporation in the *Siege of Melayne*', in *Pulp Fictions*, pp. 22–44 (p. 23).

> 'Hade thou noghte, Marye, yitt bene borne,
> Na had noghte oure gud men thuis bene lorne.
>   The wyte [blame] is all in the.
> Thay faught holly in thy ryghte
> That thus with dole to dede er dyghte.
>   A Marie, how may this bee?'
> The Bischoppe was so woo that stownd
> He wolde noghte byde appon the grownnd
>   A sakerynge[45] for to see;
> Bot forthe he went – his handis he wrange—
> And flote[46] with Marye ever amange
>   for the losse of oure menyee.   (lines 553–64)

Warm affirms that 'Turpin's major function in the world of the poem is to re-establish the primacy of religious authority, and forcefully reassert the importance of religion in a world increasingly guided by secular powers',[47] but is silent regarding this outburst, which makes all the familiar pagan-materialist 'mistakes' about religion. Turpin here is in fact reminiscent of the comically enraged title character of *The Sowdone of Babylone*, who thrice throws his idols into the fire. Unlike the Sultan, whose priests make him retrieve his gods from the fire and do vigorous penitence, Turpin is not made to show remorse. In fact, he next refuses to say mass, or to say good morning to Charlemagne.

Shepherd, placing Turpin's speech in the context of other crusade narratives in which 'expressions of anger at the Godhead ... attend the propaganda and the historical accounts', argues that it is appropriate, and even 'normative', within crusaders' vassal-and-lord concept of their service to God.[48] Suzanne Conklin Akbari suggests 'it is important not to overemphasise the significance of Turpin's action toward Mary', pointing out that saint-abuse is a somewhat common practice in the Middle Ages.[49] Whatever is true of medieval *praxis* – and it seems a little dangerous to rely on historical practice to make sense of this (or any) romance – it would seem to impose an artificial limitation not to give this speech its due. While the holy-war context pointed out by Shepherd mitigates the blasphemy, the Middle English popular-romance context does not. Turpin here fully expresses the heathen notion that a god who does not help you win is useless. As Maldwyn Mills confesses of the passage, 'it is very difficult to avoid the feeling that he is being presented as a pagan'.[50]

---

[45] That is, 'a consecration of the mass' (Lupack, *Three Middle English Charlemagne Romances*, p. 125).

[46] The poet's choice of words is noteworthy: Turpin 'flote' (line 563), that is, engaged in the colloquy generally reserved for foes: *OED* '(1) To contend, strive; also, to contend in words, chide, wrangle.'

[47] Warm, 'Identity, Narrative', p. 90.

[48] *Middle English Romances*, ed. Shepherd, pp. 389–90.

[49] Akbari, 'Incorporation in the *Siege of Melayne*', p. 27.

[50] Mills, *Six Middle English Romances*, p. xiii.

The poet has, for at least a moment, allowed the character of Turpin to take on a monstrous aspect. Like Milo's Englishness in *Turpines Story*, Turpin's condition is not permanent: the Archbishop's stirring battlefield mass and deadly prowess still lie ahead.

A speech such as Turpin's here might be shocking but funny in the *Sowdone of Babylone*, which has a wonderful comic register, but in *The Sege off Milan* it seems perverse, and it is not retracted. It is difficult not to see in it an elevation of martial and chivalric imperatives over religious ones. In this it would harmonize with the two prose texts we have already mentioned: William Caxton's *Charles the Grete*, and the Middle English *Turpines Story*. Caxton, who admonished his English audience to 'rede Froissart'[51] in order to learn about chivalry, offers a ready indication of Charlemagne's appeal for English readers. His *Charles the Grete* – a translation of the French *Ferumbras*, whose third book corresponds to the *Pseudo-Turpin* matter – shows the printer's awareness of generic imperatives: in the book's preface, Charlemagne and his paladins are committed to 'the exaltacyon of the Crysten faith and to the confusion of the hethen sarazyns and myscreaunts, whiche is a werk wel contemplatyf for to lyve wel'.[52] This passage, however, is from the part of the *Charles* preface which Caxton translated from his original (Garbin's *Fierabras*, 1483); in the portion written by Caxton there is no mention of fighting heathens, despite his willingness to promote this cause elsewhere.[53] When Charlemagne is mentioned in Caxton's own words, it is with specific reference to his 'vertues chyvalry',[54] as one of the Worthies, and – in a list of chivalric characters – as 'the grete Emperour of Allemayne and Kynge of Fraunce, whose noble actes and conquests ben wreton in large volumes with the noble faytes and actes of his douzepieres, that is to saye, Rowlond and Olyver'.[55] Heroic tales of the Frankish king were not an affront to English chivalry but rather a continuation of it.

The fifteenth-century *Turpines Story* is a Middle English translation of the highly sermonic Latin *Pseudo-Turpin* chronicle.[56] The English text departs noticeably from the Latin text's (and the tradition's) tendency to admonish warrior-heroes for their excesses: for example, the Latin text's 'wine and women' passage, in which King Marsile conveys the gift of wine and women

---

[51] *Order of Chyualry* (c. 1484); see *Caxton's Own Prose*, ed. N. F. Blake (London: Andre Deutsch, 1973), p. 126; or *The Order of Chyualry*, in *The Prologues and Epilogues of William Caxton*, ed. W. J. B. Crotch, EETS OS 176 (London: Oxford University Press, 1928), p. 83.
[52] *Charles the Grete* (1485); see Blake, *Caxton*, pp. 66–67; Crotch, *Prologues*, p. 95.
[53] See Meg Roland, 'Arthur and the Turks', *Arthuriana* 16:1 (2006), 29–42.
[54] *Caxton's Own Prose*, ed. Blake, p. 84; *Prologues and Epilogues*, ed. Crotch, p. 106.
[55] *Caxton's Own Prose*, ed. Blake, p. 139; omitted in Crotch.
[56] A chronicle which circulated in, among other languages, Old French, Anglo-Norman, medieval Welsh and medieval Irish, and whose tradition also produced the romances *Roland and Vernagu* and *Ottuel and Roland* which together form a verse translation and compression of an Old French *Pseudo-Turpin*. The Middle English *Song of Roland* incorporates Pseudo-Turpin's 'wine and women' interlude. *The Sege off Melayne* draws from Pseudo-Turpin's lore (*Middle English Romances*, ed. Shepherd, pp. 388–90).

to the Christian army, providing an apt occasion for asserting divine retribution. As Shepherd points out, the Latin text provides not only that the fornicators (and even, for good measure, the non-fornicators among them) were justly punished with death, but also introduces examples from classical history of generals who, to their confusion, brought their wives on campaign; priests are then singled out and reminded that drinking and fornication lead to eternal damnation. The Middle English *Song of Roland* preserves the episode thus:

> wyn went betwen þem, non did astert,
> þat gwynlon to toun brought, euyll him betid!
> It swymyd in ther hedis and mad hem to nap;
> they wist not what þey did, so þer wit failid.
> when they wer in bed and thought to a restid,
> they went to the women þat wer so hend,
> that wer sent fro saragos of sairsins kind:
> they synnyd so sore in þat ylk while
> that many men wept and cursid þat vile. (68–76)

Here the sermonizing is muted to the 'sore sinning' and morning-after anguish of lines 75–6. But even this is omitted in *Turpines Story*, where it is specified that Ganelon brought wine and women, and that 'the grete and þe worthy warriours, þey toke þe wynne, and þe lasse toke the women, to þeyer grete arme' (34.1122–3). *Turpine's Story* uses the wine and women to distinguish the great warriors from the lesser, but is much more sedulous to portray Ganelon's treachery – his part in putting Roland and Oliver in the rearguard – than anything else. When *Turpines Story* returns to the subject of wine and women, it is only to say:

> But þe nyht after þis, many of þe oste were dronke of þat wynne and toke many of þucke [those same] women and so were dede. Wat more?
> (35.1129–32)

Here we do not encounter the mental or spiritual anguish of the Middle English *Song of Roland* – nor is there any mention of sin. The English *Turpine*-author, Shepherd concludes, evidently 'preferred to examine the tribulations of warriors more than the lapses of sinners'.[57] The preaching of the Latin *Pseudo-Turpin* would probably have been as out of place here as it would have been in Caxton's *Charles the Grete*.

In *The Sege off Melayne*, Charlemagne himself, unable to overrule his own blasphemous bishop, represents a comic absence of that unifying energy we learn of in the biographies of the historical emperor by Einhard and Notker. Like King Edgar of *Bevis*, mentioned above, Charlemagne does not bestow

---

[57] Shepherd, 'The Middle English Pseudo-Turpin Chronicle', p. 28.

his regnal stamp on nation or narrative, but is himself measured against the heroism and gravity of his subject. If an imagined community is sought in the Middle English Charlemagne romances it is unlikely to be 'nationalist' in any stable sense of the term. These romances fall in line with Froissart's doctrine, preached by Caxton, of chivalry, and not nationhood, as the touchstone of aristocratic self-identity.

A body of romances such as the Middle English Matter of France presents yet another complicating factor in the assessment of romance nationalisms during the medieval period. While identifiable discourses of the nation can be read in some of these popular romances, other narratives present more complex challenges for the critic. As such, the corpus of Middle English romance stands as a salient reminder of the difficulties of generalizing about medieval genres, bringing us back to the truism that each text presents its own unique contexts, meanings, and problems for the reader. Medieval popular romances, despite their often highly repetitious and derivative nature, continue to demand individual detailed attention, lest we be lulled by their familiar rhythm into the belief that they speak with one voice.

6

Gender and Identity in the Popular Romance

JOANNE CHARBONNEAU and DÉSIRÉE CROMWELL

Like folktales, myths, and legends, many Middle English romances focus on constructions of identity, heroic behaviour, and an individual's defiance of or conformity to familial, social, cultural and political forces. In many of these texts, the desires of individuals are pitted against societal or familial forces lined up to thwart them: kings, treacherous lords or stewards, problematic fathers, or evil mothers-in-law. These are not always or merely archetypal or generic opponents, as the romances invest folkloric motifs with political and social resonances particular to England in post-Conquest times. Unlike folkloric stories in which monsters (such as giants and dwarfs) are powerful impediments to the success of the hero, and unlike the French or Anglo-Norman romances that emphasize sophistication and court culture,[1] these romances are often grounded in the reality of medieval English life that includes religious elements such as pilgrimages or confessions as well as political or social dangers to the heroes, often from within the domestic sphere.[2] The life of the hero in these romances becomes a positive or negative exemplum, and a bewildering number of rulers come to represent good and bad models of kingship, just or unjust rule.[3] Within these didactic frames of reference and social concerns, Middle English romances deliberately turn away from the adulterous love of their French courtly romance predecessors and focus instead on righting wrongs and re-establishing proper social order with families intact. Beginning with loss or disorder and ending with heavily imposed closure, these texts often eschew the tragic implications of other genres and resolve tensions with a final reiteration of cultural norms. Popular Middle English romance locates itself precisely at the junction between 'the kind of narrative order that finds resolution in the inviolable happy endings

---

[1] Nicola McDonald's 'A Polemical Introduction', in *Pulp Fictions*, pp. 1–21; Mehl in *Middle English Romances* notes that the 'same period that saw the emergence of the English romances, also saw the steady decline of the knight, who had been such an essential part of courtly society. Just as the knight's armour began to prove useless and obsolete during the French wars, the courtly etiquette likewise seemed to become outmoded. Where it was kept alive artificially, as was the case all over Europe, it bore no significant relation to life and had only the charm of antiquity' (p. 4).

[2] See, for example, Edward E. Foster, 'Simplicity, Complexity, and Morality in Four Middle English Romances', *Chaucer Review* 31 (1997), 401–19; *English Romance in Time*.

[3] See Matthew Holford, 'History and Politics in *Horn Child and Maiden Rimnild*', *Review of English Studies* 57 (2006), 149–68 on the importance of patrimony and rule.

and the chaos that is threatened by the giants and rapists, incubi, cannibals and necrophiliacs, to say nothing of the abusive parents and their wild offspring'.[4]

It is certainly true that these stories demonstrate the importance of and insecurities concerning gender, and the notorious reputation of Middle English romance for blurring generic distinctions allows for a range of unrestrained responses to social conditions. Gender construction is a contested ground for both male and female heroes – protagonists who do not fit easily into definable categories and who move effortlessly within or even transgress the boundaries of genre. Some romance heroes resemble those of ballads, some come straight out of pious legend, and others directly out of history and chronicle. What is most interesting is that many characters in Middle English romance are displaced figures (in disguise, in exile, in search of parents, in foreign lands, or on journeys seeking forgiveness). Thus, because the heroes operate outside the heavily scripted roles that medieval society demanded, the genre opens up a space for transgression or at least for renegotiating power and redefining identity. It is a genre of disintegration followed by assimilation, even cannibalizing from other genres (as Geraldine Heng maintains[5]) in exploring what it means to be a romance and a particularly Middle English one postdating the heyday of romance writing. These narratives thus create a fictionalized space to explore the proper behaviour of males and females, paternal authority (or abuse of it), and the importance of marriage and legitimate heirs. Often a clearly defined 'other' acts as a gauge by which the actions of the hero are measured and surprisingly often found lacking: the Saracen is a necessary Other against which the Christian knight must battle; the evil father or step-mother the Other against which the dutiful and pious child must use virtues to counter parental vices; the Otherworld of *Sir Orfeo* or the fairy mistress in *Sir Launfal* that can speak to and against the problems of worldly, aristocratic courts.

Middle English romance writers, just as their Old French predecessors, enabled their audiences to explore – within fictive and thus safe contexts – the intersections of race, ethnicity, religion, and genre while struggling towards their own national identity-building. These problematic issues as well as representations of culturally-determined others provide rich and varied possibilities of exploring the dominant culture's sense of itself and its identity *vis à vis* the perceived others, from Jews and Saracens to the vexing French, with whom the English were embroiled in the Hundred Years War during the time of romance production. It is critical to remember that boundaries and identities – generic, political, national, class – were fluid and adaptive, sometimes accommodating, other times not; sometimes heavily legislated with transgressors paying severe penalties from alienation and exile to torture

---

[4] McDonald, 'Polemical Introduction', *Pulp Fictions*, p. 16.
[5] See Geraldine Heng, *Empire of Magic: Medieval Romance and the Politics of Cultural Fantasy* (New York: Columbia University Press, 2003).

and death. Thus, issues of what constitutes right behaviour, who can cross borders, who is in and who must remain outside were highly charged in late medieval society. These contemporary issues spilled over into romance as it challenged established orders. For example, the behaviours of the Arthurian court – supposedly the model of exemplary chivalric identity – could be challenged and renegotiated by intrusions and violence from outside forces which penetrated the court unexpectedly: the Green Knight from Celtic folklore and manipulations of the fée Morgan in *Sir Gawain and the Green Knight* or the Oriental Turk of *Turke and Gowin*. Often these forces were deeply unsettling, fundamentally disruptive, and potentially deadly to the hegemonic norms associated with male identity. The unfamiliar and outside threats force those within the dominant culture to re-examine their values and behaviours and question beliefs that had been unconsciously accepted.

Gender also informs this genre from stories about calumniated wives, daughters sent into exile, sons in search of their true fathers and their own identities, to knights establishing themselves in the role of defender of the faith or unconquered fighter protecting family, land, and extended households against all outside opponents. Equally important for gender roles is the necessity of establishing patrilineal succession in a medieval English culture confronted with plagues, droughts, crop failures and political instabilities.[6] Identity formation is at the core of many of these stories. What constitutes knightly behaviour? Can a bizarre cannibalistic hero such as Richard Coeur de Lion still be a chivalric knight and national hero? Can a man such as Bevis, who devotes himself to fighting, still be a good Christian? Can a man who is the son of a devil (Gowther) be saved? Can a man born of noble blood but not raised in the proper cultural milieu still be a noble knight (Perceval)? Can a courteous knight (such as Amadace) be expected to always maintain his oath even when extreme personal sacrifice is demanded? Can a knight practise virtues such as liberality to excess and thus damage his reputation (Sir Launfal and Sir Cleges)?

These questions suggest how little these narratives resemble what is popularly construed as romances: stories of idealized knights whose adventures include rescuing damsels in distress or succumbing to romantic love, a modern construct.[7] While it is true that many romances idealize loyal and all-conquering knights – thus constructing and even valorizing a recognizable

---

[6] John Aberth, *From the Brink of the Apocalypse: Confronting Famine, War, Plague, and Death in the Later Middle Ages* (New York: Routledge, 2001); Ian Kershaw, 'The Great Famine and Agrarian Crisis in England 1315–1322', *Past and Present* 59 (1973), 3–50; and S. J. Payling, 'Social Mobility, Demographic Change, and Landed Society in Late Medieval England', *The Economic History Review* 45:1 (1992), 51–73.

[7] The term 'courtly love' was first used by Gaston Paris in 1883, and has since been used as though it were a medieval concept and universal reality. See John C. Moore, '"Courtly Love": A Problem of Terminology', *Journal of the History of Ideas* 40 (1979), 621–32; R. Howard Bloch, *Medieval Misogyny and the Invention of Western Romantic Love* (Chicago: University of Chicago Press, 1991); James A. Schultz, *Courtly Love, the Love of Courtliness, and the History of Sexuality* (Chicago: University of Chicago Press, 2006).

chivalric masculinity – other romances critique knightly identity construction and reject the fighting *ethos* by turning to a religious construction of identity focusing on penance and a turning towards God. Exceptions to male hypermasculinity also include the feminized Launfal or the churlish behaviour of Sir Perceval and Ralph the Coilyear. Other romances move away from knightly constructions of heroism by instantiating models of leadership, especially the constitution of a good ruler as dispenser of justice. Many romances are subversive in their willingness to interrogate the failures of pillars of society: a father's inappropriate and incestuous feelings towards his daughter; a steward who betrays his lord; or a knight who lies and betrays the hero through slander or false accusation. Motivated by lust, jealousy, or greed, these men in positions of authority and power abuse their privileges and become fodder for romance production. This is not a genre of simple-minded adherence to a chivalric *ethos*, but rather one that allows slipperiness and an intense interrogation of accepted values and gendered roles.

This chapter begins with the domestic sphere as the primary breeding ground for identity formation, examining how ruptures in the family affect gender roles and appropriate behaviour (absent mothers, problematic fathers, sibling rivalries, sons in search of their parentage, daughters sent out to sea in rudderless ships). A second section deals with constructions of male identity outside the domestic sphere. Many Middle English romances are concerned with male authority and challenges to it in terms of kingship: how do the just establish rightful rule in individual families as well as in kingdoms? Sometimes, romance texts approach gender and identity formation through non-Christian threats to stable identity formation. What constitutes a Christian as opposed to the quintessential Other often represented as Saracens, Jews, or supernatural creatures including wicked women with magic and power[8] such as Morgan in *Sir Gawain and the Green Knight* or Agostes in *The Grene Knight*?[9]

---

[8] Corinne Saunders, 'Erotic Magic: The Enchantress in Middle English Romance', in *The Erotic in the Literature of Medieval Britain*, ed. Amanda Hopkins and Cory James Rushton (Cambridge: D. S. Brewer, 2007), pp. 35–52. Saunders examines the nature of pleasure and desire as embodied in the Other; she argues that the 'object of desire is desirable precisely in his or her otherness, even unattainability, while the force of love is both transfiguring and alienating. It is not coincidental that there is in romance a powerful link between desire and enchantment' (p. 38). See also Barbara A. Goodman, 'The Female Spell-caster in Middle English Romances: Heretical Outsider or Political Insider', *Essays in Medieval Studies* 15 (1998), 45–56.

[9] *Sir Gawain and the Green Knight*, although not construed as a popular romance, provokes intense interrogation into issues of magic as power, female agency, and gender roles – all concerns of English popular romances. See Catherine S. Cox, 'Genesis and Gender in *Sir Gawain and the Green Knight*', *Chaucer Review* 35:4 (2001), 378–90; Colleen Donnelly, 'Blame, Silence, and Power: Perceiving Women in *Sir Gawain and the Green Knight*', *Mediaevalia* 24 (2003), 279–97; Sheila Fisher, 'Women and Men in Late Medieval English Romance', in *Cambridge Companion to Medieval Romance*, ed. Roberta L. Krueger (Cambridge: Cambridge University Press, 2000), pp. 150–64; and Cory James Rushton, 'The Lady's Man: Gawain as a Lover in Middle English Literature', in *The Erotic in the Literature of Medieval Britain*, ed. Hopkins and Rushton, pp. 27–37. Gawain's anti-feminist speech has provided many scholars with opportunities to investigate some of these issues. In particular, see Catherine Batt's 'Gawain's Antifeminist Rant, the

Joanne Charbonneau and Désirée Cromwell

Domestic sphere as gender determination

Historically, women have been defined in terms of their relationships to men in the domestic sphere and have found their self-definition by fulfilling traditional societal roles. Indeed, many of the women in these narratives are defined in relation to men or as objects of exchange between men.[10] Mothers, wives, mistresses, daughters, healers, helpers are the most recognizable gendered roles for women.[11] However, it is important to realize that uniformly idealized models of female behaviour in terms of perfect wives or dutiful daughters are not consistent across these texts, which instead offer possibilities for women to attain some social agency or self-determination[12] or at least act as impediments to male dynastic ambitions. What women want is not an insignificant issue, and feminine desires often propel these narratives so that the notion that women are merely the passive objects of male desire is highly questionable.[13] A wildly diverse range of female behaviour and types populates the romance landscape: from the pious and innocent

---

Pentangle, and Narrative Space', *The Yearbook of English Studies* 22 (1992), 117–39, and Gerald Morgan's 'Medieval Misogyny and Gawain's Outburst against Women in *Sir Gawain and the Green Knight*', *Modern Language Review* 97:2 (2002), 265–78.

[10] See Kathleen Coyne Kelly, 'The Bartering of Blauncheflur in the Middle English *Floris and Blauncheflur*', *Studies in Philology* 91:2 (1994), 101–10. Anne Clark Bartlett, in *Male Authors, Females Readers: Representation and Subjectivity in Middle English Devotional Literature* (Ithaca: Cornell University Press, 1995), discusses the problem of women as objects, even with canon law's insistence on consent: 'Medieval legal record, romance narratives, hagiography, poems, and courtesy books regularly present courtship and arranged or unhappy marriages as topics of intense concern. This is especially true for women, who were not always directly involved in the choice of a marriage partner. Although a prospective bride's consent was required by canon law, marriages often involved intense negotiations among family members, advisers, and associates. Medieval women were generally regarded as marriage objects rather than marrying agents' (pp. 71–2).

[11] David Salter, '"Born to Thraldom and Penance": Wives and Mothers in Middle English Romance', in *Writing Gender and Genre in Medieval Literature: Approaches to Old and Middle English Texts*, ed. Elaine Treharne (Cambridge: D. S. Brewer, 2002), pp. 41–59; Jennifer Fellows, 'Mothers in Middle English Romance', in *Women and Literature in Britain c. 1100–1500*, ed. Carol M. Meale (Cambridge: Cambridge University Press, 1993), pp. 41–60; Elizabeth Archibald, 'Women and Romance', in *A Companion to Middle English Romance*, ed. Henk Aertsen and Alisdair A. MacDonald (Amsterdam: VU University Press, 1990), pp. 153–69.

[12] Interestingly, many romances explore that transitional and temporary time in a woman's life between daughter in her father's home and wife and mother in her own domestic space. See Felicity Riddy, 'Temporary Virginity and the Everyday Body: *Le Bone Florence of Rome* and Bourgeois Self-Making', in *Pulp Fictions*, pp. 197–216.

[13] Feisty heroines are not uncommon in Middle English romances. Two examples that immediately come to mind are Florence of Rome knocking out the teeth of a would-be rapist and Emaré, who speaks against both her father and the Pope. For other discussions of women's agency see Arlyn Diamond, '*Sir Degrevant*: What Lovers Want', in *Pulp Fictions*, pp. 82–101; Sheryl L. Forste-Grupp, 'A Woman Circumvents the Laws of Primogeniture in *The Weddynge of Sir Gawen and Dame Ragnell*', *Studies in Philology* 99:2 (2002), 105–13; and Jane Gilbert's incisive comment about three narratives, *Lai le Freine*, *Sir Orfeo* and *The Awntyrs off Arthure*: 'The failure of Fresne's life to follow expected paths, Heurodis's incoherent alienation and the vividly disgusting corpse of Guinevere's mother all inscribe the unintelligibility of female desires and experiences when read through traditional, male-centered grids', in *Spirit*, pp. 237–57 (p. 238 n. 60).

to stereotypes from the misogynistic tradition.[14] In between these extremes are supernatural healers, absent mothers (*Emaré* and *Le Bone Florence of Rome*), too-careful and protective mothers (*Perceval*), too-dutiful daughters and wives (the patient Griselda who endures considerable hardship before she finds stability and happiness), wicked mothers-in-law and evil temptresses. Romances thus destabilize what is known or comfortable regarding a woman's station in life. One common narrative strategy is to juxtapose one of these extremes against the other: the good wife versus the evil wife (both represented in *Bevis of Hampton*), the good wife versus the wicked mother-in law (as in *Emaré* and *Octavian*), or the faithful wife versus the evil temptress or adulterous wife (as in *Generides*). In *Octavian*, for example, the good wife and daughter, Florence, is driven out of her husband's home when her cruel mother-in-law not only asserts that Florence's twin sons are bastards, but then arranges for a pretend lover to be found in Florence's bed. Even in the absence of a direct juxtaposition between good and evil archetypes, the distinctive construction of female identity depicted in any given romance stands in stark contrast to their opposing roles in other romance texts. The good daughter or faithful wife thus acts as antidote to the unfaithful and adulterous wife of other romances. In *King Horn*, for example, Rymenild's role as good daughter and loyal lover of Horn speaks to the evil of the Queen in *Generides*, who is unfaithful to her husband and king by having an affair with his steward, aiding her lover in his usurpation of her husband's throne, and sending false reports via messenger to the lovers Clarionas and Generides. The depiction of Saracen women (for example, Josian in *Bevis of Hampton*) who become loving and loyal wives to the western knights – of course, after their conversions – problematizes cultural ideas about both gender and non-Christians. Non-Christian women, recognized for their potentiality to represent values and virtues implicit in Christianity (just as the lump of flesh could be transformed through baptism into a noble baby in *King of Tars*), thus function by pointing to the failures of fictive Christian women whose evil could disrupt social and familial cohesion.

Romance texts not only inscribe instability and contradictory roles for women, but also focus on a change in status for many women within the texts, often from good daughters to abandoned and exiled ones, from loathly lady to fair maiden, from wife to nun, and from daughter to wife and mother. These shifting roles destabilize or blur traditional roles of women by creating potential threats to the norms and thus social order.[15] Several romances begin with a good daughter or wife who is later exiled and, who, in her liminal state, forges a new identity beyond the scripted, familiar one. *Emaré*, for

---

[14] Myra Seaman, 'Engendering Genre in Middle English Romance: Performing the Feminine in *Sir Beves of Hamtoun*', *Studies in Philology* 98:1 (2001), 49–75.

[15] Felicity Riddy discusses the domestic sphere and marriage in her chapter 'Middle English Romance: Family, Marriage, Intimacy', in *Cambridge Companion to Medieval Romance*, pp. 235–52.

example, problematizes the heroine's identity through the absence of a mother so that she is placed in the unnatural position of surrogate wife. She becomes the object of her father's incestuous desire, and although his noblemen and the Pope himself – all symbols of the highest male authority – align themselves with the father's unnatural desire, Emaré finds the strength to reject the marriage as morally wrong, causing her angry father to cast her out to sea in a rudderless boat. She must create a new identity no longer subject to the rules of the domestic sphere or to the man to whom she was once subservient.[16] When Emaré finally reaches land, she renames herself Egaré ('the outcast'), thus underscoring her new identity outside the domestic sphere.

The tales of *Sir Eglamour of Artois* and *Torrent of Portyngale* also raise serious questions about fathers' treatment of daughters.[17] *Eglamour* raises the very real possibility of incest (twice in its mere 1375 lines, once father-daughter and once mother-son). Both texts explore the inappropriate desires of these fathers that are often thwarted or ignored;[18] they address obliquely the problems of succession and inheritance when the ruler is childless or only has a daughter. Both texts, profiling many families without sons, directly acknowledge the social-climbing aspirations of earls wanting to marry kings' daughters. The recalcitrance of the fathers is even couched in terms of preserving the *status quo* and preventing the lower classes from rising, even if it means resorting to murder. These romances, by intermingling conflicted gender identities with social and political concerns, raise questions about how unnatural sexual desires within families intersect with other kinds of instabilities and insecurities.

Le Bone Florence of Rome foregrounds female agency while inscribing just how unstable and difficult female self-determination is. Florence's self-assured position as beloved daughter in her father the Emperor of Rome's court in control of her own body and her own marriage contract, disintegrates when her father is killed in battle, and her own action of sending her husband off to avenge his death before consummating the marriage precipitates unforeseen consequences. Her independence is fleeting, as outside evils undermine her efforts at self-definition and honourable behaviour. Beaten almost to death and staving off rape attempts by her brother-in-law Miles, Florence manages to escape with her virginity intact, but then has to rely on

---

[16] See Anne Laskaya's treatment of *Emaré* in 'The Rhetoric of Incest in the Middle English *Emaré*', in *Violence against Women in Medieval Texts*, ed. Anna Roberts (Gainesville: University Press of Florida, 1998), pp. 97–114.

[17] Joanne Charbonneau, 'Transgressive Fathers in *Sir Eglamour of Artois* and *Torrent of Portyngale*', in *Discourses on Love, Marriage, and Transgression in Medieval and Early Modern Literature*, ed. Albrecht Classen (Tempe: Arizona Center for Medieval and Renaissance Studies, 2004), pp. 243–65. For a detailed and insightful investigation into incest, see Elizabeth Archibald, *Incest and the Medieval Imagination* (Oxford: Oxford University Press, 2001).

[18] María Bullón-Fernández, *Fathers and Daughters in Gower's 'Confessio Amantis': Authority, Family, State and Writing* (Cambridge: D. S. Brewer, 2000) explores the problematics of this relation in Gower.

her own resources, the efficacy of prayer, and the generosity and kindness of strangers to forge a new definition of self. The trajectory of Florence's life outside her originally nurturing domestic sphere is replete with horrifying external threats (would-be rapists, accusation of murder, betrayals, exile as a solitary figure, shipwreck and near death), but stabilizes finally as she transfigures into a nun, healer, and then wife and mother – all comfortable and gender-sanctioned roles within inscribed spaces. This text raises the positive possibility of a woman's agency, but the costs working against a good outcome are not insignificant, and Florence ends back in a safe domestic sphere.

Lai le Freine investigates in complex ways gendered roles for women ranging from highly negative representations of motherhood to positive women with some agency. The text begins with Freine's problematic mother who abandons one of her twin daughters (fearful of being called adulterous according to common ideas about motherhood) before moving on to the abbess (a surrogate mother who is loving and nurturing and an antidote to Freine's biological mother) to Freine herself, whose name and identity are associated with nature (the ash tree) and not her socially constructed identity. Freine's agency includes taking a lover while enclosed in the nunnery, a move contrary to all socially accepted ideas of female behaviour.[19] The text problematizes her agency and independence when she is rejected by her lover, who is forced to renounce his beloved who has no social status for a supposedly more appropriate wife (her own sister). In fulfilling his public obligation, Sir Guroun compromises his personal integrity, and the text ends problematically when he marries Freine, his true love, but only once he learns of her noble lineage. The text does not endorse the innate nobility of Freine and instead reinforces culturally enforced notions of lineage. Although Freine marries the man she loves, she was willing to accommodate his socially mandated wife and renounce her own desires for the social and political good. Ultimately, Freine becomes a wife enclosed once again in a safe sphere. These texts explore women's search for identity outside the parameters of the domestic sphere, but always end with the women securely repositioned and contained within the household in their gendered roles as good wives and potential or actual mothers.

Obviously, there are many romances that seem to support the over-simplified, overgeneralized view that women are passive, patient, pietistic with no subjectivity; as objects of male desire or thoroughly marginalized figures, some have no voices and no names. But even in such romances, women are rarely completely passive even when they seem to have the least control over their lives, as when they are exiled in a rudderless boat. Even here, with

---

[19] Elizabeth Archibald, '*Lai le Freine*: The Female Foundling and the Problem of the Romance Genre', in *Spirit*, pp. 39–55; and Michelle Freeman's 'The Power of Sisterhood: Marie de France's Le Fresne', *French Forum* 12 (1987), 5–26, which examines the abbess and Freine's relationship as an antidote to the culturally privileged uncle–nephew relationship.

prayer and perseverance, women are agents of their own destiny and never succumb to despair.

As important as the domestic sphere is in delineating appropriate or subversive roles for women and men, four narratives defined as Breton Lays – *Sir Orfeo*, *Sir Degaré*, *Sir Gowther* and *Lai le Freine* – as well as a group of chivalric/exemplary romances (such as *Torrent of Portyngale*, *Sir Eglamour of Artois*, *Emaré*) depict serious problems within the domestic sphere: missing, abandoned, abducted, or exiled family members, problematic fathers, and estrangements from family members through rivalry or betrayals (*Havelok*, *Gamelyn*, *King Horn*, *Athelston*, Mordred in the Arthurian romances, Miles's betrayal in *Bone Florence of Rome*). All of these circumstances precipitate a crisis of identity beginning with the domestic sphere and spiralling outwards into society, affecting rulers and even the Pope himself. *Sir Degaré*, for example, explicitly states its interest in gender identity by investigating 'wat man was' Degaré, an abandoned child conceived by a fairy knight who ravishes a princess.[20] His search for identity takes him on a series of adventures that include unwittingly marrying his own mother, defending a woman and her castle from an unwanted suitor, defeating his own father in armed combat, and finally reconciling with both parents and assuming his 'rightful' identity. This tale, beginning with unknown parents, sets the stage for the male child to discover noble, courteous, and chivalric behaviour, thus performing the very acts that identify his true worth and birthright so that he already is what he is seeking to be.

Another Breton Lay, *Sir Gowther*, takes problematic families to an extreme as Gowther rejects everything associated with the domestic sphere, nurture, or the feminine: as an infant, he rips off his own mother's nipple, kills nine women who try to nurse him, and later rapes wives and murders their husbands, and burns nuns. This tale deliberately problematizes Gowther's identity by beginning the story with patterns of disruption, deceptions and unnatural events.[21] The normal male dynastic desire for an ancestral line is tainted by the husband's monstrous threats and repudiation of his own wife: 'Y tro thu

---

[20] Rachel Moss examines the difference between being male and being a man and the uncertain psychological space between adolescence and manhood for the titular heroes in *Lybeaus Desconus* and *Sir Degaré* in her recent conference presentation, 'Boys in the Woods: Outsiders and the Search for Masculine Identity in Middle English Romance', Gender and Difference in the Middle Ages, Edinburgh, Scotland, 11–13 January 2008. Thus, individual gender identity is dependent on the knowledge of family identity, as the male hero's conflict with the father is as essential as union with the father in allowing the hero to establish his identity as simultaneously 'belonging' and 'other', as a son to a hero and as a hero himself.

[21] Jeffrey Jerome Cohen, *Of Giants: Sex, Monsters, and the Middle Ages* (Minneapolis: University of Minnesota Press, 1999); Jane Gilbert, 'Unnatural Mothers and Monstrous Children in *The King of Tars* and *Sir Gowther*', in *Medieval Women: Texts and Contexts in Late Medieval Britain: Essays for Felicity Riddy*, ed. Jocelyn Wogan-Browne et al. (Turnhout: Brepols, 2000), pp. 329–44; and chapter 9, 'Women and the Wild', in Dorothy Yamamoto, *The Boundaries of the Human in Medieval English Literature* (Oxford: Oxford University Press, 2000), pp. 197–224.

be sum baryn, / Hit is gud that we twyn; / Y do bot wast my tyme on the.'[22] Gowther, then, is conceived from the real desire of parents for a child, a desire that, because thwarted and frustrated, is transformed into something ugly and monstrous: blame and renunciation, and then desperation as the about-to-be-cast-off wife falls into the common folkloric trap of wishing for a child no matter what. In this case, the wished-for son literally is begotten by the devil who assumes her husband's shape. Gowther's birth thus becomes a vindication of the woman's fertility and usefulness *vis-à-vis* procreation, but it is far from straightforward. In the middle section of the poem, Gowther is not quite man: his penance is not to speak and to eat only from a hound's mouth until he receives a token from God that his sins are forgiven. He must wait in this intermediate, animal state without speech and without the behaviours associated with civilized man. He is literally and symbolically set apart from God and men by living under the high table with dogs as companions. Truly about identity and transformations, this tale combines gender and genre in unexpected ways as the tale tracks the trajectory of the eponymous hero from devil's son to saint with stages in between that represent diverse and sometimes irreconcilable identities (pilgrim, unspeaking beast, Hob the Fool, chivalric knight, husband to royalty, ruler of empire).[23]

Other Breton Lays defy conventional gendered roles in their narrative structures: *The Erl of Toulous* and *Sir Orfeo* fall into this category. In *The Erl of Toulous*, the Empress has to remind her husband of his duties and obligations as a just ruler when he wrongfully seizes the lands of Sir Barnard. The remainder of the story treats the chaste love of Sir Barnard and the Empress and their final marriage after false accusations, further injustices, and the convenient death of the Emperor. Unusual in its portrayal of a chaste queen who is also political advisor and model of justice (in opposition to male injustices), the tale juxtaposes a woman's power, justice, superior morality, and sexual chastity with male treachery, lechery, and injustice. Sir Barnard, however, stands out as the anomalous male, who is a match for the queen in terms of fidelity, chastity, and truth. The tale overturns many stereotypical attributes of women and instead depicts males filled with anger and lust who are untrustworthy and morally deficient.

Sir Orfeo examines the interdependence of male and female roles by daring to explore the ways in which the male is lost without his female counterpart. The king as much as his wife is bereft and cannot function without his necessary other half. This narrative explores love, truth, and good stewardship as well as the serious repercussions when both queen and king lose their social and regnal roles and assume identities that alienate them from a sense of their socially conceived selves. It inscribes political stability in terms

---

[22] Lines 56–58 from Advocates Manuscript of *Sir Gowther* in *The Middle English Breton Lays*, ed. Anne Laskaya and Eve Salisbury (Kalamazoo, MI: Medieval Institute Publications, 1995).
[23] Joanne A. Charbonneau, 'From Devil to Saint: Transformations in *Sir Gowther*', in *Matter of Identity*, pp. 21–8.

of the recovery of the faithful wife.[24] Instead of winning the queen through traditional male force of arms in tournaments, Orfeo uses music (often associated with the feminine). Other texts also challenge the conventional privileging of the male over female by subverting female inferiority and positing instead a mutuality with the interlocking lives between the male and female heroes. *Bevis, Emaré, Havelok, Horn Child, King Horn, Sir Isumbras*,[25] *Sir Triamour*, and *Floris and Blanchefleur* all challenge culturally sanctioned notions of gender roles that necessitate the female as inferior, passive, and powerless in relationships.

Other texts undermine the male's independence and self-determination by carving out a space within which women serve a critically important function as catalysts for knightly pursuits. In these works, male ambitions are not independent of female input, and in fact the feminine becomes the driving force propelling male identity formation. In *Bone Florence of Rome*, Florence refuses to consummate her marriage with Emere until he takes revenge on the elderly Garcy, who waged war on her father. In *Guy of Warwick*, the Earl's daughter, Felice, scorns Guy and subjects him to multiple tests before she acquiesces to his marriage pleas. Guy, in turn, distinguishes himself in battle before both the Emperor of Germany and of Constantinople. In *Ipomadon*, the daughter of the Duke of Calabria asserts that she will wed only the most able knight, leading Ipomadon to abandon hunting and devote himself instead to knightly pursuits such as tournaments. These texts in particular offer a unique space in which women play pivotal roles – and the motivations and desires of these women shape not only the narrative course, but the identities of the males who pursue them. It is not a simple case of male dominance and hierarchical importance, but a complicated nexus of male and female desires.

Constructions of masculinities outside the domestic sphere

While the domestic sphere acts as a major ground for identity formation for both females and males – in terms of their roles of husbands, fathers, sons – many other venues provide sites to examine gender roles for males. Social, religious, and cultural contexts as well as the familial offer opportunities for the valorization of the perfect knight and defender of the faith, the importance of constructions of kingship that allow both males and females to flourish under just rule, and the exploration of homosocial desire in male friendships. Threats to these stable, positive, and power-wielding gendered roles include evil stewards, powerful women (often supernatural or otherworldly),

---

[24] Ellen M. Caldwell, 'The Heroism of Heurodis: Self-Mutilation and Restoration in *Sir Orfeo*', *Papers on Language and Literature* 43 (2007), 291–311.

[25] Rhiannon Purdie, 'Generic Identity and the Origins of *Sir Isumbras*', in *Matter of Identity*, pp. 113–24.

traitors and usurpers, violent opponents ranging from giants to Saracens, and sometimes life-transforming experiences that change the chivalric hero to a penitent, pilgrim or solitary soul seeking repentance, forgiveness, and spirituality.

In many romance narratives, the most culturally sanctioned role for adult males is clearly that of the chivalric knight, and certainly examples abound from the idealized, hypermasculine fighting men of Arthurian romances to the eponymous heroes (Sir Degrevant, Sir Eglamour, Sir Gawain, Sir Perceval, Sir Torrent, Sir Triamour, Sir Tristrem, Squire of Low Degre, Partonope of Blois) to the militant Christian warriors fighting in the Holy Land or against Saracens (Bevis, Guy, Richard, Octavian, the heroes of the Charlemagne romances, Sir Isumbras and the males in *Three Kings Sons*). While still working within the knightly tradition, *Sir Launfal* and *Sir Amadace* represent not the ideal, but the excess of the important social virtue of *largesse* or liberality. Both involve atypical heroes. *Sir Amadace* interrogates knightly excess in depicting not just one case, but two – both with serious consequences. First, Amadace, forced to leave his domestic space because of shame caused by excessive generosity, encounters a grieving widow whose husband, like Amadace, spent his fortune and was left owing thirty pounds to a creditor. Paying off this debt and allowing a proper burial of this knight, Amadace then becomes truly penniless until a White Knight (later revealed as the ghost of the grateful dead knight) directs him to arms and wealth so he can re-establish his knightly identity. The next part of the narrative shifts focus to the importance of keeping one's word and the honour of a loving wife. When the White Knight reappears to claim his half of Amadace's winnings, including his wife and child, Amadace's wife insists that he keep his pledge and is about to be cut in half when the White Knight reveals his true identity and commends the couple for their honouring of the pledge. This romance, with motifs from folklore as well as chivalric tales, treats concerns about wealth and generosity, honesty, and a woman's willingness to sacrifice herself for her husband's honour. The second text, *Sir Launfal*, also may be seen as vindicating a spendthrift knight. Launfal loses his fortune, leaves the Arthurian court in disgrace, and then meets a fairy mistress who gives him back riches as well as her love, rescues him at the end from false accusation, and vindicates his truth-telling.[26] In a true gender-bending reversal, she rescues him, and he rides out of court (the site of his knightly identity) behind his mistress, who now holds the literal reins, as they disappear into her kingdom in a rejection of the Arthurian court and its debased values in which fidelity, truth, and kindness are no longer practiced. Other critiques of chivalric values occur in *Lancelot of the Laik* (in which Amuntas, clerk and advisor to Arthur, rebukes Arthur for his failure to observe the duties of a king), the stanzaic *Morte Arthur* (in which Guinevere rejects her adulterous relationship with

---

[26] Elizabeth Williams, '"A damsel by herselfe alone": Images of Magic and Femininity from *Lanval* to *Sir Lambewell*', in *Romance Reading*, pp. 155–70.

Lancelot and chooses instead a penitent's life filled with self awareness of her personal failings) and *Awntyrs off Arthure* (in which Guinevere's mother appears from the dead to warn of the consequences of sin).

The interrogation of the chivalric code can take the form of serious failures in terms of lack of courtesy or violations of oaths to even more severe moral failings in terms of violence against women, betrayals, and would-be usurpation of power by those very persons most expected to be loyal: brothers or stewards. Male violence against women occurs shockingly frequently. A few examples will have to suffice: Athelston kicks his wife and kills their unborn child in rage; in *Bone Florence of Rome*, Miles beats Florence and hangs her up by her hair, and other males try to rape her or set her up for murder; in the *Jeaste of Sir Gawain*, after Gawain has sex with a woman in a pavilion, she is severely beaten by her brother and then wanders off into the woods and disappears from the text; in *Perceval of Galles* the woman whose ring Perceval steals at the beginning is bound to a tree as her lover, the Black Knight, thinks she was faithless. These negative representations of the abuse of male privilege and authority are equally possible in this genre that accommodates views that speak against idealized male portraits of heroism and military strength.

Other failures in the chivalric code occur when a steward or male in a position of trust falsely accuses the hero or heroine. In *Athelston*, the envious Wymound falsely accuses Egeland and Edyff of treason; there are false charges of seduction in *Bevis*; Guinevere is falsely accused of poisoning a Scottish knight and condemned to death in stanzaic *Morte Arthur*; Lunet is accused of treason and about to be burned but is saved in *Ywain and Gawain*; a steward ambushes the hero but is killed in both *Sir Degrevant* and *Squire of Low Degree*; the false steward Maddock betrays the queen in *Sir Triamour* and tries to kill her in the forest; Earl Godard, wanting to seize the throne of Denmark, sends Havelok to a fisherman to be killed; Fikenild betrays Horn by telling the king that Horn has seduced his daughter in *King Horn*. English popular romance writers thus manipulate their received genre in order to raise serious issues about male identity formation by depicting failures in the system including betrayal of one's lord or mistress. The dangers of treachery and usurpation carry over to romances that provide *exempla* of good and bad kingship – the highest male authority. Tales of wicked or tyrannical rulers (in *Alexander Buik*, *Apollonius of Tyre*, *Arthour and Merlin*, and *Bone Florence of Rome*) perhaps depict the most far-reaching consequences of abuse of male privilege. However, these cases are offset by the good rulers, for example, in *Arthour and Merlin*; or in *Three Kings Sons*, in which King Alfour of Sicily will not allow his daughter to marry the Turkish prince in order to save his land; and in *Bone Florence of Rome*, in which Florence's father who defends his country against the tyrannical Garcy. Romance texts thus explore problematic gender roles all the way up the social and political hierarchy to kings, the ultimate secular male power.

Other texts do not pinpoint flaws in the dominant code or individual failures – catastrophic as they may be – but rather offer other possibilities of masculine identities, thus implicitly questioning the very adherence to a worldly, aristocratic, or chivalric set of values. Situating males outside the role of typical chivalric knight, these popular romances thus point to other kinds of gendered roles available to them. For example, Grim's generosity to Havelok, the loyal steward in *Sir Orfeo*, male bonding in *Amis and Amiloun* and *Eger and Grime*, and championing the poor as in *Gamelyn* and *Gest of Robin Hood*[27] all open up other possibilities of valued masculinities beyond the fighting knight. Sometimes religious or spiritual values supersede chivalric ones. *Robert of Cisyle* is such a text in that it interrogates the value of a successful secular ruler when an angel asks the King of Sicily about his identity late in the text: 'What art thou?' and Robert answers that he is a fool and worse. Robert's identity swiftly degenerates from influential King of Sicily to madman/knave who is appointed court fool to one who has to eat and sleep with hounds – much like Gowther. Only when he repents of his pride does the angel who had assumed his kingship disappear and allow him to reassume his previous identity. In this narrative, the king learns that as king he must have humility and rules only at the pleasure of God, who determines his role in the earthly society. Thus his gendered conception of self, reinforced by power structures in his society as well as his own sense of his authority as ruler, is fundamentally challenged and superseded by a different set of rules.

Historical accounts of sieges and conquests – filled as they were with examples of treachery and evil as well as heroic actions – provided ground for the Middle English romance writers as they struggled with notions of lineage (as many heroes trace their ancestry back to Troy[28]) or the distinguishing factors of English law contrasted with other kinds of law (secular and religious). English romance writers also combed classical antiquity and history for moral lessons that would illuminate contemporary problems of intrigues, usurpations, political manoeuvrings, patronage, and good kingship versus tyrannical rule – all reflections of problematic or conflicted masculinities. Of these kinds of romances, Lydgate's *Troy Book*, popular as attested by twenty-three manuscripts and fragments, and *Siege of Thebes*, memorialized in thirty-one manuscripts, stand out in their resonances concerning truth, honour and love with moral messages on kingship and the dangers of using force. Like other romances, these works mine contrasting figures for moral

---

[27] See John M. Coggeshall, 'Champion of the Poor: The Outlaw as a Formalized Expression of Peasant Alienation', *Southern Folklore Quarterly* 44 (1980), 23–58.

[28] Pamela Luff Troyer's discussion of *The Seege of Troy* points to the possibility of the use of historical matter as a ground for contesting an ideal imaginary past and for considering dishonourable figures such as Aeneas and Hector as historical ancestors from whom the English would not want to be descended. See her 'Smiting High Culture in the "fondement": *The Seege of Troye* as Medieval Burlesque', in *Fantasies of Troy: Classical Tales and the Social Imaginary in Medieval and Early Modern Europe*, ed. Alan Shepard and Stephen D. Powell (Toronto: Centre for Reformation and Renaissance Studies, 2004), pp. 117–31.

points so that Amphion represents the ideal king and Eteocles the bad king in *Siege of Thebes*. Patterning, doublings and triplings reinforce moral messages about ineffectual rulers, a theme dominant in other texts such as *Ipomadon*, *Robert the Devil*, and *Octavian* in which abuse of power is contrasted with other more rightful kinds of power: spiritual values as well as social justice and rightful law. These texts challenge masculine prerogatives and privilege by bringing to light abuses and failures in male-dominated power structures. The commonalities that run through all these texts represent a kind of historical mythologizing and a self-conscious engagement with the past and issues of national identity as they become clarified through negotiations with other realms (other nations, other religions, other ethnicities, other masculinities and femininities).

Anxieties about gender surface in these romances in terms of contested masculinities and issues of female subjectivity. The genre accommodates conflicting views from proto-feminist texts that gesture towards women's autonomy to culturally sanctioned texts that promulgate social order in terms of appropriate marriages, continuation of noble lineages, and containment of women. Potentially disruptive women, resistant voices to patriarchal aims and dynastic concerns, and power-hungry or magic-wielding women populate the romance landscape as do pious women, good mothers, and docile wives. Hypermasculine, effeminate, penitential and religious men are equally possible in this commodious and fluid genre that defies generalities and allows multiplicities of vision and conflicting perspectives on gender.

7

The Metres and Stanza Forms of Popular Romance

AD PUTTER

Introduction: verse and prose

Discussions of versification and prosody tend (as in this *Companion*) to be tucked away in discrete chapters or sections, as if these were purely technical subjects without wider relevance. In fact, metre is a central entry point to questions of performance, theme, style, and cultural context. Verse form naturally shapes thought and expression; it also reveals the poet's sense of belonging – his ideas about the kind of work he was writing and the performance he envisaged – and gives us clues about the date, provenance, and reliability of the texts in which poems have come down to us. For all these reasons, metrical analysis should not be as tedious as it often is.

The topic is especially relevant to Middle English romance, for which verse appeared until the very end of the Middle Ages to be the only viable option.[1] In France, romance writers discovered prose in the late twelfth century but, centuries later, English writers remained wedded to verse even while adapting French prose. For example, the prose romances *L'estoire del saint graal*, *Merlin*, *Lancelot*, and the *Mort Artu*, which form part of the monumental Vulgate Cycle (c. 1215–35), were all initially translated into verse: into four-beat couplets in *Arthour and Merlin* (c. 1250–1300), into loose alliterative verse in *Joseph of Arimathie* (c. 1350), into an extended ballad stanza ($a^4b^4a^4b^4a^4b^4a^4b^4$) in the *Stanzaic Morte Arthur* (c. 1400), and into more four-beat couplets in Henry Lovelich's *History of the Holy Grail* (c. 1440) and *Merlin* (c. 1445).[2] The first translation of Arthurian matter into prose, the *Prose Merlin*, dates from the middle of the fifteenth century, and only at this late stage was there a widespread shift from verse to prose. Another example of the lateness of prose is furnished by the various adaptations of Hue de Rotelande's Anglo-Norman *Ipomedon* (c. 1185, in octosyllabic couplets). The earliest translation, *Ipomadon A* (late fourteenth century), is in

---

[1] This and the following paragraph expand on some observations in Ad Putter, 'Late Romance', in *Readings in Medieval Texts: Interpreting Old and Middle English Literature*, ed. David Johnson and Elaine Treharne (Oxford: Oxford University Press, 2005), pp. 337–53.

[2] See Helen Cooper, 'The *Lancelot-Grail Cycle* in England: Malory and his Predecessors', in *A Companion to the Lancelot-Grail Cycle*, ed. Carol Dover (Cambridge: D. S Brewer, 2003), pp. 147–62.

tail-rhyme; early in the fifteenth century it was translated again into couplets in *Ipomydon B*; yet only around 1460 did an English adapter finally opt for the (to us) obvious medium of prose in *Ipomedon C*.[3]

The reasons for the transition to prose in the second half of the fifteenth century are various. One important factor is that the traditional forms of versification, though very suitable for oral delivery, had come to seem outmoded and lowbrow in the eyes of a growing audience of readers.[4] Fifteenth- and early sixteenth-century poets with courtly and artistic aspirations responded to the changing fashions by experimenting with newly-prestigious 'Chaucerian' forms, such as the rhyme-royal stanza – as used in the stanzaic *Generydes* (c. 1440) and *Partenay* (late fifteenth century) – or Chaucer's longer five-beat heroic couplets, used in, for example, the Scottish *Launcelot of the Laik* (late fifteenth century) and *Clariodus* (early sixteenth century), and intermittently in *Parthenope of Blois* (mid fifteenth century). Prose eventually emerged as an alternative. As the language associated with historical truth and moral gravity,[5] it also avoided the stigma of wild improbability increasingly associated with romance. This stigma is reflected in a new sense of the word *romance*, 'an extravagant fiction',[6] and the consequent avoidance of the word (from the late fifteenth century up to the early seventeenth) in the titles and prologues of romances, where it had once been the term of choice.[7] While couplet and tail-rhyme romances certainly continued to be read in the age of print, it appears from the titles chosen by the early printers – for example, *The historye of Guy of Warwick* (Pynson, 1500?), *The lyfe of Ipomydon* (c. 1522), *The book of the moste victoryous prince Guy of Warwick* (Copland 1565) – that they shared the prejudice against 'old romances', or at least were shrewd enough to realize that romances would fare better in the marketplace when packaged as historical matter.[8]

In the thirteenth and fourteenth centuries these changes in taste still lay in the future, however, and if we are to appreciate popular romances properly, we need to rid ourselves of the prejudice that prose is the obvious medium for longer narratives. In the following pages I would like to consider the kinds of choices that recommended themselves to the poets of Middle English romance.

---

[3] Jordi Sánchez-Martí discusses the different versions and their audiences in 'Reading Romance in Late Medieval England: The Case of the Middle English *Ipomedon*', *Philological Quarterly* 83 (2004), 13–39.

[4] See Derek Pearsall, 'The English Romance in the Fifteenth Century', *Essays and Studies*, n.s. 29 (1976), 56–83.

[5] See Gabrielle Spiegel, *Romancing the Past: The Rise of Vernacular Prose Historiography in Thirteenth-Century France* (Berkeley: University of California Press, 1993).

[6] *OED* s.v. *romance*, sb. 6. The sense is first attested in 1497. Further examples are given by Reinald Hoops, *Der Begriff 'Romance' in der mittelenglischen und frühneuenglischen Literatur* (Heidelberg: Carl Winters, 1929), pp. 67–9.

[7] Hoops, *Der Begriff 'Romance'*, p. 65.

[8] For these and other references to printers' titles, see *STC*, nos. 807, 12540, 12452, 14128.

Couplets

The main poetic form which they inherited from Old English was alliterative verse. The alliterative long line was written in half lines linked by alliteration, with two beats in each half line. In Middle English, the alliterative tradition was continued most notably by Laȝamon, who, however, linked his half-lines not (or not merely) by alliteration but (also) by end rhyme. The two systems, alliteration and rhyme, sit side by side in lines such as the following:

> Þa him séide **Ár**thur **á**thelest kíngen:
> 'Ich æm Árthur þe k**íng** Brúttene deorl**íng** ...'   (13019–20)[9]
>
> [Then Arthur, noblest of kings, said to him: 'I am Arthur the king, beloved of the Britons.']

Laȝamon's increasing use of rhyme is usually attributed to the influence of 'foreign' metres, but it needs to be remembered that rhyme had already begun to infiltrate Late Old English verse, and that after the Norman colonization of Britain French metres became indigenous, and so were practised, not just by 'foreigners', but also by Englishmen speaking and writing the French of England. The most important French metres for narrative verse were the octosyllabic rhyming couplet and the metres associated with the *chanson de geste*, written in lines of ten or twelve syllables grouped together in sections (*laisses*) on the basis of rhyme or assonance. The octosyllabic couplet was the form that Laȝamon and the poets of *Havelok*, *Sir Tristrem*, and *Amis and Amiloun*, to name just a few examples, encountered in their sources,[10] while the poet of *Horn* had before him twelve-syllable lines (alexandrines) such as the following:

> 'Deu!' fait il en sun quoer, 'si el l'ad enamé?
> Ele est fille le rei, mun seignur avué:
> Si çoe ne fust par lui, mut sereit avilé ...'   (665–7)[11]
>
> ['God', he says in his heart, 'what if she has fallen in love with him? She is the daughter of the king, my sworn lord: if this is not done through him, she would be greatly dishonoured.']

---

[9] Ed. and trans. W. R. J. Barron and S. C. Weinberg, *Laȝamon's Arthur* (Harlow: Longman, 1989). I have modernized 'eth' and have added accent marks to indicate the beats and bold lettering to indicate alliteration and rhyme.

[10] Laȝamon's main source was Wace's *Brut*; *Sir Tristrem* is based on the Anglo-Norman *Tristan* by 'Thomas'; Gaimar's *Histoire des Engleis* and the *Lai d'Haveloc* are the closest known analogues to *Havelok*; *Amis and Amiloun* corresponds most closely to the Anglo-Norman *Amys e Amillyoun*. All these sources and analogues are in rhymed octosyllabic couplets.

[11] Thomas, *The Romance of Horn*, ed. M. K. Pope, Anglo-Norman Text Society 9, 10, 12, 13 (Oxford, 1955–64).

The *laisse* continues in this vein: each line is divided by a caesura and each ends in -*é*, until the next *laisse* brings a new rhyme sound.

I have chosen to illustrate the Old French alexandrines (rather than the octosyllabic couplet) for the obvious reason that students of English literature may never have come across the measure of the *chanson de geste*: keeping a single rhyme going for a long time is difficult in Germanic languages, and I don't know of any narrative poet who tried it in Middle English.[12] The octosyllabic couplet, on the other hand, could easily be accommodated in English, and no one acquainted with Chaucer or Gower needs to be shown what it is. The poet of *Havelok* was the first writer to develop a workable English equivalent in a romance. Here are his opening lines (with my suggested scansion, explained in n. 13):

```
      /   x (/)  x  / x   /
      Herknet to me, godë men
        / x   /    x x  / x   /
      Wives, maydnes, and allë men
      x  x / x   / x    (/)  x    / x
      Of a tale þat ich you wile tellë,
        x (/) x  x   / x    /   x / x
      Wo-so it wil here and þer-to duelle.
       x /  x x   / x / x / x
      þe tale is of Hauelok imaked:
        x  (/) x  /    x / x    x x
      While he was litel he yede ful naked   (1–6)[13]
```

Although the syllable count is not as strict as that in the Anglo-Norman analogues, the rhythm is nevertheless carefully controlled. Were it not for the poet's tolerance of double off-beats (and the imprecise rhymes in some lines[14]), *Havelok* could pass for a couplet poem in strict iambic tetrameter (its emphatically headless start being in fact a conventional opening gambit

---

12 The poet of *Ferumbras* (see below, pp. 125–8) wrote some alexandrines in his draft version (514–26) but they rhyme in couplets (internally and medially) and he corrected them to septenaries in his final version. See Stephen H. A. Shepherd, 'The Ashmole *Sir Ferumbras*: Translation in Holograph', in *The Medieval Translator: The Theory and Practice of Translation*, ed. Roger Ellis (Cambridge: D. S. Brewer, 1989), pp. 103–22.

13 *Havelok*, ed. G. V. Smithers (Oxford: Clarendon Press, 1987). See also Smithers, 'The Scansion of *Hauelok*', in *Middle English Studies Presented to Norman Davis*, ed. D. Gray and E. G. Stanley (Oxford: Oxford University Press, 1983), pp. 195–234. In my scansion of this and other passages, I have added diaereses to indicate pronounced final *-e*, and underlining for vowels likely to have been elided in pronunciation. In my scansion / denotes a beat that coincides with strong linguistic stress, x an unstressed syllable. The symbol (/) indicates a syllable that takes the beat not because it is inherently strongly stressed (or needs to be pronounced as such in performance) but because expectation inclines us to perceive them as accented. As I have emphasized elsewhere (Ad Putter, Judith Jefferson, and Myra Stokes, *Studies in the Metre of Alliterative Verse*, Medium Aevum Monographs [Oxford: Society for the Study of Medieval Languages and Literature, 2007], p. 150), this is not a metrical licence but a natural consequence of our habit of perceiving the second in a series of three weakly stressed syllables with a slight secondary accent.

14 See Smithers, pp. lxxiii–lxxiv.

in iambic verse[15]). In non-autograph manuscripts, we should always be conscious of the fact that scribal errors obscure the poet's metrical system to a greater or lesser extent.[16] In *Havelok*, the variation between the two surviving witnesses, Oxford, Bodleian Library MS Laud Misc. 108 and the fragmentary version of Cambridge University Library MS Add. 4407 (containing 57 lines only) is so enormous that only four lines have the same prosodic shape in both witnesses (342, 343, 359 and 546). Of these only one (343) falls short of iambic perfection.[17]

Havelok illustrates one important strand in the Middle English couplet tradition, an Anglicization of the French octosyllabic couplet. Other examples of this species include, for example, *Ywain and Gawain* and *Lai le Freine*. However, Middle English couplet romances could assume very different metrical guises. Consider the following passage from *King Horn*:

> Hit was upon a someres day,
> Also ihc you telle may,
> Muri, the gode king,
> Rod on his pleying
> Bi the se side,
> As he was woned ride.
> He fond bi the stronde
> Arived on his londe,
> Shipes fiftene,
> Wiþ Sarazins kene.   (29–38)[18]

I have deliberately withheld any scansion in order to confront readers with the difficult question raised by some Middle English romances: what kind of poetry is this? The first two lines of the passage might give the reassuring impression that we are on familiar ground:

> x / x / x / x   /
> Hit was upon a someres day
> / x /   x / x /
> Also ihc you telle may

Yet we soon run into lines such as 33 and 37 (confirmed by 137, 143, 169, etc.) that cannot possibly be scanned as iambic. There is a theory that such lines are scribal,[19] but that theory sits uneasily with the manuscript tradition,

---

[15] Cf. *Pearl*, line 1.
[16] In the above-cited passage, I suspect the poet wrote 'wo' rather than 'wo-so' in line 4.
[17] The line reads 'He was fayr man and wicth'. Did the poet write 'He was a fayr man and a wicth'?
[18] I cite the edition by Jennifer Fellows in *Of Love and Chivalry: An Anthology of Middle English Romance* (London: Dent, 1993), based on Cambridge University Library, MS Gg. 4.27(2). Variant readings from the other two manuscripts have been checked in the edition by Rosamund Allen (New York: Garland, 1984).
[19] W. H. French, *Essays on King Horn* (New York: Cornell University Press, 1940).

where none of the lines I have mentioned is contested. What *is* contested is the manuscript layout. In the Auchinleck MS the 'couplets' are actually written as single lines, while the scribe of CUL MS Gg. 4.27, who wrote predominantly in short couplets, nevertheless lapses into long lines so repeatedly (33–4, 37–8, 39–40, 85–6, 101–2, etc.) that he must have been working from an exemplar that also had the long-line arrangement.

If the poem is displayed in long lines, the metre becomes immediately recognizable as a descendant of Laȝamon's rhymed long line, with four chief beats:[20]

> Hit was upon a sómeres dáy,   also ihc you télle máy,
> Múri, the gode kíng,   ród on his pleyíng
> Bi the sé síde,   as he was wóned ríde.
> He fónd bi the strónde,   aríved on his lónde,
> Shípes fifténe,   wiþ Sárazins kéne.

In this layout, the poet's verse form also becomes comprehensible as a decent approximation to the alexandrines of his source, the Anglo-Norman *Horn*. The *chansons de geste* in this measure (and presumably *Horn* too[21]) were sung to the accompaniment of the *vielle* or harp. The English poet, too, seems to have envisaged a musical performance of his work, which he himself entitled 'Hornes song' (1530) and which begins as follows:

> Álle beon he blíthe that to my sóng lýthe
> A sáng ich schal you sínge of Múrye the kínge   (1–2)[22]

---

[20] My scansion agrees with J. Schipper, *History of English Versification* (Oxford, 1910, repr. New York: AMS Press, 1971), p. 83, though I place the beat on the second rather than the first syllable of 'fiftene'. The principles at stake here (and in the metrical treatment of the adjective 'good') are discussed in Putter, Jefferson, Stokes, *Studies*, pp. 168, 208.

[21] See John Stevens, *Words and Music in the Middle Ages* (Cambridge: Cambridge University Press, 1986), p. 248. A passage from *laisse* 137 of *Horn* may tell us more about the performance of *Horn*: 'Then he [Godmund] took the harp ... When he had played his notes, he began to raise the pitch and to make the strings give out completely different notes. Everyone was astonished at his skilful handling of it. And when he had done this, he began to sing the lay of Baltof, which I mentioned just now, loudly and clearly ... Next he made the harp strings play exactly the same melody as he had just sung. He performed the whole lay for them and did not want to omit any of it.' *The Romance of Horn*, in *The Birth of Romance: An Anthology*, trans. Judith Weiss (London: Dent, 1992), p. 66.

[22] I see no reason why such statements should not be taken at face value. Chaucer's reference to *Troilus and Criseyde* as being 'red or elles *song*' (V, 1797) is ritually cited by critics who doubt the musical (and oral) transmission of the Middle English romances (see e.g. A. C. Spearing, *Textual Subjectivity* [Cambridge: Cambridge University Press, 2005], p. 38), but Chaucer's words, too, can be taken literally: *Troilus* contains a number of lyrical insets which may well have been set to music by Chaucer himself (see C. Olson, 'Chaucer and Music of the Fourteenth Century', *Speculum* 16 (1941), 64–91 (p. 73). For less sceptical discussions see L. M. Zaerr, 'Fiddling with the Middle English Romance: Using Performance to Reconstruct the Past', *Mediaevalia* 21 (1996), 47–65, and Karl Reichl, 'Comparative Notes on the Performance of Middle English Popular Romance', *Western Folklore* 62 (2003), 63–81. The only romance for which the music has survived is *Eger and Grime* (extant in the Percy Folio and early printed editions). The early-seventeenth-century Straloch lutebook (now lost, but transcribed in 1847) gives the melody of

The Metres and Stanza Forms of Popular Romance

This musical mode of performance (further discussed in Karl Reich's chapter in this volume) might provide another reason why the poet of *King Horn* resorted to a rhymed form of the alliterative long line. The measures of the *chanson de geste* and the alliterative epic were both intended for musical performance, and it seems likely that (in Jakob Schipper's words) *Horn* was 'recited like the "Song" of Beowulf – probably not without a proper musical accompaniment – by the minstrels'.[23]

The *Tristrem* stanza: bobs and wheels

To the modern ear, the rhythms of *Sir Tristrem* may sound even more outlandish than those of *King Horn*. Although the source of *Sir Tristrem*, Thomas's Anglo-Norman *Tristan*, is in octosyllabic couplets, the English poet opted for an unusual stanzaic arrangement. The romance (extant only in the Auchinleck manuscript), begins as follows:

> I was at Ertheldoun
> With Thomas spak Y thare;
> Ther herd Y rede in roun
> Who Tristrem gat and bare,
> Who was king with croun,
> And who him fosterd yare,
> And who was bold baroun,
> As thair elders ware.
> Bi yere
> Tomas telles in toune
> This aventours as thai ware.
>
> This semly somers day,
> In winter it is nought sen;
> This greves wexen al gray,
> That in her time were grene.
> So dos this world, I say,
> Ywis and noght at wene,
> The gode ben al oway
> That oure elders have bene.
> To abide,
> Of a knight is that Y mene,
> His name it sprong wel wide.   (1–22)[24]

'Greysteel' (presumably *Eger and Grime*). See J. Purser, 'Greysteil', in *Stewart Style, 1513–1542: Essays on the Court of James V*, ed. J. Hadley Williams (East Linton: Tuckwell Press, 1996), pp. 143–52.

[23] Schipper, *History*, p. 83. See also the interesting remarks by Rosamund Allen (citing John Stevens) concerning likely musical performance and the function which the manuscript paraphs and initials may have played in it: *King Horn*, p. 106.

[24] *Lancelot of the Laik and Sir Tristrem*, ed. Alan Lupack, TEAMS (Kalamazoo, MI: Medieval Institute Publications, 1994).

The poet says he has learned the story from the legendary poet Thomas of Erceldoun, who recites the history in public, *in toune*, year on year. Thanks to poets, then, there are some things that do not change, but others do. Seasons come and go, and our noble ancestors have vanished. And it is to make them last (*To abide*) that the poet, following Thomas, proposes to commemorate (*menen* = 'recount' and 'remember') one such ancestor (Rohand, Tristrem's father).

The poet's stanza form consists of an octave in alternating rhyme, followed by a bob and wheel consisting of two further three-stress lines. The bob (a short line with a single beat) invariably initiates a new rhyme sound that is echoed in the last line of the stanza; the penultimate verse rhymes with either of the octave lines. In short, the verse form is $a^3b^3a^3b^3a^3b^3a^3b^3\ c^1a^3/b^3c^3$.[25] Regrettably, the form has been spoiled by scribal error at line 11, where *ware* needs emending to *were*.[26]

The arresting effect of the bob is striking and also impressed Chaucer. In *Sir Thopas*, his parody of the popular romances, he plants the occasional bob in his tail-rhyme stanzas, as if it were a joker in the pack:

> An elf queene wol I love, ywis,
> For in this world no woman is
>   Worthy to be my make
>   In towne;
> All othere women I forsake,
> And to an elf-queene I me take
>   By dale and eek by downe!   (*Sir Thopas*, 791–6)[27]

What Chaucer heard was the bob's rhythmical irregularity (exaggerated in *Sir Thopas* by the unpredictability of its occurrence). Many other poets, including the author of *Sir Gawain and the Green Knight*, heard something else: the bob struck them as an excellent way of putting the brakes on the stanza and of making audible its approaching end. It is to this end that the bob, as well as reining in the stanza, breaks up the preceding rhymes and rhythm,[28] and that the stanza's final word always rhymes with the bob.[29] The bob is the aural promise of the end, the stanza's final rhyme its fulfilment.

---

[25] Superscript numerals denote the number of beats (in English verse) or the number of syllables (in French and Latin verse).

[26] The only other stanza where the last line does not rhyme with the bob is at 145–54: 'Al cladde / The knightes that wer fade, / Thai dede as Rohand bade.' Here b*a*de should be corrected to b*a*dde.

[27] *Riverside Chaucer*.

[28] This rhythmical *volte face* is especially marked in alliterative poetry, where the bob effects the transition from strong stress rhythm to alternating rhythm.

[29] Although stanzas with wheels (with or without bobs) are various, this general rule applies to almost all lyric verse (see the catalogue of examples in E. G. Stanley, 'The Use of Bob-Lines in *Sir Thopas*', *Neuphilologische Mitteilungen* 74 (1972), 417–26) and to all romances with wheels: *Golagros and Gawain*, *Rauf Coilyear* and *Awntyrs off Arthure* (ababababab cdddc), *The Turnament of Tottenham* (aaaa bcccb).

What can the stanza form tell us about *Sir Tristrem*? First of all, it supports the view that the romance is Northern English (Yorkshire?) rather than Scottish,[30] for it is in the North and the North-Midland regions of England that we find the only comparable examples of this stanza form. Roughly contemporary with *Sir Tristrem* is another poem in the Auchinleck MS, the *Alphabetical Praise of Women*, which uses a similar stanza form ($a^4b^4a^4b^4a^4b^4a^4b^4$ $c^1d^4c^3$).[31] It is also found in the Towneley Play of the Crucifixion, where Mary's *planctus* inspired a variation ($a^4b^3a^4b^3a^4b^3a^4b^3$ $c^1a^3c^3$) of the form:

> Alas, dede, thou dwellys to lang!
> Whi art thou hid fro me?
> Who kend the to my child to gang?
> All blak thou makys his ble;
> Now witterly thou wyrkys wrang.
> The more I will wyte the,
> Bot if thou will my hartë stang
> That I myght with him dee,
>   And byde.
> Sorë syghyng is my sang
> For thyrlyd is his hyde.   (XXIII, 461–71)[32]

The example should disabuse us of the notion that the bob is inherently comic.

A final parallel, which is also instructive for what it tells us about sudden changes in metre, is provided by Lawrence Minot's poems. Minot was a Yorkshireman who saw active service in Edward III's army. His poem on The Siege of Tournay (no. 8) starts off in octaves ($a^3b^3a^3b^3$ $a^3b^3a^3b^3$) which gleefully predict destruction for Tournay. This city had been besieged by Edward III in 1340, but when Edward III's ally, the Duke of Brabant, defected (allegedly after being bribed by Philippe de Valois), Edward abandoned the siege and Minot was forced to revise his poem. To his last octave (49–56) he added a bob-and-wheel (italicized below); as a result the poem switches mid-flow to the *Tristrem* stanza (with which the rest of the poem continues):

On bere when ȝe er broght, (deathbed)
    Þan cumes Philip to late
He hetes, and haldes ȝow noght (He keeps none of his promises to you)
    With hert ȝe may him hate.
A bare now has him soght (boar = Edward III)
    Till Turnay þe right gate. (the most direct way)

---

[30] See A. McIntosh, 'Is *Sir Tristrem* an English or a Scottish Poem', in *In Other Words: Transcultural Studies in Philology, Translation and Lexicology Presented to Hans Heinrich Meier*, ed. J. Lachlan Mackenzie and Richard Todd (Dordrecht: Foris, 1989), pp. 85–95.

[31] The poem was edited as *Lob der Frauen* by E. Kölbing, 'Kleine Publicationen aus der Auchinleck-Handschrift', *Englische Studien* 7 (1884), 101–25.

[32] *The Towneley Plays*, ed. Martin Stevens and A. C. Cawley, 2 vols, EETS SS 14 (Oxford: Oxford University Press, 1994). The *Tristrem* stanza commences at stanza 62 and finishes at stanza 69, at which point Christ commands his mother to cease her sorrow. The metre obeys.

Þat es ful wele bithoght
    To stop Philip þe strate.   (To block Phillipe de Valois's way)
        Full still.   (by stealth)
Philip was fain he moght
    Graunt sir Edward his will.

If ȝe will trow my tale,
    A duke tuk leue þat tide,
A Braban brwed þat bale,   (A man from Brabant caused that trouble)
    He bad no langer bide;   (He did not propose to say any longer)
Giftes gret and smale
    War sent him on his side;
Gold gert all þat gale   (Gold caused all harm)
    And made him rapely ride (quickly)
        Till dede: (to his damnation)
In hert he was unhale;   (dishonest)
    He come þare moste for mede. (49–70)[33] (for personal gain)

As Joseph Hall suggested (p. 65), lines 57–70 must have been added by Minot after the siege was called off. Hall drew attention to the 'awkward transition' in tense (from present to past) in lines 57–9, but the shift in metre is even more remarkable: the poem's metre is the barometer of the unexpected downturn that forced Minot to change his tune (in both senses of the word). In the case of the popular romances, too, metrical changes tend to be symptoms of changes in other domains.[34] Thus the pietistic turn of *Guy of Warwick* after the hero's marriage to Felice is registered in the Auchinleck version by the abrupt change (at line 7306) from couplets to tail-rhyme.[35] In the Fillingham *Otuel and Roland*,[36] the sudden shift (at line 1697) from a rare type of tail-rhyme stanza (aabaabccbddb) to the standard variety (aabccbddbeeb) coincides with the beginning of a new episode in the hero's life that is unparalleled in the source (the *chanson Otinel*).[37] Either the poet has changed metrical gear to signal the digression or the text is a composite of two originally distinct romances.

The analogues for the *Tristrem* stanza in Middle English poetry suggest that the stanza form was lyrical in origin. The *Alphabetical Praise of Women* and Minot's poems are both thought (by their editors) to have been songs; and the use of the form for Mary's lament is consistent with this. Its use in *Sir Tristrem* might thus suggest a musical performance. The romance itself, too, depicts a world where stories are performed by harpers (551–9) and are

---

[33] *The Poems of Laurence Minot*, ed. Joseph Hall (Oxford, 1897).
[34] Changes in verse form are not always explicable, however. *Beues of Hamtoun*, ed. E. Kölbing, EETS ES 46, 48, 65 (London, 1885–94) changes from tail-rhyme to couplets but the editor cannot find a reason for it (see p. xi).
[35] J. Zupitza (ed.), EETS ES 42, 49, 59 (London, 1883–91).
[36] M. I. O. Sullivan (ed.), EETS OS 198 (London: Oxford University Press, 1935).
[37] I owe this point to an unpublished paper by Phillipa Hardman, 'The English Charlemagne Romances – Ineptitude or Experimentation', presented at the Centre for Medieval Studies, University of Bristol, 27 April 2006.

passed down orally (from Thomas to the narrator (1–11) and from Tristan to Ysonde, along with the appropriate melodies (1283–5)).[38]

The tail-rhyme stanza

The form most closely associated with the popular romances is the tail-rhyme stanza. The most common varieties are the six-line stanza ($a^4a^4b^3c^4c^4b^3$) and the twelve-line form ($a^4a^4b^3c^4c^4b^3d^4d^4b^3c^4c^4b^3$) first found in *Amis and Amiloun*. Why did the English poet choose the tail-rhyme stanza when his source was in octosyllabic couplets? What did the form mean and what were its possibilities?

An inquiry into the historical uses of the tail-rhyme stanza may help to answer these questions.[39] Two different theories concerning the origin of the tail-rhyme stanza deserve attention. One theory is that the stanza developed out of the liturgical sequence (originally a text set to the melody of the Alleluia). Certainly, no great leap of imagination is needed to see similarities between the tail-rhyme stanza and a sequence such as the following (from the rhymed office of the popular hero 'St' Thomas of Lancaster, executed by Edward II in 1322):

> O iam Christi pietas
> atque Thome caritas
>   palam elucessit.
> Heu! nunc languet equitas
> viget et impietas,
>   veritas vilessit.
>
> Nempne Thome bonitas
> eius atque sanctitas
>   indies acressit,
> Ad cuius tumbam sospitas
> egris datur, ut veritas
>   cunctis nunc claressit.
>
> [The loving kindness of Christ / and the charity of Thomas / have now shone forth. / Yet, alas, it is in these same times that

---

[38] Robert Mannyng of Brunne's *Chronicle*, ed. Idelle Sullens (Binghamton: Binghamton University, 1996), lines 93–102, shows us that this world of oral transmission was not a figment of the *Tristrem* poet's imagination. Mannyng tells us that he knows Erceldoun's *Tristrem* 'in song, in sedgeyng tale' [a story delivered by an entertainer] (93); that, although the romance is a gem, the stanza form is too complicated for ordinary people who now tell the story (and spoil it by missing things out).

[39] The following paragraphs are much indebted to Caroline Strong, 'History and Relations of the Tail-Rhyme Strophe in Latin, French, and English', *Proceedings of the Modern Language Association* 22 (1907), 371–420. The book-length study of the Middle English tail-rhyme romances by Rhiannon Purdie, *Anglicising Romance: Tail-Rhyme and Genre in Medieval English Literature* (Cambridge: D. S. Brewer, 2008), appeared after this chapter was written.

justice languishes, / irreligion flourishes, / and truth is held in low esteem. /
Even so, it is a sure fact that the goodness / and saintly stature of Thomas / grow day by day, / for such succour attends the sick / who visit his tomb that the truth / shall now be revealed to all.][40]

If the two strophes are coupled together (according to syntax and rhyme), we end up with a twelve-line tail-rhyme poem ($a^7a^7b^6a^7a^7b^6a^7a^7b^6a^7a^7b^6$).[41] In some sequences, the tail-verse is a refrain line (as it was originally, according to Schipper [42]). Only two English translations of Latin sequences survive with music: the stanzas in these poems are six-line units, each with its own melodic line.[43]

A different theory concerning the origin of the tail-line stanza is that it developed from the septenary. This form goes back to medieval Latin song, but is already found in English in the twelfth century:

Íc am élder þánne ic wés, / a wíntre and éc a lóre (*Moral Ode*, 1)[44]

(I am older than I was in winters and also in wisdom)

The a-verse has four beats, the b-verse has three; each whole line rhymes with the next. If we were to double the a-verse, we would end up with a tail-rhyme stanza ($a^4a^4b^3c^4c^4b^3$).

Both theories concerning the history of tail-rhyme are credible, and perhaps we need both to explain its rise. It is at any rate clear that the tail-rhyme stanza, too, was originally a lyric form that was later adopted for narrative purposes. The first narrative examples are in French, *De Marcoul et de Salemon* ($a^6a^6b^5c^6c^6b^5$), where the tail verse is a refrain line, and Beneit's *Life of St Thomas* ($a^8a^8b^6a^8a^8b^6$).[45] Its early use in Anglo-Norman saints' lives[46] soon encouraged its adoption by Middle English hagiographers. Once

---

[40] Text and translation by Christopher Page, 'Secular Music', in *The Cambridge Guide to the Arts in Britain*, ed. Boris Ford (Cambridge: Cambridge University Press, 1988), pp. 235–51 (p. 245). As Page points out, 'many liturgical poems now preserved in the bulky missals and antiphonals of medieval England may yet provide a clue to the lost narrative music of the minstrels' (p. 245).

[41] In Latin and French verse, numbers represent syllables rather than beats.

[42] Schipper, *History*, p. 296.

[43] As noted by Reichl, 'Comparative Notes', their music cannot provide a model for the singing of Middle English romances since their rhythmical form, $a^4a^4b^4a^4a^4b^4$, is incompatible. However, the opening stanza of the Anglo-Norman song *Eyns ne say ke pleinte fu* and its Middle English translation *Ar ne kuthe ich sorghë non*, provide a perfect fit for the Middle English tail-rhyme stanza ($a^4a^4b^3a^4a^4b^3$), and Christopher Page has used the surviving music in performances of Middle English tail-rhyme romance (personal communication). For text and music of this poem and the Middle English sequences see *Medieval English Songs*, ed. E. J. Dobson and F. Ll. Harrison (London: Faber, 1979).

[44] Cited by Schipper, *History*, p. 193.

[45] Strong, 'Tail-Rhyme Strophe', p. 388.

[46] To Strong's examples may be added *The Life of Mary Magdalene*, no. 578 in Ruth Dean, with

that had happened, it predictably spread to the pious romances of secular heroes.

This brief history of the form illuminates the nature of the Middle English tail-rhyme romances in a number of ways. First of all, the origin of tail-rhyme in *song* remains relevant in some later narrative incarnations. As Caroline Strong has argued, one reason for its popularity in Middle English romances is that the form lent itself to public recitation, which is precisely the mode of dissemination that their poets envisaged. A few opening addresses suggest a musical rendition:

> Lordinges, herkneþ to me tale
> Is merier þan þe niȝtingale,
>   Þat y schel singe. (*Beues of Hamtoun*, 1–3; cf. *Emaré*, 24)

In this example, a sung performance is implied not just by the word 'sing' but also by the comparison of the story with the nightingale. Pious legends in tail-rhyme contain similar 'minstrel addresses', which are generally absent in the couplet narratives.[47] The obvious conclusion, that tail-rhyme was a minstrels' favourite, is confirmed by Robert Mannyng of Brunne, who in his early-fourteenth-century *Chronicle* (in rhyming couplets) tells us he has avoided *ryme cowee* (tail-rhyme verse) since 'I mad noght for no disours [entertainers], / ne for no seggers [reciters], no harpours, / bot for þe luf of symple men / Þat strange Inglis not ken [know]' (75–8). 'Strange English' includes the Anglo-Norman inspired tail-rhyme form, still known in the period by its Anglo-Norman name *rime couée*.

The direct line of descent from saints' lives to tail-rhyme romances also gives food for thought, and explains the close thematic connections between the two genres. As many critics have pointed out, it is sometimes difficult to distinguish saints' lives from the 'secular hagiography' of romance,[48] and medieval writers did not usually bother: they were as happy to call a saint's life a 'romance' as to call a romance a *vita*.[49] The romance of *Sir Isumbras*, for example, borrows many motifs from the earlier *Life of St Eustace* (extant in tail-rhyme in both English and Anglo-Norman).[50] The piety of the Middle

---

    Maureen Bolton, *Anglo-Norman Literature: A Guide to Texts and Manuscripts* (London: Anglo-Norman Text Society, 1999).

[47] Caroline Strong provides some revealing statistics: 'Of the forty-nine [legends] in couplets or quatrains, printed by Horstmann [*Altenglische Legenden* (Heilbronn: Henninger, 1881)], only four have such an opening, while not one of the seven in tail-rhyme is without it' (p. 408).

[48] I take the term from Ojars Kratins, 'The Middle English *Amis and Amiloun*: Chivalric Romance or Secular Hagiography?', *Publications of the Modern Languages Association* 81 (1966), 347–54.

[49] *Amis and Amiloun* and *Sir Gowther* are both referred to as *vitae* in manuscript rubrics, and *vice versa* the verb 'romancen' is applied to the *Life of Gregory* (Oxford, Bodleian Library, MS English Poet a. 1, known as the Vernon MS, line 19) and the *Meditations on the Life & Passions of Christ*, line 1697.

[50] Both the Anglo-Norman and the English life are edited by E. Stengel, *Codicem Manuscriptum Digby 86* (Halle, 1871).

English romances is inseparable from the tail-rhyme form. That is why Guy of Warwick's conversion to a life of penance is accompanied by the change from couplets to tail-rhyme.

We also need an awareness of the evolutionary history of the tail-rhyme stanza to appreciate how and why poets exploited the form. I would like to discuss a typical example from *Amis and Amiloun*. Amiloun has become a leper; he is cared for by his faithful servant Amoraunt, who wheels him around in a pushcart:

> Than Amoraunt crud Sir Amiloun (wheeled)
> Thurch mani a cuntre, up and doun,
>   As ye may understond.
> So he com to a cite toun,
> Ther Sir Amis, the bold baroun,
>   Was douke and lord in lond.
> Than seide the knight, in that tide,
> 'To the doukes court, here biside,
>   To bring me thider thou fond.
> He is a man of milde mode;
> We shal gete ous ther sum gode,
>   Thurgh grace of Godes sond.'   (1861–72)[51]

The typical structure of the tail-rhyme stanza is clearly shown here – as is the way that structure conditions expression. In terms of both metre and sense, the twelve lines naturally divide into four 'panels'[52] – each of which is a complete unit of sense (hence the editorial full stops after 1863, 1866, 1869, 1872). Each of the four panels, too, divides into a couplet and a tail-line, of which the former is generally devoted to 'action' and the latter to reflection or elaboration. Since the tail-lines pause, the first of the couplet lines appropriately begin by signalling the resumption of the story (*Than, So, Than*).

Put pejoratively, the tail-lines are often redundant tags: we can omit them without losing track of the 'story'. A more considered way of putting the matter is that the tail-line is generally the place *outside the story* where poets can address the audience ('As ye may understand'[53]), make pious exclamations ('Iblesced mot he be!', 1836) and express Christian sentiment ('Thurgh grace of Goddes sond', repeated at 222, 2397).[54] It is also the place where poets stand back from the story to express moral approval or disapproval ('Wel ivel mot sche thrive!', 1752) or reflect on its pathos ('Gret doil it

---

[51] Fellows (ed.), *Of Love and Chivalry*.
[52] I take the term from Urs Dürmüller, *Narrative Possibilities of the Tail-Rhyme Romance* (Bern: Francke Verlag, 1974), p. 29.
[53] This is not as inane in Middle English as it sounds in Modern English: the sense is 'as you may believe with confidence'.
[54] Roger Dalrymple provides an exhaustive catalogue of pious formulae in *Language and Piety in Middle English Romance* (Cambridge: D. S. Brewer, 2000). Most of them can be found in tail-verses.

was to se!', 1884). Once we take into account the history of the tail-rhyme stanza and the metrical form of the poets' sources, this 'redundancy' of the tail-line can be understood more sympathetically. Because tail-rhyme poets were often adapting Anglo-Norman sources in couplets, they were naturally inclined to pause in the tail-line: the French couplets could be transposed into English ones if they played a waiting game in the tail-verse. The point is that the stanza form (which was originally lyrical) made this entirely appropriate. Indeed, from a historical perspective, what is odd about the tail-rhyme romances is their use of the metre for narrative ends, not the emotive, evaluative or 'phatic' content of the tail lines themselves.[55] No-one in his right mind would think of dismissing a tail-verse like 'Alleluia' in a Latin sequence as a 'redundant tag',[56] for in this setting we are conscious that the function of the verse is not just 'to tell a story' but to include in the speech act an entire community (who know the refrain, just as the audience of the romances know the formulae of the tail-verse). This is all the more true of *song*, where any emptiness of the words is immediately filled by the music. The tail-rhyme stanza of the popular romances retains some of this lyrical and liturgical potency, and it might be considered a *virtue* of its narrative redundancy that it foregrounds the sound world and re-orientates the speaker towards his audience (*qua* listeners, fellow-feelers and fellow-believers).

The possible influence of the septenary on the tail-rhyme stanza is also relevant, however. The poem that makes the issue pertinent to the genre of popular romance is the Ashmole *Sir Ferumbras*, an adaptation of the Old French *chanson de geste Fierabras*. From a metrical perspective, the most interesting moment in *Sir Ferumbras* occurs just after Roland and his French compatriots have captured the Saracen leader Aspayllard in a daring *sortie* and return safe and sound to the castle, where the princess Floripas is waiting:

```
        x  /  x  /      x   / x  /    x  /   x  /     x    /
        Þe ȝeatë þanne þay made faste; þe draȝtbrigge vp droȝ she.
        x  /    x   x  / x   /  x /   x    x  / x  / x /
        Þe Saraȝyns þay habbeþ sore agaste; and þay buþ in sauëte.
        x    /    x   /  x   (/) x /   x /   x / x / x /
        Now buþ þus barouns of honour ycome aȝen into þe tour;
                       x /    x   / x  / x
                       Flo[rippe] þay gunnë callë
        x  /   x      / x / x  /  x    /      x  /  x  x  / x   /
        To hure þay by-toke Aspaylard, and prayed hure kep him in syker warde
                  x   /   x   /  x   / x
                  For þing þat myght be-fallë.   (3409–14)[57]
```

---

[55] The term 'phatic' denotes uses of language for no other purpose than that of affirming community, as in 'As y you tel may' (1839).

[56] The example is not hypothetical. See J. Schipper, *History*, p. 296.

[57] *Sir Ferumbras*, ed. Sidney J. Herrtage, EETS ES 34 (London, 1889). I have represented the *punctus elevatus* by a semi-colon. The scansion of 'by-tok' (/x) is counter-intuitive to modern English speakers but there is good evidence that prefixes could take the beat. See Hoyt Duggan,

Line 3411 begins a new section (coinciding with a new *laisse* in the source), marked palaeographically by a large capital *N* and verbally by the recapitulation of the situation. Before that break the poet has matched the alexandrines of his source with septenaries. To make these septenaries look more familiar, it might help to set them out as quatrains:

>Þe ȝeate þanne þay made faste
>>þe draȝtbrigge vp droȝ she.
>
>Þe Saraȝyns þay habbeþ sore agaste,
>>and þay buþ in sauete.

The rhythms are basically those of the ballad stanza, with three-stress verses following four-stress ones.

The poet's metre in his new section also morphs into something much more familiar once it is realized that the short lines (3412, 1414), again three-beat lines following four-beat couplets, are actually the tail-verses of a tail-rhyme stanza. This is clearly reflected in the manuscript, where the verses are laid out in the manner characteristic of tail-rhyme romances:

>Now buþ þus barouns of honour
>>ycome aȝen into þe tour;   } Flo[rippe] þay gunne calle
>
>To hure þay by-toke Aspaylard,
>>and prayed hure kep him in syker warde } For þing þat myght be-falle

This lay-out was so strongly associated with the tail-rhyme strophe that it is imitated in the best texts of Chaucer's *Sir Thopas*. As Rhiannon Purdie writes, the early manuscripts 'exaggerate and glory in the characteristically lop-sided pattern of the tail-rhyme stanza, somewhat at the expense of readability'.[58] Purdie's criticism of the 'awkwardness' of the manuscript layout should be balanced by an appreciation that it enhances the 'readability' of the versification. Not only does it make visible the rhyme scheme, it also brings out the connection between the septenary and the tail-rhyme stanza. If (as many scholars believe) the latter arose by the doubling of the a-verse in the former, then the characteristic tail-rhyme layout (in which the tail-line is represented as the complement of both couplet lines) becomes entirely rational. The metrical change in *Sir Ferumbras* from septenary to tail-rhyme is also much less disruptive than might at first appear: the poet may well have thought of the latter as a variation on the former.

'Stress Assignment in Middle English Alliterative Poetry', *Journal of English and Germanic Philology* 89 (1990), 309–29. 'Saracens' is normally disyllabic in the poet's usage, as indicated by the spellings 'Sarȝyns' and 'Sarsyns' (3042, 3052).

[58] Rhiannon Purdie, 'The Implications of Manuscript Layout in Chaucer's *Tale of Sir Thopas*', *Forum for Modern Language Studies* 41 (2005), 263–74.

Standards of metrical correctness: rhythm and rhyme

Many romances survive in such garbled form that it is easy to gain the impression of laxity in rhyme and metre. Without access to a reliable text it is difficult to be sure whether this impression is due to the poet or that of his scribes. This makes *Sir Ferumbras* valuable for yet another reason. Not only is the poem an autograph, but a section of the poet's original draft (with his own corrections) has accidentally survived on a loose sheet that was used in the book's cover. This puts us in a unique position to study the poet's metrical intentions. If we compare his draft with his final version it becomes clear that rhyme and metre mattered to him. As we have seen already, his septenaries rhyme with each other both at line ending and in the middle (before the caesura). Many (though not all) of the poet's changes to his earlier draft edit out or tidy up false medial rhymes (e.g. helm/wel, 294–5, Berard/doȝepers, 422–3, sore/were, 633–4) and final rhymes (e.g. botel/del, 511–12, stonde/sounde, 518–19). Small changes of spelling, too, reveal his desire to improve rhymes (e.g. 'Olyuere' for 'Olyuer' at 500–1, 'Rolandre' for 'Roland' at 524–5, 'felde' for 'fyld' at 532–3). The poet also tried for the most part to smooth the rhythm of his verse (see e.g. 388, 608, 638), though he was obviously not the kind of poet who found this easy. At line 380, he needed three attempts to get it right. Below are his first draft, his corrected draft, and his final version:

> And hast mad þy avy wiþ xij men for to fiȝte[59]
>
> & now hast mad þy avy wiþ xij men for to fiȝte
>
> & hast also y-mad envy; wiþ christene men to fiȝte (done a hostile deed)

It is easy to see why the poet was not satisfied with his first attempt: it is hard to find four beats in the a-verse. The addition of 'now' in the second attempt improves at least the run-up ('& nów hast mád / þy avý') though the only way of reading the verse with four beats is to accent the possessive pronoun and impose a caesura between the clashing stresses. At the third attempt the poet avoids any awkwardness by making good use of a metrical doublet (mad/y-mad).

Having said all this, the poet was evidently not as careful a prosodist as Chaucer, let alone Gower. Double off-beats are common, and the poet tolerated clashing stress in the a-verse. When the syntax demands a pause between the adjacent stresses, this does not create problems:

> Ac hé ys a mán / héȝ of mód   (417a)
> Térry is sóne / dúk Berárd   (422a)

---

[59] Presumably *avy* = *anvy* ('envy, hostile act').

But on occasion the poet is happy to ignore the flow of syntax:

> Fýrumbrás ís my náme   (362a)
> Wíþ my swérd þát is hére   (431a)

There may be those who like this roughness and think it less artificial than the controlled verse of Chaucer or Gower; others may think that nothing could be *more* artificial than the accentuation demanded by a-verses such as 362 and 431, and that the point of controlled verse is not to create artificiality but to protect us from it.

With regard to rhyme, too, the poet was less exacting than Chaucer and Gower, but it would be unfair to construe this as incompetence. Examples of so-called 'imperfect rhymes' are so numerous both in *Ferumbras* (e.g. men/hem, 458–9, non/hom, 637–9, helm/herm, 460–1, stroke/hot, 578–9) and in other popular romances that they may not have struck listeners as 'imperfect' at all.[60] On closer inspection these rhymes turn out to be rule governed: they are based on assonance reinforced by the final consonants, which belong to the same phonetic category, for example, nasals (m/n), liquids (l/r) or plosives (k/t).[61] Because of these correspondences, such imperfect rhymes *sound* perfectly acceptable to the ear, as their persistence in oral verse (ballads, nursery rhymes, and so on) confirms.

It is only in the age of print that assonantal rhymes became intolerable. For example in *Sir Eglamour*, composed consistently in the tail-rhyme stanza, all four medieval manuscripts acquiesce in imperfect rhymes (e.g. ane/fame or oon/fome, 25–6), while all the printed editions 'correct' the rhyme (to ane/bane or one/bone). Such corrections occur so consistently (e.g. 685–6, 923–4) that we can speak of a conscious editorial policy. The explanation for it is that by the sixteenth century the printed romances were mainly being marketed for a *reading* public rather than groups of *listeners*. The imperfect rhymes that had satisfied the ear offended the eye and were therefore revised out of existence. The tendency in the early printed romances to make rhymes *look* perfect by manipulating accidentals of spelling is another symptom of this new tyranny of the eye. The printed *Lyfe of Ipomydon* is a perfect source of evidence in this regard, for we know that the printer (Wynkyn de Worde) used the surviving manuscript version (British Library, MS Harley 2252) as his copy-text.[62] The most obvious rationale behind minute adjustments in

---

[60] For examples in *Horn* see E. G. Stanley, 'Rhymes in English Medieval Verse: From Old English to Middle English', in *Medieval Studies Presented to George Kane*, ed. E. D. Kennedy, R. Waldron and J. S. Wittig (Cambridge: D. S. Brewer, 1988), pp. 19–54. It is worth citing Stanley's conclusion: 'while recognising that Chaucer, a great poet, is an accurate rhymer, unusually so among Middle English poets, it is not necessary for a poet to rhyme accurately to be a good poet' (p. 54).

[61] Smithers posits 'at least ten classes of assonance that are based on phonetic affinity' (*Havelok*, p. lxxxiii).

[62] See Carol Meale, 'Wynkyn de Worde's Setting-Copy for *Ipomydon*', *Studies in Bibliography* 35 (1982), 162–73.

spelling (e.g. <y> for <i>, <ou> for <o>, omission or addition of final –*e*) was the desire to create rhymes to please eyes as well as ears.[63]

Before I conclude I would like to mention three verse forms I cannot discuss in detail; I should say this is due to lack of space rather than of interest, since each has its own charms and each poses problems that require further research. The *Stanzaic Morte* exhibits an eight-line stanza ($a^4b^4a^4b^4a^4b^4a^4b^4$) whose lineage is far from certain. Is it a popular 'favourite', as W. P. Ker thought,[64] or is it, as has recently been claimed, 'unique in both French and English ... "technically a marriage between the continuous octosyllabic couplets of French romance and the stanzas of lyrical poetry"'?[65] I think the first description is closer to the mark, for, although the form is indeed lyrical in origin, various political songs offer earlier narrative adaptations.[66] Especially interesting are the concatenating[67] stanzas of Laurence Minot's narrative about Edward III's campaign in Normandy. In modern editions, this poem (no. 7) numbers 172 lines, so one can see why Minot repeatedly called it a 'romance'.[68] And it would be 96 lines longer if editors had not decided that the next poem (no. 8, on Edward's siege of Calais) was a different poem. In fact, these two are one, for the concatenation links the last stanza of poem 7 with the first of poem 8. The octave had a special vogue in the literature of prophecy. It is found in the prologue to *Thomas of Erceldoune*, in *Als Y Yod on a Monday*, and in the Metrical Version of the *Revelations of Methodius*. Its use in the Stanzaic *Morte* is therefore neither as innovative nor as courtly as some critics have claimed. Much more remarkable than its stanza form is its highly focused use of concatenation. The poet systematically interlinked the moving (and apparently original[69]) stanzas that tell of the final meeting

---

[63] See the list of differences in spellings in *The Lyfe of Ipomydon*, ed. T. Ikegami (Tokyo: Seijo University, 1985), 2 vols, II, pp. liv–lvi.

[64] W. P. Ker, 'Metrical Romances, 1200–1500', in *The Cambridge History of English Literature*, ed. E. A Ward and A. R. Waller, 14 vols (Cambridge: Cambridge University Press, 1907–16), I, pp. 308–34.

[65] Carole Weinberg, 'The Stanzaic *Morte Arthure*', in *The Arthur of the English*, ed. W. R. J. Barron (Cardiff: University of Wales Press, 1999), pp. 100–11 (p. 101), citing S. E. Knopp, 'Artistic Design in the Stanzaic *Morte Arthure*', *English Literary History* 45 (1978), 563–82 (p. 567).

[66] See the brief history of the stanza form provided by Alfred Jeanroy, *Les origins de la poésie lyrique en France au moyen âge* (Paris: Champion, 1904), pp. 377–86. English and Anglo-Norman poems in the form may be found in *The Political Songs of England*, ed. Thomas Wright (London: Camden Society, 1839; repr. Hildesheim: Georg Olms, 1968), including the English 'Song on the Times' (pp. 195–205).

[67] 'Concatenation' is the interlinking of stanzas by the repetition of one or more words from the last line(s) of a stanza in the first line(s) of the next.

[68] *Poems of Laurence Minot*, ed. Joseph Hall. The poems have the same numbers in the most recent edition by Richard Osberg, *The Poems of Laurence Minot, 1333–1352*, TEAMS (Kalamazoo, MI: Medieval Institute Publications, 1996). Hoops, in *Der Begriff 'Romance'*, plausibly infers from Minot's use of the term *romance* that his poems 'are like short romances, or more precisely, they represent the transition from romances to ballads' (p. 55; my translation).

[69] No such parting scene appears in the Vulgate Cycle, except in a later interpolation in a unique manuscript of the French *Mort Artu*. The Stanzaic *Morte* may (but need not) have known a similar version. See Edward Donald Kennedy, 'The Stanzaic *Morte Arthur*: The Adaptation of a French Romance for an English Audience', in *Culture and the King: The Social Implications of the*

of Lancelot and Guinevere to heighten the drama of their last moments of togetherness.[70]

A romance in which concatenation occurs systematically is *Sir Percyvell of Gales*,[71] which is in a sixteen-line tail-line stanza (aaabcccbdddbeeeb). This stanza form, too, raises questions. How did it develop? Where else is it used? I can only suggest some partial answers. In medieval romance, the strophe is also found in *Sir Degrevaunt* and *The Avowing of Arthur*; later in the sixteenth century it is employed in various comic tales.[72] An obvious theory of its origin is that it arose as an elaboration of the twelve-line tail-rhyme stanza, but the relationship between the two is far from straightforward. Rhythmically, the three medieval romances in the sixteen-line tail-rhyme stanza seem to me closer to the alliterative measure rather than the alternating rhythm of the shorter tail-rhyme romances.[73] All three romances share an unusually high amount of concatenation, which again connects them with rhymed alliterative poems (such as the *Awntyrs off Arthure*).[74]

The metre of these rhymed alliterative romances, which I have mentioned only *en passant*,[75] also merits further investigation, especially in the light of recent discoveries about the metre of unrhymed alliterative verse. While it used to be thought that all that mattered in alliterative verse is number of beats and alliteration, there is a growing realization that poets in the unrhymed tradition also observed rules concerning the number and distribution of unstressed syllables. This raises the obvious question of which (if any) of these newly discovered rules apply to poems in the rhymed tradition. Although there have been a few forays into this territory,[76] these questions are largely unanswered.

These alternative metres, the *abababab* stanza, the sixteen-line tail-rhyme stanza, and the rhymed alliterative tradition, add further variation to the

---

Arthurian Legend, ed. Martin B. Schichtman and James P. Carley (New York: SUNY, 1994), pp. 91–112.

[70] See S. J. Jaech, 'The Parting of Lancelot and Gaynor: The Effect of Repetition in the Stanzaic Morte Darthur', *Interpretations* 15 (1984), 59–69.

[71] The few exceptions are probably due to scribal error. For a different view, see D. Carling and V. J. Scattergood, 'One Aspect of Stanza-Linking', *Neuphilologische Mitteilungen* 75 (1974), 79–91.

[72] See e.g. the retelling of Chaucer's 'Miller Tale', *The Miller of Abington*, printed by Richard Jones (London, 1575), repr. Chadwyck-Healey, *English Literature On-Line* (1992). The brief introduction to the tale (in couplets) is evidently a later addition.

[73] It has been argued, plausibly in my view, that its triplets and tail verses correspond rhythmically to alliterative a-verses and b-verses respectively. See Franz Finsterbuch, *Der Versbau der mittelenglischen Dichtungen Sir Perceval of Gales und Sir Degrevant* (Vienna: Wilhelm Braumüller, 1919).

[74] See Margaret P. Medary, 'Stanza-Linking in Middle English Verse', *The Romanic Review* 7 (1916), 243–70.

[75] See above.

[76] See R. Kennedy, 'New Theories of Constraint in the Metricality of the Strong-Stress Long Line, Applied to the English Rhymed Alliterative Corpus, c. 1400', in *Métriques du Moyen Age et de la Renaissance*, ed. Dominique Billy (Paris: l'Harmattan, 1999), pp. 131–44, and Ad Putter, 'Weak e and the Metre of Richard Spalding's *Alliterative Katherine Hymn*', *Notes and Queries*, n.s. 52 (2005), 288–92.

The Metres and Stanza Forms of Popular Romance

impressive repertoire of metrical forms in the Middle English romances.[77] The metres of the French and Anglo-Norman sources and analogues seem restricted and predictable by comparison: they are either in octosyllabic couplets or in the metres of the *chanson de geste* (the decasyllable or alexandrine in *laisses*). There is no such homogeneity in Middle English, and even forms that are superficially similar, such as the couplet or the tail-rhyme stanza, conceal large differences. The couplets of *Horn* have more in common with the long lines of La3amon than with the verses of *Havelok*, and the couplet form in the Fillingam *Firumbras* is different again: its poet used six-stress lines with a medial caesura, an extremely unusual choice in romance, but one that matches the alexandrines in the source.[78] Similarly, the rhythms of *Sir Percyvell of Gales* may have more in common with alliterative verse than with *Amis and Amiloun*, even though both are technically tail-rhyme romances.

This variety is a sign of a metrical adventurousness that is found everywhere in Middle English poetry, which lacked an established metrical norm for narrative verse. The greatest challenge for the poets of Middle English romance was to find a substitute for the measures of the *chansons de geste*, which French and Anglo-Norman poets had perfected as the medium for oral and musical performance. The adaptation of lyrical forms (e.g. the tail-rhyme stanza, the *Tristrem* stanza, and the *ababab* stanza of the Stanzaic *Morte*) provided solutions for those Middle English poets who intended their works to be recited or sung. The tail-rhyme stanza, of course, survived into the age of print,[79] and so could obviously be read as well as heard, yet the reinvention of romance as reading matter also left traces in versification, in the editing out of 'imperfect rhymes' and the efforts to make rhymes orthographically visible.

The rhythms and rhymes of poetry thus have much to say to those who would listen. The subject is much too important to be left to the metrists.

---

[77] For the sake of completeness I should add the quatrain (abab) found e.g. in *The Sowdone of Babylone*, *The Knight of Courtesy*, and a fragmentary version of *Parthenope of Blois*, and in the body of *Thomas of Erceldoune*.

[78] I owe this point to Marianne Ailes and Phillipa Hardman, 'How English are the English Charlemagne Romances', in *Boundaries in Medieval Romance*, ed. Neil Cartlidge (Cambridge: D. S. Brewer, 2008), pp. 43–55 (p. 46).

[79] And beyond. When William Wordsworth used it in his Lucy poem 'Three years she grew in sun and shower', the evolution of the form had come full circle: the strophe had returned to its lyrical origin.

8

Orality and Performance

KARL REICHL

Introduction

But the Minstrels continued a distinct order of men for many ages after the Norman Conquest [...]. I have no doubt but most of the old heroic ballads in this collection were composed by this order of men; for although some of the larger metrical romances might come from the pen of the monks or others, yet the smaller narratives were probably composed by the minstrels who sang them. From the amazing variations which occur in different copies of the old pieces, it is evident they made no scruple to alter each other's productions; and the reciter added or omitted whole stanzas according to his own fancy or convenience.

'This collection' refers to the *Reliques of Ancient English Poetry* by Thomas Percy, first published in 1765. Percy appended 'An Essay on the Ancient Minstrels in England', from which the introductory quotation comes. The picture painted by Percy of the minstrel as both the performer and composer of popular Middle English romances was already in his time severely criticized, a criticism that led Percy to some modifications in later editions of his essay.[1] When reading Percy's essay today, almost 250 years after its first publication, it is gratifying to see that progress in philology has given us reliable editions of most Middle English romances, and that advances in palaeography, codicology and historical linguistics have put our interpretations of these texts on a reasonably firm basis. It is, however, also somewhat discouraging to realize that the figure of the minstrel is still shrouded in mystery and that his role in the creation, transmission and performance of Middle English romances continues to be a matter of dispute.[2]

---

[1] Joseph Ritson's 'Dissertation on Romance and Minstrelsy', in which he criticizes Percy, was first published in 1790. The quotation above comes from the re-edition of the fourth edition of Percy's *Reliques* (1794); Thomas Percy, *Reliques of Ancient English Poetry*, ed. with intro. Henry B. Wheatley, 3 vols (London: Sonnenschein, Lebas, & Lowrey, 1886), I, 347–8.

[2] There is a rich literature on the medieval minstrel; see Walter Salmen, *Der fahrende Musiker im europäischen Mittelalter*, Die Musik im alten und neuen Europa 4 (Kassel: Bärenreiter, 1960) (musical aspects); John Southworth, *The English Medieval Minstrel* (Woodbridge: The Boydell Press, 1989) (English minstrels; for the general reader); Christopher Page, *The Owl and the Nightingale: Musical Life and Ideas in France 1100–1300* (Berkeley: University of California Press,

Orality and Performance

One thing seems uncontroversial: the Middle English popular romances were meant to be heard. Many of them begin with the narrator addressing his audience and asking them to listen to his tale. Here are some examples:

For Goddes love in Trinyte,	
Al that ben hend* herkenith to me,	well-bred
I pray yow, paramoure*... (*Amis and Amiloun*)	if it please you
Herkneþ to me boþe eld & ȝing*,	old and young
For Maries loue þat swete þing ... (*King of Tars*)	
God graunt hem heven blis to mede*	reward
Þat herken to mi romaunce rede	
Al of a gentil kniȝt. (*Guy of Warwick*)[3]	

How literally are we to take this pose of a narrator who tells a story aloud to his listeners? Does this imply that romances like the ones quoted above were basically performed aloud? What does 'perform' mean: read from a manuscript or delivered from memory without the help of a book? And who did the performing, a specialist in public entertainment or, in the case of a reading performance, anyone who was literate? There are more questions we would like to have an answer for than these. Some concern the performers, some the narratives. If romances were recited by professional entertainers, what was the manner of their recital? Were they speaking, chanting or perhaps singing? Did they accompany themselves on a musical instrument? As to the narratives, were they memorized and reproduced verbatim or were there variations according to entertainer, occasion and audience? How were the romances transmitted? Only in writing or also orally? And how were they composed? With pen in hand or in the manner of oral poetry in illiterate or partly illiterate societies?

In this chapter only some of these questions can be addressed. From the corpus of Middle English romances I will focus on those romances that are generally termed 'popular romances'. Without entering into the intricacies of a discussion of the term 'popular', I will simply take as the prototype of a popular romance a tail-rhyme romance like *Sir Isumbras*, that is, an anonymous romance of short or middle length, which is in verse and can be loosely characterized as 'popular by destination'.[4] By implication, I will exclude all romances with 'literate' authors like Chaucer, Gower or Lydgate and all prose romances.

1989) (French minstrels); Wolfgang Hartung, *Die Spielleute im Mittelalter: Gaukler, Dichter, Musikanten* (Düsseldorf: Patmos, 2003).

[3] Quoted from *Of Love and Chivalry: An Anthology of Middle English Romance*, ed. Jennifer Fellows (London: Dent, 1993), p. 73 (*Amis and Amiloun*); *The King of Tars*, ed. Judith Perryman, Middle English Texts 12 (Heidelberg: Winter, 1980), p. 73 (*King of Tars*); *The Romance of Guy of Warwick*, ed. Julius Zupitza, vol. 2, EETS ES 49 (London, 1887), p. 384 (*Guy of Warwick*, part 2).

[4] On the distinction between 'popular by origin' and 'popular by destination', see *The Early English Carols*, ed. Richard Leighton Greene, 2nd edn (Oxford: Clarendon Press, 1977), p. cxviii.

Romance reading

In one of the most elaborate descriptions of female beauty in Middle English, in the Harley lyric entitled in most anthologies 'The Fair Maid of Ribblesdale', the beautiful woman has 'a mury mouht to mele, / wiþ lefly rede lippes lele, / romaunz forte rede' (a merry mouth for speaking and lovely red and beautiful lips for the reading of romances).[5] If the fair maid of Ribblesdale did indeed read romances, she would have read them aloud. This is what the young woman in Chaucer's *Troilus and Criseyde* does, who reads the *Thebais* to Criseyde and two other ladies: 'they thre / Herden a mayden reden hem the geste / Of the siege of Thebes' (II. 82–84). Similarly, in the quotation above from the beginning of the second part of *Guy of Warwick* the audience is said to be listening to the reading of a romance ('Þat herken to mi romaunce rede').

How are we to understand references to the reading of romances? There are basically four possibilities: (1) a text from a manuscript is read silently in private or (2) it is read aloud, either to oneself or (3) to a group of listeners; and there is finally the possibility (4) that 'reading' a tale means narrating it without a text.[6] Like its Old English antecedent, the Middle English verb *rēden* comprises a great number of meanings. They can be roughly grouped into two clusters of related meanings, one with 'reading' and the other with 'advising' at its respective centre.[7] It is only the first cluster that concerns us here. It is interesting to note that many of the quotations from the meaning-group 'reading' in the *MED* point to reading aloud. With the growth of literacy during the medieval period the number of readers steadily increased. This entailed a shift from the predominance of public reading to an ever growing number of private readers and hence to the development of silent reading in addition to reading aloud. Although the broad outlines of this development from public reading to private silent reading are incontestable, the details are far from clear. Paul Saenger has argued that silent reading began in the Western world in the seventh century and became standard in the late Middle Ages, while other scholars have maintained that public reading remained the most common form of reading until the late Middle Ages, at any rate in some spheres.[8] Whatever the precise relationship between public and private reading in late medieval England, the numerous appeals to pay attention and

---

[5] *The Harley Lyrics: The Middle English Lyrics of MS. Harley 2253*, ed. G. L. Brook, 3rd edn (Manchester: Manchester University Press, 1964), p. 38; on the meaning of *lele* here, see *MED* s.v. *lēl* adj. & n., meaning 2(b).

[6] The relevance of this fourth sense to Middle English romance is discussed by Ad Putter, 'Middle English Romances and the Oral Tradition', in *Medieval Oral Literature*, De Gruyter Lexikon, ed. Karl Reichl (Berlin: De Gruyter, 2009)

[7] See *MED* s.v. *rēden* v. (1); compare also *rēder(e* n. (1) and *rēding(e* ger. (1).

[8] On Saenger's argumentation, based on the development of word separation in medieval manuscripts, see Paul Saenger, *Space between Words: The Origins of Silent Reading* (Stanford, CA: Stanford University Press, 1997). The position that public reading prevailed in England and

Orality and Performance

to listen in a great number of Middle English romances suggest that these narratives were meant to be heard rather than read in private. This does not exclude the possibility that romances were also read in private (silently or *sotto voce*). In fact, some romances lack an appeal to a listening audience, and once a text has been written down, there is, of course, no bar to its being read in private.

The question here is rather whether the *primary* reception of the Middle English romances, especially the so-called popular romances, was aural or 'visual'; in other words, whether these romances were composed to be heard or to be read on one's own. The main evidence for a primary oral/aural reception consists in the narrator's addresses to his listeners. But how trustworthy are expressions like 'Lystyngs, lordyngs', 'Herkneþ to me'? It has been proposed that such lines are conventional, part and parcel of various stylistic features associated with the popular romance. Terms like 'fictitious orality' or 'the pretence of a recital situation' have been used to deny the literal acceptance of these appeals to the listener. No doubt, conventional traits of a genre do continue to be employed beyond their original *raison d'être*. Virgil begins his *Aeneid*, like Homer his *Iliad*, with the verb 'to sing', but only Homer's epics were sung, not the later literary epics modelled on Homer. It can similarly be expected that the narrator's call for attention was introduced into works for which a listening audience was never intended. As D. H. Green has shown for German literature between 800 and 1300, the fictitious nature of such requests for attention must, however, be the exception and their literal use the rule.[9] It seems strange to interpret the numerous indications of an oral presentation and aural reception given in medieval texts as fictitious rather than literal. The overwhelming majority of such indications seem to point to oral delivery. This has long been maintained both for medieval literature in general and Middle English literature in particular, especially for the romances.[10] Indeed, as Paul Zumthor has persuasively argued, 'vocality' must be considered one of the central characteristics of medieval poetry.[11]

As the semantic analysis of *rēden* in the *MED* shows, a number of citations support meanings such as 'to recite', 'to narrate', 'to perform song or music'. A citation supporting the last-named meaning comes from *Horn*

France in the late Middle Ages is held by Joyce Coleman, *Public Reading and the Reading Public in Late Medieval England and France* (Cambridge: Cambridge University Press, 1996).

[9] See D. H. Green, *Medieval Listening and Reading: The Primary Reception of German Literature 800–1300* (Cambridge: Cambridge University Press, 1994). Green offers an extensive analysis of the verbs of hearing, speaking, singing and reading in Middle High German; he sees oral/aural reception as the primary mode of reception for genres such as heroic poetry; Green also criticizes the concept of 'Hörerfiktion' (fictious listener reception) (pp. 10–12).

[10] Early seminal contributions to the problem of oral delivery are Ruth Crosby, 'Oral Delivery in the Middle Ages', *Speculum* 11 (1936), 88–110, and for the Middle English romances, Albert C. Baugh, 'Improvisation in the Middle English Romance', *Proceedings of the American Philosophical Society* 103 (1959), 418–54; 'The Middle English Romance: Some Questions of Creation, Presentation, and Preservation', *Speculum* 42 (1967), 1–31.

[11] Paul Zumthor, *La lettre et la voix: De la «littérature» médiévale* (Paris: Seuil, 1987).

Childe. While a refugee at King Houlac's court, Horn excels as a huntsman and a musician: 'Harpe & romance he radde ari3t' (line 286). Here *rēden* is construed with both *romance* and *harpe* and clearly does not mean 'to read' but rather 'to perform'.[12] A similar range of meanings can also be established for Middle High German *lesen*, meaning 'to read (silently)', 'to read (aloud)', and 'to narrate, recount, tell'.[13] From the evidence both in Middle English and in comparable medieval traditions it can be concluded that the reading of romance is generally to be understood as reading a romance aloud to an audience; in some cases it might even mean telling a romance or performing a romance without the help of a written text (the fourth possibility mentioned above).[14]

Performers and performance

In an episode in *Havelok* we find among the various forms of entertainment at Havelok's coronation feast also the reading of romances:

> Hwan he was king, ther mouthe men se
> The moste ioie that mouhte be –
> Buttinge with sharpe speres,
> Skirming with taleuaces that men beres,
> Wrastling with laddes, putting of ston,
> Harping and piping ful god won,
> Leyk of mine, of hasard ok,
> Romanz-reding on the bok.
> Ther mouthe men here the gestes singe,
> The glevmen on the tabour dinge ...   (lines 2321–30)[15]

> [When he became king one could witness the most splendid festivities imaginable: thrusting sharp spears, fencing with large shields, carried by men, wrestling of young men, stone-throwing, a great deal of harping and piping, games of dice and gambling, reading romances from a book. There one could hear the singing of *gestes* and minstrels beat the tabour ...]

There can be no doubt that here the romances were read aloud, and it is quite likely that the person reading the romances was the same as the singer of *gestes*, of heroic or adventurous romances. We know that the *gestes* in the specialized meaning of *chansons de geste* were indeed sung by the medieval minstrel, and as minstrels (gleemen) playing the tabour, a small drum, are

---

[12] See *MED s.v. rēden*, meaning 5b. (c).
[13] Green, *Medieval Listening and Reading*, pp. 316–23.
[14] On the meaning of romance reading, see also Jordi Sánchez-Martí, 'Reading Romance in Late Medieval England: The Case of the Middle English *Ipomedon*', *Philological Quarterly* 83 (2004), 13–39.
[15] *Havelok*, ed. G. V. Smithers (Oxford: Clarendon Press, 1987), p. 64. For parallels to this scene see *ibid.*, pp. 168–9.

Orality and Performance

mentioned in the following line, it is highly probable that all three activities, the reading of romances, the singing of *gestes* and the playing of music, were carried out by the minstrel, the public entertainer.

The figure of the public entertainer has many facets in medieval society. A number of terms are used in different medieval languages. In English the terms *minstrel* and *jogelour* (*jongleur*) occur, as in the romance of *Kyng Alisaunder*:

> Mery it is in halle to here þe harpe;
> Þe mynstrales synge, þe jogelours carpe.[16]

In this passage the minstrels sing and the *jongleurs* 'carp'. In Modern English 'to carp' has meanings such as 'to talk in a peevish way'; a similarly pejorative meaning can also characterize the Middle English verb ('to gossip, speak frivolously').[17] In addition, however, there are a number of different meanings. In many cases the meaning is simply 'to talk, speak', as in *carpen the sothe*, 'to speak the truth'. The verb is also used in phrases and contexts that imply the telling of a story, in some cases connected to music. It seems therefore plausible that *carpen* can also mean 'to recite' or even 'to sing'. A musical context is indicated in the introductory stanza of the rhymed tale of *The Hermit and the Outlaw*. The narrator asks his audience to be quiet and listen to his tale, otherwise they cannot enjoy his performance. Both singing and 'carping' are coupled with the playing of musical instruments:

> A man, that wylle synge or carpe,
> Be hyt wyth geterne* or wyth harpe,   gittern (a plucked lute)
>   Be hyt never so schrylle,
> 3yf anothyr be ludder* than he,   louder
> Lyttyl lykynge ys in hys gle*,   performance (glee)
>   But men be fast* and stylle.[18]   quiet

Apart from the nouns *minstrel* and *jongleur* on the one hand and the verbs *singen* and *carpen* on the other, a number of further terms occur in Middle English. In the romance of *Firumbras* (Fillingham MS) singing and 'carping' are said to be the activity of minstrels and *disours*:

> Ful mery it is to here the harpe,
> Dysours and mynstrels to synge and to carpe.[19]

---

[16] Oxford, Bodleian Library, MS Laud Misc. 622, lines 5980–5981; *Kyng Alisaunder*, ed. G. V. Smithers, 2 vols, EETS OS 227, 237 (London: Oxford University Press, 1952–57), I, 313.

[17] Compare *MED s.v. carpen*. The examples given for the pejorative meaning in the *MED*, listed under 3, are not entirely convincing. Among them is also the quotation above from *Kyng Alisaunder*. See also Henry Holland Carter, *A Dictionary of Middle English Musical Terms* (Bloomington: Indiana University Press, 1961), pp. 65–6 (*s.v. carpen* vb.).

[18] Lines 7–8; Max Kaluza, 'Kleinere Publikationen aus me. Handschriften', *Englische Studien* 14 (1890), 165–88 (p. 171).

[19] Lines 416–17; *Firumbras and Otuel and Roland, Edited from MS. Brit. Mus. Addit. 37492*, ed. Mary Isabelle O'Sullivan, EETS OS 198 (London: Oxford University Press, 1935), p. 15.

The functions of the *disour* seem to have been identical to those of the minstrel, although on account of the word's etymology ('speaker', ultimately from French *dire*) one might think of the *disour* as being more closely associated with speaking and story-telling than with singing and performing songs. There are, however, quotations which speak against this. In one of the Middle English versions of the *Sayings of Cato* there is a warning not to esteem 'disouris song; / Ful ofte þei lien and singen wrong.'[20] But in some texts the *disour* is also presented as a teller of tales, as in John Gower's *Confessio Amantis*, where in a story illustrating the vice of flattery the Emperor is entertained by his minstrels and *disours*:

> Whan he was gladdest at his mete,
> And every menstral hadde pleid,
> And every Disour hadde seid
> What most was plesant to his Ere*,   ear
> Than ate laste comen there
> His Macons*... [21]   masons

In some of the manuscripts a variant of *disour* is *gestour*, another technical term denoting (according to the *MED*) 'one who recites metrical romances or tells stories'.

When discussing the various types of medieval entertainers and their functions, it is best to remember that not only in Britain, but in medieval Europe in general, the minstrel, *jongleur*, *juglar*, *giullare*, *spilmann* etc. could be and very often was different things. We have to distinguish between the entertainer (1) as a musician (instrumentalist), (2) as an acrobat, (3) as a jester, (4) as a performer of songs, and (5) as a performer of epic and narrative poetry. It goes without saying that these functions overlap and cannot always be separated neatly from one another. Also the terminology for the medieval entertainer and the relevant sources are far from unambiguous. In some cases the word *jongleur* might denote the entertainer as acrobat, in others, as in the quotations above, it denotes the performer of poetry. As a rule, the singer of songs plays also an instrument and is hence also a musician. The jester might just fool around to amuse his audience, but he might also perform shorter narrative forms such as *fabliaux* and hence include in his repertoire shorter epic poetry. All of these activities are listed in Langland's *Piers Plowman* as the typical skills of the minstrel by Activa Vita, who is able to amuse an audience, but lacks the full panoply of a minstrel's gifts and tricks:

> Ac for I kan noither tabre* ne trompe · ne telle none gestes,   to drum
> Farten, ne fythelen* · at festes, ne harpen,   to fiddle

---

[20] Compare *MED* s.v. disour.
[21] Bk VII, lines 2422–7; *The English Works of John Gower*, ed. G. C. Macaulay, 2 vols, EETS ES 81, 82 (London: Oxford University Press, 1900–1), II, p. 299. On MS variants see *John Gower*, ed. Macaulay, II, p. 299. Compare *MED* s.v. gestour.

Iape* ne Iogly · ne gentlych pype,	to joke, act as buffoon
Ne noyther sailly* ne saute* · ne synge with the gyterne[22]	dance – tumble

As to the mode of performance, we have encountered the verbs 'to read', 'to carp', 'to say', and 'to sing'. This suggests that narratives could be performed in two basic modes, they could be spoken (read aloud, recited) or they could be sung. The singing of *gestes*, as in the quotation from *Havelok*, is comparatively well documented for the French *chansons de geste*. A number of melodies have been preserved, some as *contrafacta*, and there is also some theoretical discussion in Johannes de Grocheio's treatise *De musica* (c. 1300). The melodies to which the *chansons de geste* were sung are predominantly syllabic (one note per syllable) and stichic (the same melody or melodic formula per line). As the metre of the *chanson de geste* differs from that of Middle English poetry, none of these melodies or melodic fragments fits any of the English romances. The accentual metre (as well as some of the the stanzaic patterns) of Middle High German is closer to Middle English. There is some evidence of the singing of Middle High German narrative, most of it indirect such as melodies from the repertoire of the *Meistersinger* and of later ballads like the *Jüngere Hildebrandslied* (c. 1500). Basically, we get a similar picture to that of the melodic structure of the *chansons de geste*; the melodies are fairly simple, with a limited melodic range (ambitus), and they tend to be built up of only few melodic motifs. These melodies confirm the general idea of narrative song as indicated in the French sources, but do not lend themselves as models for Middle English romances. What all this evidence does tell us, however, is that narratives destined for oral performance by a public entertainer were often if not regularly sung. Perhaps the word 'sing' should also be understood as 'chanted', suggesting a type of melody like that used in Gregorian chant for the singing of the gospel.[23] The absence of melodies for Middle English romances does not prove that romances were not sung. The music of the Middle English lyrics, too, is by comparison with the Provençal, French and German traditions only poorly preserved; and yet we know with certainty that many of the lyrics still extant were sung. There is no reason not to understand *singen* in its literal meaning in lines such as 'Ther mouthe men here the gestes singe'. None of these performance modes – reading aloud, speaking/reciting and singing/chanting – seems to have been used exclusively; every one of them was employed, its choice depending on the occasion, the kind of performer and the type of narrative.

---

[22] B passus XIII, lines 231–4; *The Vision of William Concerning Piers the Plowman in Three Parallel Texts together with Richard the Redeless by William Langland*, ed. Walter W. Skeat, 2 vols (London, 1886), I, p. 400; compare C passus XVI, lines 205–8 (*ibid.*, p. 401). Instead of 'saute' some MSS have 'sautrien' (play the psaltery). On the musical performance of Middle English romance, see also Putter in this volume.

[23] For a survey of the musical performance of narrative in the Middle Ages, see John Stevens, *Words and Music in the Middle Ages: Song, Narrative, Dance and Drama, 1050–1350* (Cambridge: Cambridge University Press, 1986), pp. 199–267.

When romances were sung (or chanted), did the minstrel accompany himself on an instrument? Singing is generally mentioned in a context of music making, and hence also in connection with musical instruments. Two instruments are closely associated with the medieval entertainer, the harp and the fiddle. Both instruments come in different forms and have varying names. The most prominent member of medieval bowed string-instruments is the fiddle (Middle English *fithele*) or *vièle*. The medieval English harp is the *cithara anglicana*, which (from a musicological point of view) is more properly a lyre.[24] Its connection to the performance of romance has already been seen in the quotation from *Horn Childe* above ('Harpe & romance he radde ariȝt'). Minstrels are often called harpers, as in another passage of *Horn Childe*. When King Hatheolf's realm is attacked by Irish invaders, he bids his retinue to get ready for war:

> He bad þe harpour leuen* his lay: leave
> 'For ous bihoueþ anoþer play,
> Buske armour & stede*.'[25]   steed

Here the harper/minstrel is pictured as performing a *lai*. In *King Horn*, it is the hero himself who plays a *lai* with his harp:

> He sette him on the benche,
> His harpe for to clenche*.   pluck
> He makede Rymenhilde lay,
> And heo makede 'Walaway.'[26]

By *lai* we are most probably to understand a Breton *lai*, which was traditionally thought to have been sung to the accompaniment of a harp.[27] A number of Middle English and French *lais* expressly state this, and Chaucer still echoes this convention in the prologue to 'The Franklin's Tale'. Interestingly he mentions both singing and reading (aloud, no doubt), reminding us that two modes of performance were possible, of which singing is presumably the older and more traditional one:

> Whiche layes with hir instrumentz they* songe   i.e. the 'olde Britouns'
> Or elles redden hem for hir plesaunce ...

---

[24] See Mary Remnant, *English Bowed Instruments from Anglo-Saxon to Tudor Times* (Oxford: Clarendon Press, 1986); Christopher Page, *Voices and Instruments of the Middle Ages: Instrumental Practice and Songs in France 1100–1300* (London: Dent, 1987), pp. 111–25.

[25] Lines 157–9; *Horn Childe and Maiden Rimnild*, ed. from the Auchinleck MS, National Library of Scotland, Advocates' MS 19.2.1, ed. Maldwyn Mills, Middle English Texts 20 (Heidelberg: Winter, 1988), p. 86.

[26] Lines 1477–80, Cambridge University Library MS Gg. 4. 27(2); *Of Love and Chivalry*, ed. Fellows, p. 39.

[27] There is also the lyrical *lai* and the somewhat loose use of the word *lai* as song in Middle English; see *MED* s.v. *lai* n.(2).

An example of singing narrative poetry and playing the fiddle or *vièle* comes from *Piers Plowman*. After Sloth has confessed his sins, Repentance warns him of bad minstrels and their influence and admonishes him to have holy minstrels who 'fiddle the story or *gest* of Good Friday' instead.[28] It has been shown that the Old French *chansons de geste* were almost certainly recited to the accompaniment of a *vièle*.[29] The use of a bowed instrument for the performance of narrative is widely attested in oral traditions – among them that of the South Slavs – and can be supposed to have existed also in medieval England. In fourteenth-century France a minstrel who recited or sang lyrical or narrative poetry to his own accompaniment was called a *menestrel de bouche*.[30] There are, however, also passages in Middle English romances that point to a dissociation of singing/reciting and playing (harp or fiddle). One of them occurs in *Thomas of Erceldoune*:

> 'To harpe or carpe, whare so thou gose,
> Thomas, thou sall have the chose sothely.'
> And he saide, 'Harpynge kepe I none,
> ffor tonge es chefe of mynstralsye.'
>
> ['Thomas, you shall assuredly have the choice of harping or reciting wherever you go.' And he replied: 'I care nothing for the playing of the harp, for the tongue is the chief instrument of minstrelsy.'][31]

This reminds us again that minstrels could apparently choose between different ways of performance. Whatever the mode, we can be sure that it was of the utmost importance for a reciter, singer or reader that his voice had the power of riveting the attention of his audience, by its modulations, its volume and its expressivity, that it was, in Gower's words, 'most pleasnt to their ear'.[32]

Transmission

When we think of an entertainer as reading aloud from a manuscript, we are entitled to wonder whether any of the manuscripts still extant might have

---

[28] 'And fithel the, with-out flaterynge of gode Friday the storye (C gest)'; B passus XIII, 447 (C passus VIII, 107); *Piers the Plowman*, ed. Skeat, I, p. 412 (C: *ibid.*, p. 413).
[29] See Laura M. Wright, 'More on the Meanings and Uses of *Jongleur* and *Menestrel*', *Romance Studies* 17 (1990), 7–19.
[30] Nigel Wilkins, *Music in the Age of Chaucer* (Cambridge: D. S. Brewer, 1979), p. 132.
[31] Quoted and translated in Michael Chesnutt, 'Minstrel Reciters and the Enigma of the Middle English Romance', *Culture and History* 2 (1987), 48–67 (p. 52).
[32] For a discussion of the performance of medieval and Middle English romance in a comparative framework, see Karl Reichl, 'Comparative Notes on the Performance of Middle English Popular Romance', *Western Folklore* 62 (2003), 63–81, and Karl Reichl, 'Turkic Bard and Medieval Entertainer: What a Living Epic Tradition Can Tell Us about Oral Performance of Narrative in the Middle Ages', in *Performing Medieval Narrative*, ed. Everlyn Birge Vitz, Nancy Freeman Regalado and Marilyn Lawrence (Cambridge: D. S. Brewer, 2005), pp. 167–78.

served such a purpose. Léon Gautier thought that among the manuscripts preserving the *chansons de geste*, seven were *manuscrits de jongleur*. He formulated this idea in the first edition of his *Les épopées françaises* of 1865–68 and elaborated it in the second edition. Martín de Riquer added to these the Spanish manuscripts of the *Cantar de mio Cid* and the fragment of *Roncesvalles*. He describes these manuscripts as small in size (c. 16–17 x 10–12cm), written without great care and lacking in ornamentation, and he adds: 'Ils ne semblent pas avoir été copiés pour être conservés dans une bibliothèque, mais bien pour s'intégrer au bagage d'un jongleur errant.'[33] Among the manuscripts containing Middle English romances, some have been thought to be minstrel manuscripts, among them Oxford, Bodleian Library, MS Ashmole 61. It is characterized as a 'holster book', that is, as a book of the size to fit into the holster or leatherbag attached to a saddle. MS Ashmole 61 is like other holster books of oblong shape; it measures about 42 x 14.5cm and could presumably have been thus designed to be carried around in a holster. Its contents comprise five romances, *Sir Isumbras, Earl of Toulous, Libeaus Desconus, Sir Cleges* and *Sir Orfeo*. In addition it contains a number of pious poems, among them the legend of St Eustace, which is closely connected to the group of tail-rhyme romances to which *Sir Isumbras* belongs. There are also two humorous stories in verse, *Sir Corneus* (a version of the *Lai du Cor*) and *King Edward and the Hermit*, a story based on the motif of the king in disguise meeting a faithful and often somewhat rude subject who proves his mettle and is in the end rewarded. MS Ashmole 61 is a miscellany with a decided slant for popular narrative and seems to be a fitting source for a minstrel.[34]

Doubts have, however, been expressed as to the allocation of this and other manuscripts to a minstrel milieu.[35] In the case of MS Ashmole 61, one wonders whether a late medieval lay household might not suit the interests reflected in the contents just as well if not better. Among the religious poems, we find an English version of Robert Grosseteste's allegory of the Four Daughters of God from his *Chasteau d'Amour*, John Maidstone's metrical translation of the Penitential Psalms and a shortened version of the *Pricke of Conscience*. These are all popular works, but their edifying and devotional bias seems more appropriate for family reading than for public entertain-

---

[33] For the list, including the Oxford MS of the *Chanson de Roland*, see Léon Gautier, *Les épopées françaises: Études sur les origines et l'histoire de la littérature nationale*, seconde édition, entièrement refondue, 3 vols (Paris, 1878), I, p. 226, n. 1; for a discussion see *ibid.*, pp. 224–9. See also Martín de Riquer, 'Épopée jongleresque à écouter et épopée romanesque à lire', in *La technique littéraire des chansons de geste: Acte du Colloque de Liège (septembre 1957)* (Paris: Société d'Édition «Les Belles Lettres», 1959), pp. 75–82 (p. 77).

[34] On the manuscript's contents see Gisela Guddat-Figge, *Catalogue of Manuscripts Containing Middle English Romances* (Munich: W. Fink, 1976) pp. 249–52; on 'holster books', pp. 30–6.

[35] Among others by Lynne Blanchfield, 'Rate Revisited: The Compilation of the Narrative Works in MS Ashmole 61', *Romance Reading*, pp. 208–20; John C. Hirsh, '*Havelok* 2933: A Problem in Medieval Literary History', *Neuphilologische Mitteilungen* 78 (1977), 339–49; Andrew Taylor, 'The Myth of the Minstrel Manuscript', *Speculum* 66 (1991), 43–73.

ment. Similar observations can be made with regard to other manuscripts. The very fact that they have been produced by a scribe places these manuscripts in a context of writing, copying, and scribal editing, which obscures any connection they might have had to the public entertainer. It is difficult to prove the use of a manuscript by an English minstrel and sceptics will hence never be persuaded that minstrel manuscripts are anything but a myth.

While it may be problematic to connect any of the Middle English romance manuscripts to the activity of a public performer, the texts themselves have induced the editors of various romances to speculate about their oral transmission, at least in part.[36] One such romance is *Sir Launfal*, in which Thomas Chestre is named as author. This Middle English *lai* is preserved in only one manuscript; it clearly goes back to the Middle English *Sir Landevale*, a fairly free translation of Marie de France's *Lanval*. Comparing several variants between *Sir Landevale* and Chestre's *Sir Launfal*, S. T. Knight affirms that the relationship between *Sir Launfal* and *Sir Landevale* is such that Chestre must have had an 'oral experience' of *Sir Landevale*. He further surmises that Chestre might have been a minstrel. Be that as it may, the variation between the two Middle English versions of Marie de France's *lai* points to both aural and oral processes at work in the course of transmission and adaptation from *Sir Landevale* to *Sir Launfal*.[37] Editors of other romances have similarly assumed orality somewhere in the chain of transmission. G. V. Smithers, in his edition of *Kyng Alisaunder*, comes to the conclusion that the variant readings of the romance in London, Lincoln's Inn, MS Hale 150 (MS L, one of the holster books) are of such a nature that they must have arisen in the course of oral transmission:

> In fact, some of the corruptions in L are hardly explicable in terms of scribal transmission. The kind and the degree of error contained in it are such as would arise in oral transmission of a text, and specifically in a copy based on (and perhaps designed as) the version of a minstrel. There is no knowing from textual evidence alone how far back this stage of oral transmission lies behind L.[38]

The variant readings Smithers lists as 'auditory rather than palaeographical errors' suggest oral transmission but cannot prove it. The same is true of other studies. Nicolas Jacobs, who has devoted a number of studies to the transmission of the romance of *Sir Degarre* from the text in the Auchinleck MS to that in the Percy Folio MS and has developed a fine grid for the

---

[36] A full list of these various romances can be found in Ad Putter, 'A Historical Introduction to Medieval Popular Romance', in *Spirit*, pp. 1–15. While most scholars, however, doubt a relationship of this and similar MSS to the medieval minstrel, it has been shown that the scribal revisions in MS L point to use of the MS texts for performance; see Simon Horobin and Alison Wiggins, 'Reconsidering Lincoln's Inn MS 150', *Medium Ævum* 77 (2008), 30–53.
[37] See S. T. Knight, 'The Oral Transmission of *Sir Launfal*', *Medium Ævum* 38 (1969), 164–70.
[38] *Kyng Alisaunder*, II, pp. 11–12. Smithers adds: 'it may have been meant to fit the pocket of an itinerant minstrel [...]' (p. 12).

description of scribal variation and textual corruption, accepts the possibility of memorial transmission, although he maintains a basically written textual history.[39] The effects of memorization on textual variation have also been assumed for the romance of *Arthour and Merlin*. William E. Holland sees the type of variation found in some of the manuscripts containing the romance as 'due to faulty reproduction of a memorized text'.[40] He bases his claim not only on the evaluation of variant readings but also on the analysis of formulaic diction, conducted in the spirit of formula analysis as proposed by the oral-formulaic theory. In contrast to other applications of this methodology to medieval texts, it is not the oral composition of the romance which is to be proved, but only the orality of (part of) the transmission of the text.

However likely an oral transmission of some of the romances that have come down to us might be, there are no certain proofs of this. When it came to vernacular texts like the popular romances, medieval scribes felt apparently no great obligation to copy their texts carefully and few restrictions about altering and changing them. As they were reading (*sotto voce*) several lines before copying them, 'aural' corruptions could easily creep in, especially when a text was known to them through having heard it read or performed repeatedly.[41] 'Memorial transmission' and 'scribal transmission' can in this way easily become identical. Just as it is problematic to identify a minstrel manuscript, so it is difficult to point to an incontestable instance of memorial transmission. Memorial transmission must remain hypothetical, though perhaps in some cases the best hypothesis for accounting for textual variation.[42]

Composition

When speaking of oral poetry, it is customary to distinguish between oral performance, oral transmission and oral composition. Scholars are agreed on the widespread oral performance of Middle English romances – though in different modes – and have been willing to allow the possibility of memorial

---

[39] See Nicolas Jacobs, *The Later Versions of 'Sir Degarre': A Study in Textual Degeneration* (Oxford: Society for the Study of Medieval Languages and Literature, 1995), pp. 63, 98.

[40] William E. Holland, 'Formulaic Diction and the Descent of a Middle English Romance', *Speculum* 48 (1973), 89–109 (p. 96).

[41] For an early discussion of the interrelation of reading and writing, see H. J. Chaytor, *From Script to Print: An Introduction to Medieval Vernacular Literature* (Cambridge: W. Heffer & Sons, 1945), pp. 5–21. For the idea that scribes acted as oral singers in the transmission of *King Horn*, see James Hurt, 'The Texts of *King Horn*', *Journal of the Folklore Institute* 7 (1970), 47–59.

[42] Memorial transmission is also argued for in Baugh's seminal articles of 1959 ('Improvisation') and 1967 ('The Middle English Romance'). For a summary discussion of memorial transmission with regard to the Middle English romances, see Murray McGillivray, *Memorization in the Transmission of the Middle English Romances* (New York: Garland, 1990). For an assessment of the oral factor in editing Middle English texts, especially romances, see Tim William Machan, 'Editing, Orality, and Late Middle English Texts', in *Vox intexta: Orality and Textuality in the Middle Ages*, ed. A. N. Doane and Carol Braun Pasternack (Madison, WI: University of Wisconsin Press, 1991), pp. 229–45.

Orality and Performance

in addition to written transmission. An oral background to Middle English popular romance is taken for granted, even if opinions on the details of performance and transmission vary and often oppose one another. What about oral composition? Are there any grounds for Percy's belief, quoted at the beginning of this chapter, that at least some of the shorter romances 'were probably composed by the minstrels who sang them'? With the development of the oral-formulaic theory medievalists hoped to have found a methodological tool that would prove the oral origin of a given text. In his seminal *The Singer of Tales*, Albert B. Lord showed the way of applying the insights of Milman Parry's theory of composition in performance, formulated on the basis of research in South Slavic oral epic poetry, to medieval texts.[43] In Middle English studies, the analysis of formulas and themes in narrative poetry has focused on the alliterative romances. An early application of the oral theory to Middle English alliterative poetry is Ronald A. Waldron's formulaic analysis of sixteen poems, not all of them romances, which led him to postulate a continuity between Old English and Middle English alliterative poetry and to view the *Alliterative Morte Arthure* as a distant relative of Old English heroic poetry.[44] Although Waldron's approach has been criticized, a number of studies have underlined the high incidence of formulas and themes in the *Alliterative Morte Arthure* in particular.[45] Valerie Krishna has argued persuasively that the *Alliterative Morte Arthure* should be understood as on a par with traditional and oral-derived epics; she stresses the oral background to this alliterative romance, without, however, going so far as to propose oral composition.[46]

The presence of formulas in alliterative English poetry has been acknowledged by all scholars, even if there is disagreement on the precise definition of a formula and hence on the extent to which a specific text is formulaic. Formulaic analysis as a methodological tool has, however, been questioned, most notably in Larry Benson's critique of Francis P. Magoun's application of the oral-formulaic method to *Beowulf*. If, as Benson showed, poetry of a demonstrably literate character (like the Old English translations of

---

[43] Albert B. Lord, *The Singer of Tales* (Cambridge, MA: Harvard University Press, 1960; 2nd edn, ed. Stephen Mitchell and Gregory Nagy, 2000, with a new introduction and a CD), pp. 198–221 (*Beowulf*, *Chanson de Roland*, and *Digenis Akritas*).
[44] See Ronald A. Waldron, 'Oral-Formulaic Technique and Middle English Alliterative Poetry', *Speculum* 32 (1957), 792–801. For a detailed survey of scholarship into the mid-1980s, see Ward Parks, 'The Oral-Formulaic Theory in Middle English Studies', *Oral Tradition* 1 (1986), 636–94.
[45] See, e.g., John Finlayson, 'Formulaic Technique in *Morte Arthure*', *Anglia* 81 (1963), 372–93; R. F. Lawrence, 'The Formulaic Theory and its Application to English Alliterative Poetry', in *Essays on Style and Language: Linguistic and Critical Approaches to Literary Style*, ed. Roger Fowler (London: Routledge, 1966), pp. 166–83; Rosamund Allen, 'Performance and Structure in the Alliterative *Morte Arthure*', in *New Perspectives on Middle English Texts: A Festschrift for R. A. Waldron*, ed. Susan Powell, Jeremy J. Smith and Derek Pearsall (Cambridge: D. S. Brewer, 2000), pp. 17–29 (on the performance-dependent structure of the romance).
[46] See Valerie Krishna, 'Parataxis, Formulaic Density, and Thrift in the *Alliterative Morte Arthure*', *Speculum* 57 (1982), 63–83.

the *Metra* of Boethius) can also be highly formulaic, a high frequency of formulas cannot be used as proof of an oral origin.[47] The same argument applies to Middle English poetry, where formulaic diction is all-pervasive in the popular romances, both among the romances of the 'alliterative revival' and those in other metres, in particular the tail-rhyme stanzas. Formulas and themes are first and foremost elements of style; they are the hallmark of romance as a popular genre. They have the appearance of a style which one would naturally associate with an oral milieu, but are no certain indications of oral composition.

One might ask, however, why a style that carries all the marks of orally performed narrative poetry was so widespread in texts that have not been composed orally. One answer is that these popular romances were written for minstrels and have hence incorporated stylistic traits that make them suitable for performance by a public entertainer. *Sir Torrent of Portyngale* is one of the tail-rhyme romances exhibiting this style to an almost excessive extent. As early as 1842 James Orchard Halliwell proposed that the textually corrupt state of this romance could best be explained by seeing it as the transcript of an oral performance:

> ... the romance of Torrent of Portugal [...] contains so many obvious blunders and omissions, that it may be conjectured with great probability to have been written down from oral recitation.[48]

Halliwell does not elaborate on his conjecture. His view that the romance is textually corrupt is shared by all students of the poem, most of whom would agree with J. Burke Severs's assessment: 'The extant version abounds in trite phrases, repetitive incidents, trivial details, and feeble elaborations, all bespeaking the work of a crude hack-writer.'[49]

The hack-writer, whether crude or not, is a figure that has often been evoked by critics to explain the 'orally coloured' style of the Middle English popular romance. How are we to imagine such a figure? He is not just a translator or a writer, who creatively adapts some foreign source text for an English audience. He is no Chaucer, Lydgate, Malory or Caxton. A hack writer is, as the *OED* puts it, 'a literary drudge, who hires himself out to do any and every kind of literary work; hence, a poor writer, a mere scribbler'. The picture of the hack writer has been graphically painted by Laura Hibbard Loomis in her article on the Auchinleck MS and a possible London bookshop of 1330–40. According to Loomis the authors of the Auchinleck romances were

---

[47] See Larry D. Benson, 'The Literary Character of Anglo-Saxon Formulaic Poetry', *Publications of the Modern Language Association* 81 (1966), 324–41.
[48] *Torrent of Portugal: An English Metrical Romance, Now First Published from an Unique Manuscript of the Fifteenth Century, Preserved in the Chetham Library at Manchester*, ed. James Orchard Halliwell (London, 1842), pp. v–vi.
[49] *Manual*, p. 127.

men of generally humble literary attainments, of no literary ambition, and nearly all of whom were possessed of the same 'patter' of well-worn clichés, the same stereotyped formulas of expression, the same stock phrases, the same stock rimes, which Chaucer was to parody in such masterly fashion in *Sir Thopas*. [...] If these, for the most part, unoriginal and ungifted translator-versifiers were not what we should call literary hacks, what were they? [50]

Although it seems unlikely that several scribes worked together in a scriptorium in London at the time and in the way Loomis proposed, her idea that the Auchinleck romances were composed by literary hacks has found general acceptance.[51] The main argument for composition in writing is the existence of French source texts for a number of these romances which the translators or adaptors sometimes followed fairly closely, but sometimes rather freely. A. C. Baugh has cited a number of convincing cases arguing for translation from written sources. The only other explanation of the closeness between French source and English translation would be the hypothesis of a bilingual minstrel, a conceivable but unlikely hypothesis according to Baugh.[52]

This negative view of the style of the popular romances, in particular the tail-rhyme romances, and of their presumed authors, the literary hacks, is not shared by all scholars. One dissenting voice is that of A. McI. Trounce.[53] In an attempt to vindicate the poetic qualities of the popular tail-rhyme romance, Trounce analysed a group of twenty-three romances and tried to show that they formed a linguistically and stylistically homogeneous group. Trounce argued that these romances were composed for oral performance and that they originated in East Anglia. Although a number of his points have to be modified in the light of more recent scholarship, the idea that the tail-rhyme romances are composed in a distinctive and highly conventional style and language can hardly be doubted. Trounce calls the language of these romances a ' "lingua communis" of the minstrels'.[54] It is indeed noteworthy that these romances incorporate traits of different Middle English dialects, in particular in the rhyming words, which are mutually inconsistent and must yet have been part of the original poem. The dialectally mixed language has

---

[50] Laura Hibbard Loomis, 'The Auchinleck Manuscript and a Possible London Bookshop of 1330–1340', *Proceedings of the Modern Language Association* 57 (1942), 595–627 (pp. 607–8).

[51] On the 'Loomis bookshop theory' see Timothy A. Shonk, 'A Study of the Auchinleck Manuscript: Bookmen and Bookmaking in the Early Fourteenth Century', *Speculum* 60 (1985), 71–91.

[52] 'Oral composition would be conceivable only on the assumption that he was truly bi-lingual and could have sung or recited the story in French as well as English. This is conceivable but the less likely of the two possibilities' (Baugh, 'Improvisation', p. 432). The existence of bilingual minstrels has been postulated for the early Middle English period by both E. K. Chambers, *The Medieval Stage*, 2 vols (London: Oxford University Press, 1903), I, p. 76, and Alois Brandl, 'Spielmannsverhältnisse in frühmittelenglischer Zeit', in *Sitzungsberichte der königlich preussischen Akademie. der Wissenschaften, Philos.-hist. Classe* 41 (Berlin, 1910), pp. 873–92 (p. 880).

[53] See A. McI. Trounce, 'The English Tail-Rhyme Romances', *Medium Ævum* 1 (1932), 87–108, 168–82; 2 (1933), 34–57, 189–98; 3 (1934), 30–50.

[54] Trounce, 'Tail-Rhyme Romances', 2 (1933), p. 49.

been noticed by many editors. Gregor Sarrazin, for instance, in his edition of the Northern *Octavian*, explained this mixture of various dialects in the following manner:

> Clearly, we find only rarely a completely pure, consistent dialect in minstrel poetry. Like others in his profession, our minstrel will have got about a good deal in England ... [55]

B. Vogel remarks *à propos* the dialect of *Sir Tristrem* that 'it is quite conceivable that the poem is really a peculiar example of the eclecticism of which certain medieval "carpenters of romance" were capable'.[56] Judith Perryman talks of a 'romance *koiné*' when characterizing the dialect of *The King of Tars*.[57] The language and style of these romances are undoubtedly modelled on the art of the popular entertainer and we might be justified in speaking with Trounce and others of a 'minstrel idiom'.[58]

Even if some kind of a minstrel idiom can be detected in the popular romances, the romances themselves differ considerably in poetic achievement. L. H. Loomis grudgingly admitted that 'a few poems, like *Orfeo*, have genuine charm'. It is only the less successful romances whose authorship is ascribed to hacks, while the more highly esteemed representatives of the genre are as rule thought to have been composed by clerics. The Northern and the Southern versions of *Octavian* can serve as illustrations. Dieter Mehl, in his study of the Middle English romances of the thirteenth and fourteenth centuries, writes about the Northern version: 'The narrative technique of the poem does not give the impression that it was composed by or for a minstrel.' He adds, 'The artistic unity of the poem and the skilful organization of the plot suggest an educated scribe rather than an improvising minstrel.' The Southern version, on the other hand, has been seen less favourably. Mehl talks about its 'ballad-like technique' and finds that the author is 'a far less careful artist ... thinking in terms of oral recitation'. In sum, the Southern version is a 'rather artless product, which was possibly written down from memory'; it is characterized by clichés and the 'careless stringing together of episodes'.[59] Clearly, in such a scenario the minstrel as author is ruled out in the case of an artistically polished romance and replaced by the hack in the case of a more trivial representative of the genre.

Although the main lines of critical opinion as expressed in the writings of A. C. Baugh are undoubtedly convincing, some qualifications can

---

[55] *Octavian: Zwei mittelenglische Bearbeitungen der Sage*, ed. Gregor Sarrazin (Heilbronn, 1885), p. xvi (my translation). Sarrazin does, however, place the original dialect of the Northern *Octavian* in Kent and thinks of the northern dialect traits as acquired by the minstrel on his travels.

[56] B. Vogel, 'The Dialect of *Sir Tristrem*', *Journal of English and Germanic Philology* 40 (1941), 538–44.

[57] Perryman, *King of Tars*, p. 17.

[58] See Karl Reichl, *Spielmannsidiom, Dialektmischung und Kunstsprache in der mittelenglischen volkstümlichen Epik* (Paderborn: Schöningh, 2002).

[59] Mehl, *Middle English Romances*, pp. 115–17, 119.

Orality and Performance

nevertheless be made.[60] Baugh saw the romances basically as works written for minstrels and explained those variants in the transmission of the texts that could not be explained as scribal as being due to the performance of minstrels. These performance variants could have become recorded in writing either by a minstrel dictating to a scribe or by a minstrel becoming a scribe himself.[61] Cases of oral singers writing down their own versions of traditional epics are known; some of the singers Parry and Lord interviewed handed over their songs in manuscript form. Even more relevant to the medieval situation in England are traditions where it is acceptable for singers to use manuscripts while performing oral epics, as in some of the local traditions in Uzbekistan. Here the fact that manuscripts of traditional poetry are in existence guarantees a basic textual stability. It can be shown that the types of textual variations that are found in different performances by the same or different singers of an epic match exactly those found in popular romances transmitted in more than one manuscript.[62] Interestingly, in some of the areas where oral epic poetry has been cultivated, there is in addition to the singer of tales also the professional reader of tales. In other words, we find an intensive interaction between a purely oral tradition and a literate/oral tradition. This oral-literate continuum is precisely what we believe to have been the case in medieval England. While on the literate end of the continuum writing (as regards composition and transmission) and reading (as regards performance) predominate, on the oral end the voice of the singer was in the foreground, singing or reciting, with or without the accompaniment of an instrument. It does not seem too far-fetched to see in some of the manuscript variants of the Middle English popular romances traces of differing performances by public entertainers. Whether these public entertainers actually composed some of these romances, cannot be ascertained. Their role in shaping the style of the popular romance, however, is undeniable. The popular romance was meant to be orally performed, and it is as orally performed narratives that they should and can be appreciated.

---

[60] For an interpretation of Middle English romance as primarily orally performed and partially orally transmitted works of written literature, see Nancy Mason Bradbury, *Writing Aloud: Storytelling in Late Medieval England* (Urbana: University of Illinois Press, 1998).

[61] See Baugh, 'Improvisation', p. 437; 'The Middle English Romance', pp. 30–1.

[62] See my discussion of these traditions in 'The Middle English Popular Romance: Minstrel versus Hack Writer', in *The Ballad and Oral Literature*, ed. Joseph Harris (Cambridge, MA: Harvard University Press, 1991), pp. 243–68, and in 'Medieval Perspectives on Turkic Oral Epic Poetry', in *Inclinate Aurem: Oral Perspectives on Early European Verbal Culture: A Symposium*, ed. Jan Helldén, Minna Skafte Jensen and Thomas Pettitt (Odense: Odense University Press, 2001), pp. 211–54.

9

Popular Romances and Young Readers

PHILLIPA HARDMAN

The phrase 'popular romance' has received extensive scrutiny in two recent collections of critical essays on Middle English romance, where various binary configurations have been offered to explore its semantic field: popular/courtly romances;[1] popular/official culture.[2] Nicola McDonald celebrates the 'inherent unorthodoxy' of popular romance,[3] as she seeks to expose the conventional prejudices of critical discourse from the eighteenth to the twentieth centuries but, despite noting the popularity of medieval romance judged by the diversity of its audience,[4] her argument draws attention to critical prejudice in relation to age. McDonald alludes to the early reading habits of Sir Walter Scott, 'whose recollection of reading Percy as a boy in the mid 1780s confirms the logic that identifies romance with childish intellects'.[5] Why should boyhood reading construct the texts read as inferior? The young Scott was at the same time reading the works of Shakespeare, Spenser, Ariosto, Richardson, Fielding, Smollett and Mackenzie.[6] Dickens creates a similar collection of books for the boy David Copperfield, and addresses the issue of the child reading texts not specifically defined as fit for children: 'I have been Tom Jones (a child's Tom Jones, a harmless creature) for a week together.'[7] Such texts are understood to be available, even if on different terms, to readers of all ages, and this is an equally important consideration in relation to the readership of medieval popular romance.

The label 'popular romance' is indeed often used to convey a critical estimate of texts as unsophisticated and appropriate for a non-learned readership. Recent scholarly discussions have on the whole not sought to oppose these estimations outright, but rather to re-evaluate them in terms appropriate to medieval experiences of narrative instead of modern critical preconcep-

---

[1] Ad Putter, 'A Historical Introduction', in *Spirit*, pp. 1–15 (p. 2).
[2] Jane Gilbert, 'A Theoretical Introduction', in *Spirit*, pp. 15–38 (pp. 17, 18, 28).
[3] Nicola McDonald, 'A Polemical Introduction', in *Pulp Fictions*, pp. 1–21 (pp. 2, 4).
[4] 'Polemical Introduction', p. 12.
[5] 'Polemical Introduction', p. 8.
[6] J. G. Lockhart, *Memoirs of Sir Walter Scott*, ed. A. W. Pollard, 5 vols (London: Macmillan, 1900; repr. 1914), I, pp. 27–30.
[7] Charles Dickens, *The Personal History of David Copperfield*, ed. Trevor Blount (Harmondsworth: Penguin, 1966), p. 106. Blount notes the importance of these books to Dickens himself as a boy (p. 952).

tions. Thus Ad Putter, for example, interrogates the alternative term 'crude', often used of popular romance, in the case of *Sir Percyvell of Gales*, arguing persuasively that the 'raw' quality of the prominent story structure is a positive strength in this and comparable Middle English romances, where a desire for logical, sequential action is the overriding formative concern, privileging the characteristic effects of 'a sense of direction and a sense of narrative shape' above the complex plot, non-linear narrative and richness of allusion in a text such as Chrétien's *Conte du Graal*.[8] This different aesthetic requires readers to be alert to elements of sophistication within its own field, where, for example, patterns of symmetry, repetition, and recurrence can create powerfully satisfying structures of meaning.[9] What I want to suggest is that these positive 'crude' qualities of the storytelling would also be likely to attract young readers of *Sir Percyvell of Gales*, those temporarily in a 'raw' condition themselves, wanting polish and schooling, who might well be drawn to identify with the youthful hero of this romance in his adventures and learning experiences.

Another construction of 'popular' literature refers it to writing in the vernacular. Putter argues that the designation 'popular' could describe the target audience of all Middle English romances, as opposed to courtly aristocrats reading romances in French.[10] But there is an interesting qualification of this view in William of Nassyngton's defence of his use of the English tongue in *Speculum vitæ* (c. 1370), based on the claim that English functions as the inclusive language in a trilingual society not only because it is accessible to courtly (French-speaking) and non-courtly listeners alike, as well as to learned (those proficient in Latin) and unlearned, but also because it can be understood by 'alde and yonnge'.[11] William reminds us that language acquisition is age-related: young readers and hearers of Middle English texts might be only temporarily monoglot. This distinction is well illustrated in Caxton's preface to the *History of Jason* (1477), undertaken 'for the honour & worship' of Edward IV. The English translation is offered not for the King's own use, 'as I doubte not his good grace hath it in frensh / which he wel vnderstandeth', but for Edward Prince of Wales, then six or seven years old, 'to thentent / he may begynne to lerne rede Englissh'.[12] Caxton's dedicatory strategy is founded on the expectation that a child's education would progress

---

[8] Ad Putter, 'Story Line and Story Shape in *Sir Percyvell of Gales* and Chrétien de Troyes's *Conte du Graal*', in *Pulp Fictions*, pp. 171–96 (p. 192).
[9] See also, for example, Putter's essay 'The Narrative Logic of Emaré', in *Spirit*, pp. 157–80; and my discussion of these effects in the Middle English Tristan poem, 'The True Romance of *Tristrem and Ysoude*', in *Cultural Encounters*, pp. 85–99.
[10] Putter, 'Historical Introduction', in *Spirit*, p. 2.
[11] Prologue to *Speculum vitæ*, quoted in Nicholas Watson, 'The Politics of Middle English Writing', in *The Idea of the Vernacular: An Anthology of Middle English Literary Theory 1280–1520*, ed. Jocelyn Wogan-Browne et al. (Exeter: University of Exeter Press, 1999), pp. 331–52 (pp. 336–7).
[12] *The Prologues and Epilogues of William Caxton*, ed. W. J. B. Crotch, EETS OS 176 (London: Oxford University Press, 1928), pp. 33–4.

from learning to read English to later understanding of French. If the production of romance in English is predicated on an audience or readership lacking competence in French, then it seems that such a readership ought to include the young as well as the non-courtly.

So far, my argument has simply been that young readers should be taken into account among the potential target audience of Middle English romance. This is hardly a contentious position: Nicholas Orme, for example, in his survey of the reading experiences of medieval children, observes that the characteristic features of medieval romance as a genre were 'likely to attract children and adolescents, as well as their elders'.[13] What seems odd is how infrequently the question of a youthful readership is considered in discussions of Middle English romance, by comparison with, for instance, a female readership.[14] Carol Meale even characterizes H. S. Bennett's suggestion that printed romances were 'suitable for an audience of schoolboys who had mastered the alphabet' as 'near-dismissal of the romances',[15] a reaction implying discomfort with the idea of romances as appropriate for young readers.

Something similar can be seen in discussions of individual texts: as noted above, the romance of *Sir Percyvell of Gales* centres on the experiences of a young hero (he grows up from birth to the age of sixteen in the course of the story), but Putter's sensitive recuperation of this 'crude' text never considers the possibility of a youthful audience. Likewise, Elizabeth Archibald discusses the Middle English *Lai le Freine* with attention to the female focus of the story and the possibility of a woman patron, but no consideration of the likely appeal that the story of a girl from birth to the age of twelve would have for young readers.[16] On the other hand, Felicity Riddy's reading of the Middle English *Le Bone Florence of Rome* as a bourgeois narrative focused on the issue of female chastity is enriched by her contextualizing recognition of its meaning as a 'family' romance, not only in its representation of kinship ties but in its function within a family readership, where the young daughter reads a 'parental fantasy' of her future: to be made chaste and honourable as maiden and wife.[17] The relative scarcity of such readings is all the more surprising in view of the fact that not only are many Middle English romances concerned with families, as Archibald points out,[18] but that a large number have a child protagonist. As Edmund Reiss remarks, 'it seems beyond

---

[13] Nicholas Orme, 'Children and Literature in Medieval England', *Medium Ævum* 68 (1999), 218–46 (p. 230).

[14] See, for example, Gilbert's choice of women as the representative 'relatively disenfranchised' group within the romance audience for discussion in 'A Theoretical Introduction', in *Spirit*, pp. 23–4.

[15] Carol M. Meale, 'Caxton, de Worde, and the Publication of Romance in Late Medieval England', *The Library*, 6th series 14 (1992), 283–98 (p. 290).

[16] Elizabeth Archibald, '*Lai le Freine*: The Female Foundling and the Problem of the Romance Genre', in *Spirit*, pp. 39–55.

[17] Felicity Riddy, 'Temporary Virginity and the Everyday Body: *Le Bone Florence of Rome* and Bourgeois Self-making', in *Pulp Fictions*, pp. 197–216 (p. 212).

[18] Archibald, '*Lai le Freine*', in *Spirit*, pp. 41–2.

coincidence that so many of the heroes of romance are children. In fact, all of the earliest Middle English romances – that is, those before 1300 – are about children: *King Horn, Floris and Blauncheflur, Arthour and Merlin, Havelok, Sir Tristrem, Amis and Amiloun, Guy,* and *Bevis*.'[19] So marked is the presence of children in Middle English popular romances that it might even be thought of as a defining feature. For example, following the methodology of Yin Liu's study of genre in Middle English romance, we note that the heroes of five of Reiss's eight romances (Horn, Havelok, Tristrem, Guy and Bevis) feature prominently in the medieval lists of romance subjects analysed by Liu as evidence of contemporary estimates of 'typical' romance.[20] Another five subjects included in these lists are also represented in Middle English romances concerning child protagonists or substantially about children (*Sir Percyvell of Gales, Libeaus Desconus, Kyng Alisaunder, Octavian,* and *Sir Isumbras*). Thus, judging by 'goodness-of-example' (based on the extant texts) it is possible to suggest that a concern with children is one significant attribute of the complex category 'Middle English romance'. Reiss does not infer from the predominance of child-centred narratives that an important aspect of Middle English popular romance is its appeal to a youthful readership; rather, he emphasizes the significance of self-discovery, the 'search for identity', in these and other similar stories as 'what romance is actually most about'.[21] Yet the two observations are of course complementary: the narrative of self-making, embodied in stories of children and adolescents, is of obvious interest to young people.

It is notable that the formation of the young protagonist in these romances frequently involves parental concern for the child's education. This may be represented through formal schooling as in, for instance, the father's care for the upbringing of his daughter in *Le Bone Florence of Rome*, where the curriculum of reading, writing, and music is distinctly specified within the programme of honourable nurture (55–63).[22] Or it may be through an eccentric version of parental care, such as the story of Percyvell's mother, who initially keeps her son in ignorance – 'Nowther nurture ne lare / Scho wolde hym none lere' (231–2) – in an attempt to protect him from the fate of his father, killed in a tournament, but who belatedly fulfils her traditional maternal role as educator by offering Percyvell a crash course of first, religious instruction (235–52), and then the formation appropriate to his role in society, just as expressed in contemporary conduct books (397–416).[23] Orme

---

[19] Edmund Reiss, 'Romance', in *The Popular Literature of Medieval England*, ed. Thomas J. Heffernan (Knoxville: University of Tennessee Press, 1985), pp. 108–30 (p. 119).
[20] Yin Liu, 'Middle English Romance as Prototype Genre', *Chaucer Review* 40 (2006), 335–53. The lists are those contained in *Richard Coeur de Lyon* (2), *Cursor Mundi*, *Speculum vitæ*, Chaucer's *Sir Thopas*, and the *Laud Troy Book*.
[21] Reiss, 'Romance', p. 119.
[22] *Le Bone Florence of Rome*, ed. Carol Falvo Heffernan (Manchester: Manchester University Press, 1976).
[23] *Ywain and Gawain, Sir Percyvell of Gales, The Anturs of Arther*, ed. Maldwyn Mills (London: Dent, 1992).

suggests that 'the presence of children and educational themes in medieval story literature, in short, is so large as to raise the question whether the authors of such works had children in mind as part of their audience', though he adds that 'such a question is difficult to answer conclusively, and full of pitfalls'.[24] However, it does seem that in a large number of Middle English romances the prominence of the 'educational theme' is such as to warrant the question why else it should have been included, if not to be of interest or use to those engaged with the process of education, either as parents or children. Here, Riddy's richly detailed imagining of the family context for a reading of *Le Bone Florence of Rome* as a narrative of self-making offers a valuable paradigm for exploring the audience of many another popular romance which may be understood as presenting a 'parental fantasy' of a young person's future life.

As has often been observed, the great majority of Middle English popular romances are preserved in manuscript miscellany volumes, many of which appear to have been compiled as household collections of family reading.[25] Some contain 'primer' material, directly expressing the function of the household as an educational environment in which children are taught to read and are given instruction in the elements of their faith, and conduct texts explicitly aimed at the young, giving them formation in etiquette and other requirements for taking their place in society. In this context, the prevalence of popular romances concerning children and their education in all these household manuscripts suggests that such narratives were seen as particularly suitable texts for transmitting core parental cultural values to young readers, and that it would be worth examining them in their manuscript settings.

It is not surprising that six of Reiss's pre-1300 child-centred romances are found in the Auchinleck MS (c. 1331–40), the earliest major collection of Middle English romances. Thorlac Turville-Petre argues that the book is themed to express the national pride of its English owner: a 'handbook of the nation';[26] however, as he points out, the variety of the texts and the explicit mention of an audience consisting of 'children and wimmen and men / Of twelue winter elde and mare' (*IMEV* 1760, fol. 70) further identify this as a book 'designed for the household',[27] where, as William of Nassyngton implies, the use of English makes the texts accessible to all, even if some members of the family can also read French or Latin. This designation as a household, family book seems to me more significant than the disputed social status of the owner, whether 'aspirant middle-class' or unrefined 'English upper class'.[28] The chief concerns of the volume are markedly similar to

---

[24] Orme, 'Children and Literature', p. 231.
[25] See, for example, Putter, 'A Historical Introduction', in *Spirit*, pp. 4–7; Felicity Riddy, *Sir Thomas Malory* (Leiden: Brill, 1987), pp. 14–30.
[26] Thorlac Turville-Petre, *England the Nation: Language, Literature and National Identity, 1290–1340* (Oxford: Clarendon Press, 1996), p. 112.
[27] Turville-Petre, *England the Nation*, p. 136.
[28] Derek Pearsall, in *The Auchinleck Manuscript, National Library of Scotland Advocates' MS 19.2.1*,

those identified by Riddy in the fifteenth-century household manuscripts, located 'among educated townspeople or members of the gentry', analysed by her in relation to Malory's concerns in *Morte Darthur*: 'history, good manners, right living and the next world'.[29] All exhibit the same anxieties about worldly success, conventionally imaged in the romances as renown, riches, and lordly power, when seen in relation to the values of eternity, and these anxieties, as Riddy points out, were shared by merchants and nobility alike.[30] What all these concerns suggest is a book that preserves the shared values of an English, Christian, well-established family.

The popular romances in the Auchinleck MS express the interests and concerns of the family in a form particularly suitable for sharing them with the young. In the light of earlier discussion of the use of the English language for the young, and the presence in the manuscript of a copy of the so-called Battle Abbey Roll, it is notable that many of them are translations from Anglo-Norman texts. This could suggest a programme of making available to younger readers the traditionally valued narratives of their cultural heritage, as members of an English family conscious of Norman ancestry. Equally notable is the question of length: as I have discussed elsewhere, there is good evidence for the view that small books and short texts, including short romances, were deemed suitable for child readers and were produced specifically for them,[31] and there are some unusual aspects of the Auchinleck romances that can interestingly be related to the question of length.

Guy of Warwick is one of the longest of popular English romances, at around twelve thousand lines. The Auchinleck version, the earliest, presents a translation of the Anglo-Norman text uniquely reconfigured as three linked but separate shorter narratives. The first tells the story of Guy from his exemplary childhood as a page in the court of the Earl of Warwick, through his sorrows and love-service for the Earl's daughter, Felice, his chivalric adventures abroad and knight-fellowship with Sir Tirri, to his return to England after seven years' absence, where he is welcomed by King Athelstan and saves England from destruction by a dragon. The story ends as the dragon's head is hung up at Warwick to general wonder, completing Guy's youthful proving of his worth. This narrative follows the form of the Anglo-Norman original, in couplets. The second Guy story is told in tail-rhyme stanzas, and begins with a two-stanza prologue to this new 'romaunce', giving an introductory portrait of the hero: 'Balder bern was non in bi, / His name was hoten sir Gij' (fol. 146v), and a brief account of his foreign adventures and dragon-slaying. It then marks his achievement of adult status and worldly success as he succeeds to his father's estate and founds his own family by marrying

---

intro. Derek Pearsall and I. C. Cunningham (London: Scolar Press, 1977), p. viii; Turville-Petre, *England the Nation*, p. 138.

[29] Riddy, *Sir Thomas Malory*, pp. 13, 30.
[30] Riddy, *Sir Thomas Malory*, pp. 26–8.
[31] Phillipa Hardman, '"This litel child, his litel book": Narratives for Children in Late-Fifteenth-Century England', *Journal of the Early Book Society* 7 (2004), 51–66.

Felice and begetting a son. But no sooner is this accomplished than the narration makes clear the very different direction the story will take: '& seþþen wiþ sorwe & sikeing sare / Her ioie turned hem into care / As 3e may forward here' (fol. 148). Guy is described as 'prince proude in pride' and from this point on the narrative follows his progress as he does penance for his pride of life and manslaughter, concealing his identity under the guise of a poor pilgrim.[32] His exploits abroad and return to England closely mirror the events of the first story, thus offering a different perspective on the conventional narrative of chivalric adventure, now concluding with the hero's renunciation of renown, reward, and the ties of friendship (Tirri), lordship (Athelstan), and marriage (Felice), to end his days in a hermitage. The paired narratives give a striking example of the anxiety around the conflict between worldly success and Christian values.

The third romance carved out of the Anglo-Norman *Gui de Warewic* is the narrative of Reinbrun, Guy's son, which has been excerpted from its place in the source and given an independent existence. It is clearly linked as a pendant to the tail-rhyme *Guy*, in which Guy forecasts to Felice the prowess of their unborn son, plans his education as a 'gentil man', and leaves his sword for the child (fols 148v–149). The story of Guy's change of life, however, is erased from *Reinbrun*, in which Guy's absence is never explained – after fathering Reinbrun in the opening stanzas, he features chiefly as the standard of chivalry, referred to by all throughout the narrative, and as the key to Reinbrun's identity. Just as Guy was constantly identified as 'of England', Reinbrun is made known to all as 'Gij is sone'. The scope of the story matches that of the couplet *Guy* narrative, covering the childhood and education of the hero, his serving a young lady at court (though without the love interest), adventures in foreign lands (Reinbrun having been sold to piratical merchants at the age of seven), and concluding with the return of the young hero to England, ready to claim his inheritance.

The material provided in the Anglo-Norman romance has thus been reworked to produce two self-contained romances of self-making, embodying 'parental fantasies' of a son's progress from careful nurture to the verge of adult self-establishment through the successful overcoming of extreme challenges to his identity as an English 'gentil man'. Between the two, the story of Guy's penitential pilgrimage balances these narratives of worldly achievement with a representation of the fearful question posed by the prospect of eternity, in the terms of the knightly model of earthly success: 'How sall we fare', as Gawain asks in the Thornton *Awntyrs of Arthur*, we 'þat fowndis to fyghte' and 'wynnes wirchippis & welthis by wyghtenes of handis?' (Lincoln Cathedral Library, MS 91, fol. 156v).

A different procedure has been used to produce another pair of linked but separate short romances in *Roland and Vernagu* and *Otuel*, both unique to this

---

[32] For extensive discussion of this theme, see Andrea Hopkins, *The Sinful Knights: A Study of Middle English Penitential Romance* (Oxford: Oxford University Press, 1990).

manuscript. For the first, in tail-rhyme stanzas, episodes from the *Pseudo-Turpin Chronicle* have been combined to create a two-part story dealing with Charlemagne's exploits against the King of Spain and his Saracens, followed by the confrontation of Roland and Vernagu, champions of the Christian and Saracen faiths.[33] As Turville-Petre observes, the Vernagu episode offers 'doctrinal instruction basic enough for any child "of twelue winter elde"',[34] in which the articles of the Creed are expounded in a lively dialogue between the rival champions, and this was perhaps a motive for selecting it. The common thread between the episodes is the emphasis laid on miraculous occurrences: new miracles are added in the English version, including the appearance of an angel to assure Roland of victory over the unregenerate Vernagu. The romance ends with a link to the following narrative: 'To Otuel also ȝern, / Þat was a Sarraȝin stern, / Ful sone þis word sprong' (878–80). Despite this, the romance of *Otuel* does not read like a continuation of *Roland and Vernagu* but begins as an independent narrative, with its own prologue and in a different metrical form, couplets. It functions, like *Reinbrun* after *Guy*, as a parallel story that mirrors the structure of the previous text in its two parts, the combat between Roland and Otuel (nephew of Vernagu) as Christian and Saracen champions (1–668) and the battle between Charlemagne and the Saracen King of Spain. Perhaps to enhance the parallel, in this version of *Otinel* there is extra emphasis on the miraculous nature of Otuel's conversion, and, in both *Otuel* and *Roland and Vernagu*, passages have been added to the source material at the beginning of the narrative to establish a stereotypical opposition between the good and evil rulers, with the Saracen kings represented as habitual and unprovoked destroyers of Christians. The short format and simple moral certainties of these two Charlemagne romances would certainly be compatible with the idea of young readers or listeners, but there are further additions that seem specifically aimed at using the romances to teach important lessons in conduct.

The passage in *Roland and Vernagu* in which the protagonists work through the articles of Christian belief is closely based on the *Pseudo-Turpin Chronicle*, but the episode has been given a frame that aligns it more obviously with the concerns of popular romance. At the end, Roland's despatching of Vernagu is reworked to include a detailed account of their combat and a typically triumphal conclusion as Roland cuts off the giant's head; while at the beginning, Vernagu's curiosity about the Christian faith is sparked by his admiration for Roland's courteous behaviour towards him. In the midst of the battle, Vernagu asks leave of Roland to sleep, which Roland grants (611–19), assuring him of safety, as he would never slay a sleeping knight (620–5). This emphasis on Roland's honourable knightly conduct is significantly different

---

[33] Based on an Anglo-Norman copy of *Johannes*, chapters I–XIV, XLIX–L, XXXIII–XLI (*The Old French Translation of the Pseudo-Turpin Chronicle*, ed. Ronald N. Walpole, 2 vols (Berkeley: University of California Press, 1976).

[34] Turville-Petre, *England the Nation*, p. 135.

from the antiquarian observations in the Latin and French texts about truces between Christians and Saracens. Even more striking is the elaboration in the Middle English romance of Roland's gesture when he places a stone beneath the sleeping Vernagu's head. In the *Pseudo-Turpin Chronicle*, Rollant's daring action is a sign of his own eager spirit (*de grant corage*; *alacer*), intended (wittily?) to let the giant sleep more pleasantly (*plus volentiers*; *libentius*); when he awakes, Fernagu makes no mention of the stone. In *Roland and Vernagu*, the episode is reconfigured as a lesson in polite behaviour. Vernagu lies down to sleep on the ground and begins to snore, but Roland, knowing it is rude to laugh at this ridiculous occurrence, lays a stone under his head to stop the snoring (629–37), and is rewarded for this act of knightly courtesy by Vernagu's grateful offer of friendship (641–9). The Middle English text thus provides both a plausible reason for Vernagu to tell Roland of his secret vulnerability – for Roland asks as a friend (653) – and also a practical lesson in the benefits of chivalrous conduct as a way of winning friends.

The Auchinleck *Otuel* shows a similar concern with appropriate knightly behaviour in the additions made to this free adaptation of the *chanson-de-geste Otinel*. For example, when Roland and his fellows have captured the Saracen Clarel, in this version alone their discussion as to what to do with him includes the question: 'Lordinges, what is nou ȝoure red, / Wole we smiten of his hed?' (849–50), and, after two of the peers have rejected this course of action for the practical reason that, if spared, Clarel might be grateful and return the favour, the third provides the chivalrous argument: 'where he do, or he ne doþ, / Hit where sschame to ous, iwis, / To sslen a man þat ȝolden him is' (860–2). Like the Vernagu episode, then, this incident is skilfully arranged to work as a lesson in the principles and practicalities of knightly conduct. The Auchinleck *Otuel* also gives evidence of unusual interest in the junior members of the knightly class, squires and bachelors, with additional material provided to create new roles for squires in the scenes of Otuel's arrival at court and of Oger's escape from prison, and to extend the role of the beardless knight-bachelor who rides to help the peers (1443–562). The new episode of the 'noble skuier' who helps Oger get out of prison 'wiþ queintize' is an example of pure *Boy's Own* fantasy, where it is the quick-witted squire instead of the famous peer himself (as in *Otinel*) who master-minds the escape, bringing Oger armour and horse and tricking the porter into letting them go (1629–62). The earlier squire-scene is less exciting, but more educational. When Otuel arrives at court, despite being 'ful of rage' (71) he behaves with exemplary good manners, taking a squire by the hand and explaining politely that he has messages for Charles, Roland and Oliver (85–6). The squire responds with minutely described courtesy that reads like a lesson from a conduct manual on the duties of squires towards messengers (89–98). Indeed, the theme of the messenger's protected status runs through the whole episode (71–370), for the simple assurance of immunity given in *Otinel* has here uniquely been elaborated into a series of five challenges to the court's professed knightly code, all answered with the same formula:

> Þau3 Otuwel speke outrage,
> For he was comen on message,
> King Charles þat was heende and god
> Nolde soffre him habbe nou3t bote god.   (329–32)

The typical romance scene of the hostile challenger has thus been reconfigured to include an object-lesson on the principle of guaranteed protection for messengers.

Most of the child-related Auchinleck romances are short, some because they are cast in an intrinsically short narrative form, such as the Breton lay (*Lay le Freine*, *Sir Degaré*), some because they are heavily abbreviated (*Tristrem*). The parallels between the linked romances discussed above are comparable with other instances, such as the incorporation of incidents and details from *Tristrem* in the narrative of *Horn Childe*, producing two parallel short narratives.[35] However, the most striking fact about the popular romances of the Auchinleck MS is the sheer preponderance of narratives centred on children or family groups, and of these, how many include material that seems especially appropriate for parental guidance of young readers in the way it endorses the value of lessons on chivalric or courtly accomplishments or religious instruction, through specifying details of the youthful development of their heroes. There is not scope here to examine them all, but it is interesting to compare the following details: in *Amis and Amiloun*, not only do the opening stanzas trace the exemplary development of the protagonists at ages five, seven, twelve and fifteen, but there is extensive treatment of the service performed by the twelve-year-old Amoraunt for his lord, Amiloun; in *Sir Degaré*, the young hero is 'Wel inorissched' by his foster-parents at age ten, taught 'of clergise' by a hermit for another ten years, and at twenty: 'Man for him self þat he wes, / Staleworht to don ech werk / And of his elde so god a clerk' (294–6); in *Beues of Hamtoun*, the seven-year-old Beves's master proposes a plan for the recovery of his inheritance that sounds like the plot of many a family romance (364–72), and when Beves is fifteen, a Saracen knight alerts him to his lack of religious education, having left Christendom when he was 'boute seue winter old' (595). In *Lay le Freine*, the abbess undertakes to 'teche & beld' (237) the young girl until she is twelve years old, when Freine first asks the abbess to 'wis & rede' (242) her about her family; in *Horn Childe*, Horn's father selects a master 'þat al þewes couþe' (37) of hunting, harping, chess and all other games, a curriculum in which Horn is proficient at fifteen. The young Tristrem also receives teaching for fifteen years, first set to study books and then following the courtly curriculum (*Tristrem*, 278–97).

As the earliest collection of Middle English popular romances in a 'family' manuscript, the Auchinleck MS sets useful parameters for discussion of

---

[35] See *Horn Childe and Maiden Rimnild*, ed. Maldwyn Mills, Middle English Texts 20 (Heidelberg: Winter, 1988), pp. 55–6, 62, 69–70, 77, and notes to the text.

later examples. Riddy has examined the late-fifteenth-century collection, Cambridge University Library, MS Ff.2.38, in her discussion of the family reading context for *Le Bone Florence of Rome* – it would be interesting to see similar analyses of the remaining 'family' narratives which, as she points out, have male protagonists, as texts that might embody 'parental fantasies' appropriate for the sons of the house. As the editors of the facsimile edition of CUL MS Ff.2.38 note, it preserves three of the same set of romances from the Auchinleck MS (*Guy*, *Bevis*, and *Sir Degaré*),[36] and it is worth remarking that both manuscripts also contain a copy of *The Seven Sages of Rome*, which shares many attributes with the romances, including a strong focus on the topic of education.[37] A similar collection of texts is found in London, British Library, MS Cotton Caligula A.ii, and Tony Davenport, in a discussion of the unique short Middle English *Chevalere Assigne*, has drawn attention to a thematic interest in the education of boys within the manuscript.[38] It is thus interesting to note that its unique copy of the Southern version of the popular romance *Octavian* includes material (not present in the French source or the Northern *Octavian*) to balance the description of young Florent's upbringing in Paris with an account of how young Octovian is brought up by their self-supporting mother in Jerusalem, set at five-plus 'To lerne gramer, þat wyll dyscryue / The Donet' (629–30), and able at fifteen 'to bere spere and scheld' (657). Frances McSparran points out that a similar scene occurs in *Emaré* in the same manuscript, where the mother also supports herself by needlework and 'taw3te her sone nortowre' (731).[39]

Although the Lincoln Thornton manuscript (c. 1440) is often grouped with these manuscripts described as household miscellanies, it differs from most others in several respects. Discussion has largely centred on its status as a gentleman scribe's own-use collection of texts;[40] certainly, it does not contain the primer material that identifies other household miscellanies as having obvious application to the education of the young. However, it does include the text known as *John Gaytryge's Sermon* or *The Lay Folks' Catechism*, an expanded English version of Archbishop Thoresby's digest of the essential elements of Christian doctrine for the instruction of the laity. The introduction explains that parents are responsible for passing this teaching on to their children as soon as they are old enough to learn (fol. 214). This

---

[36] *Cambridge University Library MS Ff.2.38*, intro. Frances McSparran and P. R. Robinson (London: Scolar Press, 1979), p. x.

[37] For discussion of this text, see Nicole Clifton, '*The Seven Sages of Rome*, Children's Literature, and the Auchinleck manuscript', in *Childhood in the Middle Ages and the Renaissance: The Results of a Paradigm Shift in the History of Mentality*, ed. Albrecht Classen (Berlin: De Gruyter, 2005), pp. 185-201.

[38] Tony Davenport, 'Abbreviation and the Education of the Hero in *Chevalere Assigne*', in *Matter of Identity*, pp. 9–20 (p. 17).

[39] *Octovian Imperator*, ed. Frances McSparran, Middle English Texts 11 (Heidelberg: Winter, 1979), p. 103.

[40] *The Thornton Manuscript (Lincoln Cathedral MS 91)*, intro. D. S. Brewer and A. E. B. Owen (London: Scolar Press, 1975), p. ix.

pattern of expectation seems to offer a useful framework for thinking about the function of the large collection of Middle English popular romances in the manuscript – as a repertory of narrative texts that embody the values and interests of parents and are to be shared with their children when they are old enough to learn. The Thornton MS contains seven popular romances, in three of which the narrative largely turns on the issue of land disputes (*The Erl of Toulous*, *Sir Degrevant*, and *The Awntyrs of Arthure*), and in the other four of which children are represented in central or substantial roles in stories dealing with the reunification of families and rediscovery of true parentage after trials and separation (*Octavian*, *Sir Isumbras*, *Sir Eglamour*, and *Sir Percyvell of Gales*). The selected romances can thus be seen to relate to two areas of major concern to gentry families: maintaining possession of their lands, and ensuring the succession of their heirs and continuation of the family. In each group, one romance stands out from the others as presenting a simple, logical plot focused on the fortunes of a single hero – *Percyvell* and *Degrevant*, inviting comparison with the short romances from the Auchinleck MS.

In the Middle English *Percyvell* the topic of education is so prominent, mention of 'nurtoure' so frequent, that the text may be considered as offering an analysis of the educational process, weighing the relative effects upon the child of nature and nurture. As Maldwyn Mills notes, '*wilde* is a key word in this romance' to denote Percyvell and his actions,[41] and its stock opposite *tame* and the common sense 'uncultivated' point to its appropriateness for a pattern of meaning in which Percyvell's 'enduring lack of polish' creates an extended implied contrast between the 'natural' Percyvell as he is now, and how he should have been at his age, if properly educated. The story begins with the successful career of Percyvell the elder, the hero's father, a 'noble man' who is rewarded for his knightly service at King Arthur's court with marriage to the king's own sister, extensive lands, fine robes, and other moveables (21–36). The father intends his son to replicate his own success – the child is to be called 'Als his ffadir highte byforne: / Yonge Percyvell' (107–8), and from birth is set to follow his father's career in the jousting field: 'For he wolde his son were gette / In the same wonne' (119–20).[42] The father's untimely death causes the mother to abjure all such knightly education for their son in favour of a simple, safe upbringing in the woods, but in another logical addition to the source material, the English romance has her keep just one of her husband's weapons for the son's use when old enough, which he duly uses to provide the 'marte' (207), the animal carcasses for butchery that the family need to supplement the goat's milk they had for 'lyves fode' (186–8).[43] It is thus not by instinctive skill in the art of hunting that Percyvell

---

[41] *Ywain and Gawain, Sir Percyvell of Gales, The Anturs of Arther*, ed. Mills, pp. 193, xxiv. Mills argues that his lack of polish indicates an affinity with heroes of folk-tale rather than romance.
[42] As Putter observes, both these details are unique to this version of the Perceval story ('Story Line and Story Shape in *Sir Percyvell of Gales*', in *Spirit*, p. 178).
[43] The implied distinction between Percyvell's 'marte' and the art of hunting is made explicit in the

shows his innate gentility, but in the form of the questions about the weapon that he asks his mother:

> 'Swete modir,' sayde he,
> 'What manere of thyng may this bee
> That ye nowe hafe taken mee:
> What calle yee this wande?' (197–200)

As Tony Davenport notes of similar passages in the Middle English *Chevalere Assigne*, the child's questions represent 'actual medieval teaching practices'[44] and the pedagogical content, covering the terminology proper to the exercise of arms, is the appropriate curriculum for a boy in a noble family. After fifteen years without further instruction, the mother marks her son's expected emergence from childhood by advising him to pray that God help him 'A gude man for to bee / And longe to duelle here' (239–40); not surprisingly, Percyvell has to ask again: '"Swete moder," sayde he, / "Whatkyns a godd may that be …?"' (241–2), and when his imperfect understanding leads him to misconstrue the mounted knights he meets as gods, he feels the need of further maternal instruction: seeing a horse,

> He saide, 'When I come to my dame,
> And I fynde hir at hame,
> Scho will telle the name
> Off this ilke thynge!' (337–40)

Nevertheless, despite the boy's uncouth behaviour, King Arthur immediately recognizes in his 'vesage free' the likeness of his noble father (585–8). The young Percyvell's continuing misconstructions (confusing mares and horses; taking literally his mother's teaching about 'mesure'; having to resort to smithy techniques against his enemies because he is too 'ill … kende' (1675) to know better) would afford knowing pleasure to a well-instructed audience; at the same time the narrative raises interesting questions about the relative roles of natural gifts and taught skills, focused in the reaction of the lady Lufamour:

> Grete wondir had Lufamour
> He was so styffe in stour
> And couthe so littill of nurtour,
> Als scho had there sene. (1564–7)

Percyvell's delayed coming-of-age is inventively represented in his finally apprehending the difference between a 'stede' and a 'mere' and awakening from his reverie – 'The childe wann owt of study / That he was inn sett' (1710–11) – to determined and effective action:

---

romance of *Tristrem*, where Tristrem teaches huntsmen how to dress the deer correctly and not as if mere butchered farm animals, 'Martirs as it were' (452–62).

[44] Davenport, 'Abbreviation and the Education of the Hero', p. 14.

He says, 'Now hase thou taughte me
How that I sall wirke with the!'
Then his swerde drawes he
And strake to hym thro.   (1716–19)

The educational process in *Sir Degrevant*, on the other hand, is presented entirely straightforwardly. The narrative begins with an extended portrait of the hero, first as a knight of the Round Table in parallel with Percyvell the elder (1–32), and then as a contrast to Percyvell the younger, as the ideal product of a programme of gentle education, skilled in music and hunting, observant in practising his religion, chaste, ready to help those in need, charitable to the poor, generous to all, and successful in tournaments (33–96). Degrevant's possessions – his hounds and hawks; his lands, arable, pasture and park; his halls; his horses – are interwoven into this account as if to suggest a connection between his virtues and his wealth, and in the ensuing narrative he exercises many of his virtuous qualities while defending his property against the marauding earl. The unusually detailed way in which this text mirrors the life of the noble household has often been noted;[45] however, in the Thornton MS there are a few unique readings that render Degrevant a little less socially elevated. He is not related to King Arthur in this version (26–7), and is of more modest means, owning a hundred rather than a thousand pounds' worth of land, for example (65–9); perhaps this would have provided a better fit with the readership of the Thornton version, and the 'parental fantasy' of filial achievement that is one of its possible functions. Arlyn Diamond argues that the unusually potent construction of Melidor's sphere of influence in this romance gives her a partnership role with Degrevant in the formation of 'the ideal household',[46] implying that the 'parental fantasy' embodied in the narrative might be equally appropriate for daughters.

The last manuscript collection of romances to be discussed here also differs from the model of the Auchinleck MS, CUL MS Ff.2.38, and BL MS Cotton Caligula A.ii: Edinburgh, National Library of Scotland, MS Advocates' 19.3.1 was constructed as a series of separate booklets.[47] Each of the three short verse romances in the collection, *Sir Gowther*, *Sir Ysumbras* and *Sir Amadace*, forms the major text in a small book, in which each romance is accompanied by a courtesy poem addressed to a young child, suggesting that these little books were prepared for children to read.[48] The three romances clearly share the educational agenda of the courtesy books accompanying

---

[45] See, for example, Arlyn Diamond, '*Sir Degrevant*: What Lovers Want', in *Pulp Fictions*, pp. 82–101; W. A. Davenport, '*Sir Degrevant* and Composite Romance', in *Insular Romance*, pp. 111–31.
[46] Diamond, '*Sir Degrevant*: What Lovers Want', p. 98.
[47] For fuller discussion, see *The Heege Manuscript: A Facsimile of National Library of Scotland MS Advocates 19.3.1*, intro. Phillipa Hardman, Leeds Texts and Monographs, n.s. 16 (Leeds: Leeds Studies in English, 2000).
[48] See Mary Shaner, 'Instruction and Delight: Medieval Romances as Children's Literature', *Poetics Today* 13 (1992), 5–15; Hardman, *The Heege Manuscript*, pp. 22–28.

them, not only in the virtues of humility, piety, and generosity demonstrated by the hero of each, but also in the more specific sense of good manners. In *Sir Amadace*, for example, the concern with gentle nurture is quite explicit in comments that repeatedly spell out how the hero's courteous manners in salutation and leave-taking and honourable behaviour in keeping his word serve to demonstrate his gentle birth. *Sir Gowther*, on the other hand, like *Sir Percyvell of Gales*, offers an eccentric reflection of conventional education: in this case, the hero's youth is constructed as an extreme antitype of gentle nurture in which he kills his wet-nurses, terrorizes his parents, and refuses to practise his religion. Nevertheless, by the age of fifteen, the recalcitrant Gowther reveals natural abilities corresponding to the concerns of noble education in his skill with weapons, his horsemanship, and his love of hunting. Alcuin Blamires reads this story of a boy fathered by the devil as addressing 'profound medieval anxieties about the production of heirs, and particularly of violent and ungovernable heirs' through Gowther's demonic behaviour that 'makes him the total antithesis of all feudal responsibility and courtly *mesure*'.[49] It should not be overlooked, however, that the untaught naïf, Percyvell, although truly begotten and recognized by King Arthur as the living image of his noble father, is equally lacking in *mesure*, repeatedly threatening to kill Arthur, for example, if he should thwart the boy's will (*Sir Percyvell of Gales*, 383–4, 527–8). The common factor is the lack of education, whether caused by the child's rejection of discipline or by the parent's withholding of instruction, and the prominence of this theme of nurture in so many Middle English popular romances would seem to indicate a readership in which the business of providing and acquiring a gentle education is an issue of prime importance.

---

[49] Alcuin Blamires, 'The Twin Demons of Aristocratic Society in *Sir Gowther*', in *Pulp Fictions*, pp. 45–62 (pp. 52–3).

10

Modern and Academic Reception of the Popular Romance

CORY JAMES RUSHTON

The reception of popular medieval romance in England has always been inextricably linked with academic study of both the history of the language and of medieval society. Popular genres tend to evolve, often resisting coalescence around particular texts or authors, and the medieval romance lives on today through being subsumed in a variety of cultural contexts (the western, for example). Those medieval romances which have survived the passage of time, when encountered today, are found almost exclusively in the academy, and the study of their reception cannot be separated from literary history and intellectual inquiry. This leads to some unexpected observations, not only about the romance, but about the genre's relationship with other medieval artefacts and with the academy in which they have been revived.

In the context of the modern classroom, teaching the 'Tale of Sir Thopas', (Chaucer at his meta-textual best), can be a frustrating experience. Like all parody, 'Thopas' makes sense only in its 'dependent and oppositional' relationship with the popular romances it parodies,[1] romances like the ones Chaucer the Pilgrim himself names in the poem:

> Men speken of romances of prys,
> Of Horn Child and of Ypotys,
>   Of Beves and of Sir Gy,
> Of Sir Lybeux and Pleyndamour –
> But Sir Thopas, he bereth the flour
>   Of roial chivalry!   (897–902)

Modern students can only take our word, and Chaucer's, for the fame and relevance of these figures. The joke is entirely lost to time. Guy of Warwick and Horn Child, hugely popular in the Middle Ages, are virtually unknown today; Beves of Hampton shares a name with a brain-dead cartoon teenager who chortles through MTV videos with his friend Butthead, and even that reference is slipping inexorably into the ever-receding pop cultural past.

---

[1] Lee Patterson, *Temporal Circumstances: Form and History in the 'Canterbury Tales'* (New York: Palgrave MacMillan, 2006), p. 106.

Lybeaus Desconus, with his relationship to the Gawain of Malory and *Sir Gawain and the Green Knight* (henceforth *SGGK*), might have more purchase on the student imagination, but only if they have been exposed to those texts previously. *Ypotis* is an even harder sell, since it is not a romance at all, while Pleyndamour is completely unknown. In the midst of any course on medieval literature, I suspect students and casual readers might well become quite weary of hearing that every third reference is to something unknown and probably unknowable.

The Norton edition, for one, helpfully includes a selection from the stanzaic *Guy of Warwick*, so one can dutifully turn to these pages and try, perhaps with some sense of desperation, to point out just how Chaucer was imitating and parodying the metre and scansion – only to remember just how foreign those poetic elements are even in literature far more familiar to the modern student. Elsewhere in this volume, Ad Putter argues that metre should not be a dull subject (p. 111); he is right, but decades of widespread institutional disregard for prosody in favour of cultural studies militates against our success, at least until some balance between the two is found. Asking anyone to look at 'Thopas' and *Guy of Warwick*, and then to compare them with (for example) the 'Prioress's Tale' from the same *Canterbury* fragment, is therefore fraught with potential danger. Readers still struggling with the unfamiliar language will possibly have trouble differentiating between the texts – it is perhaps similar to providing readers with a page of Klingon and a page of Tolkien's Elvish and asking them to make an aesthetic case for one over the other. In the end, it is not that students and readers coming to Middle English for the first time are incapable of understanding how the metrical and stanzaic parody worked – it was simply a matter of a joke explained to death, and a joke that (to them) can only be funny in theory.

Further, there is no inherent reason to expect that many modern students would not actually prefer Guy to Thopas – both character and text. The Norton selection provides details of Guy's return to England, having proven his suitability for marriage to his beloved Felice, and it does seem to speak to several issues in 'Thopas': the generic nature of praise for the hero, the idea of chivalry as a quest to win a beloved (Felice for Guy, the fairy queen for Thopas).[2] Yet it does not contain the action sequences which may have been among the Guy tradition's attractions, 'the love of exotic places and characters, the excitement of suspense, the clash of good and evil'.[3] It might be argued that something of a straw man has been inadvertently created by emphasizing what the romance does badly (character development) instead of what it does well (chivalric adventure and strange situations). *Guy of Warwick*

---

[2] In *The Canterbury Tales: Fifteen Tales and the General Prologue*, ed. V. A. Kolve and Glending Olsen, 2nd edn (New York: W. W. Norton, 2005), pp. 451–4.
[3] Velma Bourgeois Richmond, *The Popularity of Middle English Romance* (Bowling Green, OH: Bowling Green University Popular Press, 1975), p. 192.

was just one of many popular romances to be printed in the sixteenth century, a sure sign of its continuing appeal (see Fellows, pp. 74–75).

Part of the problem, perhaps, is the survival of key romance patterns, tropes, and themes into our own generic literatures: fantasy, certainly, but also science fiction and the western. The contemporary films and video games we tend to watch and play are all rooted in a template based, more or less, on the medieval popular romance with its addiction to the fantastic and its resolute avoidance of long conversation and complex characterization. Stories like Guy's had 'become a staple of a younger generation's reading' by the late Middle Ages,[4] and in a sense this has either again become or remained the case. While it is conventional to note the success of the medievalist Tolkien's *Lord of the Rings* (and that of the genre it essentially created, including *Star Wars*) when discussing the potential currency of medieval romance, the pattern which underlies *Guy of Warwick* is far more widespread than this. Virtually every adventure video game, from the *Halo* series to *Resident Evil*, is based on the idea of the quest in which an individual leaves civilization, encountering the strange and marvellous on the way, and often returns with a firmer sense of his or her own identity – if only in the sense that the protagonist now knows what he or she is capable of accomplishing, rather than the medieval requirement that the protagonist have a new sense of social position. Certainly, the medieval romance is distant enough from us chronologically to provide many moments of confusion and alterity, but much of today's popular narrative has, at its core, a deep relationship with popular medieval narrative.

Readers (including and perhaps overwhelmingly students) often respond well to several of these texts, reacting to the sudden transitions through a lens of cinematic experience and appreciating both the barrelling forward momentum and the opaque emotional lives of the characters: the brief flash of electricity between the self-exiled Orfeo and his abducted queen Heurodis, who is trapped in the retinue of the Fairy King, as they catch each other's eye; the can-do attitude of Havelok the Dane, so familiar from generations of Disney films, at least until the various slaughters start; Launfal's tumble into the mud, mocked by observers, as he reaches his lowest point before his return to fairy-induced glory. These conversations have the potential to be sophisticated: the role of Ubbé in *Havelok* can lead to an interesting discussion of political allegiance and the historical relationship between England and Denmark, and students are often sensitive to all the potential interpretative registers of Sir Orfeo's exile: is he dead, is he a Christ-figure? While Peter Lucas shares the general critical consensus on the romance when he declares *Sir Gawain and the Green Knight* 'more sophisticated' than other romances, he can still compare it with an earlier romance in a striking manner:

---

[4] Seth Lerer, *Chaucer and His Readers: Imagining the Author in Late Medieval England* (Princeton: Princeton University Press, 1993), p. 95. See Hardman's chapter in this volume, for an exploration of Guy's appeal to younger readers.

> Whereas *Sir Gawain* is concerned with relative questions, *Sir Orfeo* is concerned with absolute questions. Hence the differences of outcome. Gawain's success or failure is a matter of ambiguity ... But Orfeo's success is necessarily absolute, since the breakdown of his relationships with his wife and his people would have dealt a scarcely bearable blow to his society as then constituted.[5]

This focus on 'absolute questions' may be the secret to the pedagogical success of the popular romance: it allows for the possibility, however elusive in practice, of an absolute answer. This in turn facilitates deeper and more daring engagements with the issues encountered along the way towards that elusive certainty.

None of this long preamble to a tale should be taken as an argument for the superiority of the popular romance as a subject for pedagogy – the rewards of teaching Chaucer or Langland can be readily apparent at the end of a course, when the difficulties of their works become the subject for intelligent student discourse rather than a source of student anxiety. What I am suggesting is that the popular romance may be a useful tool for pedagogy, and that this may be the case because of cultural changes which have taken place well away from academia (but which may be partially and paradoxically rooted in the early reception of the romance itself). If Derek Pearsall could once argue that the only reason to read most popular romances was so that the reader could appreciate the 'Tale of Sir Thopas' and 'savour the more its delicious absurdity',[6] the time may now have come when the best reason to read 'Thopas' is to appreciate the rich field of story from which it grew.

Romance and the Gentleman

David Matthews has convincingly argued that the modern study of romance is rooted in a deep desire for the pageantry of the Middle Ages; Percy, in his *Reliques*, compiled to recommend himself to the aristocratic Percy family with which he had no real connection despite the shared surname, can be credited with having 'developed a romantic, conservative Middle English designed to cement the relations between the ruling class and a certain type of aesthetic persona', the literary-scholar.[7] This pattern would be replicated as it moved into the gentleman's clubs of the nineteenth century. The medieval romances and ballads found in the Percy Folio were the initial agents of this development, but it was not their literary merit which recommended them. Chaucer,

---

[5] Peter J. Lucas, 'Earlier Verse Romance', in *Readings in Medieval Texts: Interpreting Old and Middle English Literature*, ed. David Johnson and Elaine Treharne (Oxford: Oxford University Press, 2005), pp. 229–40 (pp. 238–9).

[6] Derek Pearsall, *The Canterbury Tales* (London and New York: Routledge, 1993), pp. 161–2.

[7] David Matthews, *The Making of Middle English, 1765–1910* (Minneapolis: University of Minnesota Press, 1999), especially pp. 3–24 (p. 23); see also the chapter by Maldwyn Mills and Gillian Rogers in this volume.

even at this early date, was in a separate category, a real author who (despite his linguistic difficulties) could stand with Shakespeare and later members of the literary and cultural canon.[8] The romances, on the other hand, 'were best studied for the pictures of "customs and opinions" they provided, as the material for a positivist historicism in which questions of literary value were largely bypassed'; Percy actually 'rewrote the poems, and did so in a process that reinvented them for his time'.[9] This sense of the romance as a location for historical information, perhaps better still for historical colour, continued until at least Frederic Madden's time, when he could declare that *Havelok the Dane* has 'value ... as an accurate picture of the manners and customs of former times'.[10] As literary objects, the romance could be dismissed as (in Percy's phrase) 'barbarous productions of a rude age', a dismissal which remained in effect until relatively recently.[11] For Nicola McDonald, Percy's publication of the *Reliques* 'signals the modern abuses of romance'.[12]

It is Pearsall, again, who provides the more recent negative assessment, pronouncing it 'difficult to understand why poems that are so bad according to almost every criteria of literary value should have held such a central position in the literary culture of their own period'.[13] McDonald is correct to point to the class implications of this judgment, exploring the manner in which Pearsall's valuation of individual romance texts is linked directly to the presumed individual audience.[14] This assessment is, of course, replicated in all periods – Hollywood does not produce a continual stream of aesthetically beautiful and thematically challenging films, and modern book culture is currently dominated by Dan Brown and J. K. Rowling. If it is difficult to see how medieval romance became central to the Middle Ages, it must be equally difficult to understand why the *Star Wars* saga continues to be so popular. It should come as no surprise that Brown, Rowling, and George Lucas have all created texts descended almost directly from the medieval romances Pearsall dismisses, and that the cultural continuity implied by this descent is integral to the renewed interest in medieval popular narrative. As no less an authority than Helen Cooper notes, '*Star Wars* has its quest, its princess, its Jedi knights, and its giant hairy monster' – albeit one who 'has to have his hand held when the going gets tough'.[15] McDonald states that 'Academic communities have long been resistant to popular art and to the kind of pleasure it produces; the denial of "lower" forms of enjoyment ... is one of the most important

---

8   Tim William Machan, *Textual Criticism and Middle English Texts* (Charlottesville: University Press of Virginia, 1994), p. 47.
9   Matthews, *Making of Middle English*, pp. 11–13.
10 *The Ancient English Romance of Havelok the Dane; Accompanied by the French Text: With an Introduction, Notes, and a Glossary*, ed. Frederick Madden (London, 1828), p. iii.
11 Percy, *Reliques*, I, p. vi.
12 McDonald, 'Introduction', in *Pulp Fictions*, p. 5.
13 Derek Pearsall, 'Understanding Middle English romance', *Review* 2 (1980), 105–25 (p. 105).
14 McDonald, 'Introduction', in *Pulp Fictions*, p. 9.
15 Helen Cooper, *The English Romance in Time: Transforming Motifs from Geoffrey of Monmouth to the Death of Shakespeare* (Oxford: Oxford University Press, 2004), p. 21.

ways in which consumers and critics of high culture ... assert their cultural credentials and intellectual credibility.'[16] While this appears to be changing on the surface, with an increased academic interest in the popular culture of all periods, resistance to the medieval romance can still be found, just as more conservatively pedagogical factions resist courses devoted to Harry Potter and mount sporadic defences of the literary canon. For Percy and his successors, the denial of these lower forms was enforced through recourse to the historical rather than literary value of the romance, thus justifying their interest in the texts without validating the texts themselves.

It was this sense of the historical combined with the genre's links to the aristocracy, however, that kept the romance in sight. Matthews has capably explored the sheer oddness of the text-producing gentleman's clubs of the nineteenth century, a trend initiated by the Roxburghe Club, named for the duke whose auction of the Valdarfer Boccaccio of 1471 was commemorated in an annual dinner at which members were expected to produce editions of Middle English texts, predominantly romances.[17] Many of the period's most influential scholar-gentlemen either belonged to or did work by proxy for the Roxburghe Club and its imitators; Sir Walter Scott, for example, joined the Roxburghe Club in 1823. The dominance of the gentleman's clubs did not, and could not, last forever. With limited print runs and little editorial stringency, the clubs rarely pretended to be giving Middle English literature to the masses. Frederick J. Furnivall's foundation of the Early English Text Society in 1864 (followed by the Extra Series in 1867 and the Chaucer and Ballad Societies in 1868) acted as a catalyst for both the increasing importance of a consistent methodology and a new emphasis on placing books into libraries; EETS was based on the principles of a democratizing subscription service open to any interested institutions and individuals. Although not all of the Society's productions were of equal or lasting value, the success of Furnivall's plan is demonstrated by the presence of EETS texts in many major libraries, and by the strong presence of EETS in the bibliographic notes to a volume like this one.

Medieval popular romance remained, and arguably had always been, a special interest. While this chapter can comfortably assume the survival and evolution of romance motifs in the generic literature and film of the twentieth and twenty-first centuries, that only means that medieval romance has the capacity now to be more popular than it has been since perhaps the fifteenth century. Chaucer, in the meantime, went from strength to strength, the only medieval English author who could legitimately be called 'a commercial property'.[18] He further maintained a relatively strong presence in the universities: the father of English poetry; a precursor and source for Shakespeare, Dryden, Blake, and Wordsworth; the inventor of the Wife of Bath, with all

---

[16] McDonald, 'Introduction', in *Pulp Fictions*, p. 11.
[17] Matthews, *Making of Middle English*, pp. 85–109.
[18] Matthews, *Making of Middle English*, p. 168.

her proto-feminist possibility, and the Pardoner, with all his ambiguous and critically exciting sexual indeterminacy. Chaucer changed with the times, a fluid figure that nonetheless provided a kind of stable origin for English language and letters.[19] The romance, on the other hand, seemed rooted to its own history – that was partially why it was seen to have any value at all. Chaucer, of course, played (however inadvertently) a major role in keeping the romance in its place, and so we return to Thopas.

Thopas and Thomas

If the purpose of 'Thopas' was to mock popular romance into a position of distinct inferiority vis-à-vis Chaucer's own works, it has succeeded all too well. Perhaps Chaucer had not intended to produce such a long-standing impediment to the romance being taken seriously; Lee Patterson has recently argued that 'Thopas' might be a kind of literary lightning rod for Chaucer's wider Canterbury project:

> As a literary performance, then, the Tale of Sir Thopas stages virtually every criticism that literary orthodoxy could have leveled against the Chaucer of the *Canterbury Tales* ... In its mocking of both literary ambition and chivalric achievement, as in its deliberate adoption of socially disregarded modes of literary production, it represents a disengagement from the adult world.[20]

For N. F. Blake, there are no clues in Chaucer's language itself to indicate that 'Thopas' is a parody at all; as Wim Tigges summarizes the position, the tale can 'only be seen as parodic because of text-external comments (in particular the interruption of the Host'.[21] One of these 'text-external comments' is the admirable Parson's insistence that he 'kan nat geeste "rum, ram, ruf"', that he cannot or will not tell a 'geeste' or romance, because he is 'a southren' (and therefore sophisticated) man (X.43–2). If Chaucer appeared to have signed the death warrant for the popular romance's feasibility within modern intellectual circles, consigning it to near-permanent marginality, this is in spite of romance's widespread popularity in the print culture of the sixteenth century (as discussed by Fellows, above), a popularity which seems to have been shared by 'Thopas'.

The distinction between modern academics and Chaucer's initial audience is necessary, given the widespread evidence that 'Thopas' was taken

---

[19] For a more complicated and engaging discussion of some of these issues, see Thomas A. Prendergast, *Chaucer's Dead Body: From Corpse to Corpus* (New York and London: Routledge, 2004).
[20] Patterson, *Temporal Circumstances*, p. 105.
[21] N. F. Blake, *The English Language in Medieval Literature* (London: J. M. Dent, 1977), pp. 125–6; Wim Tigges, 'Romance and Parody', in *Companion to Middle English Romance*, ed. Henk Aertsen and Alasdair A. MacDonald (Amsterdam: VU University Press, 1990), pp. 129–51 (p. 137).

at least semi-seriously in the sixteenth century as a model for deliberately archaic poetry (as in Spenser and Drayton).[22] The curious conflation of poetry which is associated with children and is itself indicative of English poetry's own 'youth' signals the later position of the romance in literary history: it becomes the target for Tudor educational reform on the one hand, and a guide to medieval mannerisms on the other. In both cases, romance becomes something which needs to be moved past as both the individual and the society come to maturity. Where earlier critics (Percy among them) saw the romance as dangerous, Nicola McDonald reminds us that, 'Given its diminished modern status, we simply cannot believe that medieval romance bears worrying about.'[23] If Chaucer really had used the romance to signal his own lack of importance as a mere 'frivolous player of literary games',[24] an author who enters his own creation only to be 'hooted off the stage',[25] he has nevertheless played some role in reducing the romance itself to inconsequentiality. It is not just Pearsall who has used 'Thopas' to make back-handed comments on the popular romance; Sir Thopas, 'as he priketh north and est' (VII.757), has perhaps slain more texts than he has giants. Many critics now believe that young readers would have enjoyed exactly the elements it shares with non-parodic popular romance:

> ... those features that made condemnable both to Renaissance and modern scholars: its fast, almost manic pace; its violent drama of the giant and his threats; and, most pointedly, its presentation of its hero as a kind of child.[26]

If Chaucer's intentions for 'Thopas' had been to provide an entertainment for children, or some combination of the juvenile (in its non-pejorative sense) and the parodic (in any sense of the term), then the use of 'Thopas' as a stick with which to beat popular romance might no longer be of much use.

One fruitful method for examining how the popular romance has been defined against Chaucer's 'Thopas' is to look at the reception of a poem which, unlike most of the popular romances, may have a known author, Chaucer's contemporary, Thomas Chestre, composer of the aforementioned *Sir Launfal*, as the poem itself tells us in a rare moment of authorial self-identification (1039–41);[27] he may also have written one of the poems mentioned in 'Thopas', *Lybeaus Desconus* (a translation of the Old French romance *Li Beaux Desconus* by Renaut de Beaujeu).[28] Further, Chaucer and Chestre

---

[22] J. A. Burrow, 'Sir Thopas in the Sixteenth Century', in *Middle English Studies Presented to Norman Davis*, ed. Douglas Gray and E. G. Stanley (Oxford: Clarendon Press, 1983), pp. 69–91.
[23] McDonald, 'Introduction', in *Pulp Fictions*, pp. 3–4.
[24] Patterson, *Temporal Circumstances*, p. 105.
[25] Jill Mann, *Feminizing Chaucer*, rev. edn (Cambridge: D. S. Brewer, 2002), p. 99.
[26] Lerer, *Chaucer and His Readers*, p. 95.
[27] In Stephen H. A. Shepherd, *Middle English Romances* (New York: W. W. Norton, 1995).
[28] Maldwyn Mills, 'The Composition and Style of the "Southern" *Octavian, Sir Launfal*, and

may have known one another: Burrow notes the presence of a 'Thomas de Chestre' in the same 1360 list of ransomed soldiers in which Chaucer himself appears.[29] Putter invokes the latent desire to link these two named authors and simultaneously sounds a warning: 'It would be nice to think that this "Thomas de Chestre" entertained Chaucer with his romances in his period of captivity, though the surname "Chestre" is so common that the identification must remain speculative.'[30] This view of Chestre as a central figure in Chaucer's development is itself underdeveloped, but the appearance of Lybeaus in the Thopas list has proven too suggestive to ignore entirely.

Chestre does not suffer in comparison with Chaucer alone, but with his own antecedent sources; in the case of *Sir Launfal*, this source is *Lanval* by the equally daunting Old French poet Marie de France. While Myra Stokes appreciates the 'robust inventiveness and consistency that adapt the story into a more aggressive whole, centred on a less passive hero with more to endure', she also insists that the 'modern reader cannot ... but notice in it the absurdities Chaucer exposed: the jejune rhythm, the reliance on tags and formulaic clichés, the elf-queen and the giant, and so on'.[31] Chaucer's parody retroactively rewrites *Sir Launfal* in a way that Chestre, it seems, could never retroactively rewrite *Lanval*. Stokes points to several areas in which 'Chestre's tale is not without distinct emphases of an interesting kind', arguing that 'it conveys vividly the mortifications and exaltations attendant upon economic fortunes'. Stokes locates the popularity of the text not in distribution – there are more manuscripts of *Lanval* than of *Sir Launfal* – but in exactly those facets of the narrative which tend towards wish-fulfilment (tournament success, for example) or the blurring of the public/private boundary so central to Marie's narrative. Still, Stokes's tone is one of vague apology, even as she dismisses some traditional criticisms of the poem. For example, she notes that the oft-deprecated manner in which Launfal uses his invisible squire to win tournaments is little different than the use James Bond makes of 'the technological wizardry that stands in for magic in the twentieth-century mix of these time-honoured ingredients'.[32] Increasingly, other critics have begun to take *Sir Launfal* on its own terms: for example, Carol O'Toole cogently argues for the poem's intense interest in the decline of aristocratic values during the reign of Richard II.[33] Complicating matters further, Carol J. Nappholz has argued that 'Chestre consciously set out to write a humorous piece rather than a serious

---

Libeaus Desconus', *Medium Ævum* 31 (1962), 88–109. Opinion remains divided, although many now provisionally accept Chestre as the author of *Lybeaus* despite the cautions of Stephen H. A. Shepherd, *Middle English Romances*, p. 218, n. 8.

29 John Burrow, 'Romance', in *The Cambridge Companion to Chaucer*, ed. Piero Boitani and Jill Mann, 2nd edn (Cambridge: Cambridge University Press), pp. 143–59 (p. 159, n. 3).
30 Ad Putter, 'An Historical Introduction', in *Spirit*, p. 13.
31 Myra Stokes, '*Lanval* to *Sir Launfal*: A Story Becomes Popular', in *Spirit*, pp. 56–77 (p. 59).
32 Stokes, '*Lanval* to *Launfal*', pp. 71–2.
33 A representative sampling of recent work on *Sir Launfal* includes: Carol O'Toole, 'Social Disorder and Discontent in Thomas Chestre's *Sir Launfal*', *PaGes* 6 (1999), University of Dublin website: http://www.ucd.ie/pages/99/articles/otoole.pdf, accessed May 3, 2008; Dinah Hazell,

romance.'[34] If she is right, Chestre must be given credit for not only seeing the parodic potential in the popular romance just as Chaucer did, but for successfully engaging with the genre: as noted above, readers can still enjoy *Sir Launfal* without the depth of apparatus required by 'Thopas'.

At the conclusion of his discussion of 'Thopas', Pearsall asks, 'If we did not know it were by Chaucer, it would have to be by someone else: would anyone, one wonders, ever think, in such a case, that it was purposely bad?'[35] This remains a good question – Chaucer's imitation of the romance at its most derivative is too perfect to guarantee such an assumption. The reception of the 'Tale of Gamelyn', popular enough to exist in twenty-five manuscript copies of the *Canterbury Tales*, but rarely accepted as actually by Chaucer, might suggest otherwise. T. A. Shippey notes that 'The poem's apparent medieval popularity is accordingly borrowed from Chaucer', who might have planned to give the story to the Knight's Yeoman, who has no tale in the collection as it has come down to us; Shippey argues that Chaucer routinely betrays a dislike of the yeomanry, his 'class enemies', and the rough and violent tale of the outlaw Gamelyn might have been tailored to serve his ideological ends. Yet the tale has been of little interest to literary critics, partly because its common attribution to the Cook (who already has a tale) is unconvincing. 'Gamelyn' is generally left to historians, who consider it 'a major source and object of study'.[36] In that, it remains in the category of medieval historical texts once inhabited by *Havelok* and other romances, as well as the secondary category of Chaucerian apocrypha. But by the same token, we could reverse Pearsall's question: would it have taken so long for *Sir Launfal* to be accepted as worthy of serious critical attention if some scribe had written it into the *Canterbury Tales*? Disguised by the pilgrimage frame, would anyone have thought to wonder if *Sir Launfal* was Chaucer's?

Green Knights

As with 'Sir Thopas', but in a shorter period of time, another great medieval text, *Sir Gawain and the Green Knight*, has caused other medieval romances (particularly Arthurian romances) to suffer in comparison with itself. Complicated and ambiguous, *Sir Gawain* has become the perfect object for critical study: Gawain's human failings and the court's apparent failure to understand or accept his resulting shame seem to have made it acceptable to professors looking for a medieval text which fits into their historical survey courses.

'The Blinding of Gwennere: Thomas Chestre as Social Critic', *Arthurian Literature* 20, ed. Keith Busby and Roger Dalrymple (Cambridge: D. S. Brewer, 2003), pp. 123–43.

[34] Carol J. Nappholz, 'Launfal's "Largesse": Word-Play in Thomas Chestre's *Sir Launfal*', *English Language Notes* 25:3 (1988), 4–9 (p. 9).

[35] Pearsall, *Canterbury Tales*, p. 165.

[36] T. A. Shippey, '*The Tale of Gamelyn*: Class Warfare and the Embarrassments of Genre', in *Spirit*, pp. 78–96 (p. 79).

The Green Knight's final 'explanation leaves a number of loose ends that increase the ambiguity of Gawain's experience'.[37] The popular romance has a strong tendency to leave fewer loose ends, at least under its own terms, forcing literary critics to pry a text open rather than to simply pick up the 'loose ends'. *Sir Gawain* looks, at least thematically, like a modern short story, with its ironic detachment from the chivalric ethos and its refusal to allow easy answers. Yet it would appear that the very willingness to defy medieval generic expectations which makes *Sir Gawain* a fixture on modern course syllabi is what made it necessary for at least one medieval poet to rewrite it. *Sir Gawain* has few of the generic markers of the popular romance (a successful love affair; a battle; a triumphant return to court, often with the antagonist in tow), and those features which it does have (magical transformation, a long journey) are often read in isolation from popular analogues or interpreted ironically. The fifteenth-century ballad *The Grene Knight*, found in the Percy Folio, fulfils all the above requirements where *Sir Gawain* refuses to do so, and further deletes anything which might trouble easy enjoyment of the story. Of course, in traditional criticism the latter text can only be seen as negatively transformative: 'all the mystery, suspense, and power have evaporated' in *The Grene Knight*,[38] although some criticism has begun to read the later poem as 'a clarification and normalization of the complex narrative' of its forebear.[39]

Sir Gawain quickly moved into the premier position in this project of recovery, a romance which rose above its tarnished generic field. Several nineteenth-century editions began this process: Madden's anthology publication (particularly *Sir Gawain and the Green Knight*), Jessie Weston's *The Legend of Sir Gawain* in 1897 (including *SGGK*), and Richard Morris's 1864 edition of *Sir Gawain and the Green Knight* (one of the first texts produced for the democratizing Early English Text Society), the edition which first achieved widespread placement in public and university libraries. This edition, subsequently revised by Israel Gollancz, was to see three reprints after 1897, before Gollancz revised it a second time in 1912; this testifies, as Paul Reichardt argues, to 'Gollancz's fascination with the editorial problems of this particular poem'.[40] Of course, this kind of sustained publishing schedule is only possible if there is public and institutional interest in the text. Ironically, but understandably given the evolution of *Sir Gawain*'s critical reception, the most recent and complete edition of Gawain poems does not

---

[37] Sachi Shimomura, *Odd Bodies and Visible Ends in Medieval Literature* (New York: Palgrave MacMillan, 2006), p. 151.
[38] Robert W. Ackerman, 'English Rimed and Prose Romances', in *Arthurian Literature in the Middle Ages: A Collaborative History*, ed. R. S. Loomis (Oxford: Clarendon Press, 1959), pp. 480–519 (p. 497).
[39] David O. Matthews, 'Narrative and Ideology in *The Grene Knight*', *Neophilologus* 78 (1994), 301–14 (p. 312).
[40] Paul F. Reichardt, 'Sir Israel Gollancz and the Editorial History of the Pearl Manuscript', *Papers on Language and Literature* 31 (1995), 145–63 (pp. 148–9).

include *Sir Gawain and the Green Knight* at all. While this decision is a fair one given the number of editions of *Sir Gawain* in print, it still serves to reinforce the critically-imposed gap between the Gawain corpus and its most famous text.[41] This insistence is mirrored in the naming of the anonymous poet of the manuscript which contains *Sir Gawain and the Green Knight* and three other texts, none of them romances: this figure is commonly called the *Gawain*-poet, as if no other Gawain texts existed.

Some critics have begun to recognize that this gap is more artificial than we have been led to believe, starting perhaps with Arlyn Diamond, in her 1976 article on *Sir Gawain* as an alliterative romance.[42] Diamond points to the emphasis on pseudo-history, shared with texts like *The Siege of Jerusalem* and the Alliterative *Morte Arthure*, or even *Beowulf*; this historical bent seems linked with an attention to the ways in which a 'sophisticated control of social behaviour' acts to patrol the borders between civilized order and the chaos of the world.[43] These similarities are not restricted to alliterative verse, and are found across the entire range of poems in which Gawain is a central figure. Thematic similarities abound, starting with a mysterious outside force which seems to threaten Arthur or his court (as in *The Wedding of Sir Gawain and Dame Ragnelle*, *The Awntyrs off Arthur*, and *The Turke and Gawain*). Gawain's reputation with women plays a role in several texts, providing a context for the Lady of Hautdesert's feigned disappointment in the controlled libido of the Gawain with whom she is resolutely flirting.[44] Even the *Gawain*-poet's placing of the action in wild Wales, away from the civilized centre represented by Camelot, finds parallels in most of the Gawain romances. This is not to undervalue the importance of *Sir Gawain*'s French antecedents, explored for example by Ad Putter.[45] The root of *Sir Gawain*'s power might be exactly its careful negotiation of multiple traditions encoded in a staggering number of individual texts.

Most Middle English Gawain romances depict Gawain not only negating a threat to Arthur or his court, but show him leading that threat into the court, adding its strength to Arthur's. *Sir Gawain* leaves the Green Knight in his isolated wilderness, but *The Grene Knight* brings him into the fellowship of the Round Table. Here named Bredbeddle rather than Bertilak, the revised Green Knight later helps Arthur in his conflict against King Cornwall in *King Arthur and King Cornwall*, also found in Percy. The troubling appearance of Morgan le Fay in *Sir Gawain* is a reminder that the blood Gawain shares with

---

[41] *Sir Gawain: Eleven Romances and Tales*, ed. Thomas Hahn (Kalamazoo: Medieval Institute Publications, 1995). This edition is used in the present chapter for *The Grene Knight*.
[42] Arlyn Diamond, '*Sir Gawain and the Green Knight*: An Alliterative Romance', *Philological Quarterly* 55 (1976), 10–29.
[43] Diamond, 'Alliterative Romance', pp. 11–21.
[44] Cory James Rushton, 'The Lady's Man: Gawain as a Lover in Middle English Literature', in *The Erotic in the Literature of Medieval Britain*, ed. Amanda Hopkins and Cory James Rushton (Cambridge: D. S. Brewer, 2007), pp. 27–37 (p. 29).
[45] Ad Putter, '*Sir Gawain and the Green Knight' and French Arthurian Romance* (Oxford: Oxford University Press, 1995).

Arthur – and in which he takes such pride – is also blood he shares with a sorceress who is, in the wider tradition, dedicated to destroying Arthur;[46] as Joanne Charbonneau and Desiree Cromwell point out in this volume, Morgan and the Green Knight are prime examples of the kind of 'deeply unsettling, fundamentally disruptive' assaults on the male 'hegemonic norms' of the Middle Ages (p. 98 above). Elizabeth Scala argues that Morgan appears at the end of *Sir Gawain* 'to stand behind and guarantee the disruptive function of "magic," and thereby supply for "magic" a determinate meaning' which 'screens for the poem its repressed knowledge of the indeterminate nature of language'.[47] According to Larry D. Benson, even 'the uninspired author of *The Grene Knight* realized' that 'Morgan's scheme is too weak a foundation' for the earlier poem, and accordingly 'he supplied an entirely new motivation for the evil enchantress'.[48]

In fact, he supplies an entirely new evil enchantress, replacing Morgan with Agostes, Bredbeddle's mother-in-law, who is determined to help her unnamed daughter to win Gawain's love (*GK* 43–51). The critical tradition seems to be unable to find something of worth in both poems at the same time: Morgan is trivial, but Agostes makes sense; Morgan allows for the irruption of the problematic, but Agostes is too simple a plot device. As Shimomura points out, Morgan's magic is never seen directly: '… all magical transformations occur, as it were, off-stage, outside the view of the poem. Magic exists exclusively as the narrative connection' while 'the real point of Gawain's adventures seems to be – not surprisingly – Gawain's own transformations. These are not magical transformations, but rather shifts in how he and others view him.'[49] But if 'Morgan threatens to tell a different story than the one legitimated at the surface of *Sir Gawain and the Green Knight* – a surface reality that at best can be described as wish-fulfilment fantasy',[50] a fantasy of Gawain's (or Camelot's) near-perfection, the poem remains troubled by Morgan's threatened narrative, a narrative which manifests itself in a defiance of genre: Gawain does not get the girl, the Green Knight does not join Arthur's court, there is no final battle between the hero and his enemies (green or blood-related or anything else).

The author of *The Grene Knight* recuperates and brings this hint of wish-

---

46 Michael W. Twomey, 'Morgain la Fée in *Sir Gawain and the Green Knight*', in *Text and Intertext in Medieval Arthurian Literature*, ed. Norris J. Lacy (New York: Garland, 1996), pp. 91–115 (pp. 107–8).
47 Elizabeth Scala, *Absent Narratives, Manuscript Textuality, and Literary Structure in Late Medieval England* (New York: Palgrave MacMillan, 2002), p. 62.
48 Larry D. Benson, *Art and Tradition in 'Sir Gawain and the Green Knight'* (New Brunswick, NJ: Rutgers University Press, 1965), p. 34.
49 Shimomura, *Odd Bodies*, p. 153.
50 Scala, *Absent Narratives*, p. 67; Ivo Kamps, 'Magic, Women, and Incest: The Real Challenges in *Sir Gawain and the Green Knight*', *Exemplaria* 1 (1988), 313–36; Sheila Fisher, 'Taken Men and Token Women in *Sir Gawain and the Green Knight*', in *Seeking the Woman in Late Medieval and Early Renaissance Writings*, ed. Sheila Fisher and Janet Halley (Knoxville: University of Tennessee Press, 1989), pp. 71–105 (p. 75).

fulfilment to a logical conclusion (which is not to say *the* logical conclusion, only one possibility given the internal logic of the romance). The troubling gender issues of *Sir Gawain* are occluded by the later text's insistence that Bredbeddle is in total control, that his desire to join the Round Table can make use of his wife's desire for Gawain.[51] Benson argues that the poet's desire is to allow 'the audience to share the narrator's omniscience and to enjoy from the standpoint of their superior knowledge the predicament in which the hero finds himself' even as it distances that audience from sharing the protagonist's tension and amazement.[52] Matthews takes the argument further: the romance's generic tendency to address the reader (as in *GK*, 38, 84, 270, 276) suggests the narrator's lack of duplicity and a willingness to lead the reader 'without bias through the plot' – here meaning both the plot of the poem and the plot hatched by Agostes and her daughter, with Bredbeddle's partial complicity. Bredbeddle is himself a 'rebellious reader who usurps authority, overturns the role that Agostes intends for him, and becomes the hero of the story'; Bredbeddle rebels against the story Agostes places him in, and subsequently his court 'is masculinised, purged of its feminine plotting by the two knights'.[53] The ballad's fantasy of male control over its own female characters, and thus over the troubling earlier text in which the women seemed to win, may also be a fantasy of generic purity. That this fantasy, when seen against the sheer diversity of the popular romance, is itself unattainable has been an increasing interest for scholars.

Conclusion

McDonald argues that 'popular romance's degraded academic status' is rooted in the 'same assumptions and anxieties' that had prompted earlier attempts to censor the romance's wilder excesses.[54] By the same token, her assertion that the romances no longer attract moral, political, or cultural attention is quickly becoming untrue, in part because of the efforts of scholars like herself. Popular romance's concern with gender roles has attracted the attention of scholars interested in the possibilities open to both men and women, at least in certain social strata. The close engagement between this genre and both ethnic identity and what we might call proto-nationalism (see in this volume Charbonneau and Cromwell, pp. 96–110, and Rouse and Crofts, pp. 79–95) has meant that the popular romance has become a fruitful field for high theory, particularly the post-colonial. In turn, these theories have started to affect the study of 'high texts' like *Sir Gawain and the Green Knight*, which has recently been the subject of post-colonial readings which refuse to

---

[51] Rushton, 'Gawain as Lover', pp. 32–3.
[52] Benson, *Art and Tradition*, p. 171.
[53] Matthews, 'Narrative and Ideology', pp. 308–12.
[54] McDonald, 'Introduction', in *Pulp Fictions*, p. 4.

allow the poem's famous ambiguity to claim for itself a position of aesthetic isolation from real-world concerns.[55]

Bernard Cerquiglini once stated that to be a medievalist is to have a position on the *Song of Roland*, a stand echoed even more forcefully by Peter Haidu and others since; as Michael Calabrese notes concerning the 'Prioress's Tale', 'Reading and teaching the Prioress's Tale ... have become not only literary exercises – comparing analogues, studying character, tracing patterns of imagery, and so forth – but also a moral exercise in how we negotiate the past, heal its wounds, and prepare our own culture's future.'[56] The popular romance, complicit in the power struggles of the Victorian era as much as the medieval, and concerning itself with the privileged aristocratic class, has paradoxically been marginalized by mainstream academic discourse. English medieval romance is now increasingly championed by scholars dedicated to recovering history's lost voices: women, Saracens, English regionalisms long obscured by the central metropole of London. Further, the rise of the popular romance is linked with a new attention to other popular texts, including the modern generic productions which are descended from them. *Star Wars* or *The DaVinci Code* can tell us something about our own culture, and about our mental descent from earlier societies; the romance is no longer seen as a cultural dead end, but as a key component in the way we construct ourselves. The popular romance is moving back into the centre of literary studies on grounds that Percy and others might have recognized: these romances tell us something about life in the Middle Ages, but they also tell us something about life in the Twenty-first Century.[57] Because they are largely anonymous, they can do so in a less complicated manner than Chaucer or Langland (or even Malory). Just as the romance hero's journey is often a circular one, from court to the wilderness and back to court again, so too the journey of the popular romance has been from the centre to the margins and then back again.

---

[55] Patricia Clare Ingham, *Sovereign Fantasies: Arthurian Romance and the Making of Britain* (Philadelphia: University of Pennsylvania Press, 2001), pp. 107–36; Rhonda Knight, 'All Dressed Up with Someplace to Go: Regional Identity in *Sir Gawain and the Green Knight*', *Studies in the Age of Chaucer* 25 (2003), 259–84; Lynn Arner, 'The Ends of Enchantment: Colonialism and *Sir Gawain and the Green Knight*', *Texas Studies in Language and Literature* 48:2 (2006), 79–101.

[56] Michael Calabrese, 'Performing the Prioress: "Conscience" and Responsibility in Studies of Chaucer's Prioress's Tale', *Texas Studies in Language and Literature* 44:1 (2002), 66–91 (p. 66); Bernard Cerquiglini, 'Roland à Roncevaux, ou la trahison des clercs', *Littérature* 42 (1981), 40–56 (p. 40).

[57] See Umberto Eco, *Travels in Hyperreality* (New York: Harcourt, 1986).

Bibliography

Manuscripts

Aberystwyth, National Library of Wales
MS 572
MS Porkington 10

Cambridge, Cambridge University Library
MS Add. 4407
MS Ff.1.6 (Findern MS)
MS Ff.2.38
MS Gg.4.27(2)

Cambridge, Gonville and Caius College
MS 107/176
MS 175

Cambridge, Trinity College
MS O.2.13

Edinburgh, National Library of Scotland
MS Advocates' 19.2.1 (Auchinleck MS)
MS Advocates' 19.3.1

Lincoln, Lincoln Cathedral Library
MS 91 (Lincoln Thornton MS)

London, British Library
MS Additional 14408
MS Additional 27879 (Percy Folio)
MS Additional 31042
MS Cotton Caligula A.ii
MS Cotton Galba E.ix
MS Cotton Vespasian A.iii
MS Cotton Nero A.x
MS Egerton 2862
MS Harley 2252
MS Harley 3810
MS Royal 17.B.43
MS Sloane 1044

London, Lincoln's Inn
MS Hale 150

Manchester, Chetham's Library
MS 8009

Naples, Biblioteca Nazionale
MS XIII.B.29

Oxford, Bodleian Library
MS Ashmole 33
MS Ashmole 61
MS Douce 228
MS Douce 261
MS Douce 324
MS Eng. Poet. D.208
MS Laud Miscellany 108
MS English Poet a. 1 (Vernon MS)
MS Rawlinson C 86
MS Rawlinson D 82
MS Rawlinson Poet. 34
MS Rawlinson Poet. 168

Princeton University Library
MS Garrett 140
MS Taylor

Printed primary sources (editions, facsimiles, reference material)

Amis and Amiloun, ed. MacEdward Leach, EETS OS 203 (London: Oxford University Press, 1937)

Amis and Amiloun, Robert of Cisyle, and Sir Amadace, ed. Edward E. Foster (Kalamazoo, MI: Medieval Institute Publications, 1997)

The Ancient English Romance of Havelok the Dane; Accompanied by the French Text: With an Introduction, Notes, and a Glossary, ed. Frederick Madden (London, 1828)

An Anonymous Short English Metrical Chronicle, ed. Ewald Zettl, EETS OS 196 (London: H. Milford for Oxford University Press, 1935)

Arber, Edward, *A Transcript of the Registers of the Company of Stationers of London 1554–1640 AD*, 5 vols (London: privately printed, 1875–94).

Arthur, ed. Frederick J. Furnivall, EETS OS (London, 1869)

The Auchinleck Manuscript, National Library of Scotland Advocates' MS 19.2.1, intro. Derek Pearsall and I. C. Cunningham (London: Scolar Press, 1977)

Athelston: A Middle English Romance, ed. A. McI. Trounce, EETS OS 224 (London: Oxford University Press, 1951, reprinted 1957, 1987, 2002)

Beues of Hamtoun, ed. E. Kölbing, EETS ES 46, 48, 65 (London, 1885–94)

Bodel, Jean, *La Chanson des Saisnes*, ed. A. Brasseur, 2 vols (Geneva: Droz, 1989)

Boeve de Haumtone and Gui de Warewic, trans. and intro. Judith Weiss (Tempe: Arizona Center for Medieval and Renaissance Studies, 2008)

Bibliography

Le Bone Florence of Rome, ed. Carol Falvo Heffernan (Manchester: Manchester University Press, 1976)
Cambridge University Library MS Ff.2.38, intro. Frances McSparran and P. R. Robinson (London: Scolar Press, 1979)
Carter, Henry Holland, *A Dictionary of Middle English Musical Terms* (Bloomington: Indiana University Press, 1961)
Caxton's Own Prose, ed. N. F. Blake (London: Andre Deutsch, 1973)
Caxton, William, *The Prologues and Epilogues of William Caxton*, ed. W. J. B. Crotch, EETS OS, 176 (London: Oxford University Press, 1928)
The Canterbury Tales: Fifteen Tales and the General Prologue, ed. V. A. Kolve and Glending Olsen, 2nd edn (New York: W. W. Norton, 2005)
Chaucer, Geoffrey, *The Riverside Chaucer*, gen. ed. Larry D. Benson (Boston: Houghton Mifflin, 1987)
Cursor Mundi, ed. Richard Morris, EETS OS 57 (London, 1874)
Dean, Ruth J., with Maureen B. M. Boulton, *Anglo-Norman Literature: A Guide to Texts and Manuscripts* (London: Anglo-Norman Text Studies, 1999)
Deloney, Thomas, *The Works of Thomas Deloney*, ed. F. O. Mann (Oxford: Clarendon Press, 1912)
The Early English Carols, ed. Richard Leighton Greene, 2nd edn (Oxford: Clarendon Press, 1977)
The English Charlemagne Romances, Part II: 'The Sege off Melayne' and 'The Romance of Duke Rowland and Sir Otuell of Spaine' together with a fragment of 'The Song Roland', ed. Sidney J. Herrtage, EETS ES 35 (London, 1880)
Fellows, Jennifer, ed., *Of Love and Chivalry: An Anthology of Middle English Romance* (London: Dent, 1993)
The Findern Manuscript: MS Cambridge University Library Ff.1.6, ed. Richard Beadle and A. E. B. Owen (London: Scolar Press, 1978)
Firumbras and Otuel and Roland, Edited from MS. Brit. Mus. Addit. 37492, ed. Mary Isabelle O'Sullivan, EETS OS 198 (London: Oxford University Press, 1935)
Fragments of an Early Fourteenth-Century Guy of Warwick, ed. Maldwyn Mills and Daniel Huws, Medium Ævum Monographs, n.s. 4 (Oxford: Blackwell for the Society for the Study of Mediæval Languages and Literature, 1973)
Gower, John, *The English Works of John Gower*, ed. G. C. Macaulay, 2 vols, EETS ES 81, 82 (London: Oxford University Press, 1900–1)
Guddat-Figge, Gisela, *Catalogue of Manuscripts Containing Middle English Romances* (Munich: W. Fink, 1976)
Guy of Warwick, ed. J. Zupitza, EETS ES 42, 49, 59 (London, 1883-91)
Guy of Warwick: nach Coplands Druck, ed. Gustav Schleich, Palaestra 139 (Leipzig: Mayer & Müller, 1923)
The Harley Lyrics: The Middle English Lyrics of MS. Harley 2253, ed. G. L. Brook, 3rd edn (Manchester: Manchester University Press, 1964)
Havelok, ed. G. V. Smithers (Oxford: Clarendon Press, 1987)
The Heege Manuscript: A Facsimile of National Library of Scotland MS Advocates 19.3.1, intro. Phillipa Hardman, Leeds Texts and Monographs, n.s. 16 (Leeds: Leeds Studies in English, 2000)
Horn Childe and Maiden Rimnild, ed. from the Auchinleck MS, National Library of Scotland, Advocates' MS 19.2.1, ed. Maldwyn Mills, Middle English Texts 20 (Heidelberg: Winter, 1988)

Index of Middle English Verse, ed. Carleton Brown and Rossell Hope Robbins (New York: Columbia University Press for the Index Society, 1943)

Ipomadon, ed. Rhiannon Purdie, EETS OS 316 (Oxford: Oxford University Press, 2001)

King Horn, ed. Rosamund Allen (New York: Garland, 1984)

The King of Tars, ed. Judith Perryman, Middle English Texts 12 (Heidelberg: Winter, 1980)

King Orphius, Sir Colling, The brother's lament, Litel Musgray: Poems from Scottish Manuscripts of c. 1586 and c. 1630 lately discovered, ed. Marion Stewart and Helena M. Shire (Cambridge: The Ninth of May, 1973)

Kyng Alisaunder, ed. G. V. Smithers, 2 vols, EETS OS 227, 237 (London: Oxford University Press, 1952–57)

Laneham, Robert, *Robert Laneham's Letter: Describing a Part of the Entertainment unto Queen Elizabeth at the Castle of Kenilworth in 1575*, ed. F. J. Furnivall (London: Kegan Paul, Trench, Trübner, 1907)

Lancelot of the Laik and Sir Tristrem, ed. Alan Lupack, TEAMS (Kalamazoo, MI: Medieval Institute Publications, 1994)

Laȝamon's Arthur, ed. and trans. W. R. J. Barron and S. C. Weinberg (Harlow: Longman, 1989).

Libeaus Desconus, ed. Maldwyn Mills, EETS OS 261 (Oxford: Oxford University Press for EETS, 1969)

Life of St Eustace, ed. E. Stengel, *Codicem Manuscriptum Digby 86* (Halle, 1871)

Lockhart, J. G., *Memoirs of Sir Walter Scott*, ed. A. W. Pollard, 5 vols (London: Macmillan, 1900; repr. 1914), I

The Lyfe of Ipomydon, ed. T. Ikegami, 2 vols (Tokyo: Seijo University, 1985), II.

Mannyng, Robert, of Brunne, *Chronicle*, ed. Idelle Sullens (Binghamton: Binghamton University, 1996)

A Manual of the Writings in Middle English 1050-1500: I. Romances, gen. ed. J. Burke Severs (New Haven: Connecticut Academy of Arts and Sciences, 1967)

Medieval English Romances, ed. A. V. C. Schmidt and N. Jacobs (London: Hodder & Stoughton, 1980)

Medieval English Songs, ed. E. J. Dobson and F. Ll. Harrison (London: Faber, 1979)

The Middle English Breton Lays, ed. Anne Laskaya and Eve Salisbury (Kalamazoo, MI: Medieval Institute Publications, 1995)

Middle English Dictionary (online version) <http://quod.lib.umich.edu/m/med/>

Middle English Metrical Romances, ed. W. H. French and C. B. Hale (New York: Russell & Russell, 1930)

Middle English Romances, ed. Stephen H. A. Shepherd (London: W. W. Norton, 1995)

The Miller of Abington (London, 1575), repr. Chadwyck-Healey, *English Literature On-Line* (1992)

Minot, Laurence, *The Poems of Laurence Minot*, ed. Joseph Hall (Oxford, 1897)

Minot, Laurence, *The Poems of Laurence Minot, 1333–1352*, ed. Richard Osberg, TEAMS (Kalamazoo, MI: Medieval Institute Publications, 1996)

Bibliography

Der mittelenglische Versroman über Richard Lowenherz, ed. K. Brunner (Vienna and Leipzig, 1913)
The Noble and Renowned History of Guy Earl of Warwick ... (Coventry, Warwick and Leamington, 1829)
Octavian: Zwei mittelenglische Bearbeitungen der Sage, ed. Gregor Sarrazin (Heilbronn, 1885)
Octovian Imperator, ed. Frances McSparran, Middle English Texts 11 (Heidelberg: Winter, 1979)
Of Arthour and of Merlin, II, ed. O. D. Macrae-Gibson, EETS OS 279 (Oxford: Oxford University Press, 1979)
The Old French Translation of the Pseudo-Turpin Chronicle, ed. Ronald N. Walpole, 2 vols (Berkeley: University of California Press, 1976)
The Order of Chyualry, in *The Prologues and Epilogues of William Caxton*, ed. W. J. B. Crotch, EETS OS 176 (London: Oxford University Press, 1928)
Otuel and Roland, ed. M. I. O. Sullivan, EETS OS 198 (London: Oxford University Press, 1935)
Oxford Dictionary of National Biography (Oxford: Oxford University Press, 2008)
Oxford English Dictionary (Oxford: Oxford University Press, 2008)
Percy, Thomas, *Bishop Percy's Folio Manuscript: Ballads and Romances*, ed. J. W. Hales and F. J. Furnivall, 4 vols (London, 1867–8)
Percy, Thomas, *Reliques of Ancient English Poetry*, ed. with intro. Henry B. Wheatley, 3 vols (London: Sonnenschein, Lebas, & Lowrey, 1886)
Remnant, Mary, *English Bowed Instruments from Anglo-Saxon to Tudor Times* (Oxford: Clarendon Press, 1986)
Robin Hood and Other Outlaw Tales, ed. Stephen Knight and Thomas Ohlgren, TEAMS series (Kalamazoo, MI: Medieval Institute Publications, 1997).
The Romance and Prophecies of Thomas of Erceldoune, ed. James A. H. Murray, EETS OS 61 (London, 1875)
The Romance of Guy of Warwick, ed. Julius Zupitza, vol. 2, EETS ES 49 (London, 1887)
The Romance of Horn, in *The Birth of Romance: An Anthology*, trans. Judith Weiss (London: Dent, 1992)
Sentimental and Humorous Romances, ed. Erik Kooper, TEAMS series (Kalamazoo, MI: Medieval Institute Publications, 2006)
The Seven Sages of Rome, ed. K. Brunner, EETS OS 191 (London: H. Milford for Oxford University Press, 1933)
A Short-Title Catalogue of Books Printed in England, Scotland, & Ireland, and of English Books Printed Abroad, 1475–1640, ed. W. A. Jackson, F. S. Ferguson and Katharine F. Pantzer, rev. edn, 3 vols (London: Bibliographical Society, 1976–91)
A Short-Title Catalogue of Books Printed in England, Scotland, and Ireland, ed. A. W. Pollard and G. R. Redgrave, rev. W. A. Jackson and F. S. Ferguson, 3 vols (London: Bibliographical Society, 1986)
Sir Eglamour of Artois, ed. Frances E. Richardson, EETS OS 256 (London: Oxford University Press for the Early English Text Society, 1965)
Sir Ferumbras, ed. Sidney J. Herrtage, EETS ES 34 (London, 1889)
Sir Gawain: Eleven Romances and Tales, ed. Thomas Hahn (Kalamazoo: Medieval Institute Publications, 1995)

Sir Orfeo, ed. A. J. Bliss (Oxford: Oxford University Press, 1954)
Six Middle English Romances, ed. Maldwyn Mills (London: Dent, 1973)
Sources and Analogues of the Canterbury Tales, II, ed. Robert M. Correale and Mary Hamel (Cambridge: D. S. Brewer, 2005)
Stanzaic Guy of Warwick, ed. Alison Wiggins, TEAMS series (Kalamazoo, MI: Medieval Institute Publications, 2004)
Thomas, *The Romance of Horn*, ed. M. K. Pope, Anglo-Norman Text Society 9, 10, 12, 13 (Oxford, 1955–64)
The Thornton Manuscript (Lincoln Cathedral MS 91), intro. D. S. Brewer and A. E. B. Owen (London: Scolar Press, 1975)
Three Middle English Charlemagne Romances, ed. Alan Lupack (Kalamazoo: Medieval Institute Publications, 1990)
Torrent of Portugal: An English Metrical Romance, Now First Published from an Unique Manuscript of the Fifteenth Century, Preserved in the Chetham Library at Manchester, ed. James Orchard Halliwell (London, 1842)
The Towneley Plays, ed. Martin Stevens and A. C. Cawley, 2 vols, EETS SS 14 (Oxford: Oxford University Press, 1994)
The Vision of William Concerning Piers the Plowman in Three Parallel Texts together with Richard the Redeless by William Langland, ed. Walter W. Skeat, 2 vols (London, 1886)
Weiss, Judith, trans., *The Birth of Romance: An Anthology* (London: Dent, 1992)
Wogan-Browne, Jocelyn, Nicholas Watson, Andrew Taylor and Ruth Evans, eds, *The Idea of the Vernacular: An Anthology of Middle English Literary Theory 1280–1520* (Exeter: University of Exeter Press, 1999)
Wright, Thomas, ed., *The Political Songs of England* (London: Camden Society, 1839; repr. Hildesheim: Georg Olms, 1968)
Ywain and Gawain, Sir Percyvell of Gales, The Anturs of Arther, ed. Maldwyn Mills (London: Dent, 1992)

Secondary sources

Aberth, John, *From the Brink of the Apocalypse: Confronting Famine, War, Plague, and Death in the Later Middle Ages* (New York: Routledge, 2001)
Ackerman, Robert W., 'English Rimed and Prose Romances', in *Arthurian Literature in the Middle Ages: A Collaborative History*, ed. R. S. Loomis (Oxford: Clarendon Press, 1959), pp. 480–519
Ailes, Marianne, '*Gui de Warewic* in its Manuscript Context', in *Guy of Warwick: Icon and Ancestor*, ed. Alison Wiggins and Rosalind Field (Cambridge: D. S. Brewer, 2007), pp. 12–26
Ailes, Marianne and Phillipa Hardman, 'How English are the English Charlemagne Romances', in *Boundaries in Medieval Romance*, ed. Neil Cartlidge (Cambridge: D. S. Brewer, 2008), pp. 43–55
Akbari, Suzanne Conklin, 'Incorporation in the Siege of Melayne', in *Pulp Fictions of Medieval England*, ed. Nicola McDonald (Manchester: Manchester University Press, 2004), pp. 22–44
Allen, Rosamund, 'Performance and Structure in the Alliterative *Morte Arthure*', in *New Perspectives on Middle English Texts: A Festschrift for R. A. Waldron*,

ed. Susan Powell, Jeremy J. Smith and Derek Pearsall (Cambridge: D. S. Brewer, 2000), pp. 17–29

Anderson, Benedict, *Imagined Communities: Reflections on the Origin and Spread of Nationalism*, rev. edn (London: Verso, 1991).

Archibald, Elizabeth, 'The Breton Lay in Middle English: Genre, Transmission and the Franklin's Tale', in *Medieval Insular Romance*, ed. Judith Weiss, Jennifer Fellows and Morgan Dickson (Cambridge: D. S. Brewer, 2000), pp. 55–70

Archibald, Elizabeth, *Incest and the Medieval Imagination* (Oxford: Oxford University Press, 2001)

Archibald, Elizabeth, '*Lai le Freine*: The Female Foundling and the Problem of the Romance Genre', in *The Spirit of Medieval Popular Romance*, ed. Ad Putter and Jane Gilbert (Harlow: Longman, 2000), pp. 39–55

Archibald, Elizabeth, 'Women and Romance', in *A Companion to Middle English Romance*, ed. Henk Aertsen and Alisdair A. MacDonald (Amsterdam: VU University Press, 1990), pp. 153–69

Arner, Lynn, 'The Ends of Enchantment: Colonialism and *Sir Gawain and the Green Knight*', *Texas Studies in Language and Literature* 48:2 (2006), 79–101

Arthur, Ross G., 'Emaré's Cloak and Audience Response', in *Sign, Sentence, Discourse: Language in Medieval Thought and Culture*, ed. Julian N. Wasserman and Lois Roney (Syracuse: Syracuse University Press, 1989), pp. 80–92

The Arthur of the English, ed. W. J. R. Barron (Cardiff: University of Wales Press, 1999)

Barnes, Geraldine, *Counsel and Strategy in Middle English Romance* (Cambridge: D. S. Brewer, 1993)

Barron, W. R. J., *English Medieval Romance* (Harlow: Longman, 1987)

Bartlett, Anne Clark, *Male Authors, Females Readers: Representation and Subjectivity in Middle English Devotional Literature* (Ithaca: Cornell University Press, 1995)

Batt, Catherine, 'Gawain's Antifeminist Rant, the Pentangle, and Narrative Space', *The Yearbook of English Studies* 22 (1992), 117–39

Baugh, Albert C., 'Improvisation in the Middle English Romance', *Proceedings of the American Philolopshical Society* 103 (1959), 418–54

Baugh, Albert C., *A Literary History of England* (London: Routledge and Kegan Paul, 1948)

Baugh, Albert C., 'The Middle English Romance: Some Questions of Creation, Presentation, and Preservation', *Speculum* 42 (1967), 1–31

Bawcutt, Priscilla, 'English Books and Scottish Readers in the Fifteenth and Sixteenth Centuries', *Review of Scottish Culture* 14 (2001/2), 1–12

Benskin, Michael, 'The "Fit"-Technique Explained', in *Regionalism in Late Medieval Manuscripts and Texts*, ed. Felicity Riddy (Cambridge: D. S. Brewer, 1991), pp. 9–26

Benson, Larry D., *Art and Tradition in 'Sir Gawain and the Green Knight'* (New Brunswick, NJ: Rutgers University Press, 1965)

Benson, Larry D., 'The Literary Character of Anglo-Saxon Formulaic Poetry', *Proceedings of the Modern Language Association* 81 (1966), 324–41

Blake, N. F., *The English Language in Medieval Literature* (London: J. M. Dent, 1977)
Blamires, Alcuin, 'The Twin Demons of Aristocratic Society in *Sir Gowther*', in *Pulp Fictions of Medieval England*, ed. Nicola McDonald (Manchester: Manchester University Press, 2004), pp. 45–62
Blanchfield, Lynne S., 'Rate revisited, the compilation of the narrative works in MS Ashmole 61', in *Romance Reading on the Book: Essays on Medieval Narrative presented to Maldwyn Mills*, ed. Jennifer Fellows, Rosalind Field, Gillian Rogers and Judith Weiss (Cardiff: University of Wales Press, 1996), pp. 208–20
Bloch, R. Howard, *Medieval Misogyny and the Invention of Western Romantic Love* (Chicago: University of Chicago Press, 1991)
Bradbury, Nancy Mason, 'The Traditional Origins of *Havelok the Dane*', *Studies in Philology* 90 (1999), 115–42
Bradbury, Nancy Mason, *Writing Aloud: Storytelling in Late Medieval England* (Urbana: University of Illinois Press, 1998)
Brandl, Alois, 'Spielmannverhältnisse in frühmittelenglischer Zeit', in *Sitzungsberichte der königlich preussischen Akademie. der Wissenschenschaften, Philos.-hist. Classe* 41 (Berlin, 1910), pp. 873–92
Brewer, Derek, 'Escape from the Mimetic Fallacy', in *Studies in Medieval English Romances*, ed. Derek Brewer (Cambridge: D. S. Brewer, 1988), pp. 1–10
Brewer, Derek, 'The Popular English Metrical Romances', in *A Companion to Romance: From Classical to Contemporary*, ed. Corinne Saunders (Oxford: Blackwell, 2004), pp. 45–64
Brewer, Derek, *Symbolic Stories: Traditional Narratives of the Family Drama in English Literature* (Cambridge: D. S. Brewer, 1980)
Bullón-Fernández, María, *Fathers and Daughters in Gower's 'Confessio Amantis': Authority, Family, State and Writing* (Cambridge: D. S. Brewer, 2000)
Burlin, Robert B., 'Middle English Romance: The Structure of Genre', *Chaucer Review* 30 (1995), 1–14
Burrow, J. A., '*Sir Thopas* in the Sixteenth Century', in *Middle English Studies Presented to Norman Davis*, ed. Douglas Gray and E. G. Stanley (Oxford: Clarendon Press, 1983), pp. 69–91
Burrow, John, 'Romance', in *The Cambridge Companion to Chaucer*, ed. Piero Boitani and Jill Mann, 2nd edn (Cambridge: Cambridge University Press), pp. 143–59
Burton, Julie, 'Romance, Folktale and Shakespeare', in *Studies in Medieval English Romances*, ed. Derek Brewer (Cambridge: D. S. Brewer, 1988), pp. 176–97
Calabrese, Michael, 'Performing the Prioress: "Conscience" and Responsibility in Studies of Chaucer's Prioress's Tale', *Texas Studies in Language and Literature* 44:1 (2002), 66–91
Caldwell, Ellen M., 'The Heroism of Heurodis: Self-Mutilation and Restoration in *Sir Orfeo*', *Papers on Language and Literature* 43 (2007), 291–311
Calkin, Siobhain B., *Saracens and the Making of English Identity* (London, New York: Routledge, 2005)
Campbell, Kofi, 'Nation-building Colonialist-style in *Bevis of Hampton*', *Exemplaria* 18:1 (2006), 205–32

Bibliography

Carling, D. and V. J. Scattergood, 'One Aspect of Stanza-Linking', *Neuphilologische Mitteilungen* 75 (1974), 79–91

Carroll, M. C. and R. Tuve, 'Two Manuscripts of the Middle English *Anonymous Riming Chronicle*', *Proceedings of the Modern Language Association* 46 (1931), 115–54

Cartlidge, Neil, 'Sir Orfeo in the Otherword: Courting Chaos', *Studies in the Age of Chaucer* 26 (2004), 195–226

Cartlidge, Neil, ' "Thereof seyus clerkus": Slander, Rape and *Sir Gowther*', in *Cultural Encounters in the Romance of Medieval England*, ed. Corinne Saunders (Cambridge : D. S. Brewer, 2005), pp. 135–47

Chambers, E. K., *The Medieval Stage*, 2 vols (London: Oxford University Press, 1903)

Charbonneau, Joanne A., 'From Devil to Saint: Transformations in *Sir Gowther*', in *The Matter of Identity in Medieval Romance*, ed. Phillipa Hardman (Cambridge: D. S. Brewer, 2002), pp. 21–8

Charbonneau, Joanne A., 'Transgressive Fathers in *Sir Eglamour of Artois* and *Torrent of Portyngale*', in *Discourses on Love, Marriage, and Transgression in Medieval and Early Modern Literature*, ed. Albrecht Classen (Tempe: Arizona Center for Medieval and Renaissance Studies, 2004), pp. 243–65

Chaytor, H. J., *From Script to Print: An Introduction to Medieval Vernacular Literature* (Cambridge: W. Heffer & Sons, 1945)

Chesnutt, Michael, 'Minstrel Reciters and the Enigma of the Middle English Romance', *Culture and History* 2 (1987), 48–67

Cerquiglini, Bernard, 'Roland à Roncevaux, ou la trahison des clercs', *Littérature* 42 (1981), 40–56

Coggeshall, John M., 'Champion of the Poor: The Outlaw as a Formalized Expression of Peasant Alienation', *Southern Folklore Quarterly* 44 (1980), 23–58

Cohen, Jeffrey J., *Of Giants: Sex, Monsters, and the Middle Ages* (Minneapolis and London: University of Minnesota Press, 1999)

Coleman, Joyce, *Public Reading and the Reading Public in Late Medieval England and France* (Cambridge: Cambridge University Press, 1996)

Cooper, Helen, *The English Romance in Time: Transforming Motifs from Geoffrey of Monmouth to the Death of Shakespeare* (Oxford: Oxford University Press, 2004)

Cooper, Helen, 'Guy as Early Modern English Hero', in *Guy of Warwick: Icon and Ancestor*, ed. Alison Wiggins and Rosalind Field (Cambridge: D. S. Brewer, 2007), pp. 185–99

Cooper, Helen, 'The *Lancelot-Grail Cycle* in England: Malory and his Predecessors', in *A Companion to the Lancelot-Grail Cycle*, ed. Carol Dover (Cambridge: D. S Brewer, 2003), pp. 147–62

Cooper, Helen, 'Romance after 1400', in *The Cambridge History of Medieval English Literature*, ed. David Wallace (Cambridge: Cambridge University Press, 1999), pp. 690–719

Cooper, Helen, 'Thomas of Erceldoune: Romance as Prophecy', in *Cultural Encounters in the Romance of Medieval England*, ed. Corinne Saunders (Cambridge: D. S. Brewer, 2005), pp. 171–87

Coote, Lesley, *Prophecy and Public Affairs in Later Medieval England* (York: York Medieval Press, 2000)

Cox, Catherine S., 'Genesis and Gender in *Sir Gawain and the Green Knight*', *Chaucer Review* 35:4 (2001), 378–90
Crane, Ronald S., *The Vogue of Medieval Chivalric Romance during the English Renaissance* (Menasha: University of Wisconsin Press, 1919)
Crosby, Ruth, 'Oral Delivery in the Middle Ages', *Speculum* 11 (1936), 88–110
Dalrymple, Roger, *Language and Piety in Middle English Romance* (Cambridge: D. S. Brewer, 2000)
Dannenbaum, Susan Crane, '*Guy of Warwick* and the Question of Exemplary Romance', *Genre* 17 (1984), 351–74
Davenport, Tony, 'Abbreviation and the Education of the Hero in *Chevalere Assigne*', in *The Matter of Identity in Medieval Romance*, ed. Phillipa Hardman (Cambridge: D. S. Brewer, 2002), pp. 9–20
Davenport, W. A., '*Sir Degrevant* and Composite Romance', in *Medieval Insular Romance*, ed. Judith Weiss, Jennifer Fellows and Morgan Dickson (Cambridge: D. S. Brewer, 2000), pp. 111–31
de Riquer, Martín, 'Épopée jongleresque à écouter et épopée romanesque à lire', in *La technique littéraire des chansons de geste: Acte du Colloque de Liège (septembre 1957)* (Paris: Société d'Édition «Les Belles Lettres», 1959), pp. 75–82
Delany, Sheila, 'A, A and B: Coding Same-Sex Union in *Amis and Amiloun*', in *Pulp Fictions of Medieval England*, ed. Nicola McDonald (Manchester: Manchester University Press, 2004), pp. 63–81
Delany, Sheila, 'The Romance of Kingship: *Havelok the Dane*', in Delany, *Medieval Literary Politics* (Manchester: Manchester University Press, 1990), pp. 61–72
Diamond, Arlyn, '*Sir Degrevant*: What Lovers Want', in *Pulp Fictions of Medieval England*, ed. Nicola McDonald (Manchester: Manchester University Press, 2004), pp. 82–101
Diamond, Arlyn, '*Sir Gawain and the Green Knight*: An Alliterative Romance', *Philological Quarterly* 55 (1976), 10–29
Dickens, Charles, *The Personal History of David Copperfield*, ed. Trevor Blount (Harmondsworth: Penguin, 1966)
Donatelli, Joseph, 'The Percy Folio Manuscript: A Seventeenth-Century Context for Medieval Poetry', *English Manuscript Studies, 1100–1700* 4 (1993), 114–33
Donnelly, Colleen, 'Blame, Silence, and Power: Perceiving Women in *Sir Gawain and the Green Knight*', *Mediaevalia* 24 (2003), 279–97
Donovan, Mortimer J., 'Middle English *Emare* and the Cloth Worthily Wrought', in *The Learned and the Lewed: Studies in Chaucer and Medieval Literature*, ed. Larry D. Benson (Cambridge, MA: Harvard University Press, 1974), pp. 337–42
Doody, Margaret A., *The True Story of the Novel* (Rutgers, NJ: Rutgers University Press, 1996)
Duggan, Hoyt, 'Stress Assignment in Middle English Alliterative Poetry', *Journal of English and Germanic Philology* 89 (1990), 309–29
Dürmüller, Urs, *Narrative Possibilities of the Tail-Rhyme Romance* (Bern: Francke Verlag, 1974)
Echard, Siân, 'Of Dragons and Saracens: Guy and Bevis in Early Print Illustra-

tion', in *Guy of Warwick: Icon and Ancestor*, ed. Alison Wiggins and Rosalind Field (Cambridge: D. S. Brewer, 2007), pp. 154–68

Eckhardt, Caroline D. and Bryan A. Meer, 'Constructing a Medieval Genealogy: Roland the Father of Tristan in "Castelford's Chronicle"', *Modern Language Notes* 115:5 (2000), 1085–1111

Eco, Umberto, *Travels in Hyperreality* (New York: Harcourt, 1986)

Edwards, A. S. G., 'The Contexts of the Vernon Romances', in *Studies in the Vernon Manuscript*, ed. Derek Pearsall (Cambridge: D. S. Brewer, 1990), pp. 159–70

Edwards, A. S. G., 'The *Speculum Guy de Warwick* and Lydgate's *Guy of Warwick*: The Non-Romance Middle English Tradition', in *Guy of Warwick: Icon and Ancestor*, ed. Alison Wiggins and Rosalind Field (Cambridge: D. S. Brewer, 2007), pp. 81–93

Edwards, A. S. G., 'William Copland and the Identity of Printed Middle English Romance', in *The Matter of Identity in Medieval Romance*, ed. Phillipa Hardman (Cambridge: D. S. Brewer, 2002), pp. 139–47

Evans, Murray J., *Rereading Middle English Romance: Manuscript Layout, Decoration, and the Rhetoric of Composite Structure* (Montreal and London: McGill-Queen's University Press, 1995)

Falk, Oren, 'The Son of Orfeo: Kingship and Compromise in a Middle English Romance', *The Journal of Medieval and Early Modern Studies* 30 (2000), 247–74

Faust, G. P., *Sir Degare: A Study of the Texts and Narrative Structure*, Princeton Studies in English 11 (Princeton, NJ: Princeton University Press, 1935)

Fellows, Jennifer, '*Bevis redivivus*: The Printed Editions of *Sir Bevis of Hampton*', in *Romance Reading on the Book: Essays on Medieval Narrative presented to Maldwyn Mills*, ed. Jennifer Fellows, Rosalind Field, Gillian Rogers and Judith Weiss (Cardiff: University of Wales Press, 1996), pp. 251–68

Fellows, Jennifer, 'The Medieval and Renaissance *Bevis*: A Textual Survey', in *Sir Bevis of Hampton in Literary Tradition*, ed. Jennifer Fellows and Ivana Djordjević (Cambridge: D. S. Brewer, 2008), pp. 80–113

Fellows, Jennifer, 'Mothers in Middle English Romance', in *Women and Literature in Britain 1150–1500*, ed. Carol M. Meale (Cambridge: Cambridge University Press, 1993; 2nd edn 1996), pp. 41–60

Fellows, Jennifer and Ivana Djordjević, eds, *Sir Bevis of Hampton in Literary Tradition* (Cambridge: D. S. Brewer, 2008)

Fellows, Jennifer, Rosalind Field, Gillian Rogers and Judith Weiss, eds, *Romance Reading on the Book: Essays on Medieval Narrative presented to Maldwyn Mills* (Cardiff: University of Wales Press, 1996)

Fewster, Carol, *Traditionality and Genre in Middle English Romance* (Cambridge: D. S. Brewer, 1987)

Field, Rosalind, 'The Curious History of the Matter of England', in *Boundaries in Medieval Romance*, ed. Neil Cartlidge (Cambridge: D. S. Brewer, 2008), pp. 29–42

Field, Rosalind, 'From *Gui* to *Guy*: The Fashioning of a Popular Romance', in *Guy of Warwick: Icon and Ancestor*, ed. Alison Wiggins and Rosalind Field (Cambridge: D. S. Brewer, 2007), pp. 44–60

Field, Rosalind, 'Romance as History, History as Romance', in *Romance in*

Medieval England, ed. M. Mills et al. (Cambridge: D. S. Brewer, 1991), pp. 163–73

Field, Rosalind, 'The King Over the Water: Exile-and-Return Revisited', in *Cultural Encounters in the Romance of Medieval England*, ed. Corinne Saunders (Cambridge: D. S. Brewer, 2005), pp. 41–53

Field, Rosalind, 'Romance in England, 1066–1400', in *The Cambridge History of Medieval English Literature*, ed. David Wallace (Cambridge: Cambridge University Press, 1999), pp. 152–76

Finlayson, John, 'Definitions of Middle English Romance', *Chaucer Review* 15 (1980), 43–62, 168–81

Finlayson, John, 'Formulaic Technique in *Morte Arthure*', *Anglia* 81 (1963), 372–93

Finlayson, John, 'Legendary Ancestors and the Expansion of Romance in *Richard Coer de Lyon*', *English Studies* 79 (1998), 299–308.

Finsterbuch, Franz, *Der Versbau der mittelenglischen Dichtungen Sir Perceval of Gales und Sir Degrevant* (Vienna: Wilhelm Braumüller, 1919)

Fisher, Sheila, 'Taken Men and Token Women in *Sir Gawain and the Green Knight*,' in *Seeking the Woman in Late Medieval and Early Renaissance Writings*, ed. Sheila Fisher and Janet Halley (Knoxville: University of Tennessee Press, 1989), pp. 71–105

Fisher, Sheila, 'Women and Men in Late Medieval English Romance', in *Cambridge Companion to Medieval Romance*, ed. Roberta L. Krueger (Cambridge: Cambridge University Press, 2000), pp. 150–64

Forste-Grupp, Sheryl L., 'A Woman Circumvents the Laws of Primogeniture in *The Weddynge of Sir Gawen and Dame Ragnell*', *Studies in Philology* 99:2 (2002), 105–13

Foster, Edward E., 'Simplicity, Complexity, and Morality in Four Middle English Romances', *Chaucer Review* 31 (1997), 401–19

Fowler, David C., *A Literary History of the Popular Ballad* (Durham, NC: Duke University Press, 1968)

Fowler, Elizabeth, 'The Romance Hypothetical: Lordship and the Saracens in *Sir Isumbras*', in *The Spirit of Medieval Popular Romance*, ed. Ad Putter and Jane Gilbert (Harlow: Longman, 2000), pp. 97–121

Freedman, Paul, 'The Medieval Other: The Middle Ages as Other', in *Marvels, Monsters and Miracles: Studies in the Medieval and Early Modern Imaginations*, ed. Timothy S. Jones and David A. Sprunger (Kalamazoo: Medieval Institute Publications, 2002), pp. 1–24.

Freeman, Michelle, 'The Power of Sisterhood: Marie de France's Le Fresne', *French Forum* 12 (1987), 5–26

French, W. H., *Essays on King Horn* (New York: Cornell University Press, 1940)

Gautier, Léon, *Les épopées françaises: Études sur les origines et l'histoire de la littérature nationale*, seconde édition, entièrement refondue, 3 vols (Paris, 1878)

Gilbert, Jane, 'A Theoretical Introduction', in *The Spirit of Medieval Popular Romance*, ed. Ad Putter and Jane Gilbert (Harlow: Longman, 2000), pp. 15–38

Gilbert, Jane, 'Putting the Pulp into Fiction: The Lump-Child and Its Parents in

The King of Tars', in *Pulp Fictions of Medieval England*, ed. Nicola McDonald (Manchester: Manchester University Press, 2004), pp. 102–23

Gilbert, Jane, 'Unnatural Mothers and Monstrous Children in *The King of Tars* and *Sir Gowther*', in *Medieval Women: Texts and Contexts in Late Medieval Britain: Essays for Felicity Riddy*, ed. Jocelyn Wogan-Browne et al. (Turnhout: Brepols, 2000), pp. 329–44.

Goffman, Erving, 'Territories of the Self', in *Relations in Public: Microstudies of the Public Order* (New York: Basic Books, 1971), pp. 28–41.

Goodman, Barbara A., 'The Female Spell-caster in Middle English Romances: Heretical Outsider or Political Insider', *Essays in Medieval Studies* 15 (1998), 45–56

Green, D. H., *Medieval Listening and Reading: The Primary Reception of German Literature 800–1300* (Cambridge: Cambridge University Press, 1994)

Gurevich, Aron, *Medieval Popular Culture: Problems of Belief and Perception*, trans. Janos M. Bak and Paul A. Hollingsworth (Cambridge: Cambridge University Press, 1988)

Halverson, John, '*Havelok the Dane* and Society', *Chaucer Review* 6 (1971–2), 142–51

Hanna, Ralph, *London Literature, 1300–1380* (Cambridge: Cambridge University Press, 2005)

Hardman, Phillipa, 'Compiling the Nation: Fifteenth-Century Miscellany Manuscripts', in *Nation, Court and Culture: New Essays on Fifteenth-Century English Poetry*, ed. Helen Cooney (Dublin: Four Courts Press, 2001), pp. 50–69

Hardman, Phillipa, 'Fitt Divisions in Middle English Romances: A Consideration of the Evidence', *Yearbook of English Studies* 22 (1992), 63–80

Hardman, Phillipa ' "This litel child, his litel book": Narratives for Children in Late-Fifteenth-Century England', *Journal of the Early Book Society* 7 (2004), 51–66

Hardman, Phillipa, ed., *The Matter of Identity in Medieval Romance* (Cambridge: D. S. Brewer, 2002)

Hardman, Phillipa, 'A Mediaeval "Library In Parvo" ', *Medium Ævum* 47 (1978), 262–73

Hardman, Phillipa, 'The True Romance of *Tristrem and Ysoude*', in *Cultural Encounters in the Romance of Medieval England*, ed. Corinne Saunders (Cambridge : D. S. Brewer, 2005), pp. 85–99

Hartung, Wolfgang, *Die Spielleute im Mittelalter: Gaukler, Dichter, Musikanten* (Düsseldorf: Patmos, 2003)

Hazell, Dinah, 'The Blinding of Gwennere: Thomas Chestre as Social Critic', *Arthurian Literature* 20, ed. Keith Busby and Roger Dalrymple (Cambridge: D. S. Brewer, 2003), pp. 123–43

Heng, Geraldine, *Empire of Magic: Medieval Romance and the Politics of Cultural Fantasy* (New York: Columbia University Press, 2003)

Heng, Geraldine, 'The Romance of England: *Richard Coer de Lyon*, Saracen, Jews, and the Politics of Race and Nation', in *The Post-Colonial Middle Ages*, ed. Jeffrey J. Cohen (New York: St Martin's Press, 2000), pp. 135–72

Hibbard (Loomis), Laura A., *Mediæval Romance in England: A Study of the Sources and Analogues of the Non-Cyclic Metrical Romances* (New York and London: Oxford University Press, 1924)

Hirsch, John C., '*Havelok* 2933: A Problem in Medieval Literary History', *Neuphilologische Mitteilungen* 78 (1977), 339–49

Hodnett, Edward, *English Woodcuts 1480–1535* (Oxford: Oxford University Press, 1973)

Holford, Matthew, 'History and Politics in *Horn Child and Maiden Rimnild*', *Review of English Studies* 57 (2006), 149–68

Holland, William E., 'Formulaic Diction and the Descent of a Middle English Romance', *Speculum* 48 (1973), 89–109

Hoops, Reinald, *Der Begriff 'Romance' in der mittelenglischen und frühneuenglischen Literatur* (Heidelberg: Carl Winters, 1929)

Hopkins, Amanda, 'Veiling the Text: The True Role of the Cloth in *Emaré*', in *Medieval Insular Romance*, ed. Judith Weiss, Jennifer Fellows and Morgan Dickson (Cambridge: D. S. Brewer, 2000), pp. 71–82

Hopkins, Andrea, *The Sinful Knights: A Study of Middle English Penitential Romance* (Oxford: Oxford University Press, 1990)

Horobin, Simon, and Alison Wiggins, 'Reconsidering Lincoln's Inn MS 150', *Medium Ævum* 77 (2008), 30-53

Hudson, Harriet E., 'Construction of Class, Family, and Gender in Some Middle English Popular Romances', in *Class and Gender in Early English Literature*, ed. Britton J. Harwood and Gillian R. Overing (Bloomington and Indianapolis: Indiana University Press, 1994), pp. 76–94

Hudson, Harriet E., 'Towards a Theory of Popular Literature: The Case of the Middle English Romances', *Journal of Popular Culture* 23 (1989), 31–50

Hurt, James, 'The Texts of *King Horn*', *Journal of the Folklore Institute* 7 (1970), 47–59

Hutton, W. H., *The English Church from the Accession of Charles I to the Death of Anne (1625-1714)* (London: Macmillan, 1903)

Huws, Daniel, 'MS Porkington 10 and its Scribes', in *Romance Reading on the Book: Essays on Medieval Narrative presented to Maldwyn Mills*, ed. Jennifer Fellows, Rosalind Field, Gillian Rogers and Judith Weiss (Cardiff: University of Wales Press, 1996), pp. 188–207

Ingham, Patricia Clare, *Sovereign Fantasies: Arthurian Romance and the Making of Britain* (Philadelphia: University of Pennsylvania Press, 2001)

Jacobs, Nicolas, *The Later Versions of 'Sir Degarre': A Study in Textual Degeneration*, Medium Ævum Monographs, n.s. 18 (Oxford: Society for the Study of Medieval Languages and Literature, 1995)

Jacobs, Nicolas, '*Sir Degarre, Lay le Freine, Beves of Hamtoun* and the "Auchinleck Bookshop"', *Notes and Queries*, n.s. 29 (1982), 294–301

Jaech, S. J., 'The Parting of Lancelot and Gaynor: The Effect of Repetition in the Stanzaic *Morte Darthur*', *Interpretations* 15 (1984), 59–69

Jeanroy, Alfred, *Les origins de la poésie lyrique en France au moyen âge* (Paris: Champion, 1904)

Kaluza, Max, 'Kleinere Publikationen aus me. Handschriften', *Englische Studien* 14 (1890), 165–88

Kamps, Ivo, 'Magic, Women, and Incest: The Real Challenges in *Sir Gawain and the Green Knight*', *Exemplaria* 1 (1988), 313–36

Kelly, Kathleen Coyne, 'The Bartering of Blauncheflur in the Middle English *Floris and Blauncheflur*', *Studies in Philology* 91:2 (1994), 101–10

Kennedy, Edward Donald, 'The Stanzaic *Morte Arthur*: The Adaptation of a

French Romance for an English Audience', in *Culture and the King: The Social Implications of the Arthurian Legend*, ed. Martin B. Schichtman and James P. Carley (New York: SUNY, 1994), pp. 91–112

Kennedy, R., 'New Theories of Constraint in the Metricality of the Strong-Stress Long Line, Applied to the English Rhymed Alliterative Corpus, *c.* 1400', in *Métriques du Moyen Age et de la Renaissance*, ed. Dominique Billy (Paris: l'Harmattan, 1999), pp. 131–44

Ker, W. P., 'Metrical Romances, 1200–1500', in *The Cambridge History of English Literature*, ed. E. A Ward and A. R. Waller, 14 vols (Cambridge: Cambridge University Press, 1907–16), I, pp. 308–34

Kershaw, Ian, 'The Great Famine and Agrarian Crisis in England 1315–1322', *Past and Present* 59 (1973), 3–50

Knight, Rhonda, 'All Dressed Up with Someplace to Go: Regional Identity in *Sir Gawain and the Green Knight*', *Studies in the Age of Chaucer* 25 (2003), 259–84

Knight, Stephen, 'The Characteristic Mode of 'Sir Orfeo', *Balcony: The Sydney Review* 5 (1966), 17–24

Knight, Stephen, '"Harkeneth aright": Reading *Gamelyn* for Text not Context', in *Tradition and Transformation in Medieval Romance*, ed. Rosalind Field (Cambridge: D. S. Brewer, 1999), pp. 15–27

Knight, S. T., 'The Oral Transmission of *Sir Launfal*', *Medium Ævum* 38 (1969), 164–70

Knopp, S. E., 'Artistic Design in the Stanzaic *Morte Arthure*', *English Literary History* 45 (1978), 563–82

Kölbing, E., 'Kleine Publicationen aus der Auchinleck-Handschrift', *Englische Studien* 7 (1884), 101–25

Kratins, Ojars, 'The Middle English *Amis and Amiloun*: Chivalric Romance or Secular Hagiography', *Publications of the Modern Languages Association* 81 (1966), 347–54

Krishna, Valerie, 'Parataxis, Formulaic Density, and Thrift in the *Alliterative Morte Arthure*', *Speculum* 57 (1982), 63–83

Laskaya, Anne, 'The Rhetoric of Incest in the Middle English *Emaré*', in *Violence against Women in Medieval Texts*, ed. Anna Roberts (Gainesville: University Press of Florida, 1998), pp. 97–114

Lavezzo, Kathy, ed., *Imagining a Medieval English Nation* (Minneapolis: University of Minnesota Press, 2004)

Lawrence, R. F., 'The Formulaic Theory and its Application to English Alliterative Poetry', in *Essays on Style and Language: Linguistic and Critical Approaches to Literary Style*, ed. Roger Fowler (London: Routledge, 1966), pp. 166–83

Lawton, David A., '*Scottish Field*: Alliterative Verse and Stanley Encomium in the Percy Folio', *Leeds Studies in English*, n.s. 10 (1978), 42–57

Lee, Stuart D. and Elizabeth Solopova, *The Keys of Middle Earth* (Basingstoke and New York: Palgrave, 2005)

Lerer, Seth, *Chaucer and His Readers: Imagining the Author in Late Medieval England* (Princeton: Princeton University Press, 1993)

Levine, Robert, 'Who Composed *Havelok* for Whom?', *Yearbook of English Studies* 22 (1992), 95–104

Liu, Yin, 'Middle English Romance as Prototype Genre', *Chaucer Review* 40 (2006), 335–53

Liuzza, Roy Michael, 'Representation and Readership in the Middle English *Havelok*', *Journal of English and Germanic Philology* 93 (1994), 504–19

Loomis, Laura H., 'The Auchinleck Manuscript and a Possible London Bookshop of 1330–1340', in *Adventures in the Middle Ages: A Memorial Collection of Essays and Studies* (New York: B. Franklin, 1962), pp. 150–87

Loomis, Laura H., 'The Auchinleck Manuscript and a Possible London Bookshop of 1330–1340', *Proceedings of the Modern Language Association* 57 (1942), 595–627

Lord, Albert B., *The Singer of Tales* (Cambridge, MA: Harvard University Press, 1960; 2nd edn, ed. Stephen Mitchell and Gregory Nagy, 2000, with a new introduction and a CD)

Love, Harold, *Scribal Publication in Seventeenth-Century England* (Oxford: Clarendon Press, 1993)

Lucas, Peter J., 'Earlier Verse Romance', in *Readings in Medieval Texts: Interpreting Old and Middle English Literature*, ed. David Johnson and Elaine Treharne (Oxford: Oxford University Press, 2005), pp. 229–40

Machan, Tim William, 'Editing, Orality, and Late Middle English Texts', in *Vox intexta: Orality and Textuality in the Middle Ages*, ed. A. N. Doane and Carol Braun Pasternack (Madison: University of Wisconsin Press, 1991), pp. 229–45

Machan, Tim William, *Textual Criticism and Middle English Texts* (Charlottesville: University Press of Virginia, 1994)

Mann, Jill, *Feminizing Chaucer*, rev. edn (Cambridge: D. S. Brewer, 2002)

Matthews, David, *The Making of Middle English, 1765–1910* (Minneapolis: University of Minnesota Press, 1999)

Matthews, David, 'Narrative and Ideology in *The Grene Knight*', *Neophilologus* 78 (1994), 301–14

McDonald, Nicola, 'A Polemical Introduction', in *Pulp Fictions of Medieval England*, ed. Nicola McDonald (Manchester: Manchester University Press, 2004), pp. 1–21

McDonald, Nicola, ed., *Pulp Fictions of Medieval England: Essays in Popular Romance* (Manchester: Manchester University Press, 2004)

McGillivray, Murray, *Memorization in the Transmission of the Middle English Romances* (New York: Garland, 1990)

McIntosh, Angus, 'Is *Sir Tristrem* an English or a Scottish Poem', in *In Other Words: Transcultural Studies in Philology, Translation and Lexicology Presented to Hans Heinrich Meier*, ed. J. Lachlan Mackenzie and Richard Todd (Dordrecht: Foris, 1989), pp. 85–95

McIntosh, Angus, M. L. Samuels and Michael Benskin, *A Linguistic Atlas of Late Medieval English*, 4 vols (Aberdeen: Aberdeen University Press, 1986)

Meale, Carol M., 'Caxton, de Worde, and the Publication of Romance in Late Medieval England', *The Library*, 6th series 14 (1992), 283–98

Meale, Carol, 'Wynkyn de Worde's Setting-Copy for *Ipomydon*', *Studies in Bibliography* 35 (1982), 162–73

Medary, Margaret P., 'Stanza-Linking in Middle English Verse', *The Romanic Review* 7 (1916), 243–70

Bibliography

Mehl, Dieter, *The Middle English Romances of the Thirteenth and Fourteenth Centuries* (London: Routledge and Kegan Paul, 1968)
Menuge, Noël James, 'The Wardship Romance: A new Methodology', in *Tradition and Transformation in Medieval Romance*, ed. Rosalind Field (Cambridge: D. S. Brewer, 1999), pp. 29–43
Mills, Maldwyn, 'The Composition and Style of the "Southern" *Octavian*, *Sir Launfal*, and *Libeaus Desconus*', *Medium Ævum* 31 (1962), 88–109
Mills, Maldwyn, 'Generic Titles in Bodleian Library MS Douce 261 and British Library MS Egerton 3132A', in *The Matter of Identity in Medieval Romance*, ed. Phillipa Hardman (Cambridge: D. S. Brewer, 2002), pp. 125–38
Mills, Maldwyn, '*Sir Isumbras* and styles of tail-rhyme romance', in *Readings in Medieval English Romance*, ed. Carol M. Meale (Cambridge: D. S. Brewer, 1994), pp. 1–24
Moore, John C., '"Courtly Love": A Problem of Terminology', *Journal of the History of Ideas* 40 (1979), 621–32
Morgan, Gerald, 'Medieval Misogyny and Gawain's Outburst against Women in *Sir Gawain and the Green Knight*', *Modern Language Review* 97:2 (2002), 265–78
Nappholz, Carol J., 'Launfal's "Largesse": Word-Play in Thomas Chestre's *Sir Launfal*', *English Language Notes* 25:3 (1988), 4–9
Olson, C., 'Chaucer and Music of the Fourteenth Century', *Speculum* 16 (1941), 64–91
Orme, Nicholas, 'Children and Literature in Medieval England', *Medium Ævum* 68 (1999), 218–46
O'Toole, Carol, 'Social Disorder and Discontent in Thomas Chestre's *Sir Launfal*', *PaGes* 6 (1999). University of Dublin website: http://www.ucd.ie/pages/99/articles/otoole.pdf, accessed May 3, 2008
Page, Christopher, *The Owl and the Nightingale: Musical Life and Ideas in France 1100–1300* (Berkeley: University of California Press, 1989)
Page, Christopher, 'Secular Music', in *The Cambridge Guide to the Arts in Britain*, ed. Boris Ford (Cambridge: Cambridge University Press, 1988), pp. 235–51
Page, Christopher, *Voices and Instruments of the Middle Ages: Instrumental Practice and Songs in France 1100–1300* (London: Dent, 1987)
Parks, Ward, 'The Oral-Formulaic Theory in Middle English Studies', *Oral Tradition* 1 (1986), 636–94
Patterson, Lee, *Temporal Circumstances: Form and History in the 'Canterbury Tales'* (New York: Palgrave MacMillan, 2006)
Payling, S. J., 'Social Mobility, Demographic Change, and Landed Society in Late Medieval England', *The Economic History Review* 45:1 (1992), 51–73
Pearsall, Derek, *The Canterbury Tales* (London and New York: Routledge, 1993)
Pearsall, Derek, 'The Development of Middle English Romance', *Medieval Studies* 27 (1965), 91–116
Pearsall, Derek, 'The Development of Middle English Romance', in *Studies in Medieval English Romances*, ed. D. Brewer (Cambridge: D. S. Brewer, 1988), pp. 11–35
Pearsall, Derek, 'The English Romance in the Fifteenth Century', *Essays and Studies*, n.s. 29 (1976), 56–83

Pearsall, Derek, 'The idea of Englishness in the fifteenth century', in *Nation, Court and Culture: New Essays on Fifteenth-Century English Poetry*, ed. Helen Cooney (Dublin: Four Courts Press, 2001), pp. 15–27

Pearsall, Derek, 'Madness in *Sir Orfeo*', in *Romance Reading on the Book: Essays on Medieval Narrative presented to Maldwyn Mills*, ed. Jennifer Fellows, Rosalind Field, Gillian Rogers and Judith Weiss (Cardiff: University of Wales Press, 1996), pp. 51–63

Pearsall, Derek, 'Understanding Middle English romance', *Review* 2 (1980), 105–25

Plomer, H. R., 'Two Lawsuits of Richard Pynson', *The Library*, n.s. 10 (1909), 115–33

Powicke, Maurice, *The Thirteenth Century, 1216–1307*, 2nd edn (Oxford: Clarendon, 1962)

Pratt, Marie L., *Imperial Eyes: Travel Writing and Transculturation* (London and New York: Routledge, 1992)

Prendergast, Thomas A., *Chaucer's Dead Body: From Corpse to Corpus* (Routledge: New York and London, 2004)

Price, Paul, 'Confessions of a Godless Killer: Guy of Warwick and Comprehensive Entertainment', in *Medieval Insular Romance*, ed. Judith Weiss, Jennifer Fellows, and Morgan Dickson (Cambridge: D. S. Brewer, 2000), pp. 93–110

Purdie, Rhiannon, 'Generic Identity and the Origins of *Sir Isumbras*', in *The Matter of Identity in Medieval Romance*, ed. Phillipa Hardman (Cambridge: D. S. Brewer, 2002), pp. 113–24

Purdie, Rhiannon, 'The Implications of Manuscript Layout in Chaucer's *Tale of Sir Thopas*', *Forum for Modern Language Studies* 41 (2005), 263–74

Purdie, Rhiannon, 'Medieval Romance in Scotland', in *A Companion to Medieval Scottish Poetry*, ed. Priscilla Bawcutt and Janet Hadley Williams (Cambridge: D. S. Brewer, 2006), pp. 165–77

Purser, J., 'Greysteil', in *Stewart Style, 1513–1542: Essays on the Court of James V*, ed. J. Hadley Williams (East Linton: Tuckwell Press, 1996), pp. 143–52

Putter, Ad, 'A Historical Introduction', in *The Spirit of Medieval Popular Romance*, ed. Ad Putter and Jane Gilbert (Harlow: Longman, 2000), pp. 1–15

Putter, Ad, 'Late Romance', in *Readings in Medieval Texts: Interpreting Old and Middle English Literature*, ed. David Johnson and Elaine Treharne (Oxford: Oxford University Press, 2005), pp. 337–53

Putter, Ad, 'The Narrative Logic of Emaré', in *The Spirit of Medieval Popular Romance*, ed. Ad Putter and Jane Gilbert (Harlow: Longman, 2000), pp. 157–80

Putter, Ad, *'Sir Gawain and the Green Knight' and French Arthurian Romance* (Oxford: Oxford University Press, 1995)

Putter, Ad, 'Story Line and Story Shape in *Sir Percyvell of Gales* and Chrétien de Troyes's *Conte du Graal*', in *Pulp Fictions of Medieval England*, ed. Nicola McDonald (Manchester: Manchester University Press, 2004), pp. 171–96

Putter, Ad, 'Weak *e* and the Metre of Richard Spalding's *Alliterative Katherine Hymn*', *Notes and Queries*, n.s. 52 (2005), 288–92

Putter, Ad and Jane Gilbert, eds, *The Spirit of Medieval Popular Romance* (Harlow: Longman, 2000)

Putter, Ad, Judith Jefferson, and Myra Stokes, *Studies in the Metre of Alliterative*

Verse, Medium Aevum Monographs (Oxford: Society for the Study of Medieval Languages and Literature, 2007)

Radulescu, Raluca L., 'Ballad and Popular Romance in the Percy Folio', *Arthurian Literature* 23 (2006), 68–80

Radulescu, Raluca L., 'Genealogy in Insular Romance', in *Broken Lines: Genealogical Literature in Medieval Britain and France*, ed. Raluca L. Radulescu and Edward Donald Kennedy (Turnhout: Brepols, 2008), pp. 7–25

Ramsey, Lee *Chivalric Romances: Popular Literature in Medieval England* (Bloomington: Indiana University Press, 1983)

Reichardt, Paul F., 'Sir Israel Gollancz and the Editorial History of the Pearl Manuscript', *Papers on Language and Literature* 31 (1995), 145–63

Reichl, Karl, 'Comparative Notes on the Performance of Middle English Popular Romance', *Western Folklore* 62 (2003), 63–81

Reichl, Karl, '*The King of Tars*: Language and Textual Transmission', in *Studies in the Vernon Manuscript*, ed. Derek Pearsall (Cambridge: D. S. Brewer, 1990), pp. 171–86

Reichl, Karl, 'Medieval Perspectives on Turkic Oral Epic Poetry', in *Inclinate Aurem: Oral Perspectives on Early European Verbal Culture: A Symposium*, ed. Jan Helldén, Minna Skafte Jensen and Thomas Pettitt (Odense: Odense University Press, 2001), pp. 211–54

Reichl, Karl, 'The Middle English Popular Romance: Minstrel versus Hack Writer', in *The Ballad and Oral Literature*, ed. Joseph Harris (Cambridge, MA: Harvard University Press, 1991), pp. 243–68

Reichl, Karl, *Spielmannsidiom, Dialektmischung und Kunstsprache in der mittelenglischen volkstümlichen Epik* (Paderborn: Schöningh, 2002)

Reichl, Karl, 'Turkic Bard and Medieval Entertainer: What a Living Epic Tradition Can Tell Us about Oral Performance of Narrative in the Middle Ages', in *Performing Medieval Narrative*, ed. Evelyn Birge Vitz, Nancy Freeman Regalado and Marilyn Lawrence (Cambridge: D. S. Brewer, 2005), pp. 167–78

Reiss, Edmund, 'Romance', in *The Popular Literature of Medieval England*, ed. Thomas J. Heffernan (Knoxville: University of Tennessee Press, 1985), pp. 108–30

Richmond, Velma Bourgeois, *The Popularity of Middle English Romance* (Bowling Green, OH: Bowling Green University Popular Press, 1975)

Riddy, Felicity, 'Middle English Romance: Family, Marriage, Intimacy', in *Cambridge Companion to Medieval Romance*, ed. Roberta L. Krueger (Cambridge: Cambridge University Press, 2000), pp. 235–52

Riddy, Felicity, 'Temporary Virginity and the Everyday Body: *Le Bone Florence of Rome* and Bourgeois Self-making', in *Pulp Fictions of Medieval England*, ed. Nicola McDonald (Manchester: Manchester University Press, 2004), pp. 197–216

Riddy, Felicity, *Sir Thomas Malory* (Leiden: Brill, 1987)

Robson, Margaret, 'Cloaking Desire: Re-reading *Emaré*', *Romance Reading on the Book: Essays on Medieval Narrative presented to Maldwyn Mills*, ed. Jennifer Fellows, Rosalind Field, Gillian Rogers and Judith Weiss (Cardiff: University of Wales Press, 1996), pp. 64–76

Rogers, Gillian, 'The Grene Knight', in *A Companion to the Gawain-Poet*, ed.

Derek Brewer and Jonathan Gibson (Cambridge: D. S. Brewer, 1997), pp. 365–72

Rogers, Gillian, 'The Percy Folio Manuscript Revisited', in *Romance in Medieval England*, ed. Maldwyn Mills, Jennifer Fellows and Carol M. Meale (Cambridge: D. S. Brewer, 1991), pp. 39–44

Roland, Meg, 'Arthur and the Turks', *Arthuriana* 16:1 (2006), 29–42

Rouse, Robert A., 'An Exemplary Life: Guy of Warwick as Medieval Culture Hero', in *Guy of Warwick: Icon and Ancestor*, ed. Alison Wiggins and Rosalind Field (Cambridge: D. S. Brewer, 2007), pp. 94–109

Rouse, Robert A., 'Expectation vs Experience: Encountering the Saracen Other in Middle English Romance', *SELIM, Journal of the Spanish Society for Medieval English Language and Literature* 10 (2002), 125–40, http://www.uniovi.es/SELIM/archivos/english.htm

Rouse, Robert A., 'For King and Country? The Tension between National and Regional Identities in *Sir Bevis of Hampton*', in *Sir Bevis of Hampton in Literary Tradition*, ed. Jennifer Fellows and Ivana Djordjević (Cambridge: D. S. Brewer, 2008), pp. 79–88

Rouse, Robert A., *The Idea of Anglo-Saxon England in Middle English Romance* (Cambridge: D. S. Brewer, 2005)

Rouse, Robert A., '*In his time were gode lawes*: Romance, Law, and the Anglo-Saxon Past', in *Cultural Encounters in Medieval English Romance*, ed. Corinne Saunders (Cambridge: D. S. Brewer, 2005), pp. 69–83

Rushton, Cory James, 'The Lady's Man: Gawain as a Lover in Middle English Literature', in *The Erotic in the Literature of Medieval Britain*, ed. Amanda Hopkins and Cory James Rushton (Cambridge: D. S. Brewer, 2007), pp. 27–37

Saenger, Paul, *Space between Words: The Origins of Silent Reading* (Stanford, CA: Stanford University Press, 1997)

Salmen, Walter, *Der fahrende Musiker im europäischen Mittelalter*, Die Musik im alten und neuen Europa 4 (Kassel: Bärenreiter, 1960)

Salter, David, '"Born to Thraldom and Penance": Wives and Mothers in Middle English Romance', in *Writing Gender and Genre in Medieval Literature: Approaches to Old and Middle English Texts*, ed. Elaine Treharne (Cambridge: D. S. Brewer, 2002), pp. 41–59

Sánchez-Martí, Jordi, 'Reading Romance in Late Medieval England: The Case of the Middle English *Ipomedon*', *Philological Quarterly* 83 (2004), 13–39

Saunders, Corinne, 'Erotic Magic: The Enchantress in Middle English Romance', in *The Erotic in the Literature of Medieval Britain*, ed. Amanda Hopkins and Cory James Rushton (Cambridge: D. S. Brewer, 2007), pp. 38–52

Saunders, Corinne, ed., *A Companion to Romance: From Classical to Contemporary* (Malden, MA and Oxford: Blackwell, 2004)

Saunders, Corinne, ed., *Cultural Encounters in the Romance of Medieval England* (Cambridge: D. S. Brewer, 2005)

Scala, Elizabeth, *Absent Narratives, Manuscript Textuality, and Literary Structure in Late Medieval England* (New York: Palgrave MacMillan, 2002)

Schipper, J., *History of English Versification* (Oxford, 1910, repr. New York: AMS Press, 1971)

Schofield, W. H., *English Literature from the Norman Conquest to Chaucer* (London: Macmillan, 1906)

Bibliography

Schultz, James A., *Courtly Love, the Love of Courtliness, and the History of Sexuality* (Chicago: University of Chicago Press, 2006)
Schwegler, Robert A., 'Sources of the Ballads in Bishop Percy's Folio Manuscript' (unpublished Ph. D. dissertation, University of Chicago, 1978)
Scott, Anne, 'Language as Convention, Language as Sociolect in *Havelok the Dane*', *Studies in Philology* 89 (1992), 137–60
Seaman, Myra, 'Engendering Genre in Middle English Romance: Performing the Feminine in *Sir Beves of Hamtoun*', *Studies in Philology* 98:1 (2001), 49–75
Shaner, Mary, 'Instruction and Delight: Medieval Romances as Children's Literature', *Poetics Today* 13 (1992), 5–15
Shepard, Leslie, 'The Finding of the Percy Folio Manuscript: A Claim of Prior Discovery', *Notes and Queries* 212 (1967), 45–6
Shepherd, Stephen H. A., 'The Ashmole *Sir Ferumbras*: Translation in Holograph', in *The Medieval Translator: The Theory and Practice of Translation*, ed. Roger Ellis (Cambridge: D. S. Brewer, 1989), pp. 103–22
Shepherd, Stephen H. A., 'The Middle English Pseudo-Turpin Chronicle', *Medium Aevum* 65:1 (1996), 19–34
Shepherd, Stephen H. A., *Middle English Romances* (New York: W. W. Norton, 1995)
Shimomura, Sachi, *Odd Bodies and Visible Ends in Medieval Literature* (New York: Palgrave MacMillan, 2006)
Shippey, T. A., '*The Tale of Gamelyn*: Class Warfare and the Embarrassments of Genre', in *The Spirit of Medieval Popular Romance*, ed. Ad Putter and Jane Gilbert (Harlow: Longman, 2000), pp. 78–96
Shonk, Timothy A., 'A Study of the Auchinleck Manuscript: Bookmen and Bookmaking in the Early Fourteenth Century', *Speculum* 60 (1985), 71–91
Simons, John, 'Northern *Octovian* and the question of class', in *Romance in Medieval England*, ed. Maldwyn Mills, Jennifer Fellows and Carol M. Meale (Cambridge: D. S. Brewer, 1991), pp. 105–12
Smithers, G. V., 'The Scansion of *Hauelok*', in *Middle English Studies Presented to Norman Davis*, ed. D. Gray and E. G. Stanley (Oxford: Oxford University Press, 1983), pp. 195–234
Southworth, John, *The English Medieval Minstrel* (Woodbridge: The Boydell Press, 1989)
Spearing, A. C., '*Sir Orfeo:* Madness and Gender', in *The Spirit of Medieval Popular Romance*, ed. Ad Putter and Jane Gilbert (Harlow: Longman, 2000), pp. 258–72
Spearing, A. C., *Readings in Medieval Poetry* (Cambridge: Cambridge University Press, 1987)
Spearing, A. C., *Textual Subjectivity* (Cambridge: Cambridge University Press, 2005)
Speed, Diane, 'The Construction of the Nation in Medieval English Romance', in *Readings in Medieval English Romance*, ed. Carol M. Meale (Cambridge: D. S. Brewer, 1994), pp. 135–57
Spiegel, Gabrielle, *Romancing the Past: The Rise of Vernacular Prose Historiography in Thirteenth-Century France* (Berkeley: University of California Press, 1993)
St Clair, William, *The Reading Nation in the Romantic Period* (Cambridge: Cambridge University Press, 2004)

St Clair-Kendall, S. G., 'Narrative Form and Mediaeval Continuity in the Percy Folio Manuscript: A Study of Selected poems' (unpublished Ph. D. dissertation, University of Sydney, 1988)

Staines, David, '*Havelok the Dane*: A Thirteenth-Century Handbook for Princes', *Speculum* 51 (1976), 602–23

Staley, Lynne, *Languages of Power in the Reign of Richard II* (University Park: Pennsylvania State University Press, 2005)

Stanley, E. G., 'Rhymes in English Medieval Verse: From Old English to Middle English', in *Medieval Studies Presented to George Kane*, ed. E. D. Kennedy, R. Waldron and J. S. Wittig (Cambridge: D. S. Brewer, 1988), pp. 19–54

Stanley, E. G., 'The Use of Bob-Lines in *Sir Thopas*', *Neuphilologische Mitteilungen* 74 (1972), 417–26

Stevens, John, *Words and Music in the Middle Ages: Song, Narrative, Dance and Drama, 1050–1350* (Cambridge: Cambridge University Press, 1986)

Stewart, Marion, 'A Recently-Discovered Manuscript: "ane taill of Sir colling ye kny^t"', *Scottish Studies* 16 (1972), 23–39

Stokes, Myra, 'Lanval to Sir Launfal: A Story Becomes Popular', in *The Spirit of Medieval Popular Romance*, ed. Ad Putter and Jane Gilbert (Harlow: Longman, 2000), pp. 56–77

Strohm, Paul, 'Middle English Narrative Genres', *Genre* 13 (1980), 379–88

Strohm, Paul, '*Storie, Spelle, Geste, Romaunce, Tragedie*: Generic Distinctions in the Middle English Troy Narratives', *Speculum* 46:2 (1971), 348–59

Strohm, Paul, 'The Origins and Meaning of Middle English *Romaunce*', *Genre* 10 (1977), 1–28

Strong, Caroline, 'History and Relations of the Tail-Rhyme Strophe in Latin, French, and English', *Proceedings of the Modern Language Association* 22 (1907), 371–420

Taylor, Andrew, 'The Myth of the Minstrel Manuscript', *Speculum* 66 (1991), 43–73

Thompson, John J., 'The Compiler in Action: Robert Thornton and the "Thornton Romances" in Lincoln Cathedral MS 91', in *Manuscripts and Readers in Fifteenth-Century England*, ed. Derek Pearsall (Cambridge: D. S. Brewer, 1983), pp. 113–24

Thompson, John J., 'The *Cursor Mundi*, the "Inglis tong", and "Romance"', in *Readings in Medieval English Romance*, ed. Carol M. Meale (Cambridge: D. S. Brewer, 1994), pp. 99–120

Thompson, John J., 'Looking Behind the Book: MS Cotton Caligula A.ii. part 1, and the experience of its texts', in *Romance Reading on the Book: Essays on Medieval Narrative presented to Maldwyn Mills*, ed. Jennifer Fellows, Rosalind Field, Gillian Rogers and Judith Weiss (Cardiff: University of Wales Press, 1996), pp. 171–87

Thompson, John J., *Robert Thornton and the London Thornton Manuscript* (Cambridge: D. S. Brewer, 1987)

Tigges, Wim, 'Romance and Parody', in *Companion to Middle English Romance*, ed. H. Aertsen and Alasdair A. MacDonald (Amsterdam: VU University Press, 1990), pp. 129–51

Trounce, A. McI., 'The English Tail-Rhyme Romances', *Medium Ævum* 1 (1932), 87–108, 168–82; 2 (1933), 34–57, 189–98; 3 (1934), 30–50

Troyer, Pamela Luff, 'Smiting High Culture in the "fondement": *The Seege of*

Bibliography

Troye as Medieval Burlesque', in *Fantasies of Troy: Classical Tales and the Social Imaginary in Medieval and Early Modern Europe*, ed. Alan Shepard and Stephen D. Powell (Toronto: Centre for Reformation and Renaissance Studies, 2004), pp. 117–31

Tsai, Christine Li Ju, 'Parents and Children in Middle English Romance: Personal, National, and International Relations in the Thirteenth to Fifteenth Centuries' (unpublished Ph.D. thesis, University of Kent at Canterbury, 2006)

Turville-Petre, Thorlac, 'Afterword: The Brutus prologue to *Sir Gawain and the* Green Knight', in *Readings in Medieval English Romance*, ed. Carol M. Meale (Cambridge: D. S. Brewer, 1994), pp. 340–6

Turville-Petre, Thorlac, *England the Nation: Language, Literature and National Identity, 1290–1340* (Oxford: Clarendon Press, 1996)

Turville-Petre, Thorlac, '*Havelok* and the History of the Nation', in *Readings in Medieval English Romance*, ed. Carol M. Meale (Cambridge: D. S. Brewer, 1994), pp. 121–34

Twomey, Michael W., 'Morgain la Fée in *Sir Gawain and the Green Knight*', in *Text and Intertext in Medieval Arthurian Literature*, ed. Norris J. Lacy (New York: Garland, 1996), pp. 91–115

Vogel, B., 'The Dialect of *Sir Tristrem*', *Journal of English and Germanic Philology* 40 (1941), 538–44

Waldron, Ronald A., 'Oral-Formulaic Technique and Middle English Alliterative Poetry', *Speculum* 32 (1957), 792–801

Warm, Robert, 'Identity, Narrative and Participation: defining a context for the Middle English Charlemagne romances', in *Tradition and Transformation in Medieval Romance*, ed. Rosalind Field (Cambridge: D. S. Brewer, 1999), pp. 87–100

Warren, Michelle, *History on the Edge: Excalibur and the Borders of Britain, 1100–1300* (Minneapolis: University of Minnesota Press, 2000)

Watson, Nicholas, 'The Politics of Middle English Writing', in *The Idea of the Vernacular: An Anthology of Middle English Literary Theory 1280–1520*, ed. Jocelyn Wogan-Browne et al. (Exeter: University of Exeter Press, 1999), pp. 331–52

Weinberg, Carole, 'The Stanzaic *Morte Arthure*', in *The Arthur of the English*, ed. W. R. J. Barron (Cardiff: University of Wales Press, 1999), pp. 100–11

Weiss, Judith, 'Structure and Characterisation in *Havelok the Dane*', *Speculum* 44 (1969), 247–57

Weiss, Judith, Jennifer Fellows and Morgan Dickson, eds, *Medieval Insular Romance* (Cambridge: D. S. Brewer, 2000)

Wiggins, Alison, 'Are Auchinleck Manuscript's Scribes 1 and 6 the same scribe? The advantages of whole-data analysis and electronic tests', *Medium Ævum* 73 (2004), 10–26

Wiggins, Alison, 'The Manuscripts and Texts of the Middle English *Guy of Warwick*', in *Guy of Warwick: Icon and Ancestor*, ed. Alison Wiggins and Rosalind Field (Cambridge: D. S. Brewer, 2007), pp. 61–80

Wiggins, Alison, 'Synopsis', in *Guy of Warwick: Icon and Ancestor*, ed. Alison Wiggins and Rosalind Field (Cambridge: D. S. Brewer, 2007), pp. 201–13

Wiggins, Alison and Rosalind Field, eds, *Guy of Warwick: Icon and Ancestor* (Cambridge: D. S. Brewer, 2007)

Wilkins, Nigel, *Music in the Age of Chaucer* (Cambridge: D. S. Brewer, 1979)

Williams, Elizabeth, '"A damsel by herselfe alone": Images of Magic and Femininity from *Lanval* to *Sir Lambewell*', in *Romance Reading on the Book: Essays on Medieval Narrative presented to Maldwyn Mills*, ed. Jennifer Fellows, Rosalind Field, Gillian Rogers and Judith Weiss (Cardiff: University of Wales Press, 1996), pp. 155–70

Wilson, Edward, '*Sir Gawain and the Green Knight* and the Stanley Family of Stanley, Storeton, and Hooton', *Review of English Studies*, n.s. 30 (1979), 308–16

Wittig, Susan, *Stylistic and Narrative Structures in the Middle English Romances* (Austin and London: University of Texas Press, 1978)

Wright, Laura M., 'More on the Meanings and Uses of *Jongleur* and *Menestrel*', *Romance Studies* 17 (1990), 7–19

Yamamoto, Dorothy, 'Women and the Wild', in Dorothy Yamamoto, *The Boundaries of the Human in Medieval English Literature* (Oxford: Oxford University Press, 2000), pp. 197–224.

Zaerr, L. M., 'Fiddling with the Middle English Romance: Using Performance to Reconstruct the Past', *Mediaevalia* 21 (1996), 47–65

Zumthor, Paul, *La lettre et la voix: De la «littérature» médiévale* (Paris: Seuil, 1987)

Zupitza, Julius, *Zur Literaturgeschichte des Guy von Warwick* (Vienna, 1873)

Index

Akbari, Suzanne Conklin   92
Alliterative Morte Arthure   145, 176
alliterative poetry   145–46, 171
Alphabetical Praise of Women   119
Amis and Amiloun   36, 42–43, 109, 124, 159
Anderson, Benedict   79–82
Archibald, Elizabeth   152
Arthurian romances (*see also individual romances*)   32, 59–62, 107, 111, 160–63, 174–78
Arthour and Merlin   108, 144
Athelston   188
Auchinleck manuscript (NLS MS Advocates 19.2.1)   17, 37, 43, 52–55, 74–75, 81–82, 86, 119, 143, 146–47, 154–56, 158–60, 163
Awntyrs off Arthure   49, 108, 130, 156, 176

Beneit (*Life of St. Thomas*)   122–23
Benson, Larry D.   145–46, 177–78
Beowulf   145
Bevis of Hampton   72–74, 83–85, 101, 123
Blamires, Alcuin   41, 164
Bodel, Jean   34–35
Boeve de Hauntoun (AN)   12
Bond, James   173
Breton *lai*   140
   Middle English   16, 103–6
Brewer, Derek   9, 35–36
Burrow, John   173

Calkin, Siobhan Bly   79, 84
Campbell, Kofi   84
Carle off Carlile   64
Capystranus   88–89
Cartlidge, Neil   18 n. 21, 41
'Cavalier' poetry   64–65
Caxton, William   68, 93, 151–52
Cerquiglini, Bernard   179
chanson de geste   14, 125, 141
Chanson de Roland (see *Song of Roland*)
Charbonneau, Joanne   4
Charlemagne   32, 81, 94

romances of   85–95, 125–28, 156–57
Charles the Grete (Caxton)   93
Chaucer, Geoffrey   19–20, 34, 49, 112, 118, 126–29, 133–34, 140, 165–69, 170–74
   'Clerk's Tale'   55
   'Franklin's Tale'   16, 140
   'Man of Law's Tale'   19–20
   'Pardoner's Tale'   171
   'Parson's Tale'   171
   'Prioress' Tale'   166, 179
   Sir Thopas   34, 118, 126, 165–67, 171–74
   Troilus and Criseyde   116 n. 22, 134
   'Wife of Bath's Tale'   170–71
Chestre, Thomas   21–23, 143, 172–74
Chevalre Assigné   160
Chrétien de Troyes   22, 151
   Conte du Graal   151
   Yvain   22
Christianity   90–93
Cohen, Jerome Jeffrey   5, 83
Confessio Amantis   138
Cooper, Helen   9–10, 47–48, 66, 87, 169
Copland, William   68–70, 112
Cursor Mundi   34–35, 87

DaVinci Code   169, 179
Delaney, Sheila   42–43
dialect   146–47
Dickens, Charles   150

Early English Text Society   170
Edward II (king of England)   43, 56, 121
Edward III (king of England)   119
Edwards, A. S. G.   32–33
Emaré   19–20, 21, 101–2, 160
The Erl of Toulous   36, 105
escapism   29
Eucharist   90–91
Evans, Murray   34

Fairy King (*Sir Orfeo*)   17
Fierabras (OF)   93, 125
Findern MS   50–51
Floris and Blanchefleur   23–24, 55

205

Index

Fowler, Elizabeth 42
Freedman, Paul 3
Furnivall, F. J. 58, 170

Gamelyn 26–28, 45, 51 n.8, 109, 174
Gautier, Léon 142
Gaveston, Piers 43
Grene Knight 62, 65–66, 174–78
gender 43–44, 96–110
Generydes 112
Gollancz, Israel 175
Gower, John 127, 133, 138, 141
Green, D. H. 135
Grey, Sir Thomas (*Scalicronica*) 46
Grosseteste, Robert 142
Gui de Warewic (AN) 12–16, 156
Gurevich, Aron 3–4
Guy of Warwick 17, 37, 74–75, 82–84, 106, 123, 133, 155–56, 165–67

Hales, J. W. 58
Hall, Joseph 120
Halo (video game) 167
Halverson, John 9
Hardman, Phillipa 53 n.16
Havelok the Dane 9, 24–28, 37, 40–41, 114–15, 136, 167–69
Heng, Geraldine 80–81, 85, 97
History of Jason (Caxton) 151
Hoccleve, Thomas 53
holster books 142
Horn (AN) 113, 116
Horn Childe 53, 55, 135–36, 140
Hue de Rotelande 12, 111
Hundred Years' War 81, 83

Ipomadon (AN) 12, 111
Ipomadon (ME) 111–12
Ipomydon, Lyfe of (printed) 128–29

Jacobs, Nicolas 143–44
Jane Eyre 28
Jeaste of Sir Gawain 107
John of Fordun 46

Ker, W. P. 129
King Arthur and King Cornwall 61, 176
King Horn 101, 115, 117
King of Tars 44–46, 148
Knight, Stephen 16 n. 17, 26, 143
Kyng Alisaunder 37, 137, 143
Lai la Freine (ME) 39–40, 103, 115, 152, 159
Lancelot 61–62

Launcelot of the Laik 107, 112
Langland, William (see also *Piers Plowman*) 138
Laud Troy Book 34
Laȝamon 113–14
Le Bone Florence of Rome 31 n. 2, 44–45, 49, 102–03, 106, 152–54, 160
Liber Regum Anglie 55–56
Linguistic Atlas of Late Medieval England 56–57
Loomis, Laura Hibbard 146–47
Lord, Albert B. 145
Lucas, Peter 167
Lord of the Rings (see also Tolkien, J. R. R.) 167
Lupack, Alan 87, 90
Lybeaus Desconus 45, 166, 172
Lydgate, John 10, 109, 133

Madden, Frederic 169, 175
Malory, Thomas (*Morte D'Arthur*) 155, 179
Mannyng, Robert (Brunne) 46, 123
Manuscripts (*see also individual manuscripts*) 32–33, 49–66
  Aberystwyth, National Library of Wales MS 572 74
  Aberystwyth, National Library of Wales MS Porkington 10 50 n.2
  Cambridge University Library MS Add. 4407 115
  Cambridge University Library MS Ff.1.6 (see *Findern* MS)
  Cambridge University Library MS Ff.2.38 53, 56, 67–68
  Cambridge University Library MS Gg.4.27(2) 115 n.18, 116
  Cambridge, Gonville and Caius College MS 107/176 74
  Cambridge, Gonville and Caius College MS 175 68 n.12
  Cambridge, Trinity College MS O.2.13 72
  Edinburgh, National Library of Scotland, MS Advocates' 19.2.1 (see Auchinleck)
  Edinburgh, National Library of Scotland, MS Advocates' 19.3.1 54, 163–64
  Lincoln Cathedral Library MS 91(Lincoln Thornton) 31, 46, 50–51, 53, 68–70, 156, 160–63
  London, British Library MS Add 14408 74

Index

London, British Library MS Add 27879 (*see* Percy Folio)
London, British Library MS Add 31042 (London Thornton) 54, 86–87
London, British Library MS Add 37492 (Fillingham) 120, 131, 137
London, British Library MS Cotton Caligula A.ii 52–53, 54–55
London, British Library MS Cotton Galba E.ix 56
London, British Library MS Cotton Vespasian A.iii 35 n.13
London, British Library MS Cotton Nero A.x (*Gawain*-poet) 51 n.7, 176
London, British Library MS Egerton 2862 49–50, 68–70
London, British Library MS Harley 2252 128
London, British Library MS Harley 3810 17 n.18
London, British Library MS Royal 17.B.43 34 n.9
London, British Library MS Sloane 1044 74
London, Lincoln's Inn MS Hale 150 54, 143
Manchester, Chetham's Library MS 8009 54, 72–73
Naples, Biblioteca Nazionale MS XIII. B.29 54, 56
Oxford, Bodleian Library MS Ashmole 33 56
Oxford, Bodleian Library MS Ashmole 61 53–55, 142–43
Oxford, Bodleian Library MS Douce 228 51
Oxford, Bodleian Library MS Douce 261 50–51, 56
Oxford, Bodleian Library MS Douce 324 53
Oxford, Bodleian Library MS Eng. Poet. D.208 ???
Oxford, Bodleian Library MS English Poet a.1 (see *Vernon Manuscript*)
Oxford, Bodleian Library MS Laud Miscellany 108 53
Oxford, Bodleian Library MS Rawlinson C 86 53
Oxford, Bodleian Library MS Rawlinson D 82 53
Oxford, Bodleian Library MS Rawlinson Poet. 34 75–76
Oxford, Bodleian Library MS Rawlinson Poet. 168 53
Princeton University Library MS Garrett 140 56 n.26
Princeton University Library MS Taylor 9 51
Marie de France 143, 173
Lanval 173
Matters 34–35
  of Britain (see *Arthurian romances*)
  of England 5, 25–26, 38, 47–48, 79–86
  of France 85–95, 125–28, 156–57
Matthews, David 168–71, 178
Mehl, Dieter 40, 87, 90, 148
Mills, Maldwyn 33, 74–75, 92, 161
Minot, Lawrence 119–20, 129
minstrels 132–33, 136–41
  in *Havelok* 136–37
  in *The Hermit and the Outlaw* 137
  in *Horn Childe* 135–36, 140
  in *Kyng Alisaundir* 137
Morgan le Fay 99, 176–77
motifs
  address to the audience 123, 133
  lions as helpers 22
  outlaws 25–27, 59
  Rash Promise 17
  Saracens 45–46, 83–95, 101, 156–57, 159
McDonald, Nicola 10, 31, 150, 169–70, 178
McSparran, Frances 160

Northanger Abbey (Jane Austen) 28

Octavian 21–23, 101, 109, 148
Orme, Nicholas 152–54
Otuel 86, 120, 156–59

Parry, Milman 145
Parthenope of Blois 112
Patterson, Lee 165 n. 1, 171
Pearsall, Derek 79–80, 168, 174
Percy, Bishop Thomas 57, 132, 150, 169–70
Percy Folio 57–66, 70–72, 132, 168–69, 175
Perryman, Judith 148
Piers Plowman 138–39, 141
Pricke of Conscience 142

Printed romances 67–78, 112, 128–29
Pseudo-Turpin Chronicle 156–58

Index

Putter, Ad 19–20, 151, 176
Pynson, Richard 70, 72–74, 76, 112

Radulescu, Raluca L. 62–63
Ramsey, Lee 6
Reinbrun 156
Reiss, Edmund 152
Resident Evil (video game) 167
Richard Coeur de Lion 34, 36, 80–81, 85, 88
Riddy, Felicity 152–54, 160
Ritson, Joseph 132 n.1
Robert of Cisyle 109
Roberts, Adam 29
Robin Hood 59, 109
Roland 88–95 (*passim*), 156–57
Roland and Vernagu 86, 156–58
Romances, *see individual titles*
   Anglo-Norman 11–16, 96
   anthologies 10, 166
   classification 31–48
   class in 25–28
   definition 7
   in the early modern period 67–78
   family in 21–24
   genre 4, 7, 31–48, 165–79
   identity 96–110
   masculinity 106–10
   metre 111–31
   and modern readers 165–68
   national identity 79–95
   Old French
   orality and performance 120–21, 132–48
   parody 165–67
   reception 9–11, 16, 165–79
   stanza form
      tail rhyme stanza 121–26
      Tristrem stanza (bob and wheel) 117–21
   women in 43–44 100–106
   woodcuts 73–74
   and young readers 150–64, 165–67
Roxburghe Club 170
Rouse, Robert 17
Rowlande and Otuel 87
Rowling, J. K. 169–70

Saenger, Paul 134
Sayings of Cato 138
Scala, Elizabeth 177
Scalicronica (Sir Thomas Grey) 46
Schipper, Jakob 117, 122
Scotichronicon 46–47

Scott, Sir Walter 150, 170
Sege off Melayne 88–95
Seven Wise Masters 55
Shepherd, Stephen H. A. 88–89
Shimomura, Sachi 175 n. 37, 177
Short English Metrical Chronicle 55
Siege of Jerusalem 87
Siege of Thebes (Lydgate) 109
'Siege of Tournay' (Minot) 119–20
Sir Amadace 45, 107, 163–64
Sir Cleges 45
Sir Degaré 45, 75–78, 143–44, 159–60
Sir Degrevant 45, 162–63
Sir Eglamour of Artois 68–70, 102, 128
Sir Ferumbras (Ashmole) 125–28
Sir Firumbras (Fillingham) 137
Sir Gawain and the Green Knight 32, 51 n.7, 99 n.9, 118, 167–68, 174–79
Sir Gowther 34, 37, 41, 104–5, 108–09, 163–64
Sir Isumbras 41–42, 55, 123, 133
Sir Launfal 45, 97, 107, 143, 167, 172–74
Sir Orfeo 1, 16–19, 97, 105–6, 148, 167
Sir Percyvell of Galys 46, 107, 130, 151–53, 161–64
Sir Tristrem 46, 117–21, 148, 159
Sir Tryamowre 70–72, 108
Sir Ysambrus / Sir Ysambrace 46, 163–64
Smithers, G. V. 143
Song of Roland (OF) 87, 90, 179
Song of Roland (ME) 91
South English Legendary 53
Sowdane of Babylone 92–93
Squire of Low Degree 108
Speed, Diane 80
Spenser, Edmund 172
Stanley family 65–66
Stanzaic Morte Arthur 129–30
Star Wars 169
Stokes, Myra 173
Strange Horizons (website) 29
Strong, Caroline 123

Thomas of Erceldoune 46–48, 129, 141
Thomas of Lancaster 121
Thornton manuscript (Lincoln) (*see* Lincoln Cathedral Library MS 91)
Thornton, Robert 46
Tolkien, J. R. R. 18–19, 167
Torrent of Portyngale 4, 102, 146
Townley Play of the Crucifixion 119
Tristan (AN, Thomas) 117

208

Index

Trounce, A. McI.   147
Troy   34, 109
Troy Book (Lydgate)   109
Turke and Gowin 64, 98, 176
Turpin, Archbishop   90–94
Turpines Story   86, 93–94
Turville-Petre, Thorlac   79, 156–57

Uzbekistan   149

Vernon MS   32–33

Warm, Robert   88
Wedding of Sir Gawain and Dame Ragnelle   176
William of Nassyngton (*Speculum vitae*)   151, 154

Winchester   17
Wordsworth, William   131 n. 79, 170
Wynkyn de Worde   67–78 (passim.), 128–29

Ywain and Gawain   56, 108, 115

Zumthor, Paul   135
Zupitza, Julius   74–75

Volumes already published

I: *The Orient in Chaucer and Medieval Romance*, Carol F. Heffernan, 2003
II: *Cultural Encounters in the Romance of Medieval England*, edited by Corinne Saunders, 2005
III: *The Idea of Anglo-Saxon England in Middle English Romance*, Robert Allen Rouse, 2005
IV: *Guy of Warwick: Icon and Ancestor*, edited by Alison Wiggins and Rosalind Field, 2007
V: *The Sea and Medieval English Literature*, Sebastian I. Sobecki, 2008
VI: *Boundaries in Medieval Romance*, edited by Neil Cartlidge, 2008
VII: *Naming and Namelessness in Medieval Romance*, Jane Bliss, 2008
VIII: Sir Bevis of Hampton *in Literary Tradition,* edited by Jennifer Fellows and Ivana Djordjević, 2008
IX: *Anglicising Romance: Tail-Rhyme and Genre in Medieval English Literature,* Rhiannon Purdie, 2008
X: *A Companion to Medieval Popular Romance*, edited by Raluca L. Radulescu and Cory James Rushton, 2009
XI: *Expectations of Romance: The Reception of a Genre in Medieval England*, Melissa Furrow, 2009
XII: *The Exploitations of Medieval Romance*, edited by Laura Ashe, Ivana Djordjević and Judith Weiss, 2010
XIII: *Magic and the Supernatural in Medieval English Romance*, Corinne Saunders, 2010
XIV: *Medieval Romance, Medieval Contexts*, edited by Rhiannon Purdie and Michael Cichon, 2011
XV: *Women's Power in Late Medieval Romance*, Amy Vines, 2011

www.ingramcontent.com/pod-product-compliance
Lightning Source LLC
Chambersburg PA
CBHW070803230426
43665CB00017B/2470